A Time to Rock

A Time

A SOCIAL HISTORY

to Rock

OF ROCK-AND-ROLL

David P. Szatmary

Schirmer Books
An Imprint of Simon & Schuster Macmillan
New York

Prentice Hall International
London Mexico City New Delhi Singapore Sydney Toronto

Schirmer Books
An Imprint of Simon & Schuster Macmillan
1633 Broadway
New York, NY 10019

Library of Congress Catalog Card Number: 96-7915

Printed in the United States of America

Printing Number
1 2 3 4 5 6 7 8 9 10

Library of Congress Cataloging-in-Publication Data

Szatmary, David P., 1951-
    A time to rock : a social history of rock 'n' roll / David P.
Szatmary.
        p.   cm.
    Includes bibliographical references and index.
    ISBN: 0-02-864670-3
    1. Rock music—History and criticism. 2. Rock music—Social as-
pects—United States. 3. Rock music—Social aspects—Great Britain. I.
Title.
ML3534.S96 1996   96-7915
781.66'09—dc20   CIP
                                                   MN

This paper meets the requirements of ANSI/NISO Z39.48-1992 (Per-
manence of Paper).

To My Father and Mother

Contents

Preface

This book intends to be a social history of rock-and-roll. It will place an ever-changing rock music in the context of American and, to some extent, British history from roughly 1950 to 1994. *A Time to Rock* tries to explain how rock-and-roll both reflected and influenced major social changes during the last 44 years.

A Time to Rock emphasizes several main themes, including the importance of African-American culture in the origins and development of rock music. The blues, originating in the work songs of American slaves, provided the foundation for rock-and-roll. During the early 1950s, southern African-Americans who had migrated to Chicago created an urbanized electric rhythm and blues that preceded rock-and-roll and served as the testing ground for pioneer rock-and-rollers such as Little Richard and Chuck Berry. African-Americans continued to create such new styles as the Motown sound and the soul explosion of the 1960s, the disco beat of the next decade, and, most recently, rap music.

The new musical styles often coincided with and reflected the struggle of African-Americans for equality. The electric blues of Muddy Waters gained popularity amid the beginnings of the civil rights movement during the 1950s. In the early 1960s, as the movement for civil rights gained momentum, folk protesters such as Bob Dylan and Joan Baez sang paeans about the cause. In 1964 and 1965, as Congress passed the most sweeping civil rights legislation since the Civil War, Motown artists topped the popular charts. When disgruntled, frustrated African-Americans took to the streets later in the decade, soul musicians such as Aretha Franklin shouted for respect. During the late eighties and into the nineties, hip-hoppers such as Public Enemy rapped about inequality and a renewed interest in an African-American identity.

As the civil rights struggle began to foster an awareness and acceptance of African-American culture, rock-and-roll became accessible to white teenagers. Teens such as Elvis Presley listened to late-night rhythm-and-blues radio shows that started to challenge and break down racial barriers. During the 1960s, African-American performers such as the Ronettes, the Crystals, the Temptations, and the Supremes achieved mass popularity among both African-Americans and whites. By the 1980s, African-American entertainers such as Michael Jackson achieved superstar status. Throughout the last four decades, rock music has helped integrate white and black America.

A dramatic population growth during the postwar era, the second theme of this book, provided the audience for an African-American inspired rock-and-roll. After World War II, both the United States and Great Britain experienced a tremendous baby boom. By the mid-1950s, the baby boomers had become an army of youngsters who demanded their own music. Along with their older brothers and sisters who had been born during the war, they latched onto the new rock-and-roll, idolizing a young, virile Elvis Presley who represented the hordes of postwar youth.

Rock music appealed to and reflected the interests of the baby-boom generation until the end of the seventies. The music of the Dick Clark era, the Brill Building songwriters, the Beach Boys, the Motown artists, and the early Beatles showed a preoccupation with dating, cars, high school, and teen love. As the generation matured and entered college or the work force, the music scene became more serious and was dominated by the protest music of Bob Dylan and psychedelic bands which questioned basic tenets of American society. The music became harsh and violent when college-age baby boomers were threatened by the Vietnam-era military draft and the prospect of fighting in an unpopular war. During the 1970s, after the war ended and when many of the college rebels landed lucrative jobs, glitter rock and disco exemplified the excessive, self-centered behavior of the boomers. During the 1980s, such artists as Bruce Springsteen, who matured with his audience and celebrated his fortieth birthday by the end of the decade, reflected a yearning for lost youth. Rock-and-roll became the music of a new generation, called Generation X in the popular press, only after the late 1970s when punk, MTV, rap, and grunge defined the music.

The economic climate during the postwar era serves as a third focus of this book. Favorable economic times allowed rock to flourish among the baby-boom generation. Compared to the preceding generation, which had been raised during the most severe economic depression of the twentieth century, the baby boomers in the United States lived in relative affluence. In the 1950s and early 1960s, many youths had allowances that enabled them to purchase the latest rock records. During the next 15 years, unparalleled prosperity allowed youths to consider the alternatives of hippiedom and led to the excesses and unmatched record sales of the late 1970s. The economic scene began to worsen during the late 1970s in Britain, where a new generation of youths created the sneering protest of punk, which reflected harsh economic realities.

The importance of technological advances to the development of rock, enhancing the popularity of the music by delivering it easily and inexpensively, provides another framework for *Rockin' in Time*. The electric guitar, developed by Leo Fender and popularized during the 1950s, gave rock its distinctive sound. Television brought and still brings rock to teens in their homes—Elvis Presley and the Beatles on "The Ed Sullivan Show," Dick Clark's "American Bandstand," and, currently, MTV. The portable transistor radio, and later the portable cassette tape player-recorder, provided teens the opportunity to listen to their favorite songs in the privacy of their rooms, at school, or on the streets. The inexpensive 45-rpm record allowed youths to purchase the latest hits and dominated rock sales until the 1960s, when the baby-boom generation grew older and could afford the price of an LP. Advances in the quality of sound such as high fidelity, stereo, component stereo systems, and recently the compact disc have brought the immediacy of the performance to the home.

The increasing popularity of rock music has been entwined with the development of the music industry, another focus of this book. Rock-and-roll has always been a business. At first, small independent companies such as Chess, Sun, Modern, and King recorded a commercially untested rock. As it became more popular among teens, rock-and-roll began to interest major record companies such as RCA, Decca, and Capitol, which by the 1960s dominated the field. By the 1970s, the major companies aggressively marketed their product and consolidated ranks to increase profits and successfully create an industry more profitable than network television and professional sports. In 1978, as the majors experienced a decline in sales, independent labels again arose to produce new rock styles such as punk, rap, and grunge. By the end of the 1980s, the major companies reasserted their dominance of the record industry, buoyed by the signing of new acts that had been tested by the independents and by the introduction of the compact disc, which lured many record buyers to purchase their favorite music in a different, more expensive format.

Though a business, rock music has been rebellious, which serves as the final theme of this book. Fueled by uncontrolled hormones, teenage rockers in the 1950s and early 1960s rebelled against their parents by wearing sideburns and long hair, driving fast cars, and screaming for the gyrations of Elvis Presley. In the 1960s, college-age rockers directed their frustration and anger at racial and social injustice, taking freedom rides to the South, demanding social change, and protesting the war in Vietnam. Entering the work force during the 1970s, many baby boomers submerged their anger in material excess as rock became theatrical and extravagant.

A new generation of rockers rekindled the flame of rebellion after the late 1970s. Sneering British punks, growing spiked hair, wearing ripped T-shirts, and spitting at their audiences, lashed out against economic and racial inequalities. Trying to foster a pride among African-Americans, rappers unabashedly condemned racial prejudice and its effects on African-Americans in the inner cities. In the 1990s, grunge musicians voiced the frustration and despair of their generation. Even older rock-and-rollers such as Bruce Springsteen committed themselves to specific causes such as aid to African famine victims and the crusade against apartheid. Throughout much of its existence, rebellion defined rock-and-roll.

This book places the rebellion of rock in larger racial, demographic, technological, and economic frameworks. Rather than present an encyclopaedic compilation of the thousands of well-known and obscure bands that have played throughout the years, it deals with rock-and-rollers who reflected and sometimes changed the social fabric. It does not deal with many artists, some of my favorites, who never gained general popularity and remained outside the mainstream of rock.

A Time to Rock also deals with musicians when they helped define an era. Though some creative rock musicians have changed with the times to create new styles of music that encapsulate several eras, most continue to record the music developed during their youth. This book deals with artists when they most fully reflected the world around them.

The social forces of history seldom separate into neat packages. Many of the different types of rock overlapped with one another. For example, from 1961 until the advent of the British invasion, the Brill Building songwriters, surf music, and Bob Dylan existed side by side on the charts. Though sometimes intersecting and cross-pollinating, the different periods in rock history have been divided into chapters to clearly distinguish the motivating factors behind each type of music.

A Time to Rock tries to be as impartial as possible. Even though a book cannot be wrenched from the biases of its social setting, I have attempted to present the music in a social rather than a personal context and have tried to avoid any effusive praise or disparaging remarks about any type of rock. As Sting once said, "There is no bad music, only bad musicians."

These pages explore the social history of rock-and-roll. During the more than four decades that it has been an important part of American and British culture, rock-and-roll has reflected the frustrations, hopes, joys, fears, ambitions, and desires of two generations. The different forms rock music has assumed, some of them intensely defiant, have been influenced by and have themselves affected the social climate of the United States and Great Britain.

Acknowledgments

I wish to thank several people who helped me with this book. Bill Flanagan, Timothy Leary, Michael Batt, Jamie Steiwer, Howie Wahlen, Peter Blecha, Chris Waterman, Charles Cross, Gene Stout, Jeff Taylor, Rob Innes, Adam Bratman, Carl Krikorian, Don Hood, Stephanie Haigh, Dave Wolter, and Sonny Masso provided perceptive comments on various drafts of the text. I want to thank Robert Palmer, Bob Guiccione, Jr., Alan Douglas, Mike Farrace, Gregg Vershay, and Bob Jeniker for their encouragement. My colleagues at University of Washington Extension, especially Richard Lorenzen, provided understanding and support during the writing of the book. I would especially like to thank Stewart Stern, Richard Hell, and Ed "Sugar Bear" Wells for their insights. Obviously, none of those who provided assistance can be held responsible for the contents of this book.

As in previous editions, I have others to thank for this volume. Jerry Kwiatkowski (Kaye) introduced me to the world of rock and prodded me to listen to everyone from Captain Beefheart to Eric Clapton. Mike Miller helped me explore the summer concert scene in Milwaukee. Ramona Wright, Neil Fligstein, Eileen Mortenson, Gail Fligstein, and Tom Speer did the same for me in Tucson and Seattle. On the East Coast, Dave Sharp fearlessly accompanied me on journeys to see Sid Vicious and Root Boy Slim.

I would like to acknowledge former co-workers at Second Time Around Records in Seattle—owners Wes and Barbara Geesman, Dan Johnson, Mike Schwartz, Michael Wellman, and Jim Rifleman—for adding to my understanding of rock music and the rock business. At the University of Arizona in Tucson, Donald Weinstein graciously allowed me to teach a class on the social history of rock-and-roll, the beginnings of this book; Rick Venneri did the same at the University of Washington. Students in those classes added to my knowledge of rock music. Thanks to Dudley Johnson at the University of Washington for putting me in contact with Prentice Hall.

I owe a special debt to Bob "Wildman" Campbell, who spent many hours with me analyzing the lyrics of Larry Fischer, the nuances of Tibetan Buddhist chants, Bonzo Dog Band album covers, and the hidden meaning behind the grunts of Furious Pig. Besides reading and commenting on this manuscript, he expanded my musical horizons with a series of demented tapes, which twisted this book into shape. Such a debt can never be repaid.

Many thanks to Clarence J. Stuessy of the University of Texas at San Antonio, for his review of the manuscript.

I wish to thank my parents, Peter and Eunice, for instilling in me a love of music and the written word. Thanks go to my mother for commenting on the manuscript and giving suggestions for a title. My daughter, Sara, brought me back to reality when I became overly absorbed in the manuscript and showed me that energy can be boundless. Most of all, I would like to thank my wife, Mary, for her love and companionship, her musical prowess, her editorial comments, and her indulgence of my vinyl addiction during three editions of this book.

Credits

Grateful acknowledgment is made to the following copyright holders for permission to reprint their copyrighted material.

Bruce Springsteen Music: Lyrics from "My Hometown," words and music by Bruce Springsteen, copyright © Bruce Springsteen Music. Used by permission of Bruce Springsteen Music.

Irving Music: Lyrics from "White Rabbit," lyrics and music by Grace Slick, copyright © 1967 Irving Music, Inc. (BMI). All rights reserved—International Copyright Secured.

Jondora Music: Lyrics from "Fortunate Son" by John Fogerty, copyright © 1969 Jondora Music. Courtesy Fantasy Inc.

I wish to thank the following for use of photos and help in finding them: Alligator Records, especially Bruce Iglauer; Peter Asher Management with special help from Ira Koslow; Atlantic Records; Roberta Bayley; David Bowie; Bill Graham Presents (BGP) Archives; Capitol Records; Chrysalis Records; Columbia Records; Delmark Records and Bob Koester; Brian O'Neal at D.M.B.B. Entertainment; Alan Douglas and the staff at Are You Experienced?; Elektra Records; the Estate of Elvis Presley, especially Marc Magaliff; Don Everly; Cam Garrett; Richard Hell; Isolar Enterprises; Marilyn Laverty at Shore Fire; the Library of Congress; Living Blues Archival Collection, University of Mississippi Blues Archive; MCA Records; RCA Records, especially J. Matthew Van Ryn; *Rush* Artist Management; the Seattle *Times*; Sire Records; Beverly Rupe at Specialty Records; Chris Stamp; Sun Records; and Warner Brothers Records.

I wish to pay special thanks to Barbara Krohn of the *Daily* of the University of Washington for her help in locating photos.

Every effort has been made to locate, identify, and properly credit photographers, songwriters, and song publishers. Any inadvertent omissions or errors will be corrected in future editions.

1

The Blues, Rock-and-Roll, and Racism

"It used to be called boogie-woogie, it used to be called blues, used to be called rhythm and blues. . . . It's called rock now."

Chuck Berry

A smoke-filled club, the Macomba Lounge, on the South Side of Chicago, late on a Saturday night in 1950. On a small, dimly lit stage behind the bar in the long, narrow club stood an intense African-American dressed in a bright blue suit, baggy pants, a white shirt, and a wide striped tie. He gripped an oversized electric guitar—an instrument born in the postwar urban environment—caressing, pulling, pushing, and bending the strings until he produced a sorrowful, razor-sharp cry that cut into his listeners, who responded with loud shrieks. With half-closed eyes, the guitarist peered through the smoke and saw a bar jammed with patrons who nursed half-empty beer bottles. Growling out the lyrics of "Rollin' Stone," the man's face was contorted in a painful expression that told of cotton fields in Mississippi and the experience of African-Americans in Middle America at mid-century. The singer's name was Muddy Waters, and he was playing a new, electrified music called rhythm and blues.

The rhythm and blues of Muddy Waters and other urban blues artists served as the foundation for Elvis, the Beatles, the Rolling Stones,

Jimi Hendrix, Led Zeppelin, and most other rock-and-rollers. A subtle blend of African and European traditions, it provided the necessary elements and inspiration for the birth of rock and the success of Chuck Berry and Little Richard. Despite their innovative roles, R & B artists seldom received the recognition or the money they deserved. Established crooners, disc jockeys, and record company executives, watching their share of the market shrink with the increasing popularity of R & B and its rock-and-roll offspring, torpedoed the new music by offering toned-down, white copies of black originals that left many African-American trailblazers bitter and sometimes broken.

The Birth of the Blues

The blues were an indigenous creation of black slaves who adapted their African musical heritage to the American environment. Though taking many forms and undergoing many permutations through the years, the blues formed the basis of rock-and-roll.

Torn from their kin, enduring an often fatal journey from their homes in West Africa to the American South, and forced into a servile way of life, Africans retained continuity with their past through music. Their voices glided between the lines of the more rigid European musical scale to create a distinctive new sound. To the plantation owners and overseers, the music seemed to be "rising and falling" and sounded off-key.

The music involved calculated repetitions. In this call-and-response, used often to decrease the monotony of work, one slave would call or play a lead part, and his fellow workers would follow with the same phrase or an embellishment of it until another took the lead. As one observer wrote in 1845, "Our black oarsmen made the woods echo to their song. One of them, taking the lead, first improvised a verse, paying compliments to his master's family, and to a celebrated black beauty of the neighborhood, who was compared to the 'red bird.' The other five then joined in the chorus, always repeating the same words." Some slaves, especially those from the Bantu tribe, whooped, or jumped octaves, during the call-and-response which served as a basis for field hollers.

Probably most important, the slaves, accustomed to dancing and singing to the beat of drums in Africa, emphasized rhythm over harmony. In a single song they clapped, danced, and slapped their bodies in several different rhythms, compensating for the absence of drums, which were outlawed by plantation owners, who feared that the instrument would be used to coordinate slave insurrections. One ex-slave, writing in 1853, called the polyrhythmic practice "patting juba." It was performed by "striking the right shoulder with one hand, the left with the other—all the while keeping time with the feet and singing." In contrast, noted President John Adams, whites "droned out [Protestant hymns] . . . like the braying of asses in one steady beat."

African-Americans used these African musical traits in African-

American religious ceremonies. One writer in the *Nation* described a "praise-meeting" held in 1867: "At regular intervals one hears the elder 'deaconing' a hymn-book hymn, which is sung two lines at a time, and whose wailing cadences, borne on the night air, are indescribably melancholy." The subsequent response from the congregation to the bluesy call of the minister, along with the accompanying instruments, created the rhythmic complexity common in African music.

Such African-inspired church music, later known as gospel, became the basis for the blues, which applied the music to secular themes. Bluesman Big Bill Broonzy, who recorded nearly 200 songs from 1925 to 1952, started as "a preacher—preached in the church. One day I quit and went to music." Broonzy maintained that "the blues won't die because spirituals won't die. Blues—a steal from spirituals. And rock is a steal from the blues. . . . Blues singers start out singing spirituals."

From the Rural South to the Urban North

During and after World War I, many southern African-Americans brought the blues to northern cities, especially Chicago, the end of the Illinois Central Railroad line, where the African-American population mushroomed from 40,000 in 1910 to 234,000 twenty years later. Many African-Americans left the South to escape the boll weevil, a parasitic worm that ravaged the Mississippi Delta cotton fields in 1915 and 1916. Some migrated to break loose from the shackles of crippling racial discrimination in the South. As Delta-born pianist Eddie Boyd told Living Blues, "I thought of coming to Chicago where I could get away from some of that racism and where I would have an opportunity to, well, do something with my talent. . . . It wasn't peaches and cream [in Chicago], man, but it was a hell of a lot better than down there where I was born." Once in Chicago, migrating African-Americans found jobs in steel mills, food-processing plants, and stockyards needing extra hands because of the wartime draft and a sudden cutoff of European immigration. They settled in Chicago's South and West Side neighborhoods.

The migrants to the Windy City included guitarist Tampa Red, who moved from Florida to Chicago in 1925. Pianist Eurreal Wilford ("Little Brother") Montgomery, born in 1907 on the grounds of a Louisiana lumber company, performed at logging camps until he ended up in Chicago. Big Bill Broonzy, an ex-slave's son who worked as a plowhand in Mississippi and laid railroad track in Arkansas, headed for the same destination in 1916 when drought destroyed the crops on his farm. In 1929, pianist Roosevelt Sykes, "The Honeydripper," took the same route. A few years later, harmonica wizard John Lee ("Sonny Boy") Williamson, the first Sonny Boy, migrated from Jackson, Tennessee. And about the same time, guitarist Sleepy John Estes, the son of a Tennessee sharecropper, moved to the Windy City. Remembered George Leaner, who began selling blues discs in Chicago during the 1930s: "The Illinois Central Railroad brought the blues to Chicago. With the thousands of laborers who came to work in the meat-packing plants and the steel mills came Peetie Wheatstraw, Ollie Shepard, Blind Boy Fuller, Washboard Sam, Little Brother Montgomery, Blind Lemon [Jefferson], Memphis Minnie, and Rosetta Howard."

These migrants played different styles of blues. At first, most delivered country blues. By the early 1940s, when the urban setting began to influence the music, they recorded a hybrid of blues, vaudeville styles, and newer swing rhythms, which included the boogie-woogie, rolling-bass piano, a sound that had been associated with the jump blues band of Louis Jordan. Some dubbed the early Chicago blues the "Bluebird Beat" because many of the blues artists recorded for RCA Victor's Bluebird label, started in 1933.

Lester Melrose, a white music talent-scout producer, documented the Chicago blues scene during the 1930s and 1940s. As Willie Dixon, bassist, songwriter, and talent scout, told *Living Blues*, "I started goin' up to Tampa Red's house where a lot of the other blues artists was, on 35th and State Street. He had a place up over a pawnshop. And a lotta the musicians used to go up there and write songs, lay around in there, and sleep. Lester Melrose always came there when he was in town. That was his kind of headquarters, like. And whenever he was in town, and different people had different songs that they wanted him to hear, they came by Tampa's house. . . . Big Bill Broonzy and a bunch of 'em would hang around there. And we get to singing it and seein' how it sounds. If it sounded like it was alright, then Melrose would say, 'Well, looky here, we'll try it out and see what happens.'" Melrose himself boasted that "from March 1934 to February 1951 I recorded at least 90 percent of all rhythm-and-blues talent for RCA and Columbia records." He included on his roster Big Bill Broonzy, Tampa Red, Sleepy John Estes, Roosevelt Sykes, Sonny Boy Williamson, and many others. By using the artists interchangeably, Melrose featured vocals, a guitar, and a piano to create a Chicago blues sound more enlivened and sophisticated than the more subdued country blues.

The blues became even more entrenched in northern urban areas during and after World War II, when thousands of southerners in search of work streamed into the cities. "World War I started bluesmen up North and No. II made it a mass migration," pointed out Atlantic record executive Jerry Wexler. From 1940 to 1944, estimated *Time* magazine, over 50,000 African-Americans from Mississippi alone headed for Chicago. They paid about $15 for the trip on the Illinois Central Railroad to the Windy City, the home of *The Defender*, the widely read, black-owned newspaper that encouraged southern sharecroppers to migrate to the North. From 1940 to 1950, 214,000 southern African-Americans arrived in Chicago, an increase of 77 percent in just one decade. About half the migrants came from the Mississippi Delta region, which stretched 200 miles from Memphis to Vicksburg.

Many of the Delta migrants had heard a propulsive, acoustic, personalized style of blues on their plantations. On Saturdays at parties, at picnics, and in juke joints, they listened to the moans, the heavy bass beat, and the bottleneck slide guitar of local musicians. Their favorites

Fred McDowell, Mississippi Delta blues guitarist
Photo by Chris Strachwitz, courtesy Arhoolie records

included Charley Patton, the king of the Delta blues, who played around Will Dockery's plantation during the 1920s and in 1929 recorded his classics "Pony Blues," "Pea Vine Blues," and "Tom Rushen Blues." He played with Eddie ("Son") House, a Baptist preacher who taught himself guitar at the age of 25 and in the 1930s cut such discs as "Preachin' the Blues." Robert Johnson, one of the most celebrated and legendary of the Delta blues artists, learned guitar technique from the Patton disciple Willie Brown and picked up Delta stylizings from Son House. During his brief recording career, which began in 1936, he released such gems as "Dust My Broom," "Sweet Home Chicago," "Crossroads," "Love in Vain," and "Rambling on My Mind."

Muddy Waters and Chicago R & B

Muddy Waters (a.k.a. McKinley Morganfield), who grew up in Clarksdale, Mississippi, listening to Johnson, Patton, and Son House, merged his Delta influences with the urban environment of Chicago. He had his first introduction to music in church. "I used to belong to church. I was a good Baptist, singing in church," he recollected. "So I got all of my good moaning and trembling going on for me right out of church."

Muddy bought his first guitar when he was 13. "The first one I

The Muddy Waters band, early 1950s. From left to right:
Muddy Waters (guitar), unknown, Otis Spann (piano),
Henry Strong (harmonica), Elgin Evans (drums), and
Jimmy Rogers (guitar)
Photo © MCA Records, Inc.

got," he told writer Robert Palmer, "I sold the last horse we had. Made about fifteen dollars for him, gave my grandmother seven dollars and fifty cents, I kept seven-fifty and paid about two-fifty for that guitar. It was a Stella. The peoples ordered them from Sears-Roebuck in Chicago." A young Muddy played locally around his home base, a plantation owned by Colonel William Howard Stovall. In 1941, on a trip to the Mississippi Delta in search of Robert Johnson, musicologists Alan Lomax and John Work discovered Waters, then a tenant farmer, and recorded him for the Library of Congress.

Two years later, Muddy moved to Chicago "with a suitcase, a suit of clothes, and a guitar," hoping to "get into the big record field. . . . I wanted to get out of Mississippi in the worst way," Waters told a journalist. "They had such as my mother and the older people brainwashed that people can't make it too good in the city. But I figured if anyone else was living in the city, I could make it there, too." Waters worked in a paper container factory and then as a truck driver by day, playing at parties in the evenings.

In 1944, Muddy bought his first electric guitar, an instrument probably invented and introduced for mass consumption by Leo Fender. Two years later he formed his first electric combo. Possibly the archetype of Chicago R & B artists, Muddy Waters felt compelled to electrify his sound in Chicago. "When I went into the clubs, the first thing I wanted was an amplifier. Couldn't nobody hear you with an acoustic." At least partly out of necessity, Waters combined his Delta blues with the electric guitar and amplifier, which blasted forth the tension, volume, and confusion of the big-city streets.

By combining the sounds of the country and city into a nitty-gritty, low-down, jumpy sound, Muddy Waters reflected the optimism of postwar African-Americans, who had escaped from the seemingly inescapable southern cotton fields. The urban music contrasted sharply with the more sullen country blues, born in slavery. Remembered Willie Dixon—a bassist from Vicksburg, Mississippi, and composer of such blues-rock classics as "Hoochie Coochie Man," "I'm a Man," and "Just Want to Make Love to You,"—"there was quite a few people around singin' the blues but most of 'em was singing all *sad* blues. Muddy was giving his blues a little pep." The peppy blues of artists such as Muddy Waters became known as rhythm and blues.

After four years of perfecting his electric sound in Chicago clubs, Muddy signed with Aristocrat Records, owned by Polish immigrants Leonard and Phil Chess, who operated several South Side bars, including the Macomba Lounge. At first, as Muddy told journalist Pete Welding, Leonard Chess "didn't like my style of singing; he wondered who was going to buy that. The lady [Evelyn Aron, a partner of the Chess brothers] said 'You'd be surprised.' . . . Everybody's records came out before mine, [Macomba house vocalist] Andrew Tibbs had two records before me. . . . But when they released mine, it hit the ceiling. . . . I had a hot blues out, man," Muddy remembered about his first disc, "I Can't Be Satisfied," backed with "Feel Like Going Home." "I'd be driving my truck and whenever I'd see a neon beer sign, I'd stop, go in, look at the jukebox, and see my record on there. . . . Pretty soon I'd hear it walking along the street. I'd hear it *driving* along the street."

Encouraged by success and the abandonment of the blues market by RCA and Columbia, in 1950 the brothers bought out their partner, Evelyn Aron, changed the name of the company to Chess, and began to release a series of Muddy Waters sides that became hits on the "race" charts: They first cut "Rolling Stone" backed by the Robert Johnson tune "Walkin' Blues." They followed the next year with "Long Distance Call" and "Honey Bee." By the mid-1950s, Waters had defined the raucous, urbanized, electric Delta blues, recording "Got My Mojo Working," the Delta standard "Rollin' and Tumblin'," "Mad Love," "(I'm Your) Hoochie Coochie Man," "I Just Wanna Make Love to You," and "I'm Ready," among many others. His group of the early fifties, which included Otis Spann on piano, Little Walter on harmonica, Jimmy Rogers on guitar, and Leroy ("Baby-Face") Foster on drums, stands out as one of the most explosive R & B units ever assembled.

The Wolf

Chester ("Howlin' Wolf") Burnett, Waters's musical rival at Chess, also delivered an electric version of the Delta blues. A teenaged Burnett, living on Young and Morrow's plantation near Ruleville, Mississippi, in

Hubert Sumlin (guitar) and Howlin' Wolf (seated)
at Silvio's blues club, Chicago, IL, 1960s
Photo © Ray Flerlage, Frank Driggs Collection

1926 met Charley Patton, who lived nearby on Will Dockery's plantation. As he told writer Pete Welding, "Charley Patton started me off playing. He took a liking to me, and I asked him would he learn me, and at night, after I'd get off work, I'd go and hang around." A few years later he listened to the country yodeling of another Mississippian, Jimmie Rodgers, and decided to emulate the white singer. Never mastering the yodel technique with his harsh, raspy voice, the blues singer earned a series of nicknames for his distinctive style, which included "Bull Cow," "Foot," and "The Wolf." "I just stuck to Wolf. I could do no yodelin' so I turned to Howlin'," remembered Burnett. To perfect his raspy blues, Howlin' Wolf traveled across the Delta during the next two decades and played with legendary blues artists of the area such as Robert Johnson and Rice Miller (also known as Sonny Boy Williamson II).

In 1948, at the age of 38, the Wolf plugged his Delta blues into an electric amplifier and in West Memphis formed an electric band, which at times included harp players James Cotton and Little Junior Parker. The Wolf landed a regular spot on station KWEM and began to attract attention.

Four years later, the Wolf joined the exodus to Chicago. At first, remembered Burnett's guitarist Hubert Sumlin, "he stayed at Muddy [Waters's] house for about two months. And Muddy introduced him around. Muddy was on the road a good bit in those days, so he took

Wolf and introduced him to Sylvio, Bobby and Mutt at the Zanzibar, and Ray and Ben Gold at the 708 Club. When Muddy went on the road, Wolf just stepped in his shoes in [those] three places."

A rivalry began to develop between Waters and the Wolf, who quickly established himself among the Chicago R & B crowd. Sumlin pointed out that "ever since the Wolf came to Chicago and started taking over, Muddy didn't like him too well. A kind of rivalry started up between them about who was the boss of the blues." "Every once in a while [the Wolf] would mention the fact, 'Hey man, you wrote that [song] for Muddy. How come you won't write me one like that?' But when you write one for him he wouldn't like it," recalled Willie Dixon, whom the Chess Brothers hired in 1950 as a songwriter and talent scout. Dixon "found out that all I could do was use backward psychology and tell him, 'Now here's one I wrote for Muddy, man.' 'Yeah, man, let me hear it. Yeah, that's the one for me.' And so, I'd just let him have it."

The Wolf scored a series of hits with Dixon's songs and traditional blues standards that would influence the course of rock-and-roll. He recorded his calling card, "Moanin' at Midnight"; "Killing Ground," later recorded by Jimi Hendrix; "How Many More Years," which became Led Zeppelin's "How Many More Times"; "I Ain't Superstitious," covered by Jeff Beck; and "Smokestack Lightnin'," later popularized by the Yardbirds.

Wolf's stage performances presaged later rock-and-roll antics. At the end of one performance he raced toward a wing of the stage, took a flying leap, and grabbed onto the stage curtain, still singing into his microphone. As the song built to a climax, the Wolf scaled the curtain; as the song drew to a close, he slid down the drapery. He hit the floor just as the song ended, to the screams of the audience. Recalled Sam Phillips, the genius behind Sun Records who recorded a few Howlin' Wolf songs and sold them to Chess, "God, what it would be worth on film to see the fervor in that man's face when he sang. His eyes would light up, you'd see the veins come out on his neck and, buddy, there was *nothing* on his mind but that song. He sang with his damn soul."

Other Chess Discoveries

The Chess brothers recorded other hard-driving rhythm and blues performers from the Delta. Born Ellas McDaniel in McComb, Mississippi, Bo Diddley moved to the Windy City with his family. "Oh, I played street corners until I was 19 or 20, from about 15 on," he told rock critic and musician Lenny Kaye. "Then I walked the streets around Chicago for about 12 years, before I got somebody to listen to me." Eventually, he landed a job at the 708 Club and in 1955 signed with Chess Records, where reputedly Leonard Chess gave him his stage name, Bo Diddley, "because it meant 'funny storyteller.'" That year, Diddley hit the charts with "Bo Diddley" and "I'm a Man" and subsequently with "Mona," "You Can't Judge a Book by Its Cover," and "Say Man." Though sometimes appealing to rock-and-roll fans, Diddley stood firmly rooted in the electrified Delta sound. The striking similarity between his "I'm a Man" and Muddy Waters's "Mannish Boy," both recorded in 1955, attests to Bo Diddley's Delta foundation.

Chess also recorded two pioneers of the amplified harmonica. Marion Walter Jacobs, otherwise known as Little Walter, grew up in the cotton fields of Louisiana. He learned to play the harmonica (the harp, as he called it) during his teens, patterning himself after Rice Miller, whom he discovered on "King Biscuit Time," a daily 15-minute radio show on station KFFA broadcast from Helena, Arkansas. Two years after World War II, Little Walter left home for Chicago, where he joined the Muddy Waters band. After impressing the Chess Brothers with his talent, Little Walter recorded his own compositions. In 1952, backed by the Muddy Waters group, he hit the charts with "Juke," which remained in the R & B Top 10 for 14 weeks. Little Walter quickly formed his own band, the Night Cats, and followed with "Sad Hours," "Blues with a Feeling," "You're So Fine," and in 1955 his biggest commercial success, "My Babe," a Willie Dixon composition based on the gospel song, "This Train."

Leonard Chess snagged Rice Miller (Sonny Boy Williamson II), the idol of Little Walter and the undisputed king of the R & B harmonica, when Miller moved to Milwaukee in 1955. His band included the Muddy Waters outfit and, sometimes, Robert Jr. Lockwood, who had learned guitar from Robert Johnson and for two years had played with Williamson on "King Biscuit Time." Though already a popular artist when he signed with Chess in 1955, Sonny Boy cut a number of now-classic singles for the Chicago label, including "One Way Out" covered by the Allman Brothers, and "Eyesight for the Blind," later recorded by The Who.

Bo Diddley, ca. mid 1950s
Photo courtesy Chess Records

The Independent Sweepstakes

Modern Records and its various subsidiaries, owned by Saul and Jules Bihari of Los Angeles, gave Chess its stiffest competition in the search for R & B talent. During the late forties and early fifties, the Bihari brothers made numerous scouting trips to the Mississippi Delta. They also commissioned as a talent scout pianist Ike Turner, who was then the leader of the Rhythm Kings and later gained fame as half of the Ike and Tina Turner duo.

The Biharis signed one of the most successful rhythm and blues artists, Riley "Blues Boy" King. Born on a cotton plantation near Indianola, Mississippi, the heart of the Delta, King was forced into the fields at the age of nine, working for $15 a month. "I guess the earliest sound of blues that I can remember was in the fields while people would be pickin' cotton or choppin' or somethin'," King told *Living Blues*. "Usually one guy would be plowin' by himself or maybe one guy would take his hoe and chop way out in front of everybody else and usually you would hear this guy sing most of the time. No special lyrics or anything. Just what he felt at the time. . . . When I sing and play now I can hear those same sounds that I used to hear as a kid," he added.

As with many R & B performers, King began his musical career in the church. "Singing was the thing I enjoyed doing, and when I started in school, I sang with a group: a quartet singing spirituals," King told *Downbeat*. From his father, a 15-year-old King received an eight-dollar guitar, which became the boy's constant companion. He continued to "sing gospel music, using the guitar to tune up the group I played with," he related. "When I was introduced into the army at the age of 18, I started playing around little towns, just standing on the corner. People asked me to play gospel tunes and complimented me real nicely: 'Son, if you keep it up, you're going to be real good someday.' But the people who asked me to play the blues tunes normally tipped me, many times getting me beer. So that motivated me to play the blues, you might say."

In 1949, after being discharged from the army, King hitchhiked to Memphis, Tennessee, and moved in with a cousin, Booker T. ("Bukka") White, a renowned Delta blues figure. He found a job at the Newberry Equipment Company and by the end of 1949 began singing Peptikon commercials on the black-owned radio station, WDIA. Remembered the guitarist, "This Peptikon was supposed to be good for whatever ails you, y'know, like a toothache. Anyway, they put me on from 3:30 to 3:40 and my popularity began to grow. I sang and I played by myself and I later got two men with me . . . Earl Forrest playing drums and Johnny Ace playing piano."

After a year on WDIA, King—by now called "Blues Boy," or "B. B." for short—signed a contract with Modern Records and its subsidiaries, RPM, Kent, and Crown. His music, now almost fully developed, fused his Delta influences with a piercing falsetto vocal style and a jazzy, single-note guitar attack borrowed from jazz guitarist Django Reinhardt and Texas bluesman Aaron (T-Bone) Walker, who himself had electrified the technique he had learned from country bluesman Blind Lemon Jefferson. Within a few years King's new style produced dozens of R & B classics that subsequent rock guitarists have either copied or stolen, including "Everyday I Have the Blues," "I Woke Up This Morning," and "You Upset Me Baby."

Elmore James eventually joined B. B. King at Modern Records. Born on a farm near Richland, Mississippi, James taught himself guitar by stringing a broom wire to a wall of his cabin and plunking on it. He listened to such Delta giants as Robert Johnson and Charley Patton; by the late 1940s, he had become a master of the slide guitar. Trumpet Records, started in Jackson, Mississippi, by Lillian McMurry, first recorded James. In 1952, the company released James's gut-wrenching, slashing version of Robert Johnson's "Dust My Broom." The next year, the Bihari brothers lured Elmore to Chicago, where he began to record for the Meteor label, another subsidiary of Modern. His output included a number of now-classic tunes such as "Shake Your Moneymaker," "It Hurts Me Too," "The Sky Is Crying," and "Hawaiian Boogie." Like his fellow Delta performers, Elmore James captured in his music the pain and anguish of three centuries of slavery and tenant farming. As African-American producer Bobby Robinson suggested, listen "to the raw-nerved, spine-tingling picking of the guitar and the agonized screams and the soul-stirring of Elmore James. Close your eyes, you'll see the slave ships, the auction blocks, the cotton fields, the bare backs straining, totin' that barge and liftin' that bale. You will smell the sweat, feel the lash, taste the tears and see the blood, and relive 300 years of the Blues."

The Biharis also recorded John Lee Hooker, the Delta-born guitarist who traveled north to Detroit during the postwar era. Hooker learned guitar from his stepfather, Will Moore, who had performed with Charley Patton on Dockery's plantation. He sang with various gospel groups in the Delta, left home by the age of 14, and in 1943 moved to Detroit. "At that time jobs weren't hard to get, it was during the war," recalled Hooker. "Good money, too. You could go anywhere any day and get a job, nothing to worry about too much." In the Motor City, Hooker worked by day as an orderly, as a janitor at the Dodge automobile factory and at Comco Steel, and at night played in various Detroit nightclubs. After a few years, he boasted, "I became the talk of the town around at the house parties. Finally, I met this very, very great musician, who I loved so much, I treasured him like I would a piece of gold, the great T-Bone Walker. He was the first person to get me my electric guitar."

In 1948, John Lee was spotted by record distributor Bernie Besman, who recorded Hooker on his Sensation label. For his first single he recorded "Boogie Chillin," an electric, chantlike, dark, superstitious-sounding stomp that vividly described black Detroit's main thoroughfare, Hastings Street. According to Hooker, the single "caught fire. It was ringin' all around the country. When it come out, every juke box

Little Walter Jacobs at the Chess Studios
Courtesy of MCA Records

you went to, every place you went to, every drug store you went, every-where you went, department stores, they were playin' it in there." Hook-er followed with such rhythm and blues chart climbers as "Hobo Blues," "Crawling Kingsnake Blues," "Sally Mae," "Boom! Boom!," and "I'm in the Mood," which label owner Besman leased to Modern Records.

African-American disc jockey Vivian Carter and her husband, James Bracken, founding Vee Jay Records of Chicago in 1953, noticed the success that Chess and Modern had achieved with the electrified Delta blues and jumped into the R & B field with Jimmy Reed. Born on a plantation near Dunleith, Mississippi, Reed discovered the guitar with friend and later backup musician Eddie Taylor, whose style derived from Charley Patton and Robert Johnson. He learned harmonica by "listen-ing to Sonny Boy Williams [Rice Miller]. . . . I'd slip out of the fields and go up to the house to listen to them do the 15 minutes he had to do over the radio show. He was broadcastin' for King Biscuit flour out of Helena, Arkansas." In 1941, Reed headed toward Chicago, where he worked at various steel mills and foundries. During his breaks and lunch hours, he practiced one-chord, Delta guitar shuffles and a laid-back vo-cal style that masked the biting lyrics of such songs as "Big Boss Man."

In 1953, after being rejected by Leonard Chess, who "was too tied

John Lee Hooker, mid 1950s
Frank Driggs Collection

B. B. King in concert, ca. 1968
Photo © Raeanne Rubenstein

up with Little Walter and Muddy Waters and Wolf and them, till he did-n't have no time for me," Reed signed with the newly organized Vee Jay Records. He first topped the R & B charts in 1955 with "You Don't Have to Go," and followed with a series of hits that included "Ain't That Loving You Baby," "Hush-Hush," "Honest I Do," and "Take Out Some Insurance on Me, Baby," the last covered by the Beatles in their early years.

Small, independent record companies in Los Angeles, the new home of thousands of African-Americans who had migrated to the city during World War II to secure jobs, specialized in different styles of the new R & B music. Aladdin Records, begun by brothers Leo and Edward Mesner, recorded a postwar sound that spanned the relaxed vocal stylings of Charles Brown and the more jumpy blues of Amos Milburn, who hit the charts in the early 1950s with songs about alcohol: "Bad, Bad Whiskey," "One Scotch, One Bourbon, One Beer," "Let Me Go Home, Whiskey," and "Thinking and Drinking." In 1956, the company released Shirley and Lee's "Let the Good Times Roll," which became a rallying cry for rock and rollers.

In 1945, Lew Chudd established Imperial Records in Los Angeles and achieved success with the barrelhouse, rolling piano of Antoine "Fats" Domino. Born in New Orleans, Domino learned to play piano at the age of nine and as a teenager worked in a bedspring factory by day and in local bars at night. He quickly mastered the New Orleans piano style and in 1949 signed with Imperial. He debuted with the single "Fat Man," which sold a million copies. Domino followed with a string of hits: "Ain't That a Shame," "Blueberry Hill," "Blue Monday," and "I'm Walking." From 1949 to 1962, Fats had 43 records that made *Billboard's* charts, 23 gold records, and record sales of 65 million units.

R & B record companies arose in cities other than Chicago and Los Angeles. In Cincinnati, Syd Nathan set up King Records in an abandoned ice house and recorded the jump blues of Bill Doggett and such big-band-influenced vocalists as Lonnie Johnson, Ivory Joe Hunter, and Wynonie "Mr. Blues" Harris. In 1952, African-American entrepreneur Don Robey bought the Memphis-based Duke Records and scored hits with the smooth-voiced, gospel-influenced Bobby Blue Bland and teen star Johnny Ace, a former member of the B. B. King band. In Newark, New Jersey, Herman Lubinsky jumped into the R & B field, adding such rhythm and blues vocalists as Nappy Brown and Big Maybelle to his jazz record label, Savoy. By the mid-fifties, dozens of independent companies in the major urban areas of the United States had begun to produce R & B records.

The R & B Market

The market for the new sound expanded with the number of African-Americans who flooded into northern and western cities during and after World War II. The migrants, some of them having a little extra cash for the first time, looked for entertainment but faced a number of obstacles. "Harlem folks couldn't go downtown to the Broadway theaters and movie houses," recalled Ahmet Ertegun, cofounder of Atlantic Records. "Downtown clubs had their ropes up when they came to the door. They weren't even welcome on Fifty-Second Street where all the big performers were black. . . . Even radio was white-oriented. You couldn't find a black performer on network radio. And when it came to disc jockeys on the big wattage stations, they wouldn't play a black

Fats Domino, ca. mid 1950s

record. We had a real tough time getting our records played—even Ruth Brown, who didn't sound particularly black."

For their leisure, some African-Americans in urban areas frequented segregated clubs such as the Roosevelt in Pittsburgh, the Lincoln in Los Angeles, the Royal in Baltimore, Chicago's Regal, the Howard in Washington, and the now-famous Apollo Theater in New York City. The owners of Town Hall, the only large dance hall in Philadelphia that admitted African-Americans, claimed that "swollen Negro paychecks at local war plants and shipyards" helped to increase their profits. Other African-Americans went to segregated taverns and demanded music by African-American artists on the jukeboxes.

The majority of migrants, bound closer to home by their families, found entertainment through the record. As Ahmet Ertegun suggested, most "black people had to find entertainment in their homes—and the record was it." They bought 78-rpm discs by their favorite artists in furniture stores, pharmacies, shoeshine stands, and other local businesses.

Most favored the electrified R & B sound. "The black people, particularly the black people I knew," Art Rupe, the owner of Specialty Records, recalled of the late 1940s, "looked down on country music. Among themselves, the blacks called country blues 'field nigger' music. They wanted to be citified."

At first, only African-Americans bought R & B discs. Johnny Otis, a white bandleader who grew up in a black section of Berkeley and later helped many African-American artists rise to stardom, noticed the trend: "As far as black music was concerned we had what was known as race music. Race music was Big Bill Broonzy, Peetie Wheatstraw, and things like that. Now, these things were very much part of the black community but they didn't occur anywhere else and these cats could hardly make a living plying their trade." A successful rhythm and blues recording generally sold only 400,000 copies, and, according to Jerry Wexler of Atlantic Records, "sales were localized in ghetto markets. There was no white sale, and no white radio play."

But during the early 1950s, more and more white teenagers began to become aware of R & B. At first, young southern whites started to buy records by African-American artists. As Jerry Wexler of Atlantic Records observed about his experience in the early 1950s, "We became aware that southern whites were buying our records, white kids in high school and college." In California at the same time, Johnny Otis saw the changing demographics of the R & B audiences, which were becoming dotted with white faces. In 1952, the Dolphin Record store in Los Angeles, which specialized in R & B records, reflected the trend by reporting 40 percent of its sales to whites. Eventually white teens in all parts of the country turned to rhythm and blues. In April 1955, Mitch Miller, then head of Columbia Records and later famous for the sing-along craze he masterminded, complained that "rhythm and blues songs are riding high." This " 'rock and roll' began among Negro people, was first recorded by Negro performers and had its following among Negroes in the South and also Negro urban areas in the North." But Miller noticed that "suddenly millions of white teenagers who buy most of the 'pop' records in America have latched onto rhythm and blues."

From R & B to Rock and Roll:
Little Richard and Chuck Berry

The white teens who bought R & B records favored a few showmen who delivered the most frenetic, hard-driving version of an already spirited rhythm and blues which became known as rock-and-roll. They especially idolized young R & B performers with whom they could identify. By 1955, Muddy Waters had turned 40, Howlin' Wolf was 45, Sonny Boy Williamson was 57, John Lee Hooker was 38, B. B. King was 30, and Elmore James was 37.

Little Richard and Chuck Berry, significantly younger and wilder than most R & B performers, became heroes to white teens who had discovered rhythm and blues. Little Richard, born Richard Penniman in Macon, Georgia, on December 5, 1932, sang in a Baptist church choir as a youth and traveled with his family gospel troupe, the Penniman Family. He joined various circuses and traveling shows and in the Broadway Follies met gospel R & B shouter Billy Wright, who secured a recording contract from Camden Records for the 18-year-old Little Richard. In 1951, Richard cut eight sides for Camden, which featured boogie-woogie and urban blues numbers in the style of Billy Wright.

The next year a local tough shot and killed Little Richard's father, the owner of the Tip In Inn. To support the family, Richard washed dishes in the Macon Greyhound Bus station by day and at night sang with his group, the Upsetters, at local theaters for $15 a show. "We were playing some of Roy Brown's tunes, a lot of Fats Domino tunes, some B. B. King tunes and I believe a couple of Little Walter's and a few things by Billy Wright," remembered Little Richard.

After a few years of one-night stands in southern nightclubs, Penniman began to change his style. He transformed himself from a traditional R & B singer into a wild-eyed, pompadoured madman who crashed the piano keys and screamed nonsensical lyrics at breakneck speed. Richard later recalled that "it was funny. I'd sing the songs I sing now in clubs, but the black audiences just didn't respond. They wanted blues stuff like B. B. King sings. That's what they were used to. I'd sing 'Tutti Frutti' and nothing. Then someone would get up and sing an old blues song and everyone would go wild."

On the advice of rhythm and blues singer Lloyd Price of "Lawdy Miss Clawdy" fame, Richard sent a demo tape of two rather subdued blues tunes to Art Rupe at Specialty Records in Los Angeles, which had recorded Price as well as R & B artists such as Roy Milton. The tape, according to Specialty's musical director Bumps Blackwell, was "wrapped in a piece of paper looking as though someone had eaten off it." Blackwell opened the wrapper, played the tape, and recommended that Rupe sign Little Richard.

Richard arrived in New Orleans during late 1955 for his first Specialty recording session. Reminisced Little Richard: "I cut some blues songs. During a break in the session, someone heard me playing 'Tutti Frutti' on the piano and asked about the song. We ended up recording it and it sold two hundred thousand copies in a week and a half." And a legend was born. During the next four years Richard cut a wealth of rock standards, which defined the new music: "Long Tall Sally," "Slippin' and Slidin'," "Rip It Up," "Ready Teddy," "The Girl Can't Help It," "Good Golly Miss Molly," "Jenny, Jenny," "Keep a Knockin'," and "Lucille."

Little Richard, dressed in flamboyant clothing and with a pompadour hairstyle and makeup, delivered his music in a wild stage show. His band "the Upsetters wasn't just a name; when we'd go into a place, we'd upset it! We were the first band on the road to wear pancake makeup and eye shadow, have an earring hanging out of our ear and have

The fabulous Little Richard
Courtesy of Specialty Records

our hair curled in process," remembered drummer Charles Conner. "Richard was the only guy in the band that was actually like that, but he wanted us to be different and exciting."

If anyone besides Little Richard could claim to be the father of rock-and-roll, it would be Chuck Berry. Berry, unlike almost all other R & B musicians, spent his youth in a sturdy, brick house on a tree-lined street in the middle-class outskirts of St. Louis. He first sang gospel at home with his family. As he wrote in his *Autobiography*, "Our family lived a block and a half from our church and singing became a major tradition in the Berry family. As far back as I can remember, mother's

Chuck Berry, performing his famous
"Duck Walk," ca. late 1950s

household chanting of those gospel tunes rang through my childhood. The members of the family, regardless of what they were doing at the time, had a habit of joining with another member who would start singing, following along and harmonizing. Looking back I'm sure that my musical roots were planted, then and there."

The young Berry soon heard a different music on the radio. "The beautiful harmony of the country music that KMOK radio station played was almost irresistible," recalled Berry. By his teens Berry also had become a fan of Tampa Red, Arthur Crudup, and, especially, Muddy Waters.

After a stay in reform school and various odd jobs, which included work as a cosmetologist and an assembler at the General Motors Fisher Body plant, Berry turned to rhythm and blues. He obtained his first guitar from St. Louis R & B performer Joe Sherman and, in the early fifties, formed a rhythm and blues trio with Johnny Johnson on piano and Ebby Harding on drums that played "backyards, barbecues, house parties" and at St. Louis bars such as the Cosmopolitan Club.

In the spring of 1955, 24-year-old Berry and a friend traveled to Chicago, then the mecca of urban blues. He watched the shows of Howlin' Wolf, Elmore James, and his idol, Muddy Waters. After a late-night set, Berry approached Waters for his autograph and got "the feeling I suppose one would get from having a word with the president or the pope." When Berry asked Muddy about his chances of making a record, Waters replied, "Yeah, see Leonard Chess, yeah, Chess Records over on Forty-seventh and Cottage." To Berry, Waters "was the godfather of the blues. He was perhaps the greatest inspiration in the launching of my career."

Chuck Berry took Muddy Waters's advice. The next day he rushed to the Chess offices and talked with Leonard Chess, who asked for a demo tape of original songs within a week. Berry returned with a tape that included a country song, "Ida May." Chess, remembered Berry, "couldn't believe that a country tune (he called it a 'hillbilly song') could be written by a black guy. He wanted us to record that particular song." In the studio, on the advice of Willie Dixon, Berry added "a little blues" to the tune, renamed it "Maybelline" after the trade name on a mascara box in the corner of the studio and backed it with the slow blues, "Wee Wee Hours."

Berry convinced Chess to release "Maybelline," a country song adapted to a boogie-woogie beat, which hinted at the marriage between country and R & B that would reach full fruition with the rockabillies. Within weeks Berry's upbeat song had received national airplay. The guitarist-songwriter followed with "Roll Over Beethoven (Dig These Rhythm and Blues)," "School Days," "Rock and Roll Music," "Sweet Little Sixteen," "Johnny Be Goode," "Rockin' and Rollin'," and an almost endless list of other songs. He embarked upon a whirlwind tour of the country, playing 101 engagements in 101 nights, during which he perfected antics such as the duck walk.

By 1956, Chuck Berry and Little Richard had bridged the short gap between rhythm and blues and what became known as rock-and-roll, originally an African-American euphemism for sexual intercourse. They delivered a frantic, blues-based sound to teens who claimed the music as their own.

Social Change and Rock and Roll

The popularity of a wild, teen-oriented rock-and-roll can be attributed to a number of social changes that occurred during the 1950s. Television made radio space available to more recording artists. Before the 1950s, network radio shows, many of them broadcast live, dominated the airwaves and, as Johnny Otis argued, "in the thirties and forties, black music was summarily cut off the radio." Music by African-Americans "simply was not played, black music of any kind—even a Louis Armstrong was not played on the air." After World War II, television became more popular and affordable. By 1953, more than 300 television stations in the United States broadcast to more than 27 million television sets. By absorbing the network radio shows to fill a programming void, television created air time for a greater variety of records, including discs by African-American artists.

Many of the disc jockeys who spun R & B records became diehard advocates of the music. B. Mitchell Reed, who jockeyed on the leading Los Angeles rock station, KMET FM, became "enthralled with rock" during the 1950s and convinced the management to switch from a jazz format to rock when he "realized that the roots of the stuff that I was playing—the rock—had come from the jazz and blues I'd been playing before." Even earlier than Reed's conversion to rock, the Los Angeles "dean of the DJs," Al Jarvis, "wanted the black artists to be heard" and introduced them on his show.

Rock-and-roll's superpromoter was Alan Freed. Freed, a student of trombone and music theory, began his broadcasting career in New Castle, Pennsylvania, on the classical station WKST. After a stint on a station in Akron, Ohio, in 1951 he landed a job in Cleveland on the independent station WJW. Convinced by record store owner Leo Mintz, Freed began to play R & B records on his program. He picked the howling "Blues for the Red Boy," a release by Todd Rhodes on King Records, for his theme song and named his show "The Moondog Rock 'n' Roll House Party."

Freed ceaselessly marketed the new music. In 1952 and 1953, the disc jockey organized increasingly racially integrated rock-and-roll concerts in the Cleveland area that met with enthusiastic responses. For the first, the "MoonDog Coronation Ball," he attracted 18,000 teens to an auditorium that seated 9,000 and was forced to cancel the show. By late 1954, the successful Freed landed a key nighttime spot on the New York station WINS. While there, the DJ introduced thousands of young whites on the East Coast to African-American music, consistently befriending African-American artists who recorded on the small, independent labels. Freed also managed several R & B acts and appeared

22

in movies such as "Don't Knock the Rock," "Rock, Rock, Rock," and the now-famous "Rock Around the Clock," which caused riots in the United States and Europe and further familiarized white youths with R & B, now being called rock-and-roll by Freed.

Young teens listened to disc jockeys such as Freed on a new gadget, the portable transistorized radio. First developed in 1947 at the Bell Laboratory in New Jersey, it reached the general public by 1953. Within a decade more than 12 million consumers, many of them teens, bought hand-held radios each year. It offered teens on the move an inexpensive means of experiencing the exciting new music called rock-and-roll.

The car radio served the same purpose as the portable transistor model. Marketed initially in the 1950s, it became standard equipment within a few years. By 1963, music blasted forth from the dashboards of more than 50 million automobiles speeding down the highways and back roads of the country. The car radio introduced rock-and-roll to many teens who used the automobile in such rites of passage as the school prom and the first date. In 1956, a nervous, clammy-palmed youth, sitting next to his girlfriend and behind the wheel of his father's El Dorado, could hear Chuck Berry detail his exploits with Maybelline that occurred in a similar car. The car radio helped deliver rock-and-roll to a mobile, young, car-crazy generation.

The civil rights movement helped make possible the acceptance of African-American-inspired music by white teens. In 1954, the year that the Canadian group, the Crew-Cuts, made "Sh-Boom" into rock-and-roll's first commercial success, the Supreme Court handed down *Brown v. the Board of Education of Topeka*. Convinced by the arguments of Thurgood Marshall, counsel for the NAACP and later a Supreme Court justice himself, the court unanimously banned segregation in public schools and ordered school districts to desegregate. "In the field of public education," Chief Justice Earl Warren contended, "the doctrine of 'separate but equal' has no place. Separate educational facilities are inherently unequal." By overturning the "separate but equal" doctrine of the 1896 *Plessy v. Ferguson* case, the court had strongly endorsed African-American rights and had helped to start a civil rights movement that would foster an awareness and acceptance of African-American culture, including the African-American-based rock-and-roll.

The number of youths who would feel the impact of the *Brown* decision was growing rapidly. In 1946, about 5.6 million teenagers attended American high schools. Ten years later, the number climbed to 6.8 million; in 1960 the number of teens increased to 11.8 million. Observers called it the "wartime baby boom." "No decrease is in sight this century," predicted a Census Bureau official in 1955. "We have come to consider it routine to report new all-time high records."

Many of these teens, living during prosperous times, had money in their pockets to spend on records. Between 1940 and 1954, the United States gross national product (GNP) rose from $200 billion to $360 billion, and the average yearly family income increased from about $5000 to $6200. Having more leisure time than during the war, most Americans spent much of this extra money on consumer items such as paperback novels, television sets, cameras, and electrical appliances. Teenagers received sizable allowances totaling more than $9 billion in 1957 and $10.5 billion in 1963, some of which was spent on records. In a 1960 survey of 4500 teenaged girls conducted by *Seventeen* magazine, the average teen had "a weekly income of $9.53, gets up at 7:43 A.M., and listens to the radio two hours a day." Wanting to own the songs they heard, more than 70 percent of the girls bought records with their allowances. Along with other factors, an increasingly affluent society, paved the way for the mass consumption of rock-and-roll.

By 1954, rock-and-roll was beginning to achieve a general popularity among white youths. Teens bought discs by Chuck Berry and Little Richard and soon started to dance to the music. When Ralph Bass, a producer for Chess Records, went on the road with African-American acts in the late 1940s and early 1950s, "they didn't let whites into the clubs. Then they got 'white spectator tickets' for the worst corner of the joint. They had to keep the white kids out, so they'd have white nights sometimes, or they'd put a rope across the middle of the floor. The blacks on one side, whites on the other digging how the blacks were dancing and copying them. Then, hell, the rope would come down, and they'd all be dancing together." Touring with Fats Domino, Chuck Berry also saw audiences beginning to integrate: "Salt and pepper all mixed together, and we'd say, 'Well, look what's happening.' "

Racist Backlash

The integration of white and black youths elicited a racist response from many white adults. In 1956, as white southerners lashed out against desegregation and attacked civil rights workers, a spokesman for the White Citizens Council of Birmingham, Alabama, charged that rock-and-roll—"the basic, heavy-beat music of the Negroes"—appealed to "the base in man, brings out animalism and vulgarity" and, most important, represented a "plot to mongrelize America."

Other whites expressed their fear of race mixing by complaining about the sexual overtones of rock. Testifying before a Senate subcommittee in 1958, Vance Packard, author of *Hidden Persuaders*, cautioned that rock-and-roll stirred "the animal instinct in modern teenagers" by its "raw savage tone." "What are we talking about?" Packard concluded, quoting an article from a 1955 issue of *Variety*. "We are talking about rock 'n' roll, about 'hug' and 'squeeze' and kindred euphemisms which are attempting a total breakdown of all reticences about sex." *Cash Box* similarly editorialized that "really dirty records" had been "getting air time," and suggested that companies "stop making dirty R & B records." Russ Sanjek, later vice-president of Broadcast Music, Inc. (BMI), which initially licensed most rock songs, explained the white fear of possible white and African-American sexual relations:

"It was a time when many a mother ripped pictures of Fats Domino off her daughter's bedroom wall. She remembered what she felt toward her Bing Crosby pin-up, and she didn't want her daughter creaming for Fats."

A few adults defended the music of their children. In 1958, one mother from Fort Edward, New York, found that rock eased the boredom of her housework: "After all how much pep can you put into mopping the floor to 'Some Enchanted Evening,' but try it to 'Sweet Little Sixteen' by Chuck Berry and see how fast the work gets done. (I know the above is silly, but I just had to write it because it really is true, you know.) . . . Rock and roll has a good beat and a jolly approach that keeps you on your toes," she added.

To jazz innovator Count Basie, the uproar over rock reminded him of the racist slurs hurled at his music two decades earlier. After living through the "swing era of the late 1930s when there was a lot of screaming pretty much like the furor being stirred up today," he remembered, "one comment in the 1930s, which said 'jam sessions, jitterbugs, and cannibalistic rhythm orgies are wooing our youth along the primrose path to hell.' The funny thing is, a lot of the kids who used to crowd around the bandstand while we played in the 1930s are still coming around today to catch us. A lot of them are parents in the PTA, and leading citizens."

Many whites refused to accept the Count's logic. To waylay expected integration, they tried to outlaw rock-and-roll. The Houston Juvenile Delinquency and Crime Commission blacklisted 30 songs that it considered obscene, all of them by African-American artists, which included "Honey Love" by the Drifters, "Too Much Lovin'," by the 5 Royales', "Work with Me Annie" by Hank Ballard and the Midnighters, and Ray Charles's "I Got a Woman." R & B singer Jimmy Witherspoon, living in Houston at the time, felt that "the blacks was starting a thing in America for equality. The radio stations and the people in the South was fighting us. And they were hiring program directors to program the tunes. . . . They banned Little Richard's tune ('Long Tall Sally') in Houston." In Memphis, station WDIA banned the recordings of thirty African-American rock-and-roll singers.

In some areas, violence erupted in response to the new music. In April 1956, at a Nat King Cole concert, the White Citizens Council of Birmingham, equating jazz with R & B, jumped on the stage and beat the performer. Explaining the incident, Ray Charles said it happened because "the young white girls run up and say, 'Oh, Nat!' and they say, 'No, we can't have *that!*' Come on man, shit, that's where it is." At other rock-and-roll shows, Bo Diddley reminded interviewer Lou Cohen that "we used to have funny things like bomb scares and stuff like that because we were in South Carolina where the KKK didn't want us performing."

The Music Industry vs. Rock and Roll

The music industry also organized against rock-and-roll. Crooners whose careers had taken nose dives because of the new music bitterly condemned it. Testifying before Congress in 1958, Frank Sinatra called rock "the most brutal, ugly, desperate, vicious form of expression it has been my misfortune to hear." He labeled rock-and-rollers "cretinous goons" who lured teenagers by "almost imbecilic reiterations and sly—lewd—in plain fact dirty—lyrics." By such devious means, he concluded, rock managed "to be the martial music of every sideburned delinquent on the face of the earth." A year earlier, Sammy Davis, Jr., an African-American who had achieved success by singing as a crooner, put it more succinctly: "If rock `n' roll is here to stay I might commit suicide." At the same time, crooner Dean Martin cryptically ascribed the rise of rock to "unnatural forces."

Pat Boone, ca.1958, in concert
Photo by Popsie Randolph, Frank Driggs Collection

26

Disc jockeys who lost listeners from their pop and classical programs to rock-and-roll stations similarly spoke out against their competition. In 1955, Bob Tilton of WMFM in Madison, Wisconsin, called for "some records for adults that don't rock, roll, wham, bam, or fade to flat tones." To Chuck Blower of KTKT in Tucson, the year 1955, "with the tremendous upsurge of R & B into the pop crop—the almost complete absence of good taste, to say nothing of good grammar . . . has been the worst and certainly the most frustrating pop year I have ever known." A *Billboard* survey in the same year indicated that "many jockeys believe the quality of the pop platter has seriously deteriorated in the past year. . . . Several jockeys are strongly opposed to the rhythm and blues influence in pop music."

Songwriters in the American Society of Composers, Authors, and Publishers (ASCAP) exhibited an equal disdain for rock. Because the new music usually was written by the performers themselves, professional songwriters began to scramble for work and soon complained. Lyricist Billy Rose, then a board member of ASCAP, labeled rock-and-roll songs "junk," and "in many cases they are obscene junk much on the level with dirty comic magazines." Meredith Wilson, the songwriter of *Music Man* fame, charged that "rock and roll is dull, ugly, amateurish, immature, trite, banal and stale. It glorifies the mediocre, the nasty, the bawdy, the cheap, the tasteless." Mrs. Barbara Lehrman, a listener from Brooklyn, New York, supported Wilson's contention: "Let's give the music business back to the music men," she demanded in a letter to Senator John Pastore. "Let's clear the air of ear-splitting claptrap." To reassert their control, in November 1953 ASCAP songwriters initiated a $150 million antitrust lawsuit against the three major broadcasting networks, Columbia Records, RCA, and Broadcast Music, Inc. (BMI), a song/performance licensing competitor which had been formed in 1941 by broadcasters and which catered to R & B, country music and the new rock 'n' roll. The battle eventually ended in a congressional subcommittee, but did little to squelch the popularity of rock music.

The Blanching of Rock

Many record executives complained about and successfully undermined African-American rockers and their music. Some leaders of the music industry personally disliked rock-and-roll. RCA vice-president George Marek did not "happen to like [rock] particularly, but then I like Verdi and I like Brahms and I like Beethoven." Explained Ahmet Ertegun, who had recorded R & B artists on his Atlantic Records: "You couldn't expect a man who loved 'April in Paris' or who had recorded Hudson De-Lange in the 30s when he was beginning in the business, to like lyrics like 'I Wanna Boogie Your Woogie,' and 'Louie, Louie.' He had always thought race music and hillbilly were corny, and so he thought rock 'n' roll was for morons."

More important than their personal tastes, established record executives feared the economic consequences of a new popular music that they did not control. Outdistanced by new, independent labels that had a virtual monopoly on rock acts by 1955, they worried about their share of the market, especially when white teens started to buy rock-and-roll records.

To reverse this trend, larger companies signed white artists to copy, or "cover," the songs of African-American artists, sometimes sanitizing the lyrics. Charles "Pat" Boone, a descendent of pioneer Daniel Boone who wore a white sweater and white buck shoes, became the most successful cover artist of the era. After hosting a radio program on Nashville station WSIX, Boone signed with Dot Records in early 1955 and hit the top of the charts with a cover of Fats Domino's "Ain't That a Shame." He continued to score hits with such other covers as "At My Front Door" by the El Dorados, Big Joe Turner's "Honey Hush," "Tutti Frutti" and "Long Tall Sally" by Little Richard, the Flamingos's "I'll Be Home," and Ivory Joe Hunter's "I Almost Lost My Mind," among many others. All told, Boone recorded 60 hit singles, six of them reaching the number-one spot.

Boone many times toned down the originals. He reworked T-Bone Walker's "Stormy Monday," substituting the phrase "drinkin' Coca Cola" for "drinkin' wine." When covering "Tutti Frutti," Boone explained, "I had to change some words, because they seemed too raw for me. I wrote, 'Pretty little Susie is the girl for me,' instead of 'Boys, you don't know what she do to me.' " "I had to be selective and change some lyrics, but nobody seemed to care," remembered the singer. "It made it more vanilla."

Other white singers covered songs of R & B artists first released by independent labels. The McGuire Sisters copied "Sincerely" by the Moonglows; Dorothy Collins took Clyde McPhatter's "Seven Days"; Perry Como stole "Kokomo" from Gene and Eunice; and the Crew-Cuts covered the Penguins' "Earth Angel" and took their monster hit, "Sh-Boom," from the Chords.

Some of the cover artists believed their versions furthered the development of rock-and-roll. "R & B is a distinctive kind of music; it doesn't appeal to everybody," argued Pat Boone. "So if it hadn't been for the vanilla versions of the R & B songs in the 50s, you could certainly imagine that rock 'n' roll, as we think of it, would never have happened." "Imitation may be the sincerest form of flattery, but that kind of flattery I can do without," countered LaVern Baker, who hit the R & B chart on Atlantic Records in 1955 with "That's All I Need" and "Tweedle Dee," and saw her hits covered by white singers.

To sell these imitations, Columbia, Capitol, Decca, and RCA employed new marketing techniques. The companies placed their product on racks in suburban supermarkets, which by 1956 sold $14 million worth of records and by 1957 sold $40 million of records, almost 20 percent of all record sales. In addition, Columbia and then RCA and Capitol started mail-order record clubs to further increase sales.

Many disc jockeys aided the major companies in the purge of the independent labels. Although a few jockeys such as Alan Freed refused to spin covers, most gladly played "white" music. "It was a picnic for the majors," Ahmet Ertegun of Atlantic Records told an interviewer. "They'd copy our records, except that they'd use a white artist. And the white stations would play them while we couldn't get our records on. 'Sorry,' they'd say. 'It's too rough for us.' Or: 'Sorry, we don't program that kind of music.'" Danny Kessler of the independent Okeh Records also found that "the odds for a black record to crack through were slim. If the black record began to happen, the chances were that a white artist would cover—and the big stations would play the white record. . . . There was a color line, and it wasn't easy to cross."

Industry leaders even succeeded in banning some African-American artists from the airwaves. In one instance, CBS television executives discontinued the popular "Rock 'n' Roll Dance Party" of Alan Freed when the cameras strayed to a shot of African-American singer Frankie Lymon of the Teenagers dancing with a white girl.

The introduction of the 45-rpm record by the major companies helped undermine the power of the independents. Leon Rene of the small Exclusive Records outlined the effects of the new format: "We had things going our way until Victor introduced the seven-inch vinyl, 45-rpm record, which revolutionized the record business and made the breakable, ten-inch 78-rpm obsolete overnight. . . . Competition with the majors, however, forced the independent labels to use the seven-inch 45-rpm records, and they had to reduce the price of R & B records from a dollar five to seventy-five cents, retail. This forced many independent companies out of business."

Through all of these efforts, businessmen at the head of the major companies suppressed or at least curtailed the success of the independents and their African-American performers. The McGuire Sisters' copy of "Sincerely," for example, sold more than six times as many records as the Moonglows' original. In 1955 and 1956, the covers by such white artists as Pat Boone climbed to the top of the charts, while most African-American artists received little fame or money for their pioneering efforts.

By the early 1960s, Wynonie Harris tended bar; Amos Milburn became a hotel clerk; and Muddy Waters, Howlin' Wolf, and Bo Diddley were forced to tour constantly to make a living. "With me there had to be a copy," complained Bo Diddley 20 years later. "They wouldn't buy me, but they would buy a white copy of me. Elvis got me. I don't even like to talk about it. I was Chess Records along with Muddy Waters, Koko Taylor, Etta James, Chuck Berry, Little Walter, Howlin' Wolf. Without us there wouldn't have been no Chess Records. I went through things like, 'Oh, you got a hit record but we need to break it into the white market. We need to get some guy to cover it.' And I would say, 'What do you mean?' They would never tell me it was a racial problem." Johnny Otis put the problem succinctly: African-American artists developed the music and got "ripped off and the glory and the money goes to the white artists."

The Story of Arthur "Big Boy" Crudup

The saga of Arthur "Big Boy" Crudup bears testimony to Otis's charge. Crudup, born in Forrest, Mississippi, worked as a manual laborer in the fields, logging camps, sawmills, and construction projects until his thirties. In 1941, he headed to Chicago and signed a contract with RCA. Between 1941 and 1956, Crudup released over 80 sides, including "Mean Ole Frisco Blues," "Rock Me Mama," "She's Gone," "That's All Right, Mama," and "My Baby Left Me," that have been subsequently done by Elvis Presley, Creedence Clearwater Revival, Elton John, Rod Stewart, Canned Heat, Johnny Winter, and many others. By the late 1950s, Crudup quit playing. "I realized I was making everybody rich, and here I was poor."

Arthur "Big Boy" Crudup, ca. 1941
Frank Driggs Collection

30

In 1968, Dick Waterman, an agent and manager for many blues artists, began the fight for Crudup's royalties through the American Guild of Authors and Composers. After two years he reached an agreement for $60,000 in back royalties with Hill and Range Songs, which claimed ownership of Big Boy's compositions. Crudup and his four children traveled from their home in Virginia to New York City and signed the requisite papers in the Hill and Range office, a converted four-story mansion. John Clark, the Hill and Range attorney, took the papers to Julian Aberbach, head of Hill and Range, for his signature, while Waterman, Crudup, and his children "all patted each other on the back and congratulated Arthur that justice had finally been done." But, according to Waterman, "the next thing, John Clark comes back in the room, looking stunned and pale, and says that Aberbach refused to sign because he felt that the settlement gave away more than he would lose in legal action. We all waited for the punch line, for him to break out laughing and whip the check out of the folder. But it wasn't a joke. We sat around and looked at each other." Crudup, who once said "I was born poor, I live poor, and I'm going to die poor," passed away four years later, nearly destitute.

In only a few years rock-and-roll, recorded and promoted by small independents, had become a major force in popular music. The major record labels, publishing companies, and disc jockeys, though refusing to accord independent labels and their African-American artists the success that they deserved, tried to capture the rock-and-roll teen market. In 1956, they capitalized on a fusion of African-American R & B and white country sounds that would change the face of American popular music.

2

Elvis and Rockabilly

"I love the rhythm and beat of good rock and roll music and I think most people like it too. After all, it's a combination of folk or hillbilly music and gospel singing."

Elvis Presley

Rockabilly Roots

Elvis Presley, a kinetic image in white suede shoes, an oversized, white-checkered jacket over a jet-black shirt with an upturned collar, and *no tie*. He violently shook his black zoot-suit pants as he gyrated his hips and legs. A sneering, rebellious expression covered Presley's face, and his greased hair fell over his sweat-drenched forehead. The singer grabbed a microphone as if he were going to wrench it from its metal base and barked, snarled, whimpered, and shouted into it. Elvis warded off screaming fans who pulled at his loose pants, his suit, and his shirt, lusting to tear off a piece of the raw energy that burst forth. Swaggering across the stage, he sang a sexually charged music that fused a white country past with African-American sounds. Elvis Presley, singing to hordes of adoring, frantic teens, delivered a sound called *rockabilly* that would change the direction of popular music.

White teenagers from poor southern backgrounds, growing up in the border states where black and white cultures stood face to face over a seemingly impassable chasm, concocted the pulsating mixture of African-American-inspired rhythm and blues and country and western known as rockabilly. They were teenagers such as Jerry Lee Lewis, who leapt on his piano, banged the keys with his feet, and heaved his jacket, and sometimes his shredded shirt, to the audience; the more subdued Carl Perkins, writer of "Blue Suede Shoes," "Boppin' the Blues," and many other classics; Johnny Cash, who launched his career with "The Ballad of a Teenage Queen," "Get Rhythm," and "Folsom Prison Blues"; Johnny Burnette, the cofounder of the crazed Rock and Roll Trio with brother Dorsey and Paul Burlison; the quiet, bespectacled Texan, Charles ("Buddy") Holly; and, of course, Elvis Presley, the pace setter of the new music, whose raw edge drove crowds to a frenzy. Despite the warnings of many horrified adults, these poor southern whites spread the message of rock-and-roll to millions of clamoring teenage fans and vaulted to the top of the national charts.

Most rockabillies never dreamed of such success. Presley, the king of swagger, the musical embodiment of James Dean's celluloid image, grew up in a 30-foot-long, two-room house in the poor section of Tupelo, Mississippi. His father, Vernon, sharecropped and worked odd jobs, while his mother, Gladys, did piecework as a sewing machine operator. When Elvis was born on January 8, 1935, one neighbor remembered that his parents "didn't have insurance and the doctor didn't believe in carrying his expectant mothers to the hospital, so Gladys stayed at home." During Elvis's childhood in Tupelo, noted a friend, the Presleys "lost their house and moved several times. They lived in several houses this side of the highway, on Kelly Street, then on Barry. Later the house on Barry was condemned. They was real poor. They just got by." In September 1948, the Presley family moved from Mississippi. As Elvis told it: "We were broke, man, broke, and we left Tupelo overnight. Dad packed all our belongings in boxes and put them on the top and in the trunk of a 1939 Plymouth. We just headed to Memphis. Things had to be better."

In Memphis, the standing of the Presleys did not improve initially. Vernon worked for a tool company, as a truck driver, and finally, in 1949, landed a job as a laborer at the United Paint Company. Earning less than $40 a week, he paid the rent on an apartment in the Lauderdale Courts, a federally funded housing project. Elvis attended nearby Humes High School, "a lower poverty-type school, one of the lowest in Memphis," according to one of Presley's classmates. After graduating from Humes in 1953, he did factory work at the Precision Tool Company and then drove a truck for the Crown Electric Company until he turned to music. Jane Richardson, one of two home service advisors working for the Memphis Housing Authority, summed up the condition of the Presleys during their first years in Memphis: "They were just poor people."

Other rockabilly stars came from similarly impoverished backgrounds. Jerry Lee Lewis, who scored hits in 1957 with "Great Balls of Fire" and "Whole Lotta Shakin' Goin' On," was born in September 1935 on a farm outside Ferriday, Louisiana. His father, the gaunt-faced Elmo, eked out a living doing carpentry work and by growing surplus produce on the farm. Johnny Cash was born on February 26, 1932, into a poor country family in Kingland, Arkansas. When Franklin D. Roosevelt's New Deal came to the South, the Cash family moved to Dyess, Arkansas, as part of a resettlement program for submarginal farmers. Johnny later enlisted in the Air Force and after his discharge sold refrigerators in Memphis. The boredom of the sales job prompted him to write the classic "I Walk the Line." Carl Perkins grew up only a few miles from Johnny Cash—according to Cash, "he on the Tennessee side of the Mississippi, I on the Arkansas side. We both lived on a poor cotton farm." When writing "Blue Suede Shoes," Perkins recounted, "me and my wife Valda were living in a government project in Jackson, Tennessee. Had the idea in my head, seeing kids in the bandstand so proud of their new city shoes—you gotta be real poor to care about new shoes like I did—and that morning I went downstairs and wrote out the words on a potato sack—we didn't have reason to have writing paper around."

The Rockabilly Sound

These poor youths combined the two indigenous musical forms of the rural American South: the blues and country music. As did the Delmore Brothers in the 1930s and Arthur "Guitar Boogie" Smith in the 1940s, Elvis Presley looked to both African-American and white music for inspiration. A member of the evangelical First Assembly of God Church in Tupelo, Elvis "used to go to these religious singings all the time. There were these singers, perfectly fine singers, but nobody responded to them. Then there was the preachers and they cut up all over the place, jumpin' on the piano, movin' ever' which way. The audience liked 'em. I guess I learned from them."

Elvis listened to such bluesmen of the Mississippi Delta as Big Bill Broonzy, B. B. King, John Lee Hooker, and Chester ("Howlin' Wolf") Burnett, hearing them on late-night radio and in the clubs along Beale Street in Memphis, one of the main thoroughfares of African-American musical culture in the South. According to blues great B. B. King, "I knew Elvis before he was popular. He used to come around and be around us a lot. There was a place we used to go and hang out on Beale Street. People had like pawn shops there and a lot of us used to hang around in certain of these places and this was where I met him."

The Presley sound also was steeped in the country and western tradition of the South—Roy Acuff, Ernest Tubb, Ted Daffan, Bob Wills, and Jimmie Rodgers. In late 1954, Elvis, then called the King of the Western Bop, played the Bel Air Club in Memphis with bassist Bill Black and guitarist Scotty Moore in Doug Poindexter's Starlite Wranglers. At that time, recalled Poindexter, "we were strictly a country band. Elvis worked hard at fitting in, but he sure didn't cause too many riots in them days."

Presley's first recordings revealed his dual influences: a "race" number written by Arthur ("Big Boy") Crudup, "That's All Right, Mama," and a Bill Monroe country tune, "Blue Moon of Kentucky." As Presley indicated at the time, "I love the rhythm and beat of good rock and roll music and I think most people like it too. After all, it's a combination of folk or hillbilly music and gospel singing."

Ironically, at least to self-righteous northerners, southern whites incorporated African-American sounds into their music. "The break-through didn't come, as you might expect, in the North," observed Atlantic Record cofounder Ahmet Ertegun. "No, it was 'prejudiced' white Southerners who began programming R & B. They began playing Fats Domino, Ivory Joe Hunter, Roy Milton, Ruth Brown, Amos Milburn, because young white teenagers heard them on those top-of-the dial stations and began requesting them. What the hell was Elvis listening to when he was growing up?" Added Jerry Wexler, another of the forces behind Atlantic: "Despite the Ku Klux Klan and bloodshed, the South-ern white is a helluva lot closer to the Negro psyche and black soul than your liberal white Northerner."

Millon-dollar quartet of Sun Records. From left to right: Jerry Lee Lewis, Carl Perkins, Elvis Presley, and Johnny Cash
Courtesy of Sun Records

Sun Records and Elvis

Many southern rockabillies recorded their brand of raucous black-and-white blues at the Sun Record Company in Memphis, which was owned by Sam Phillips. Phillips, growing up near Florence, Alabama, and working in the cotton fields as a boy, seldom noticed "white people singing a lot when they were chopping cotton, but the odd part about it is I never heard a black man who couldn't sing good. Even off key, it had a spontaneity about it that would grab my ear." He "got turned on to rock and roll immediately, when it was still rhythm and blues," he later related. "I always felt that rhythm and blues had a special viability." During the early 1940s, a young Phillips landed a job as a disc jockey at WLAY in Muscle Shoals, Alabama, moved to WLAC in Nashville, and ended at WREC in Memphis.

Phillips, earning certification as a radio engineer through a correspondence program, built his own recording studio in a converted radiator shop on Union Avenue in Memphis to record R & B artists, since, in his words, "there was no place in the South they could go to record, the nearest place where they made so-called race records—which was soon to be called rhythm and blues—was Chicago." He cut sides for such independent companies as Chess and Modern, with such performers as Howlin' Wolf, Big Walter Horton, Joe Louis Hill, Rosco Gordon (who began to combine R & B and country), B. B. King, and Jackie Brenston, who with the Ike Turner band cut "Rocket 88."

The R & B orientation of Sun Records began to change during the early 1950s. Many of the best African-American performers in Memphis, such as B. B. King and Howlin' Wolf, moved to Chicago, the rhythm and blues capital of the world, and the artists remaining at Sun sold only a limited number of discs. Phillips, still in his twenties, also sought a younger audience. As he told *Rolling Stone* magazine, he wanted his records to appeal "most especially to young whites, young blacks and then thirdly to the older blacks. . . . There was just no music for young people then except for a few little kiddy records put out by the major labels." Faced with a declining business in R & B, Phillips confided to his secretary that "if I could find a white man who had the Negro sound and the Negro feel, I could make a billion dollars."

Elvis Presley walked into the Sun Records studio and gave Sam Phillips the sound he sought. In 1953, an 18-year-old Presley recorded the Ink Spots' "My Happiness" as a present for his mother at the Memphis Recording Service, a section of the Sun Studio where anyone could record a 10-inch acetate for four dollars. On a Friday in January 1954, he returned and cut his second disc—a ballad, "Casual Love," and a country tune, "I'll Never Stand in Your Way." Marion Keisker, the secretary at the studio, taped the takes and rushed them to her boss.

After a few weeks, Phillips telephoned Presley to make arrangements for some recording sessions. Presley, guitarist Scotty Moore, and bass player Bill Black struggled without results until finally a disgusted Phillips "went back to the booth. I left the mikes open, and I think that

Elvis felt like, 'What the hell do I have to lose? I'm really gonna blow his head off, man.' And they cut down on 'That's All Right, Mama,' and, hell, man, they were just as instinctive as they could be."

Dewey Phillips, WHBQ disc jockey who hosted the R & B radio show "Red Hot and Blue," received the record from the Sun owner the next day. On July 10, 1954, recalled Sam Phillips, Dewey "played that thing, and the phones started ringing. Honey, I'll tell you, all hell broke loose." The disc jockey then interviewed the new local sensation. In Dewey's words, "I asked him where he went to high school and he said Humes. I wanted to get that out, because a lot of people listening thought he was colored." Within ten days, more than 5000 orders streamed into the Sun offices for the record, which hit the top position in the Memphis charts.

Elvis's live performances began to end in hysteria. "In his first public show," Phillips remembered, "we played him at a little club up here at Summer and Medenhall. I went out there that night and introduced Elvis. Now this was kind of out in the country and way out on the highway, as they say. It was just a joint. Here is a bunch of hard-drinking people, and he ain't necessarily playing rhythm and blues, and he didn't look conventional like they did. He looked a little *greasy*, as they called it then. And the reaction was just *incredible*."

The mania continued unabated during Elvis's first tour of the South. On July 4, 1955, in DeLeon, Texas, fans shredded Presley's pink shirt—a trademark by now—and tore the shoes from his feet. One female admirer from Amarillo, Texas, suffered a gash in her leg at the concert. "But who cares if it left a scar," she told a *Newsweek* reporter. "I got it trying to see Elvis and I'm proud of it. This must be what memories are made of."

Country singer Bob Luman recalled similar hysteria at Kilgore, Texas. "The cat came out in red pants and a green coat and a pink shirt and socks," he told writer Paul Hemphill, "and he had this sneer on his face and he stood behind the mike for five minutes, I'll bet, before he made a move. Then he hit his guitar a lick, and he broke two strings. So there he was, these two strings dangling, and he hadn't done anything yet, and these high school girls were screaming and fainting and running up to the stage, and then he started to move his hips real slow like he had a thing for his guitar. That was Elvis Presley when he was about nineteen, playing Kilgore, Texas. He made chills run up my back."

Presley, attracting wild-eyed, teenaged fans, began to sell records. In early 1955, the singer had a local hit with "Good Rockin' Tonight." Later that year he appeared regularly on the radio program "Louisiana Hayride" on KWKH in Shreveport, Louisiana, and made his television debut on a local version of "Hayride," which propelled "Baby, Let's Play House" to number ten and "Mystery Train" to the top slot on the national country and western chart.

The young Elvis Presley, 1956
Photo by Alfred Wertheimer, used by courtesy of RCA Records

"The Killer"

Sam Phillips, buoyed by his success with Presley, began to record other young southerners who had the same gritty, jumpy sound. A persistent Jerry Lee Lewis, nicknamed "The Killer" in high school, joined Sun in 1956. Influenced by both the gospel sound and country singer Jimmie Rodgers, Lewis first played piano publicly at the age of 14 with a local country band in a Ford dealership parking lot. Five years later, a determined Jerry Lee headed for Memphis and met Jack Clement, the producer at the Sun studio. According to Lewis, Clement "told me he didn't have time to make a tape with me, but I told him he was going to do it or I'd whip him. I had driven up to Memphis from Ferriday, Louisiana—286 miles. I sold 39 dozen eggs to pay for the gas. I said, 'You've got the time. I'm going to play the piano and you're going to put it on tape for Sam Phillips.' " He said, "'Well, if you feel that strongly about it, you must be good."

When Phillips returned from a long-deserved vacation at Daytona Beach, Clement put Lewis's "Crazy Arms" on the sound system, and the Sun owner screamed, "Where the hell did that man come from? He played that piano with abandon," Phillips later remembered. "A lot of people do that, but I could hear between the stuff that he played and he didn't play, that spiritual thing. Jerry is very spiritual."

In December 1956, Sun released Lewis's "Crazy Arms," which entered the lower reaches of the charts. For the next year, Jerry Lee backed a few lesser-known Sun acts and added drummer James Van Eaton and guitarist Roland James to his band. In 1957, Sam Phillips recorded Jerry Lee Lewis and his new band ripping through an earth-shattering version of "Whole Lotta Shakin' Goin' On" for his second Sun disc, which sold 60,000 copies regionally soon after its release.

Phillips, in dire financial straits, decided to put Sun's efforts behind the single. "I knew the only hope to make Sun a successful and big company was that we take Jerry Lee Lewis and put everything behind him and use his talent to create all the other Sun personalities," remarked Judd Phillips, Sam's brother and a Sun executive. The promotion package included a spot on the popular "Steve Allen Show"—the close rival of the "Ed Sullivan Show"—which showcased Lewis frantically banging the keys, kicking the piano stool into the audience, and shaking his mop of curly blond locks until he looked like Lucifer's incarnation. The teens in the audience erupted while the stage crew peered in disbelief. After the performance, the switchboard lit up: Scandalized voices screamed their dissatisfaction and shaky-voiced teenagers called to find out more about their new idol. In an uncharacteristic understatement, Lewis related: "Then I got on the Steve Allen Show and it busted wide open." Hits followed with "Great Balls of Fire," "Breathless," and "High School Confidential."

Jerry Lee Lewis, 1957
Frank Driggs Collection

"Blue Suede Shoes"

Lewis's success was matched by a steady stream of Sun rockabilly talents, among them guitarist-songwriter Carl Lee Perkins. Born in Tiptonville, Tennessee, on April 9, 1932, Perkins and his family moved near Jackson, Mississippi, where young Carl found work at a battery factory. Eight years later, in 1953, he bought his first guitar, a $150 Les Paul, and began to perfect a unique style. Since he seldom had the cash for new strings, he once told a reporter, "I'd slide along to where I'd had to tie a knot and push up on a string 'cause I couldn't jump over the knot. Maybe if I'd been wealthy and could have bought new strings, I'd have slid down it and not developed the pushing up on the strings and I'd have sounded like everyone else."

Carl produced a sound that resembled the music of other rockabillies. He "liked Bill Monroe's fast stuff and also the colored guys, John Lee Hooker, Muddy Waters, their electric stuff. Even back then, I liked to do Hooker's things Monroe style, blues with a country beat and my own lyrics" and began to play music that sounded very much like Presley's. Bob Neal, then a disc jockey at Memphis radio station WMPS and later Presley's manager, recalled that he and Elvis saw Perkins perform "in the fall of 1954 and we were both struck by the sound Perkins was getting. It was very similar to Elvis's own." After hearing Presley's first Sun recording, Perkins himself felt that "it was identical to what our band was doing and I just knew that we could make it in the record business after that."

Perkins and his band, which included his brothers Clayton and Jay as well as W. S. Holland, signed with Sun in 1955 and began touring from the back of a truck, charging a dollar to watch the show. That year, the Perkins band released three singles for Sun: "Movie Magg," backed by "Turn Around"; "Let the Jukebox Keep Playing," with the hard-bopping "Gone, Gone, Gone"; and in December 1955, Perkins's smash "Blue Suede Shoes," which by April 1956 topped country and western, pop, and R & B charts.

As he vied for the rockabilly crown, Perkins faced tragedy on March 21, 1956. On the way to New York City for appearances on "The Ed Sullivan Show" and "The Perry Como Hour," outside of Delaware he was involved in a car crash that killed his brother Jay and hospitalized him with a broken shoulder and skull. "I was a poor farm boy, and with 'Shoes' I felt I had a chance but suddenly there I was in the hospital," Carl recalled bitterly.

Perkins never attained the stardom of Presley who, according to Perkins, "had everything. He had the looks, the moves, the manager, and the talent. And he didn't look like Mr. Ed, like a lot of us did. . . . Elvis was hitting them with sideburns, flashy clothes and no ring on the finger. I had three kids," added Carl. After Presley hit the charts with his version of "Blue Suede Shoes," Perkins became known more for his songwriting than his performing and worked in the shadow of the King.

Johnny Cash

Johnny Cash was the other important Sun rockabilly besides Elvis, Jerry Lee Lewis, and Carl Perkins. Son of a sharecropper, Cash joined the Air Force when, in his words, "I started writing songs. I wrote 'Folsom Prison Blues' in the Air Force in 1953. I played with a little group of musicians in my barracks. I was singing Hank Snow and Hank Williams songs with them before I ever tried to sing my own songs."

Cash was also attracted to the blues. "My favorite music," he recalled, "is people like Pink Anderson, Robert Johnson, the king of the Delta blues singers, Howlin' Wolf, Muddy Waters. . . . Those are my influences in music, those are the ones I really loved."

The songwriter signed with Sun Records in 1955 and developed his own sound. As Cash told *Musician* magazine, "I kind of found myself in those first months working in the studio at Sun. I discovered, *let it flow.*" He first hit the charts with "Cry, Cry, Cry." Convincing Sam Phillips that he rather than baritone singer Tennessee Ernie Ford should record it, Cash followed with "Folsom Prison Blues." The next year, he remembered, "Elvis asked me to write him a song. . . . I just told a story about a shoeshine boy. I put it down and Elvis loved ['Get Rhythm']. But it came time for my next single release and Sam said, 'Elvis can't have that!' . . . So Sam released it with the 'Ballad of a Teenage Queen' which got the most play for a long time." Later in 1956, Cash recorded his signature song, "I Walk the Line," which eventually sold a million copies.

The Sun Rockabilly Stable

The Big Four of Sun—Presley, Jerry Lee Lewis, Perkins, and Johnny Cash—supported a battalion of lesser-known but nonetheless hell-bent rocka-billies. Billy Lee Riley was probably the most promising. The wild Riley, a part-Native American who played guitar, harmonica, drums, and bass, formed the Little Green Men in 1955. He scored hits with "Flying Saucers Rock and Roll" and "Red Hot" and drove crowds to a frenzied pitch with his onstage antics. During one memorable performance, he hung from the water pipes near the stage with one hand and clutched the microphone with the other, screaming the lyrics of a song until his face turned bright pink. Though the fans went berserk, Riley never achieved major recognition. He believed that his failure stemmed from the "distribution of Sun discs. They sent out a batch of discs all together and when there was a Perkins release, a Cash release and later Jerry Lee Lewis, the dee jays didn't want to be bothered with the rest of the bunch. The public could only afford so many at one time anyway."

Sonny Burgess, another slightly crazed rockabilly in the Sun fold, produced raw rock that attracted a local audience. A farm boy from Newport, Arkansas, Burgess heard of Sun's growing reputation and traveled to Memphis in 1955. His music, best exemplified by his minor hit "Red-Headed Woman," which sold 90,000 copies, combined a coun-

Johnny Cash, ca. 1960
Frank Driggs Collection

try Arkansas heritage and African-American rhythm and blues: "Yes, I really liked R & B, Fats Domino, Jimmy Reed, Muddy Waters," Burgess told a reporter. Burgess's gritty. R & B-inspired voice possessed the demonic quality of the true rockabilly. Authors Colin Escott and Martin Hawkins called Sonny's music "loosely organized chaos."

Ray Harris, who cut "Come On Little Mama" for Sun in 1956, exhibited similar intensity. Bill Cantrell, then a Sun employee, felt that "Ray wanted to be another Elvis. He couldn't sing and he wasn't good to look at but he didn't care. Man, he was crazy. You would go to visit him and hear him practicing there on Ogden from two blocks away. He would open the door wearing nothing but his overalls and dripping with sweat. He had an old portable tape recorder and he'd go back to singing and playing and sweating. In the studio he would throw himself around with his arms like windmills. That record 'Come On Little Mama' was a triumph for the guitar man Wayne Powers and drummer Joe Riesenthal. They had to keep up with the guy." In an understatement, *Billboard* referred to the single as "excitable."

Not all Sun rockabillies possessed the passion of Ray Harris. Some such as Roy Orbison were forced by Sam Phillips into the Sun mold. Orbison, raised in Wink, Texas, formed the Wink Westerners, later renamed the Teen Kings, while in high school. After a year of college, remembered the singer, "I met a couple of guys who had written 'Ooby

Dooby' and what convinced me I was in the wrong place at the wrong time was I heard a record by a young fellow on the jukebox called 'That's All Right.' "

Orbison headed for Memphis and in March 1956 recorded the Sun-issued "Ooby Dooby." It sold nearly a half million copies and reached number 59 on the *Billboard* singles chart, which was the best chart position of a Sun disc other than hits by the Big Four of Sun. The singer, identifiable by his sunglasses, black clothes, and a near-operatic, high-pitched, ethereal voice, followed with "Rockhouse," but only reluctantly. Said Jack Clement: "The first artist Sam gave me to record was Roy Orbison. I recorded 'Rockhouse' with Roy and it was good but Roy was not into what the Sun studio was capable of back then." "I was writing more ballads then [1957]," confirmed Roy, "but I didn't bother to ask Sam to release them. He was the boss and there was no arguing. I made some demos of things like 'Claudette' but that was about it. I would never have made it big with Sun. They just didn't have the ways to get into the audience I wanted to go for." Orbison eventually signed with Monument Records and in the early 1960s achieved popularity with a series of songs which built to powerful, dramatic, emotional crescendos: "Only the Lonely," "Running Scared," "Crying," and "Oh, Pretty Woman."

Roy Orbison, however, proved to be the exception to the Sun rule. By late 1956, Sam Phillips had groomed a stable of white country boys who willingly sang with the feeling of black men and the intensity of whirling dervishes, driving white teenaged girls to hysteria.

The Decca Challenge

The major record companies competed with Sun for the rockabilly market. Decca Records took the lead, signing Bill Haley and the Comets. Born in Michigan, Haley in 1949 formed a band, the Four Aces of Western Swing, for a radio show that he hosted on station WPWA in Chester, Pennsylvania. As the Ramblin' Yodeler, he recorded country music with the Four Aces and subsequently with the Down Homers and the Saddlemen. "My mother was a piano teacher," he told an interviewer. "My dad, who was from Kentucky, played mandolin. And I suppose that was where the country influence came from."

In 1950, Haley released a cover version of Jackie Brenston's "Rocket 88," which convinced him to combine country swing music with the R & B boogie-woogie, jump beat of Louis Jordan. "We'd begin with Jordan's shuffle rhythm," remembered Milt Gabler, the Comets' producer at Decca. "You know, dotted eighth notes and sixteenths and we'd build on it. I'd sing Jordan riffs to the group that would be picked up by the electric guitar and tenor sax, Rudy Pompilli. They had a song that had the drive of [Jordan's] Tympany Five and the color of country and western. Rockabilly was what it was called back then."

"We started out as a country western group, then we added a touch of rhythm and blues," Haley recalled. "It wasn't something we

Bill Haley and his Comets, 1957
Photo by Popsie Randolph, Frank Driggs Collection

planned, it just evolved. We got to where we weren't accepted as country western or rhythm and blues. It was hard to get bookings for a while. We were something new. We didn't call it that at that time, but we were playing rock-and-roll."

After a minor success with "Crazy Man Crazy" in 1952, Haley and the Comets signed with Decca in 1954. They first released "Rock Around the Clock," a song originally cut two years earlier by Sunny Dae, who scored only a minor hit with it. The group followed with a remake of Joe Turner's "Shake, Rattle and Roll" that hit the Top 10 in both the United States and Britain. In 1955, the Comets re-released "Rock Around the Clock," which hit the top of the charts and caused riots worldwide when it was included on the soundtrack of *Blackboard Jungle*, a movie that captured the spirit of teenage rebellion embodied by rock during the mid-1950s. According to rock critic Lillian Roxon, the furor over "Rock Around the Clock" "was the first inkling teenagers had that they might be a force to be reckoned with, in numbers alone. If there could be one song, there could be others; there could be a whole world of songs and, then, a whole world."

Haley continued to churn out hits. During 1955 and 1956, he scored with twelve Top 40 records, including "See You Later Alligator," "Burn That Candle," "Dim, Dim the Lights," "Razzle-Dazzle," and "R-O-C-K." In 1957, he appeared in two movies, *Rock Around the Clock* and *Don't Knock the Rock*, that featured his music.

Buddy Holly and the Crickets, ca. 1958
Photo courtesy MCA Records

Though predating Elvis and laying claim to the first rockabilly success, Haley never wrenched the rock crown from Presley. He delivered a smoother sound than the jagged-edged music of Presley. The singer and his Comets also offered a tamer stage show. In 1956, Haley warned that "a lot depends on the entertainer and how he controls the crowd. The music is stimulating enough without creating additional excitement," an apparent jab at Elvis. Just as important, Haley's age and appearance—pudgy, balding, and 32 years old in 1957—compared unfavorably to that of the young, virile, swivel-hipped Elvis in the eyes of teenaged rock-and-rollers driven by raging hormones.

Decca, hoping for a larger share of the teen market, signed the Rock 'n' Roll Trio to its Coral subsidiary. Growing up in Memphis, Johnny and Dorsey Burnette met Paul Burlison in 1953 at the Crown Electric factory, the same company that employed Presley as a truck driver. Initially they played in a Hank Williams style. But when Burlison backed Howlin' Wolf on a radio broadcast in West Memphis, the group started to blend country music with the electric blues.

Beale Street in Memphis "was really happening in those days, and my dad and his friends would go down there a lot and listen to the blues guys," remembered Billy Burnette, the son of Dorsey, who continued in the rockabilly tradition of his family. "They'd buy their clothes on Beale Street, at Lansky Brothers, where all the black people shopped. Right outside Memphis, there was a voodoo village, all black—real mystic kind of people. People who were into music would go over there and get charms and things like that. You know, a lot of real old line

Southern people called my dad and my uncle white niggers. Nobody was doing rock-and-roll in those days except people they called white trash. When my dad and uncle started doin' it, they were just about the first."

The path-breaking Trio caused disturbances throughout the South with "The Train Kept a Rollin'," "Rock Billy Boogie," "Tear It Up," and "Rock Therapy." In one incident, reported the Evansville, Indiana, *Courier* in late 1956, "all during Burnette's performance, the crowd of about two thousand persons kept up a continuous howl that all but drowned out the singer's voice." When Johnny Burnette tried to leave the stage, hundreds of wild-eyed girls attacked him and "tore his shirt to bits for souvenirs." According to the *Courier*, "the singer, who had all but exhausted himself in the performance, was in sad shape when he reached the car. 'I shoulda laid off that last "Hound Dog," ' he panted." In 1956, the Trio decided to quit their jobs and move to New York City with hopes of national success. After winning first prize on Ted Mack's "Amateur Hour," the Rock 'n' Roll Trio signed with Decca Records and recorded one seminal album before disbanding.

The same year, Decca discovered Charles ("Buddy") Holly, a skinny teenager from Lubbock, Texas, who wore thick-rimmed glasses and a shy grin. Holly had heard R & B through records and on radio programs such as "Stan's Record Rack," broadcast from Shreveport, Louisiana. As Holly's friend Bob Montgomery explained, "Blues to us was Muddy Waters, Little Walter, and Lightnin' Hopkins."

As with other rockabillies, Holly was also influenced by white country music, especially bluegrass and western swing. He listened to performers such as Hank Snow and Hank Williams and, in 1953, with friends Bob Montgomery and Larry Welborn, formed a country music trio that performed at the Big D Jamboree in Dallas and regularly played on the radio as "The Buddy and Bob Show." By his sixteenth birthday, Buddy already had "thought about making a career out of western music if I am good enough but I will just have to wait and see how that turns out."

The new music of rock-and-roll changed Buddy's plans. In early 1955, when Elvis arrived in Lubbock for an engagement at the Cotton Club, Holly and Bob Montgomery drove the new sensation around town. Later that night at the concert, remembered a Lubbock local, Buddy and Bob "went over to talk to Elvis. Later Buddy said to me, 'You know, he's a real nice, friendly fellow.' I guess Buddy was surprised that Elvis was so normal and would talk to him so easily, because Buddy thought of Elvis as a big star and really admired him." The next day, Holly and his group backed Elvis at the grand opening of a local Pontiac dealership. "And when the next KDVA Sunday Party rolled around, Buddy was singing Elvis songs." Added Larry Holly, Buddy's brother, "He was on an Elvis Presley kick—he just idolized the guy. And, I mean, he sounded exactly like him. He did Elvis Presley things on the Jamboree." Holly, interested in leather work at the time, even crafted a wallet with "ELVIS" emblazoned in pink letters on it and in early 1956 left the wallet at Sun Studios as a present for Presley.

Holly incorporated Presley's style to create a unique sound. By 1957, when he formed the Crickets with Joe B. Maudlin on stand-up bass and drummer Jerry Allison, he had perfected a light, bouncy, bright rockabilly that bore traces of the unique Presley sound.

Holly took his distinctive sound to the small studio of producer Norman Petty, who had already recorded hits for the Rhythm Orchids— "Party Doll" and "Stickin' with You," released under the names of singer Buddy Knox and bassist Jimmy Bowen. With Petty's help, the Crickets hit the charts in 1957 with "That'll Be the Day," the title taken from a John Wayne line in the movie *The Searchers*. They followed with a series of fresh rockabilly tunes that became rock-and-roll classics: "Peggy Sue," "Maybe Baby," "Not Fade Away," "Rave On," and "Oh Boy."

Rockabilly Sweeps the Nation

Other record companies searched for their own acts to enter the rockabilly market. Capitol Records, a major label, signed Gene Vincent, a Korean War veteran who was born Gene Vincent Craddock in the southern navy town of Norfolk, Virginia. In 1956, with his band, the Bluecaps, Vincent released the unforgettable "Be-Bop-a-Lula." According to the singer, he wrote the classic one day when he "and Don Graves were looking at this bloody comic book. It was called Little Lulu and I said, 'Hell, man, it's bebopalulu.' And he said, 'Yeah, man, swinging,' and we wrote the song. Just like that. And some man came to hear it and he bought the song for $25. Right. Twenty-five dollars! And I recorded it and told my friends that I was going to get a Cadillac, because all rock and roll singers had Cadillacs." From 1956 to 1958, in quest of his Cadillac, Vincent cut such boppers as "Dance to the Bop," "Bluejean Bop," "Race with the Devil," "She She Little Sheila," and "Crazy Legs."

Cadence Records, a small New York-based independent company owned by Archie Bleyer, scored with the Everly Brothers. Sons of country stars Ike and Margaret Everly, the two brothers, Don and Phil, toured with their parents and performed on a family radio show that aired on several stations. In 1955, the duo headed for Nashville, where they sold a few songs to a country music publishing firm owned by guitarist Chet Atkins. The next year they signed with Columbia Records and released two songs that flopped.

In 1957, the Everly Brothers signed with Cadence Records after being spotted by music publisher Wesley Rose. The duo climbed the charts with "Bye Bye Love." Their sound, dominated by bright, warm, country-style harmonies they had learned from their father, had an R & B influence. As Don pointed out, "I loved Bo Diddley; I told [country guitar master] Chet Atkins, 'That's what I want my guitar to sound like.' I said, 'Chet, have you heard Bo Diddley?' He said, 'Yeah.' 'What's he doing?' He said, 'Well, he's got an amplifier, but he's also got a tuned guitar.' The intro to 'Bye Bye Love' was inspired by Bo Diddley." "Phil and I are really a strict mixture of rhythm 'n' blues and country," added Don. After appearances on "The Ed Sullivan Show" as well as other tele-

The Everly Brothers in the studio
Courtesy of Don Everly

vision programs in 1957, the Everlys followed with the now-classic "Wake Up Little Susie," "All I Have to Do Is Dream," and "Bird Dog," racking up sales of $35 million by 1962.

Imperial, the label that featured Fats Domino as its star, snagged Ricky Nelson in the rockabilly sweepstakes. The son of jazz bandleader Ozzie Nelson and singer Harriet Hilliard, the young Nelson "used to listen to the radio and longed to be a recording artist. I wanted to be Carl Perkins. I used to go and buy every Sun record that I could get my hands on back in the Fifties 'cause they were such a really good sound."

Beginning in October 1952, Ricky played himself on his parents' television series, "The Adventures of Ozzie and Harriet." In April 1957, he covered Fats Domino's "I'm Walkin'" on the show and, after a wild teenage response to the program, released the song on Verve Records. Attesting to the importance of television, the song sold 60,000 copies in three days.

Prodded by his success and the business acumen of his father, Ricky continued to sing one of his songs on each subsequent episode of the show, ending the segments by belting out a song at the sock hop of his television high school. When Verve Records withheld royalties, Nelson signed with Imperial Records and racked up a series of hits such as "Be-Bop Baby," "Stood Up," "Travelin' Man," "Poor Little Fool," "Lonesome Town," and "Hello Mary Lou." He also scored with songs written by Johnny and Dorsey Burnette such as "Waiting in School," "Believe What You Say," and "A Little Too Much." Promoted by his parents's television show until 1966, helped by such songwriters as the Burnettes and supported by guitarist James Burton, who would back Elvis, Ricky Nelson became a rockabilly sensation.

Liberty Records jumped into the rockabilly field with Eddie Cochran. The son of two Oklahoma City country-western fans, in 1949 Eddie moved with his family to Bell Gardens, California. While thumbing through the racks of a local record store, Cochran met Jerry Capehart, who would become his songwriter-collaborator throughout his career. In 1955, the duo traveled to Nashville, signed with American Music, and recorded "Skinny Jim," which flopped. Trying to secure better distribution for their discs, Capehart flew to Los Angeles and convinced Si Waronker, president of Liberty Records, to invest in the rockabilly talent of Cochran. After releasing a few unsuccessful singles, in late 1958 Cochran alternated between an Elvis-like whimper and a gravel-voiced growl in an anthem of teenage frustration, "Summertime Blues." Cochran's bopping call to arms, nearing the top of the charts, struck a chord among teenagers, who were gaining increasing power by their numbers.

The Selling of Elvis Presley

RCA Victor lured to its label the performer who became known as the king of rock-and-roll. In 1955, the company offered Sun Records $35,000 for the rights to Elvis Presley's recorded material. Sam Phillips accepted the money and surrendered all of the Presley tapes that Sun had produced. "I looked at everything for how I could take a little extra money and get myself out of a real bind," explained Phillips. "I mean I wasn't broke, but man, it was hand-to-mouth."

In January 1956, RCA began to merchandise Elvis, for the first time using the powerful new medium of television to sell rock-and-roll. Developed during the 1920s, televised images had been offered to the public by the end of the 1930s and after World War II had become much more available. By 1953, 328 stations broadcast to nearly 27 million sets in the United States. Within three years the number of stations had nearly doubled, to 620, and the number of TV sets in American homes had increased to 37 million, showing many programs that previously had been aired on radio. At the time television was dominated by three networks: the American Broadcast Company (ABC), the Columbia Broadcasting System (CBS), and the National Broadcast Company (NBC), the last of which was owned by RCA, the Radio Corporation of America.

the most talked-about new personality in the last 10 years of recorded music

ELVIS PRESLEY
now on RCA Victor records with

I FORGOT TO REMEMBER TO FORGET
MYSTERY TRAIN...20/47-6357

Bob Neal, manager
under direction of Hank Snow Jamboree Attractions,
Col. Tom Parker, general manager
Box 417, Madison, Tennessee

RCA VICTOR

The new sensation: ad for Elvis Presley, December 3, 1955
RCA/Estate of Elvis Presley

RCA immediately slotted the photogenic Elvis for television, booking him for six Saturday night appearances on the Tommy and Jimmy Dorsey "Stage Show," a half-hour variety program hosted by the two big-band leaders. This show preceded Jackie Gleason's "The Honeymooners" and competed with "The Perry Como Hour." After Presley boosted the ratings of "Stage Show," RCA scheduled the singer for "The Milton Berle Show" and "The Steve Allen Show."

By the end of the year Ed Sullivan, who earlier had condemned Presley as "unfit for a family audience," agreed to pay the new rock star $50,000 for three appearances on his show, one of the two most popular television programs in America at the time. Sullivan booked Presley for his first appearance on September 9, 1956. Fearing a backlash from his usual viewers, the television host ordered that Elvis be filmed from the waist up, allowing the teenaged television audience only to imagine the pelvic gyrations that took place off the screen. Creating one of the most legendary moments in television history, Sullivan attracted nearly 54 million viewers, or almost 83 percent of the television audience, to his show and helped lift Presley into national prominence.

"Presley is riding high right now with network TV appearances," observed *Billboard*, and RCA's release of "Heartbreak Hotel" "should benefit from all the special plugging." A week later, the magazine reported that sales of the single had "snowballed," and in a few more weeks it reached the top of the national singles chart.

During the next few months, Presley hit the top of the chart with a number of songs, many of which he had sung on his television appearances: "I Want You, I Need You, I Love You," "Love Me Tender," "Hound Dog," "Don't Be Cruel," and "All Shook Up," the last two written by African-American songwriter Otis Blackwell, who had penned "Great Balls of Fire" for Jerry Lee Lewis. "It was television that made Elvis's success possible," related Steve Allen, who featured the singer on his show. "What his millions of young fans responded to was obviously not his voice but Elvis himself. His face, his body, his hair, his gyrations, his cute, country-boy persona."

Besides television, a new Top 40 format on radio helped promote Presley. It was pioneered in 1954 by radio chain owners Todd Storz and Gordon McLendon to rescue radio from a five-year decline caused by the popularity of television. Top 40 radio involved an instant news concept, disc jockey gags and patter, and a limited play list of roughly 40 hits that disc jockeys spun in a constant rotation.

Top 40 radio, promoting the songs of only a few artists, fueled the meteoric rise of Elvis. "There was a huge change overnight," recalled Russ Solomon, founder of the Tower Records chain. "Everybody was interested [in Presley]. At the same moment, Top Forty radio came into play. As a result there was a very dramatic change in the way you perceived selling records. Your hit titles became more and more important."

The marketing acumen of Colonel Thomas Parker contributed to Presley's hit-making success. Born in 1910, Parker got his start in carnivals. Since the circus life, according to the Colonel, "was a day-to-day living," he used his ingenuity to make money. For one of his ploys, he rented a cow pasture adjacent to the circus grounds and during the night herded the cows on the only road through the field, which served as the sole exit from the carnival. When unsuspecting circus-goers reached the exit the next day, they could either walk through ankle-deep manure or pay the Colonel a nickel for a pony ride through it.

By 1955, Parker had abandoned the circus and applied his ingenious techniques to the careers of such country singers as Roy Acuff, Minnie Pearl, Eddy Arnold, and Hank Snow. A year later, remembered one of Elvis's neighbors, the Colonel "in the most polished Machiavellian way" convinced Presley's parents to sign their son to his management company. "Colonel Tom was a salesman, I'll give him that. He sure knew how to sell." Almost immediately the Colonel began to market Elvis Presley to the media. "The Colonel doesn't sell Elvis to the public, dig?" Jon Hartmann, one of Parker's subordinates, later observed. "He sells Elvis to the people who sell to the public, and those are the media people—the television and motion picture personalities, the executives and businessmen who control the networks, the important radio people. It's like an endless trip for the Colonel. Elvis, as a product, always in the state of being sold."

In mid-1956, Hank Saperstein joined Tom Parker in the Presley media blitz. Saperstein had become successful in the advertising industry through his marketing efforts for television creations such as Lassie, Wyatt Earp, Ding Dong School, and the Lone Ranger. Not to be outdone by his competitors, he had even stuffed plastic blowguns in cereal boxes to increase the sales of Kellogg's Cornflakes. Saperstein recognized the "universality" of the Presley appeal and began to plaster Elvis's name and picture on all types of products. By 1957, Saperstein and Parker had saturated the American market.

If a loyal fan so desired, she could put on some Elvis Presley bobby socks, Elvis Presley shoes, skirt, blouse, and sweater, hang an Elvis Presley charm bracelet on one wrist, and with the other hand smear on some Elvis Presley lipstick—either Hound Dog Orange, Heartbreak Hotel Pink, or Tutti Frutti Red. She might put an Elvis Presley handkerchief in her Elvis Presley purse and head for school. Once in the classroom, she could write with her green Elvis Presley pencil, inscribed "Sincerely Yours," and sip an Elvis Presley soft drink between class periods. After school she could change into Elvis Presley bermuda shorts, blue jeans, or toreador pants, write to an Elvis Presley pen pal, or play an Elvis Presley game, and fall asleep in her Elvis Presley pajamas on her Elvis Presley pillow. Her last waking memory of the day could be the Elvis Presley fluorescent portrait that hung on her wall. All told, the fan could buy 78 different Elvis Presley products that grossed about $55 million by December 1957. In addition to 25 percent of Elvis's performance royalties, Colonel Parker received a percentage of the manufacturer's wholesale price on each item.

Reactions Against the Presley Mania

Many adults criticized the Presley mania. In one review, Jack Gould, the television critic for *The New York Times*, wrote: "Mr. Presley has no discernible singing ability. His specialty is rhythm, songs which he renders in an undistinguished whine; his phrasing, if it can be called that, consists of the stereotyped variations that go with a beginner's aria in a bathtub. . . . His one specialty is an accented movement of the body that heretofore has been primarily identified with the repertoire of the blonde bombshells of the burlesque runway. The gyration never had anything to do with the world of popular music and still doesn't." Jack O'Brien of the New York *Journal-American* agreed that "Elvis Presley wiggled and wiggled with such abdominal gyrations that burlesque bombshell Georgia Southern really deserves equal time to reply in gyrating kind. He can't sing a lick, makes up for vocal shortcomings with the weirdest and plainly planned, suggestive animation short of an aborigine's mating dance."

Others held similar opinions. Jack Mabley of *Downbeat* jazz magazine did not think "the fad of Elvis Presley is going to last much longer than the fad for swallowing goldfish." Addressing the House of Representatives, Congressman Robert MacDonald of Massachusetts viewed "with absolute horror" performers "such as Elvis Presley, Little Richard . . . and all the other hundreds of musical illiterates, whose noises presently clutter up our jukeboxes and our airways." *Time* magazine called Presley a "sexibitionist," who lived "off what most parents would agree is the fat of teenagers' heads," and *Look* accused him of dragging " 'big beat' music to new lows in taste." The magazine *America* pleaded with television and radio executives to "stop handling such nauseating stuff" so "all the Presleys of our land would soon be swallowed up in the oblivion they deserve." "Beware Elvis Presley," the magazine cautioned. Broadway composer Oscar Hammerstein, analyzing "All Shook Up," astutely noted that " 'bug' and 'shook up' don't rhyme. It's sloppy writing."

Fear of increasing juvenile delinquency underlay much of the backlash against Presley. The dark image of the alienated, shiftless, and violent street tough in a black leather jacket who dangled a cigarette from his lips had been popularized in books and films. The preoccupation with the teenage delinquent was reflected in such paperbacks as *Blackboard Jungle, Gang Rumble, The Hoods Ride In, Teen-Age Vice, Teen-Age Terror, D For Delinquent*, and countless others. It also appeared in such movies as *The Wild One* (1954), which showcased Marlon Brando as the leader of a heartless motorcycle gang, and *Rebel Without a Cause*, released the next year, starring James Dean, who with Brando symbolized teenage rebellion.

Rebel Without a Cause, explained Stewart Stern, who wrote the screenplay, dealt with "the phenomenon of what was called in those days juvenile delinquency, happening not in families that were economically deprived but in middle-class families that were emotionally deprived. Partly, people felt it had to do with the war, the fact that so many women were working for the first time away from the home, that older brothers and fathers who would have been role models for the young weren't there, and the tremendous drive for material 'things.' . . . When the kids saw that the material goods that were supposed to make their parents happy really didn't," continued Stern, "they began to doubt their parents's authority. . . . The lesson of *Rebel*," concluded the screenwriter, "was that if the kids could not be acknowledged or understood by their parents, at least they could be acknowledged by each other."

Threatened by the power of youth banding together, which they identified with juvenile delinquency, adults many times linked rock-and-roll to teen violence. On April 11, 1956, *Variety* connected rock to a "staggering wave of juvenile violence and mayhem. . . . On the police blotters, rock 'n' roll has been writing an unprecedented record. In one locale after another, rock 'n' roll shows, or disc hops where such tunes have been played, have touched off every type of juvenile delinquency." The Pennsylvania Chief of Police Association contended that rock music provided "an incentive to teenage unrest," and Pittsburgh Police Inspector Fred Good felt "wherever there's been teenage trouble lately, rock and roll has almost always been in the background." Entertainer Jackie Gleason put it succinctly, calling Elvis Presley "a guitar-playing Marlon Brando."

Teen riots increased the fear of rock-and-roll delinquents and prompted officials to bar promoters from holding rock concerts in civic buildings. In San Jose, rock fanatics routed 73 policemen and caused $3000 in damage, pressuring the mayor of nearby Santa Cruz to ban rock concerts. On May 3, 1958, violence erupted after an Alan Freed-hosted rock revue that headlined Jerry Lee Lewis. When police turned on the house lights before the show ended, Freed huffed, "I guess the police here in Boston don't want you kids to have a good time," and teens streamed into the street. As *Time* reported, "all around the arena common citizens were set upon, robbed and sometimes beaten. A young sailor caught a knife in the belly, and two girls with him were thrashed. In all nine men and women were roughed up enough to require hospital treatment." Though, as *Time* admitted, "the arena site had been the site of frequent muggings in the past" and teens probably did not participate in the violence, Boston Mayor John Hynes barred rock-and-roll shows from the city. Officials in New Haven and Newark followed the Boston example, canceling scheduled Freed-sponsored shows. After a melee among 2700 fans at a rock show, Mayor Roland Hines of Asbury Park, New Jersey, banned all rock concerts from city dance halls. Officials in nearby Jersey City did the same a few days later.

Others mobilized against Elvis Presley. In Nashville and St. Louis, angry parents burned effigies of Presley. In Ottawa, Canada, eight students of the Notre Dame convent were expelled for attending a local Elvis show. Yale University students handed out "I Like Ludwig [Beethoven]" buttons to counter the sale of "I Like Elvis" buttons. And a Cincinnati used-car dealer increased business with a sign that read: "We Guarantee to Break 50 Elvis Presley Records in Your Presence If You Buy One of These Cars Today."

Disc jockeys who broadcast classical and pop music also took action. In Halifax, Nova Scotia, station CJCH rigidly forbade the airplay of any Elvis discs. Nashville jockey "Great Scott" burned 600 Presley records in a public park, and a Chicago station manager smashed Elvis 45's during a broadcast. In Wildwood, New Jersey, a local disc jockey started an organization to "eliminate certain wreck and ruin artists" such as Elvis.

Even religious leaders spoke out against Presley. Reverend William Shannon commented in the *Catholic Sun* that "Presley and his voodoo of frustration and defiance have become symbols in our country, and we are sorry to come upon Ed Sullivan in the role of promoter. Your Catholic viewers, Mr. Sullivan, are angry." Although he had never seen Elvis, evangelist Billy Graham was "not so sure I'd want my children to see" him. Reverend Charles Howard Graff of St. John's Episcopal Church in Greenwich Village called Elvis a "whirling dervish of sex," and Reverend Robert Gray of the Trinity Baptist Church in Jacksonville, Florida, believed Presley had "achieved a new low in spiritual degeneracy. If he were offered salvation tonight, he would probably say, 'No thanks, I'm on the top.' " In his sermon "Hot Rods, Reefers, and Rock and Roll," Gray warned the youth in his congregation not to attend an upcoming Presley show.

Elvis Goes to Hollywood

RCA Victor and Colonel Parker responded to the reaction against Presley by modifying the singer's wild act. Presley's appearance on "The Steve Allen Show" provides an example. "We'd recognized the controversy that was building around Elvis and so we took advantage of it," remembered Allen. The host dressed Presley "in a tuxedo—white tie and tails—and [took] away his guitar. We thought putting Elvis in formal wardrobe to sing the song was humorous. We also asked him to stand perfectly still, and we positioned a real hound dog on a stool next to him—a dog that had been trained to do nothing but sit and look droopy." Elvis's respectable behavior on the show stood in marked contrast to his earlier hip-shaking performances and signaled the beginning of a change in image.

Throughout 1957 and 1958 and into the 1960s, Presley became more subdued. In September 1957, the rising star split with two members of his original band, Scotty Moore and Bill Black, who had helped pioneer the distinctive Presley sound; Elvis recorded with them only sporadically during the next decade. On subsequent records and in his 31 movies, starting with *Love Me Tender* and followed by such films as *G. I. Blues, Flaming Star, Wild Star, Blue Hawaii, Follow That Dream, Kid Galahad,* and *Girls! Girls! Girls!,* Elvis for the most part abandoned gut-bucket rockabilly for a soothing ballad style that reinforced his new image. "Elvis would go ahead with the program and get the picture done," remembered D. J. Fontana, the drummer who played with Elvis from 1954 to 1968. "You see, the Colonel's thought was *don't make any waves;* don't let me have to make a deal with these people."

The more mainstream Presley appealed to even more fans and sold even more albums, a total of more than 250 million by the end of his career. In the history of recorded music, only Bing Crosby neared Elvis's mark, with about 200 million records sold. Frank Sinatra, the bobby-socks sensation of the 1940s, sold only about 40 million discs.

With his newfound wealth, Elvis bought a fleet of Cadillacs, including one in his favorite color, pink; a $40,000, one-story ranch house in Memphis; and then a $100,000 mansion, Graceland, for himself and his parents. He purchased an airplane, a truckload of television sets, and hundreds of other gadgets.

Presley also began to receive awards of all types. In 1959, the Mississippi legislature passed a resolution that lauded Elvis as a "legend and inspiration to tens of millions of Americans" who "reaffirms a historic American idea that success in our nation can still be attained through individual initiative, hard work and abiding faith in one's self and his creator." A few months later, a joint session of the Tennessee legislature honored Presley.

The young, working-class Presley, ceaselessly marketed by RCA, was swept away by stardom. "My daddy and I were laughing about it the other day," he told a reporter in late 1956. "He looked at me and said, 'What happened, El? The last thing I remember is I was working in a can factory and you were still driving a truck.' We all feel the same way about it still. It just caught us up."

The rock star paid dearly for his fame. As his popularity increased, Elvis found it difficult to protect his privacy. "Even today [late sixties] I'd be willing to bet a thousand dollars he could draw a hundred people in five minutes anywhere he went," mused Neal Matthews, one of the Jordanaires, Elvis's backup singing group. "And he knows this. It's bound to make him unhappy. He'd like to be able to walk down the street like a normal human being. He can't be a person like anybody else." The "only time he could get out, really, was at night, or if he had the night off. He'd rent a skating rink or a movie house and rent it for the whole night and he and whoever'd be around would go to two, three movies after the movie theater had closed. That's the only kind of entertainment he had. He couldn't go out."

On his 1969 tour of Hawaii with Minnie Pearl, Minnie related, "There were five hundred women there and as we got out of the taxi, Elvis grabbed my arm and the women broke and mobbed us. I felt my feet going out from under me. . . . You know, everyone wants to be number one, but that one experience was enough to convince me I don't want it." As Minnie Pearl and her husband enjoyed the Hawaiian sun, "Elvis never got out of his room except to work. They say he came down in the middle of the night to swim. He couldn't come down during the day. He had the penthouse suite on the top of that thing there and we'd get out and act crazy, having the best time in the world, and we'd look up there and Elvis would be standing at the window, looking down at us."

Eventually the isolation began to affect Presley. "You know, you all are lucky," Presley told D. J. Fontana and his wife in 1968. "I'm so tired of being Elvis—I don't know what to do. I just wish I could do something else."

A depressed Elvis sometimes became violent. He destroyed several television sets, pool cues, jukeboxes, and cars. "The temper was the hardest thing to take," one friend recalled. "One day he'd be the sweetest person in the world, the next day he'd burn holes in you with his eyes." As singer Johnny Rivers concluded, Elvis "had created his own world. He had to. There was nothing else for him to do." His retreat into himself ended in drug excess and death in 1977.

Elvis Presley had been trapped by success. The gyrating, sneering Elvis, who taunted his audiences and worked them to a fever pitch, had given way to a more haggard performer bloated by drugs and alcohol and adorned by extravagant, sequined costumes, who sang ballads to the well-dressed clientele of Las Vegas nightclubs and in arenas across the country. Sometimes the old magic sneaked through the weary flesh, but most of the original vibrancy and vitality had disappeared. Elvis was transformed from an innocent country boy who belted out a new kind of music with animalistic intensity to a well-groomed, multi-million-dollar product. The change, starting when Presley signed with RCA and becoming more pronounced during the sixties, spelled the end of rockabilly. Soon, teenaged crooners schooled by Dick Clark would vie for the mantle of the King.

3

Dick Clark, Don Kirshner, and the Teen Market

"I hope someday that somebody will say that in the beginning stages of the birth of the music of the Fifties, though I didn't contribute in terms of creativity, I helped keep it alive."

Dick Clark

"Elvis in the army, Buddy dead, Little Richard in the ministry, and Berry nabbed by the Feds," became the chant of a bewildered rock-and-roll generation. Becoming an important part of American culture just three years earlier, by 1959 rock-and-roll had lost many of its heroes. Elvis Presley had been inducted into the army, Buddy Holly had been tragically killed, Little Richard had suddenly joined a fundamentalist religious sect, and Chuck Berry had been jailed.

Two young entrepreneurs—Dick Clark and Don Kirshner—produced a new crop of idols and a fresh batch of songs for rock-starved teens. Beginning in 1957, Clark found photogenic, well-groomed Italian teens, promoted them on his television show, and almost single-handedly created the Philadelphia sound. Only the payola scandal slowed Clark's success. A music publisher in the Tin Pan Alley tradition, Kirshner assembled teams of young, talented songwriters in the Brill Building in New York City and from 1960 to 1963 churned out hundreds of tunes that he placed with scores of budding girl groups. For nearly three years he helped set the direction of rock-and-roll.

From 1958 to 1963, in the absence of Presley and other rock pioneers, two businessmen reshaped rock-and-roll and made it respectable.

Lost Idols

During the late 1950s, rock-and-roll fans either lost or rejected their heroes. In October 1957, the flamboyant Little Richard renounced his jeweled bracelets and wild parties for the ministry of the Seventh Day Adventist Church. Richard had frequently threatened to quit rock. Chuck Conners, the drummer in Little Richard's band, remembered that Richard "had been talking about giving up rock 'n' roll and devoting his life to God for a long time." Then, on his way to Australia, as Little Richard looked out the window of the plane, the engines seemed to burst into flames, doused only by the saving efforts of yellow angels. A few days later in Sydney, on the fifth day of a two-week tour, Richard walked away from rock-and-roll in the middle of a show and in front of 40,000 fans. As he told it, "that night Russia sent off the very first *Sputnik* [the Soviet Union's first artificial earth satellite in outer space]. It looked as though the big ball of fire came directly over the stadium about two or three hundred feet above our heads. It shook my mind. It really shook my mind. I got up from the piano and said, 'This is it. I am through. I am leaving show business to go back to God.' " True to his word, Richard deserted his fans for Jehovah. Said the singer: "If you want to live for the Lord, you can't rock and roll too. God doesn't like it." Not until 1964 during a tour of England did Little Richard again raise the standard of rock.

A month later, 22-year-old Jerry Lee Lewis married his 13-year-old third cousin, Myra Gale Brown, who was the daughter of Lewis's bass player. It was Lewis's third marriage. Though a relatively common practice in the rural South—"I know lots of people married to thirteen-year-olds," Lewis said at the time—the marriage caused promoters to cancel the 27 shows scheduled for Lewis's 1957 tour of England. During his first performance after the marriage, the crowd greeted the rockabilly star with silence and then sporadic heckling. "I sho' hope yawl ain't half as dead as you sound," Lewis shouted to the crowd. "Go home, crumb, baby snatcher," the audience yelled back. For more than a decade, the public censured the "Killer," who gravitated more and more toward country music.

On March 24, 1958, the king of rock-and-roll, Elvis Presley, entered the armed forces for a two-year stint. On orders from his manager, Colonel Tom Parker, he refused to sing for the army and spent his time in Bremerhaven, Germany, where he met his future wife, Priscilla Beaulieu. When discharged in January 1960, Presley concentrated his efforts on motion pictures and only in 1968 returned to the stage.

The next year, two of rock's pioneers left the stage. Chuck Berry was forced from the music scene by a ruling from a federal court. In 1959, a 14-year-old girl accused Berry of transporting her from Texas to St. Louis for immoral purposes after Berry fired her as a hatcheck girl in his St. Louis club. Testimony at the trial, which dragged on for nearly two years, revealed that the girl had been a prostitute when Berry first met her and that she had come willingly to St. Louis. A judge initially found Berry guilty, but a retrial was scheduled because the magistrate referred to the performer as "this Negro." The jury in a second trial convicted Berry of a violation of the Mann Act and sentenced him to two years in the federal penitentiary at Terre Haute, Indiana.

A different sort of tragedy occurred on February 3, 1959. Rockabilly singer and songwriter Buddy Holly, the shy, bespectacled youth from Texas, died in a plane crash near Mason City, Iowa, after a show during a midwestern tour. J. P. Richardson, the disc jockey known as the Big Bopper, who in 1958 hit the charts with "Chantilly Lace," and the 17-year-old sensation Richie Valens (a.k.a. Richard Valenzuela), who had just scored hits with "La Bamba" and "Donna," were killed in the same crash.

An automobile accident robbed rock-and-roll of two other hit makers. On April 17, 1960, after a successful tour of England, Eddie Cochran, Gene Vincent, and Sharon Sheely, Cochran's girlfriend, who subsequently wrote many of Ricky Nelson's hits, rode to the airport in a chauffeured limousine. En route, near Chippenham, Wiltshire, a tire blew out, the driver lost control, and the car smashed into a lamppost. Within hours, Cochran died of multiple head injuries at Bath Hospital. Sheely and Vincent survived, but the accident destroyed Vincent's career.

The Booming Teen Market

Rock-and-roll tragedy occurred amid booming economic conditions. During the 1950s, the GNP, the indicator of U.S. economic growth, rose from $213 billion to $503 billion. The personal per capita income in the country increased from $1,526 in 1950 to $2,788 ten years later, an increase of 82 percent. Throughout the decade, unemployment fluctuated between 4 and 5.5 percent.

The recording industry, reinvigorated by rock-and-roll, shared in the general prosperity. Record sales in the United States skyrocketed from $189 million in 1950 to nearly $600 million by the end of the decade. The industry sold almost half of all discs through mail-order clubs and in supermarkets, which by the 1950s had replaced neighborhood stores. In 1959, the industry chalked up almost $200 million in sales of 45-rpm records, which usually were manufactured for teens, who could afford the comparatively inexpensive discs. Though over 5000 record labels competed for a share of the market, four major companies—RCA Victor, Columbia, Decca, and Capitol—racked up nearly 75 percent of the total sales.

Reflecting a postwar trend in U.S. business, the record industry even expanded into the international market with rock-and-roll. RCA vice-president George Marek observed in 1959 that "rock-and-roll is popular not only in this country but it has swept the world, the world

Dick Clark (center, with microphone) interviews the vocal group, The Skyliners, on "American Bandstand," ca. late 1950s

where there are no broadcasting stations even: It is relatively popular in conservative England, in Australia, India, Germany, wherever you go." An early 1960s Decca press release described the state of the music business: "The recording industry, a fledgling during the heyday of vaudeville, has shown a steady, remarkable growth until today it stands as a major factor in the world's economy."

Dick Clark and American Bandstand

Dick Clark, a marketing genius from upstate New York, delivered new stars to the increasing number of rock-and-rollers. Born in 1929, Richard Augustus Clark II attended Syracuse University and studied advertising and radio, getting, in his words, a "sound education in business administration." In 1951, he landed a part-time job as an announcer for station WOLF, and then worked for his father, who was station manager at WRUN in Utica. A short time later Clark decided to accept a job at WFIL in Philadelphia, at first announcing a radio show of popular and classical music. He later wrote: "I was a great pitchman. I sold pots and pans, vacuum cleaners, diamond rings, Mrs. Smith pies, the works. Eventually I landed the Schaefer Beer account. I did one hell of a beer spot."

In July 1956, Clark moved to WFIL's television station and hosted Philadelphia "Bandstand," which showcased local high school students dancing to popular hit records. He replaced disc jockey Bob Horn, who, in October 1952, had launched the program and four years later had resigned due to adverse publicity surrounding two drunken-driving citations.

Dick Clark initially knew little about the rock-and-roll music that the program highlighted. During his first "Bandstand" appearance as the regular host, Clark remembered, he arrived on the "set at two that afternoon with only a foggy notion of what the kids, music, and show were really about. . . . I don't understand this music," he confessed to record promoter Red Schwartz.

The new host of "Bandstand" quickly became familiar with the commercial potential of the new music. "The more I heard the music the more I enjoyed it; the more I enjoyed it, the more I understood the kids," he later related. "I knew that if I could tune into them and keep myself on the show, I could make a great deal of money." Clark—voted by his high school classmates as the "Man Most Likely to Sell the Brooklyn Bridge"—felt that behind his "bland twenty-nine-year-old face lay the heart of a cunning capitalist" who wanted to "defend my right and your right to go to a church of our choice, or to buy the record of our choice."

Clark's business savvy transformed a local telecast into a national phenomenon. To get sponsors for the show, he "traveled the advertising agency circuit on Madison Avenue" and eventually snagged the lucrative Beechnut Spearmint Gum account. After that success, *Advertising Age* predicted that Dick Clark "may replace Arthur Godfrey as the number-one personal salesman."

"Bandstand," built upon a solid advertising base by Clark, was nationally televised as "American Bandstand," premiering on August 5, 1957, on 67 stations coast to coast to more than 8 million viewers. The show aired from Philadelphia for 90 minutes every weekday afternoon and on Monday nights from 7:30 to 8:00 P.M. It featured 150 teenagers in the audience, many of whom danced to the popular hits and listened to the smooth patter of Dick Clark. "It's been a long, long time since a major network has aimed at the most entertainment-starved group in the country," Clark told *Time* magazine. "And why not? After all, teenagers have $9 billion a year to spend."

Droves of teenaged girls responded to Clark's brand of rock-and-roll. After school hours, hordes of pubescent girls rushed home and feverishly tuned into "American Bandstand." Usually with their best girlfriend or sister, they danced to the music on their living room floors, identified with the regular dancers, and fantasized about stardom on the dance floor of "American Bandstand." The girls flooded the show with up to 45,000 letters a week and helped the program gross $500,000 a year and net ratings that equaled the combined ratings of the shows telecast by two rival networks. "We love it," gushed one girl from Charleston, West Virginia. "When I hear a Beethoven symphony I don't feel anything. When I hear our kind of music, I feel something way down deep, like oatmeal." In the absence of major rock stars and working on the new medium of television, the farsighted Clark had created a rock-and-roll that emphasized the audience as much as the music.

Clark and "American Bandstand" brought a respectability to rock-and-roll that had not existed with the suggestive, greasy rockabillies. Clark himself portrayed a prim, clean-cut image. *Newsweek* referred to him as "genial and softspoken," and *Time* characterized the announcer as "personable and polite, he manages to sound as if he really means such glib disc jockey patter as, 'Let me pull up a hunk of wood and sit down with you.' "

The dancers and performers featured on "American Bandstand" mirrored the clean-cut demeanor of the host. Clark insisted upon a dress code, forcing boys to "wear a jacket and tie, or a sweater and tie. Nobody dressed that way in real life, but it made the show acceptable to adults who were frightened by the teenage world and their music. Girls couldn't wear slacks, tight sweaters, shorts, or low-necked gowns—they had to wear the kind of dresses or sweaters and skirts they wore in school. No tight toreadors or upturned collars." *Newsweek* approvingly reported that "Clark enforces strict rules: No smoking, no tight sweaters or dresses, no slacks, no hats or overcoats, no gum chewing. He also carries a supply of safety pins for 'sent' kids who come undone." "We've never had an incident," Clark boasted to *Time* in 1958.

To further purge sexuality from the airwaves, the announcer refused to say "going steady" and banned the Alligator and Dog dances as "too sexy." "We just didn't deal with sex," Clark later wrote. As music writer Arnold Shaw concluded, "Clark was, in fact, the great tranquilizer of the era, reassuring parents by his suave manners that rock-and-roll was not bad and transforming the youngsters on his show into sunshine biscuits."

One of Clark's books on teenage etiquette, *To Goof or Not to Goof*, exemplified his transmutation of teenage rebellion. The dust jacket read: "How to have morals and manners and still have fun." The contents dealt with such burning questions "to successful teenaging" as "Where do your elbows go when you're not eating? . . . How long should it take to say good night to a girl? To her father? . . . Do nice girls call up boys? . . . How far is friendly?"

Clark's Creations

Dick Clark, though showcasing a variety of rock-and-roll acts on *American Bandstand*, created a stable of mostly Italian, Philadelphia-bred youths whom he groomed, promoted, and cast as the stars of his show. One such idol was Fabian. One day in 1957, a South Philadelphia policeman, Dominick Forte, suffered a heart attack on the street. Bob Marcucci, co-owner of Chancellor Records, offered help and noticed Forte's 14-year-old son, Fabian. Impressed with Fabian's resemblance to Elvis Presley, the manager gave the youth voice and etiquette lessons for two years and then without much success tried to sell the teen by buying full-page ads in the trade papers of the music industry.

In 1959, Dick Clark agreed to promote Fabian, who lip-synced "Turn Me Loose," "Tiger," and the Elvis Presley imitation, "Hound Dog Man" on "American Bandstand." Though believing that the singer "got screams though he couldn't sing a note," Clark transformed Fabian from a $6-a-week drugstore clerk into an overnight sensation. Within a year, Clark had enabled the Philadelphia teen to sell almost a million copies of his signature song, "Tiger," appear on "The Ed Sullivan Show," and be covered in *Time* magazine. "Dick Clark was the only way to get your artist to be seen throughout the entire country in the matter of one day," commented Bob Marcucci on the importance of "American Bandstand."

Dick Clark also launched the career of Frankie Avalon, another regular on "American Bandstand" who was managed by Bob Marcucci. Born Francis Avallone, Avalon played trumpet for the Philadelphia group Rocco and the Saints, and in 1958 debuted his solo single, "DeDe Dinah," which reached the number-seven slot on the charts. Through repeated appearances on "American Bandstand," the teen scored hits with such songs as "Venus" and "Why." Remarked Frankie about "Venus": "Dick got behind it and it sold a million and a half copies. He's the greatest."

Bobby Rydell, born Robert Ridarelli in Philadelphia, followed his friend Frankie Avalon on the path to stardom. Also a member of Rocco and the Saints, Rydell started a solo career in 1958 that was unsuccessful until he joined "American Bandstand" a year later. In 1959 he scored hits with "Kissin' Time," "Volare," and "Swingin' School"; within four years he chalked up 19 Top 30 chartbusters. Along with Fabian and Frankie Avalon, Bobby Rydell became an "American Bandstand"-produced teen idol who defined the Philadelphia sound, a teenaged version of the smooth ballads delivered by such Italian crooners of the 1940s and early 1950s as Frank Sinatra, Perry Como, and Dean Martin.

Clark also brought to fame Ernest Evans, another Philadelphian who became known as Chubby Checker and popularized an international dance craze. In the summer of 1960, Clark noticed an African-American couple on "American Bandstand" "doing a dance that consisted of revolving their hips in quick, half-circle jerks, so their pelvic regions were heaving in time to the music. . . . For God's sake, keep the cameras off that couple. . . . It looked like something a belly dancer did to climax her performance," Clark screamed to his producer, Tony Mammarella.

The announcer soon realized the commercial potential of the dance and suggested that Cameo Records, a company owned partially by Clark, cover Hank Ballard's 1959 "The Twist." For a singer the company chose Chubby Checker, an African-American chicken plucker at a poultry shop who had attended high school with Fabian and Frankie Avalon. In 1960, "American Bandstand" played Checker's "The Twist" until it hit the top of the charts and earned the butcher's helper $822,459 from 1960 to 1962.

A new dance craze, started on the program, accompanied the song. To do the dance, instructed rock critic Lillian Roxon, "you put one foot out and pretend you're stubbing out a cigarette butt on the floor with the big toe. At the same time, you move your hands and body as though you're drying every inch of your back with an invisible towel. That's the twist." The twist craze reached international proportions and spawned a series of records: *Chuck Berry Twist*, the Isley Brothers' "Twist and Shout," Ray Henry's "Twist Polka," *Twist with Bobby Darin*, Sam Cooke's "Twistin' the Night Away," *Twist with the Ventures*, *Twistin' with Duane Eddy*, and many others.

Dick Clark marketed other dances and their theme songs on his television show. "Many of these dances," admitted the announcer, "came out of Philadelphia and were associated with songs done by artists on Cameo Records." Chubby Checker sang to the Hucklebuck, the Pony, the Limbo, and the Fly. Bobby Rydell popularized the Fish. The white, Philadelphia doo-wop group the Dovells introduced the Bristol Stomp and the Continental, and singer Dee Dee Sharp exhorted television viewers to do the Mashed Potato.

Though creating teen idols and dance steps for his television viewers, Clark remained at center stage. He received the attention of the trade publications and the popular press. *Time* labeled him "the Pied Piper of the teenagers." Even the teens themselves swooned over Clark. During the first year of "American Bandstand" more than 300,000 fans requested Clark's photo, and in 1958 *Life* printed a revealing shot of an awestruck 16-year-old, June Carter, during "her great moment, touching the cheek Dick Clark has just kissed." *Life*, carrying an article about the announcer and the army-bound Elvis Presley, described the power of Clark in the headline: "The Dictator at Home and the King at War."

For Clark, popularity led to wealth. The announcer collected a sizable salary each year for his work on such television programs as "American Bandstand"; "The Dick Clark Show," a concert format started in 1958; and "Dick Clark's Caravan of Stars," begun in 1959. Besides the income from his work on shows, he earned $50,000 a year spinning discs at record hops, which led to the formation of his first corporation, Click. Clark slowly gained interest in such record companies as Chancellor, which featured Fabian and Frankie Avalon; Cameo-Parkway, which recorded Bobby Rydell, Chubby Checker, and the Dovells; Swan Records; Jamie Records; Chips Record Distributing Corporation; Globe Records; and Hunt Records. He also owned the copyrights to over 160 songs including "At the Hop," "Party Time," "January Music," and "Sixteen Candles" and controlled the Mallard Pressing Corporation. During the fifties, Dick Clark held at least some share in 33 corporations. By April 8, 1958, *Time* reported that "television's newest rage consists of a jukebox full of rock 'n' roll records, a studio full of dancing teenagers and Dick Clark, a suave young (28) disc jockey full of money."

The Payola Investigation

Clark's interlocking interests became painfully public during the payola

Teen idol Frankie Avalon, squeaky clean and perfect for the whitebread market
Frank Driggs Collection

investigations of 1959 and 1960. Payola, or play for pay, had been an accepted practice in the music industry dating to the vaudeville era. "It was an era of outright payola," wrote Abel Green, editor of *Variety*. "From the opening acrobatic act, which plugged *Japanese Sandman*, *Dardanella* or some other instrumental while making with the hand-to-hand gymnastics, through the rest of the bill, there was little that the then powerful Vaudeville Managers Protective Association and the Music Publishers Protective Association could do to kayo it." "Historically, payola is an outgrowth of a music business tradition—song plugging," agreed Paul Ackerman, the music editor of *Billboard*.

The payola investigations of 1959 and 1960 began with fraud on television. In November 1959, Charles Lincoln Van Doren admitted before the House Special Committee on Legislative Oversight that he had been given answers in advance as a contestant on NBC's "Twenty-One" quiz show. "I would give almost anything I have to reverse the course of my life in the last three years," he told the committee. Reeling from the revelation, the networks discontinued many game programs: NBC canceled "Tic Tac Dough" and "The Price Is Right"; CBS eliminated all quiz shows from its schedule and fired the president of the network, who had been closely associated with "Quiz Kids," "Stop the Music," and "The $64,000 Question," the most popular show in America.

The scandal spread to the music industry with the prodding of the American Society of Composers, Authors, and Publishers (ASCAP), a song/performance-licensing concern that, through the 1950s, had attacked the interlocking interests of radio, network television, and the record companies represented by the rival licensing agent, Broadcast Music, Inc. (BMI). Concerned about rock performers such as Little Richard and Chuck Berry, who wrote their own material, the professional songwriters of ASCAP used the payola investigation as a forum to lash out bitterly against BMI and the rock-and-roll it licensed. The songwriters hired Vance Packard, author of *Hidden Persuaders*, who tried to demonstrate that "the rock and roll, hillbilly, and Latin American movements were largely engineered, manipulated for the interests of BMI, and that would be the point, that the public was manipulated into liking rock and roll." Rock music, Packard continued, "might be best summed up as monotony tinged with hysteria," which could not be sold to the discerning public without payola. "What do you think is going to happen to rock and roll songs?" asked ASCAP member and well-known songwriter Oscar Hammerstein. "There seems to be something funny to me that these songs have been so popular, so much more popular than any other new songs that have been produced, and yet don't live. They die as soon as the plug stops."

Congressmen in charge of the investigation, hoping to impress their conservative constituencies during an election year, joined in the attack on rock-and-roll. "Suppose John Smith owns a record company and then buys a broadcast station," postulated the counsel for the committee. "Suppose he dumps its personnel and its good music format to put on his own label, generally only rock and roll. . . . Now, that's not in the public interest." Without payola, "a lot of this so-called junk music, rock 'n' roll stuff, which appeals to the teenagers would not be played," stressed Congressman John Bennett of Michigan. "The good music did not require the support, the good music did not require the payment of payola," added Representative John Moss of California. Such "trash" as rock music had been "pushed" on unsuspecting teens.

The committee focused on disc jockeys who played rock-and-roll. Boston jockey Norm Prescott told the House committee that "bribery, payola, has become the prime function of this business to get the record on the air at any cost," and that he had taken almost $10,000 from various record distributors. Another Boston announcer, WBZ's Dave Maynard, admitted that a record distributor had helped finance his 1957 Mercury station wagon and his 1959 Buick, and had given him $6817 in cash. Alan Dary, also of WBZ, received cash, a hi-fi, liquor, and carpeting for his master bedroom. By 1960, investigators announced that 207 rock disc jockeys in 42 states had accepted more than $263,000 in payola. President Dwight Eisenhower instructed the committee, headed by Oren Harris of Arkansas, "to clean up this whole mess."

Some rock DJs immediately felt repercussions from the payola investigation. In Detroit, Tom Clay of station WJBK was fired after he admitted to taking $6000 in a year and a half. After defending payola "as part of American business," WJBK jockey Jack LeGoff lost his job. Don McLeod of the same station was fired two days later. In Boston, three top disc jockeys on the rock station WILD—Stan Richards, Bill Marlowe, and Mike Eliot—found themselves unemployed. And in New York, premier rock announcer Alan Freed was dismissed by WABC when he admitted that he had taken $30,650 from six record companies. Complained a bitter Freed, "what they call payola in the disc jockey business they call lobbying in Washington."

Dick Clark, perhaps the most prominent rock announcer at the time, came under especially close scrutiny. As Representative John Burnett of Michigan put it: "I think it is pretty convincing that Clark was involved with payola as all other disc jockeys, but on a much larger scale." Congressman Peter Mack of Illinois called him "the top dog in the payola field," and Representative John Moss of California began to refer to the investigations as "Clarkola."

Clark escaped the payola investigation with his job and reputation intact. Wearing a blue suit, a button-down shirt, and black loafers, the announcer uncategorically informed the House committee in April 1960 that "I have never agreed to play a record in return for payment in cash or any other consideration." When grilled about spinning records of artists who recorded for companies in which he owned an interest, a cool Clark replied softly that "I did not consciously favor such records. Maybe I did so without realizing it." The host of "American Bandstand," seldom promoting performers who wrote their own material and projecting an air of respectability to the congressional investigators, slipped through the committee unscathed. At the end of his testimony, he was told by Chairman Oren Harris: "You're not the inventor of the system or even its architect. You're a product of it. . . . Obviously," Harris concluded, "you're a fine young man."

Alan Freed, a tireless champion of black performers who wrote their own songs and had created rock-and-roll, did not fare so well. As the payola investigation ended in 1960, an unemployed Freed was charged with commercial bribery in connection with payola by an eight-member grand jury in New York. Blackballed by the music industry after the payola scare, the former disc jockey, penniless, stood trial in December 1962 and pleaded guilty to two counts of commercial bribery. He was fined $300 and given a six-month suspended sentence. Less than two years later, on March 16, 1964, Freed was charged with income tax evasion during 1957 to 1959 by another grand jury, which ordered him to pay the Internal Revenue Service almost $38,000 in back taxes. Later in the year, a broken, unemployed, despondent Alan Freed entered a California hospital, suffering from the effects of alcoholism. On January 20, 1965, he died at the age of 43.

Don Kirshner Takes Charge

The payola investigation had an immediate impact on rock-and-roll. As the established tunesmiths in ASCAP had hoped, songwriters became a dominant force in the new music. Ironically, from 1960 to 1963, a new breed of songsmiths nurtured by New York music publisher Don Kirshner outdistanced recognized Tin Pan Alley songwriters to corner the teen market. They produced romantic lyrics and upbeat melodies for and about teenage girls and placed the songs with gospel-influenced, black girl groups, which gradually became more popular than the white, male, Italian teen idols of the Dick Clark era.

Don Kirshner masterminded the takeover of rock by the songwriters. The son of a Bronx tailor, Kirshner began to write songs professionally in 1958 and hoped to reshape Tin Pan Alley for the expanding teen market. As he remembered, "My idols at the time were Max and Louis Dryfuss, who had built [the music publishing firm of] Chappell Music. I had watched some of the old movies they were in, like *Night and Day* and *Rhapsody in Blue* and had observed them molding the greats like Gershwin, Rodgers and Hammerstein, and Lerner and Lowe. . . . My philosophy—my dream," he related, "was that we were approaching a new era in the music business with room for new people to accomplish what the Dryfusses had. And I believed that if I got the chance to sit behind a desk in the music business, I'd be the guy to accomplish that."

Chasing his dream, in 1958 a 21-year-old Don Kirshner—along with Al Nevins, guitarist for the pop group the Three Suns—established Aldon Music. "Our concept," pointed out Kirshner, "was to build new writers." The business partners rented office space across the street from the famed Brill Building at 1619 Broadway, which housed the well-known publishing firms so important to the pop music of Tin Pan Alley. "The Brill Building," reminisced songwriter Mike Stoller, who collaborated with Jerry Leiber on a number of songs recorded by Elvis Presley and the Coasters, "had music publishers on every floor. Frequently in the Brill Building writers would go to peddle their songs and they'd go from door to door trying to sell them."

Kirshner quickly discovered teams of young songwriters who challenged the established firms across the street. One afternoon, just two days after he had opened his door for business, the new music publisher "was sweeping the floor with a short-sleeve shirt on." Two aspiring writers and high school chums, Neil Sedaka and Howie Greenfield, walked into the office. As Kirshner recalled, "they had just been turned down by Hill and Range [publishers] upstairs. They asked to see me. I said, 'I'm the guy!' They said, 'Come on, you're kidding us.' But they figured they had nothing to lose, so they proceeded to play six incredible songs: 'Stupid Cupid,' 'The Diary,' and 'Calendar Girl' and a few others." Kirshner took the team to the home of a friend, pop singer Connie Francis, who recorded and hit the charts with "Stupid Cupid" and later in 1958 scaled the charts with another Sedaka-Greenfield tune, "Fallin'."

Neil Sedaka, unlike almost all the other songwriters at Aldon, began to record his own material. After the Connie Francis hits, Sedaka, who was a classically trained pianist, began to sense that the singers who recorded his songs "couldn't feel it the way I could. I used to play songs for people and then play the record, and they would say, 'We like the way you do it better.' "

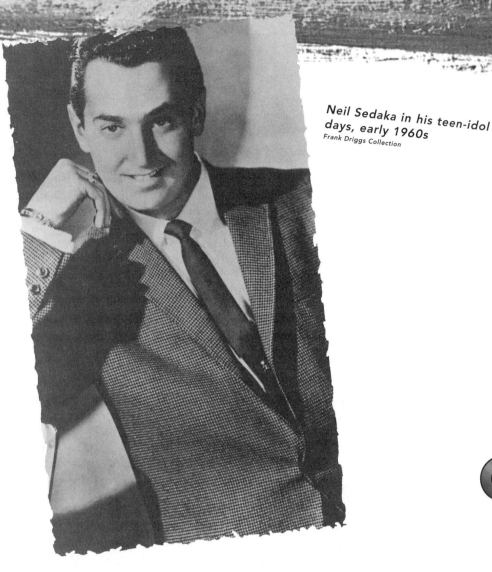

Neil Sedaka in his teen-idol
days, early 1960s
Frank Driggs Collection

In 1959, Al Nevins took Sedaka to RCA executive Steve Scholes, who told the 19-year-old songwriter: "Yes, we are looking for more teenage attractions because of our immense success with Elvis. Being that you write songs, you are very interesting." A few weeks later, RCA signed Sedaka and recorded "The Diary," which, after a $100,000 promotional campaign, became Sedaka's first hit as a singer. During the next three years, Sedaka followed with the chartbusters "Breaking Up Is Hard to Do," "Calendar Girl," "Stairway to Heaven," "Happy Birthday Sweet Sixteen," and "Oh! Carol," the last written in 1959 for his girlfriend, Carole Klein.

The Sounds on the Streets

Don Kirshner found other successful songwriters who helped extend the boundaries of doo-wop. Doo-wop originated on the streets of New York City, where groups of young African-American males, too poor to afford instruments, started to harmonize. Many groups fashioned themselves after the Ravens. Formed in 1945, the six-man group featured the deep bass tone of leader Jimmy Ricks; they released singles on Hub, National, and King Records before signing with Columbia in 1950. They hit the R & B Top 10 with "I Don't Have to Ride No More" and "Rock Me All Night Long." During the fifties, the Ravens inspired dozens of groups named after birds, including the Larks ("Heaven and Paradise"), the Swallows ("Itchy Twitchy Feeling"), the Cardinals, the Robins ("Smokey Joe's Cafe"), the Jayhawks ("Stranded in the Jungle"), and the Penguins, who perhaps achieved the greatest commercial success with "Earth Angel."

Doo-wop groups also looked to Clyde McPhatter and the Drifters for inspiration. As with most doo-wop harmonizers, McPhatter first joined a gospel group, the Dominoes, who were managed by Billy Ward. Soon after their television debut on "The Arthur Godfrey Show," the group began to record rhythm and blues numbers; in May 1951, they released the classic "Sixty Minute Man." Within two years, McPhatter bolted from the Dominoes to form the Drifters, settling on the name because the members "drifted" from one group to another. The group signed with Atlantic Records and immediately scaled the chart with "Money Honey." They followed with such hits as "Such a Night," "Honey Love," and "Bip Bam" before McPhatter left the group in 1954 for the army.

New York music entrepreneur George Goldner recorded several of the doo-wop groups that had been influenced by the Ravens and the Drifters. Born in 1919 in Manhattan, Goldner, originally a garment-district wholesaler, became interested in Latin music; in 1948, he founded Tico Records to record well-known Latin acts. In March 1954, on the advice of his friend and talent agent Cliff Martinez, he recorded the doo-wop group, the Crows, who unexpectedly attracted an R & B and pop following with "Gee."

Encouraged by his success with the Crows, Goldner established Gee Records and signed several now-legendary harmonizers, including Frankie Lymon and the Teenagers. The Teenagers, fronted by 12-year-old Lymon, practiced on street corners, in a junk-filled backyard, and on the top of a Harlem tenement house. One day Richard Barrett, the lead singer of another Goldner act, the Valentines, overheard the Teenagers as he passed by a street corner. Excitedly, he brought the boys, all in their teens except for Lymon, to the offices of Gee Records at Ninth Avenue and 49th Street, where they sang "Why Do Fools Fall In Love." Goldner asked Lymon if he had the sheet music for the song. "Nope," replied Frankie, "we don't know anything about written down music." The next day, the Teenagers recorded "Why Do Fools Fall In Love" for Gee. Released in January 1956, the song became a national hit within a few months. Goldner followed with doo-wop from such groups as the Wrens, the Dubs, the Mello-Tones, the Harptones, the Flamingos, and the Channels. "His gift was that he could recognize and manipulate talent with an uncanny ear for commercial potential," remarked Herb Cox, lead singer of the Cleftones, who hit for Gee Records with "Little Girl of Mine."

Frankie Lymon (center) and the Teenagers, ca. mid 1950s
Frank Driggs Collection

By the mid-1950s, hundreds of young African-American males, most of whom had just graduated from high school, harmonized on the streets of urban America. Most came from New York City, including the Paragons ("Florence"), the Jive Five ("My True Story"), the Jesters ("The Plea"), the Hearts ("Lonely Nights"), the Chords ("Sh-Boom"), the Charts ("Desirie"), the Halos ("Nag"), the Heartbeats ("A Thousand Miles Away"), and the Genies ("Who's That Knockin'"). From Los Angeles came the Penguins, the Olympics ("Western Movies"), the Hollywood Flames ("Buzz-Buzz-Buzz"), the Jacks ("Why Don't You Write Me") and the Medallions ("The Letter"). The Five Satins, who hit with "In the Still of the Night," and the Nutmegs ("Story Untold") came from New Haven, the Charms ("Hearts of Stone") sang on the streets of Cincinnati, the Monotones ("Book of Love") and the Fiestas ("So Fine") grew up in Newark, and the Dells ("Oh, What a Night") and the El Dorados ("At My Front Door") came from Chicago.

Many of the doo-wop groups found their names on the urban streets. Some borrowed their names from the automobiles that glided past the streets on which they sang: the El Dorados, the Cadillacs, the Edsels, the Fiestas, the Impalas, the Imperials, and the Belvederes. Dion and the Belmonts ("I Wonder Why" and "Teenager in Love"), one of the few white doo-wop groups, named themselves after Belmont Avenue in the Bronx near their home. Reflecting life in fifties urban America, these teens created a sound that would reverberate through the history of rock-and-roll.

The Girl Groups

Don Kirshner hired teams of young New York City songwriters who built upon the doo-wop tradition by writing teen-oriented songs for young African-American female vocal groups. Carole Klein, the subject of a Neil Sedaka song ("Oh! Carol") who later became known as Carole King, helped write Aldon Music's first smash hit, which set the direction of the company for the next three years. King had learned piano at the age of four and in high school formed her first band, the Co-sines. While attending Queens College in New York in 1958, she met Gerry Goffin, who started to write songs with her.

The King-Goffin team joined Aldon Music and began to compose Tin Pan Alley songs designed especially for teens. Goffin told *Time*, "Lyrics will hurt a song if they're too adult, too artistic, too correct. You should shy away from anything too deep or too happy."

In 1960, the King-Goffin duo, by then fixtures at Aldon Music, composed the teen ballad, "Will You Love Me Tomorrow." Kirshner brought the song to Mitch Miller, then the head of Artists and Repertoire (A&R) at Columbia Records, and suggested that pop balladeer Johnny Mathis sing the song. Miller, a stalwart in the music establishment, rejected the offer of the fledgling new publisher. Since, as Kirshner explained, the "A&R man was very big, and two men controlled the industry: Mitch Miller and Milt Gabler of the Decca Group," the co-owner of Aldon took the song to a New Jersey-based independent company, Scepter Records. He approached label owners Florence Greenberg and Luther Dixon "for a group they had called the Shirelles," an African-American, all-girl act that in 1959 had remade the Five Royales' "Dedicated to the One I Love" without much success. Kirshner convinced Scepter Records and the Shirelles to record "Will You Love Me Tomorrow," which became a number-one hit and, as Kirshner told it, "created Scepter Records. I mean it was a real major hit." The song became the first number-one hit by an all-girl group.

Kirshner hired other teams of songwriters who worked side by side to compose teenage-oriented tunes for other doo-wop-influenced, African-American girl groups who became some of the first female rock-and-roll performers. Paying his composers about $150 a week, he snagged the songwriting teams of Barry Mann-Cynthia Weil and Ellie Greenwich-Jeff Barry, who joined about 30 other young tunesmiths at Aldon Music during the early 1960s. "It was insane," recalled Barry Mann. "Cynthia and I would be in this tiny cubicle, about the size of a closet, with just a piano and chair; no window or anything. We'd go in every morning and write songs all day. In the next room Carole [King] and Gerry [Goffin] would be doing the same thing, and in the next room after that Neil [Sedaka] or somebody else. Sometimes when we all got to banging on our pianos you couldn't tell who was playing what. . . . All of us—me and Cynthia, Carole King and Gerry Goffin, Neil Sedaka and Howie Greenfield—were so insecure that we'd never write a hit again that we constantly wrote in order to prove we could," added Mann.

The two teams of Mann-Weil and Greenwich-Barry, sequestered in their cubicles, in 1962 and 1963 crafted a number of songs for two of the premier African-American girl groups, the Ronettes and the Crystals. Mann and Weil wrote the hits "Uptown" and "He's Sure the Boy I Love" for the Crystals and "Walking in the Rain" for the Ronettes. The more prolific Greenwich-Barry team authored "Baby, I Love You" and "Be My Baby" for the Ronettes, "Da Doo Ron Ron" and "Then He Kissed Me" for the Crystals. They also composed "Today I Met The Boy I'm Gonna Marry" and "Wait Till My Baby Gets Home" for Darlene Love, who sang lead vocal on many of the Crystals' hits.

Darlene Love (a.k.a. Darlene Wright) infused the girl-group sound with a gospel flavor. "My father was a minister, and I used to sing all the time in the church choir," remembered Love. "That's my favorite type of music, gospel music." At 16, the singer joined the Blossoms, a racially integrated female vocal group in Los Angeles which also included Annette, Nanette, and Fanita James and Grazia Nitzsche. In 1962, Darlene Love sang lead vocal on the Crystals' "He's a Rebel," infusing the song with a gospel sound. With the Blossoms, the singer cut many other gospel-influenced records officially released under the Crystals' name. Ellie Greenwich described Love as "a typical sixties soulful street gospel singer."

The Crystals, early 1960s
Photo courtesy William Morris Agency

75

The Ronettes (Ronnie Spector, center)
early 1960s. Dig those wigs!

The Aldon Music songwriters supplied singers such as the gospel-influenced Darlene Love with tunes that appealed to the teen market. Darlene Love complained that "many of the singers [in the girl groups] that sung those songs didn't really want to sing them. We called them bubblegum songs. The lyrics were really not even teenage. I say kid, you know 10 to 12, the market was geared for them."

Phil Spector, owner of Philles Records, which recorded the Crystals and the Ronettes, surrounded the teen-oriented, gospel-flavored tear-jerkers of Aldon Music with a wall of sound to create distinctive, girl-group music. Spector, born in the Bronx, moved to Los Angeles with his mother when his father died. After a short-lived success with a rock combo, the Teddy Bears, he found employment with independent producers Lester Sill and Lee Hazelwood, who in 1960 sent Spector to New York. In 1961, the 21-year-old Spector and Lester Sill, a former promotion man for Modern Records, formed the New York-based Philles Records, which Spector owned solely by 1962.

While recording the Crystals and the Ronettes for Philles, the producer perfected his now-famous wall of sound, which involved multiple instrumentation. Ronnie Bennett, the lead singer of the Ronettes, who later married and then divorced the producer, remembered that "everything was done double. I mean where most people have one guitar or one drummer we had two of everything, so that's what made that wall of sound." "Well, I know that Phil's favorite composer was Wagner, no question, power, bigness," commented Ellie Greenwich. "And a few times when I'd gone over, Phil had an office on the main floor of a building and he had an apartment upstairs, and very often he would be upstairs in his one room listening with the speakers blasting, conducting. Wagner was his idol and Wagner was power and bigness and heavy and all that and I think he was going after that in his records." Spector himself called the new sound "a Wagnerian approach to rock and roll; little symphonies for the kids." The power of Spector's production that surrounded gospel-flavored songs of teenage romance resulted in the bright, upbeat, almost ethereal girl-group sound.

The Dream

The rags-to-riches success stories of the girl groups added to the romantic appeal of the music for thousands of school-age girls. The Crystals, a group of Brooklyn teens, had been discovered by Phil Spector while auditioning in New York City. The Shirelles had begun singing at school shows and at parties, and in 1958 had been signed to Scepter Records by Florence Greenberg, the mother of one of their high school classmates, Mary Jo Greenberg. The Chantels, five New York teens who sang in the cherub choir of a local Catholic grade school, were signed to a contract when a talent scout inadvertently heard them harmonizing at a Frankie Lymon concert. In 1958, they hit the charts with "Maybe."

Other groups had similar stories. The Chiffons, a group of high school friends who sang during lunch breaks and in the neighborhood after school, were discovered by songwriter Ronnie Mack, who groomed the girls until they made their chart-topping "He's So Fine." The Dixie Cups, singing together since grade school, were spotted at a local New Orleans talent contest by singer/pianist Joe Jones, who became their manager and helped them up the charts with the Greenwich-Barry song "Chapel of Love." The Shangri-las, one of the few white girl groups of the era, grew up in a tough section of Queens, New York, and began singing together as teenagers. One day producer Shadow Morton, a friend of Ellie Greenwich, happened to hear the three girls—Mary Weiss and the Ganser twins, Marge and Mary Ann—and signed them to the new Red Bird label, which had been started by doo-wop impresario George Goldner and R & B songwriters Jerry Leiber and Mike Stoller. In 1964, when Mary was only 15, the group hit the top of the singles chart with "Leader of the Pack."

The discovery of the Ronettes—sisters Veronica and Estelle Bennett and cousin Nedra Talley—probably offered teenaged girls the most heartfelt story. In 1961, the three girls became resident dancers at the Peppermint Lounge, the focus of the twist craze in New York City. In August the group signed with Colpix Records and released four unsuccessful songs. After a show at the Peppermint Lounge in 1963, Ronnie Bennett casually walked into a bar and saw Phil Spector sitting at the piano. Their eyes fastened upon one another, and Spector softly asked Ronnie to sing. After a few bars, the producer exclaimed, "That's the voice, that's the voice I've been looking for."

Such tales of instant stardom coupled with the dramatic, romanticized music of the girl groups to create the fantasy among many young girls that they too could become famous. "You see them coming from the cities, mostly groups, off the streets, hanging around Tin Pan Alley on Broadway near the Brill Building," noticed Phil Spector at the time. "They're usually between 16 and 19, anxious to record, anxious to be a singer." Although few traveled to New York in search of their dreams, millions of girls lay in their beds, listened to their transistor radios, and fantasized about impending stardom. Songwriter Jerry Leiber characterized the era as "very naive, very innocent, full of hope, full of fantasy, full of promise." *Life* magazine referred to the new sound as "a fairy tale called the pop-record business" and identified Don Kirshner as "the grand wizard of the fairy tale."

The fantasies of teenaged girls helped Don Kirshner establish a music-publishing empire. "The fastest rising phenomenon in the business is a Tin Pan Alley octopus called Aldon Music Inc., which has 35 boys and girls busy night and day composing songs," reported *Time* in March 1963. A few months later, *The Saturday Evening Post* renamed Tin Pan Alley as "Teen Pan Alley" and told its readers that "Broadway's Brill Building, once the home of jelly-jowled, gray-headed music publishers, is now being refurbished with youthful executives who have grown up to no other kind of music than the beat of today. . . . One of the typical—and prime—figures in youth's take-over of the pop record business is a onetime unsuccessful songwriter named Don Kirshner whose knack for picking up songs has earned him a $225,000 palace in New Jersey." By the end of the year, Kirshner had sold hundreds of songs that dominated the rock charts and grossed millions of dollars.

In 1963, Don Kirshner and partner Al Nevins sold Aldon Music. "The money just kept rolling in, and the hits kept rolling in," shrugged Kirshner, "and you walk away at 28 years of age with a $2 million dollar check with your partner, it's difficult to turn down." Kirshner left for a lucrative job in the Columbia Screen Gems Television Music Division, where he supervised the record-and-music-publishing interests of the company. He had left Aldon just when the surf had begun to rise.

Surfboards and Hot Rods: California, Here We Come

"We sang about California and being young."

Dean Torrence

Eureka, a Greek word meaning "I have found it," was selected by state legislators as a motto in 1850, at the end of the great gold rush, when California became the thirty-first state. Especially during the late 1950s and early 1960s, it aptly characterized the sentiments of the droves of migrants from the Midwest and the East Coast who traveled to California with hopes of sun, fun, and jobs. A new indigenous music—a bright, bouncy sound that glorified beaches, bikinis, and hot rods—embodied and promoted the California myth.

The New American Empire

Postwar California had advantages over most other states. It enjoyed an abundance of natural resources including lumber, oil, boron minerals, mercury, thorium concentrates, and tungsten. In 1961, the state produced more fruit, vegetables, sugar beets, seed crops, walnuts, and almonds than any other state and topped the number-two farm state, Iowa, by more than $700 million in total produce. California, which offered scores of white-collar jobs to its inhabitants, by the early 1960s secured about 25 percent of all prime government defense contracts and space program money. Spearheading the computer-chip age, in

1961 the state procured almost half of the $6 billion in Defense Department research-and-development contracts; during the 1950s it had attracted 200 electronic firms such as Western Electric, Raytheon, Remington Rand, Zenith, and Motorola to the aptly named Silicon Valley. Probably most important, the state, third only to Alaska and Texas in size, boasted a wide range of terrains and climates from the desert of Death Valley to the damp, forested mountains in the north, from the central farm valley to the beaches of Malibu.

The resources of California, especially a healthy economy and the sunny, balmy climate of the southern part of the state, drew throngs of migrants after the war. In 1940, the population of the state stood at almost 7 million. Within ten years it had increased to 10.6 million, bolstered by many Texans and Oklahomans who had come to California during the war for employment in government factories. People continued to stream into California during the next decade, until by 1960 the population mushroomed to more than 15.8 million. By late 1962, with its population expanding by 1700 daily, California had more than 17 million inhabitants and had become the most populous state in the Union. About 60 percent of the people lived in the ten southernmost counties of the state. According to then-Governor Edmund "Pat" Brown, the rapid population growth "is the greatest mass migration in the history of the world."

Many of the migrants looked for the mythical California of fun and prosperity that had been promulgated by the press. In a late-1962 article, "What to Know About and Look For," *Life* focused upon the "bigness, bustle and boom" of California. It promised its readers a per capita income 25 percent above the national average, a "wide open" job market, "plenty" of houses equipped with swimming pools, 160 state parks (a third of which were beaches), and supermarkets and roadside stands that would "stagger most easterners." At the same time, *Newsweek* emphasized the "happy hedonism" of the California transplants. "Californians take their relaxation seriously," it asserted. "Unassuming and carefree, they break with the staid ways of their former communities, dip freely into credit for financing luxury items, and start experimenting in weird and wonderful ways." California, concluded a writer in a September 1962 issue of *Look*, "presents the promise and the challenge contained at the very heart of the original American dream."

Surfing U.S.A.

A buoyant surf music, born amid the California boom, reflected and promoted the myth of the California wonderland. It glorified one of the most attractive elements of the California myth: the sun-drenched Southern California beaches dotted with tanned, blonde, bikini-clad beauties.

Surfing, the sport of Hawaiian kings, was introduced to California at the turn of the century. In 1959, the sport received a boost from the movie *Gidget*, a tale about a young girl who spends a summer on the beach and falls in love with two surfers. Cliff Robertson, one of the male leads in the film, even started a surfboard business. "One day," he remembered, "production on the picture got held up while we waited for a shipment of boards to come in from Honolulu, and I got to thinking why couldn't the West Coast support a surfboard industry." With a partner, Robertson established a surfboard-manufacturing company in Venice, California. "We drew some blueprints, bought some raw materials and started to turn out ten or twelve boards a month."

The innovations of two other surfboard companies, Hobie Surfboards in Dana Point and Sweet's Surfboards in Santa Monica, further popularized the sport. Hobie Alter and Dave and Roger Sweet replaced the heavy wooden board with a lightweight polyurethane foam strip coated with fiberglass and glossed with a polyester resin that could be handled more easily, an important consideration for the teen market.

Almost immediately, young people in Southern California started to buy the foam plastic boards and took to the waves. In late September 1961, *Life* commented that "now the surf that sweeps in on the beaches bears flotillas of enthusiasts standing on long buoyant boards. . . . Surfing has become an established craze in California. There are some 30,000 [teenagers who] revel in the delights of mounting their boards on waves hundreds of feet out and riding them in." "If you're not a surfer," explained one high school boy, "you're not 'in.' If you're a good surfer, you're always in. All you've got to do is walk up and down the beach with a board and you've got girls."

By August 1963, reported *Time*, "every weekend an estimated 100,000 surfers paddle into the briny on 7 ft. to 12 ft. balsa or polyurethane boards, struggle upright into a precarious balance with nature, and try to catch the high breakers coming in." "Ninety percent are beginners," calculated Bill Cooper, executive secretary of the U.S. Surfing Association. "Half of them give it up in a year or two, but then there are more."

The new legion of predominantly male, teenaged surfers began to develop their own culture, dressing and speaking in a distinctive way. At high school, the bleached-blond surfers wore Pendleton shirts; sandals; white, tight, and somewhat short Levis; and baggies—very large, loose, boxer-style shorts. After school, they jumped into an oversized station wagon with wood-en sides ("woodie"), which transported their "polys" (surfboards), drove to the beach, and dashed toward the ocean. They ran with their "sticks" (surfboards) into the "soup" (the foaming water near the beach) and tried to catch a wave. Some would only "fun surf" on three-to-six-feet waves. Other more daring surfers would carry their "big guns" (surfboards designed for riding tall waves) into the water, pick up a "hairy" wave (a fast wave that is difficult to surf) and "shoot" (ride) it, sometimes "hot dogging" (performing tricks) to impress the "bunnies" (girls) on shore. All surfers showed disdain for the poorly skilled or fraudulent, to whom they referred as "gremlins" or "kooks." After packing up and going home, they could read magazines such as *Surfer* and *Surfer Illustrated* or watch such surfing films by director Bruce Brown as *Slippery When Wet* (1960) and *Barefoot Adventure* (1962) or the more commercial *Beach Party* (1963), *Muscle Beach Party* (1964), and *Bikini Beach* (1964), which starred two Dick Clark regulars, Frankie Avalon and Annette Funicello.

The Sound of Surf

Surfers listened to their own music, which originated with Dick Dale and his Del-Tones. Born in Beirut, Dale (a.k.a. Richard Monsour) grew up on the Southern California coast and joined the hordes of young surfers. Also a guitar enthusiast who had released a few undistinctive singles on his own label in 1960, Dale worked closely with Leo Fender, the manufacturer of the first mass-produced, solid-body electric guitar and the president of Fender Instruments, to improve the Showman amplifier and to develop the reverberation unit that would give surf music its distinctively fuzzy sound.

The Beach Boys: kings of the wild surf
Courtesy of Capitol Records

Dick Dale fused his two passions, surfing and the guitar, to create a new music for surf fanatics. "There was a tremendous amount of power I felt while surfing and that feeling of power was simply transferred into my guitar when I was playing surf music," he recalled. "The style of music I developed, to me at the time, was the feeling I got when I was out there on the waves. It was that good rambling feeling I got when I was locked in a tube with the whitewater caving in over my head. I was trying to project the power of the ocean to the people," added the guitarist. "I couldn't get the feeling by singing, so the music took an instrumental form."

During the summer of 1961, Dale and his band unveiled the new surf sound during weekend dances at the Rendezvous Ballroom in Balboa, California. The guitarist told an interviewer that "they said nobody would come to my dances because the Ballroom was too far away and nobody will drive that distance."

Loyal surfers traveled the distance to hear the music which they adopted as their own. The Rendezvous Ballroom in Balboa, remembered Pete Johnson, later a member of the surf group the Belairs, "held well over 1000 and Dale's sound was, in a word, awesome! The music was huge and throbbing, especially when combined with all those sandals stomping on the wooden floor." By late 1961, when he first arrived on the West Coast, disc jockey and producer Jim Pewter found that "the word was 'Let's go to a Dick Dale dance,' so my girl and I motivated to the Rendezvous and checked it out, only to return again and again."

Dick Dale and the Del-Tones released records for the surf crowd. In September 1961, "Let's Go Trippin'" topped the California charts and edged toward the national Top 50. Dale followed with "Surfbeat," "Surfing Drums," and "Shake 'n' Stomp," and in 1962 produced the classic surf instrumental, "Miserlou." In early 1963, Capitol Records recorded Dale and pegged him as the King of the Surf Guitar. The same year, the guitarist landed a spot in the William Asher-directed movie *Beach Party*, and by 1963 he had become a California celebrity.

The Beach Boys

The Beach Boys brought surf music to national prominence. Raised in the suburb of Hawthorne, California, the boys—leader Brian Wilson, his brothers Carl and Dennis, cousin Mike Love, and Al Jardine, a classmate of Brian's at El Camino Junior College—in 1961 began to play as Kenny and the Cadets, Carl and the Passions, and usually the Pendletones, the last a name that referred to the brand of shirt worn by most surfers.

The band smoothed the rough edges of the fuzzy, twanging surf instrumental. As with Dick Dale, the boys favored a swinging, fifties, electric guitar sound. "'Rock Around the Clock' shocked me," Brian Wilson once told a reporter. "I mean, I was so electrified by the experience—that song was really it." The group combined the rawness of fifties rock with glossy harmonies gleaned from such white vocal groups as the Four Freshmen. The blend resulted in a bright, airy, snappy sound that embodied the California myth and, as with the girl-group sound, reflected the general optimism of the Kennedy presidency.

These California teens recorded their new sound with the help of their domineering, sometimes abusive father, Murry Wilson, who managed a heavy-machinery import business and in his spare time composed songs. When asked by music publisher Hite Morgan about new songwriters, Murry suggested Al Jardine, who spoke with the publisher and agreed to record a demo for him.

In October 1961, Jardine appeared at the session with the complete band. "We've written a song about the surfing sport and we'd like to sing it for you," pestered the Wilson brothers. Morgan quietly listened to the tune and exclaimed, "Drop everything; we're going to record your song. I think it's good." Within two hours at the local Keen Recording Studio, the group recorded "Surfin'." Morgan took the demo to the local Candix label, owned by Herb Newman, who released the record in December 1961 and changed the name of the group from the Pendletones to the Beach Boys. Commented Mike Love about the name change: "We didn't even know we were the Beach Boys until the song came out. It was that kind of thing. We could have said, 'No, we're not going to be the Beach Boys.' " Within weeks, "Surfin' " topped the California charts and reached number 75 on the national Top 100.

Good luck temporarily deserted the Beach Boys. Two months after the success of "Surfin'," the Beach Boys recorded four more songs: "Surfin' Safari," "The Beach Boys Stomp," "Judy," and "Surfer Girl," the last two written by Brian for his girlfriend, Judy Bowles. Before it could release the songs, Candix Records, plagued by financial difficulties, ceased operations. Murry Wilson, by this time the manager of the group, played the demos to Decca, Liberty, and Dot Records, all of which rejected the songs because, in the estimation of an executive at Dot, "surfing music was a flash in the pan." Al Jardine, disgusted with the failures, quit the band to begin dental school and would only rejoin the group a year later.

Murry Wilson finally brought the demos to Nick Venet of Capitol Records. After listening to the songs, the producer rushed into the office of his supervisor, Voyle Gilmore, and boasted, "Boss, I've got a double-sided smash for Capitol." The label signed the Beach Boys and released "Surfin' Safari," which reached number 14 on the national singles chart. Later in the year, Capitol followed with an album of the same name which cracked the Top 35.

In May 1963, Capitol released the breakthrough Beach Boys album, *Surfin' U.S.A.*, which featured on the cover an action photo of a surfer cutting a path across a 30-foot wave and included a headline that hailed the Beach Boys as "the No. 1 surfing group in the country." "Surf's Up! Here come the Beach Boys," Nick Venet proclaimed in the liner notes on the album. "Here's the group that started the surf-dancing craze all over the country—even in places where the nearest thing to surf is maybe the froth on a chocolate shake." Venet promoted the "brawny, sun-tanned" Beach Boys as "nationwide symbols for the exhilarating sport that has taken America by storm."

The Beach Boys applied their trademark harmonies to the title track on the album, "Surfin' U.S.A.," a note-for-note reworking of Chuck Berry's "Sweet Little Sixteen," which hit the number-three slot on the national singles chart. The other selections on the album included covers of Dick Dale's "Miserlou" and "Let's Go Tripping" and other odes to surfdom such as "Lonely Sea," "Surf Jam," and "Noble Surfer." The album established the Beach Boys as the kings of surf, and *Surfin' U.S.A.* helped to spread the surfing craze throughout the nation.

During the next few months, the Beach Boys fortified their reputation. In late 1963, they scored with "Surfer Girl"; in 1964 they topped the singles chart with "I Get Around." The group reflected and enforced the California myth with their next chartbusters, "Fun, Fun, Fun," "All Summer Long," and "California Girls." By early1964, the Beach Boys had brought a bright, bouncy surf music that extolled the sun and fun to teens across the country.

Jan and Dean

Jan and Dean delivered the same message of the California surf to American teenagers. Becoming friends at Emerson Junior High School in Los Angeles, where they had football lockers next to one another, Jan Berry and Dean Torrence began their partnership by recording teen ballads. In October 1959, they reached the Top 10 with "Baby Talk" and appeared on the nationally televised "American Bandstand." They followed with such paeans to teenage love as "Heart and Soul," "A Sunday Kind of Love," "There's a Girl," and "We Go Together."

The duo joined the ranks of surfdom with the help of the Beach Boys. "When 'Surfin' came out," recalled Dean, "we heard it and liked it. I think we sensed that it was going to be good for business." Because "Jan and I were physically involved with surfing, it was just natural that we became involved with the music."

In late 1962, Jan and Dean became converted to surf music after performing with the Beach Boys. At one show, the Beach Boys first played a few songs, including "Surfin'" and "Surfin' Safari," and Jan and Dean followed with three or four songs. After getting an enthusiastic reaction from the crowd, Jan and Dean asked the Beach Boys, "Hey, do you want to do your set again, and we'll sing with you guys?" "Gee, you'll sing our songs," responded an awestruck Brian Wilson. "Sure," replied Dean, "I think your songs are really fun to sing." Jan and Dean backed the Beach Boys on two numbers, and the crowd went wild.

The collaboration convinced Jan and Dean to include a surf song on their upcoming album, which featured the song "Linda." As Dean told it, their record producer and manager Lou Adler suggested " 'Why don't you take Linda surfing, and do an album called *Jan and Dean Take Linda Surfing*. That gets it all in there.' " Dean agreed but "didn't know any surfing songs except the two that the Beach Boys had done." He called Brian Wilson and asked if the group would play the instrumental parts to "Surfin' " and "Surfin' Safari" on the album. Brian, recalled Dean, "was just totally knocked out that we were going to record his songs! He said, 'Sure, I'll get the guys,' " who dashed to the studio. While at a session, Brian sang the opening line of a new song, which he offered to Jan and Dean. The duo added lyrics and recorded it as "Surf City," a song that in 1963 went to the top of the charts and, as part of the California myth of abundance, promised "two girls for every boy." The next year, they followed with "Ride the Wild Surf" and "Sidewalk Surfin'."

By the end of 1963, surf music had become a national craze. The Surfaris recorded "Wipe Out," which reached number two on the national charts. Modeling their sound after Dick Dale, the Chantays hit the Top 5 with "Pipeline." Duane Eddy, the king of twang, recorded "Your Baby's Gone Surfin'," the Trashmen from the Midwest cut "Surfin' Bird," and the Astronauts from Colorado released "Surfin' with the Astronauts." A spate of other surf-inspired albums emerged: *Surfin' with the Challengers, Surfin' Bongos, Surfin' with the Shadows*, the Markett's *Surfers Stomp, Surfbeat* by the Surfriders, and *Surf Mania* by the Surf Teens. Chess Records even released the album *Surfin' with Bo Diddley* without informing the R & B guitarist. By the mid-1960s, the California surf had risen.

Drag City

Many of the surfer groups glorified another aspect of the sprawling Southern California landscape—the automobile. By the early 1960s, a maze of highways connected the inhabitants of Southern California. "California," *Life* informed its readers in October 1962, "has 1000 miles of freeways and blueprints for many more. It has 850 miles of expressways and 2400 miles of multilane highways."

The tangle of roads forced most Californians to own at least one automobile. "In California, a car is like an extra, highly essential part of the human anatomy," explained *Life*, which estimated that the 8.5 million cars in the state, positioned bumper to bumper, would extend over 27,000 miles. The magazine equated life in California without an automobile to "a fate roughly equal to decapitation."

The importance of cars in California led to an automobile subculture that, as with the surfers, involved distinctive dress and language. Teen-agers, mostly males, lusted for their first automobile. Rather than a staid station wagon, they cast their eyes upon "asphalt eaters" (dragsters) such as Cudas (Plymouth Barracudas) or GTOs (Grand Turismos) propelled by such huge engines as the rat motor (a 427-cubic-inch Chevy engine) or the Chrysler Hemi (a 426-cubic-inch engine equipped with hemispherical combustion chambers). Like cowboys on their horses in a California of another era, teens with greased hair and tight black pants drove their machines to seldom-used roads and waited for a

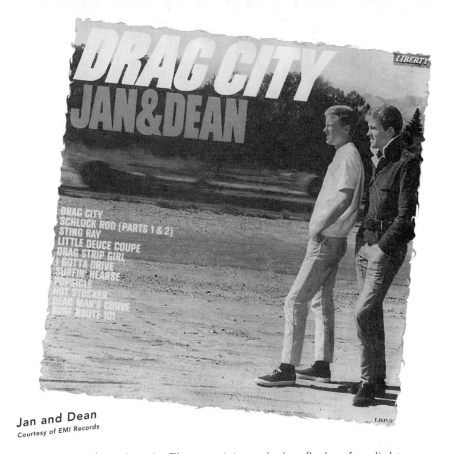

Jan and Dean
Courtesy of EMI Records

competitor to drag (race). They anticipated the flash of a light, "dropped the hammer" (released the clutch quickly) and sped away, "shutting down" (defeating) an opponent. By the end of the 1950s, the dragsters could race legally on such strips as the one at the Orange County Airport near Santa Ana. "Kids love dragging a car," gushed auto customizer Ed Roth at the time, "I mean they really love it."

The hot rod subculture was promoted through the press and on film. Bob Petersen and Bob Lindsay, two young hot rodders living near Los Angeles, in 1947 published the first issue of *Hot Rod* magazine, which would become standard reading for car-crazed California youth. Casting hot rodders as juvenile delinquents on wheels, such movies as *Hot Rod Girl* (1956), *Dragstrip Girl* (1957), *Hot Rod Gang* (1958), *Dragstrip Riot* (1958), and *Teenage Thunder* (1959) further popularized drag racing among an element less clean-cut than the surfer crowd.

Roger Christian, a Los Angeles disc jockey who was tagged "Poet of the Strip," helped surfer bands such as the Beach Boys write songs about dragsters, even though die-hard surfers considered hot rodders—or "ho-dads," as they called them—to be rivals. "Roger was a guiding light for me," revealed Brian Wilson of the Beach Boys. After Christian's late-night radio show, Brian and the disc jockey would "go over to Otto's, order a hot fudge sundae and just . . . whew! talk and talk. . . . Roger is a real car nut," he told *Life* in 1964. "His normal speech is only 40 percent comprehensible. And he has a tremendous knack for rhyming things with *carburetor*." Christian and Brian Wilson first collaborated on "Shut Down," which became a Top 20 hit. They continued their partnership with "Little Deuce Coupe," "Car Crazy Cutie,"

"Don't Worry Baby," and "Spirit of America," the last of which celebrated Craig Breedlove's three-wheeled, 7800-pound jet car.

Roger Christian began to compose songs for Jan and Dean. In 1963, at the request of Jan, Christian and Brian Wilson wrote "Drag City" for the duo, which reached the Top 10. The disc jockey penned most of the other songs on the album of the same name, including "Hot Stocker," "I Gotta Drive," "Schlock Rod," and "Dead Man's Curve," which became prophetic in 1966 when Jan Berry smashed his Stingray into a parked truck at 65 mph on Whittier Boulevard in Los Angeles and sustained serious brain damage. "For the finest reproduction," wrote Roger Christian in the liner notes for *Drag City*, "this recording should be played on a chrome reversed turn-table driven by a full-blown turntable motor equipped with tuned headers. Transmission of power should be through a four-speed box with a floor stick." The "Poet of the Strip" had, in his own words, effected "the merger of Jan and Dean and the car craze."

By 1964, several other bands had jumped on the car craze bandwagon. The Rip Chords, a studio band formed by Bruce Johnston, a neighbor of Jan Berry, and which included guitarist Glen Campbell, scored with "Hey, Little Cobra." The Nashville-based Ronny and the Daytonas hit with "G.T.O." Surf-guitar innovator Dick Dale and his Del-Tones checked in with *Mr. Eliminator*. Jerry Kole and the Stokers released the album *Hot Rod Alley*; a group called the Hot Rodders cut "Big Hot Rod"; the Roadrunners released *The New Mustang (and other Hot Rod Hits)*; the Zip Codes did *Mustang* and the T-Bones cut *Boss Drag at Hot Rod Beach*. Even car customizer Ed Roth, backed by a studio band, recorded an LP, *Rods and Ratfinks*, under the name Mr. Gasser and the Weirdos. In November 1964, *Life* noted the proliferation of "love songs to the carburetor."

By 1964, jangling harmonies celebrated the California myth. "I think we had a lot to do with the population rush to California," asserted Beach Boy Al Jardine. "People hearing the Beach Boys' songs envisioned California as sort of a golden paradise where all you did was surf and sun yourself while gorgeous blondes rubbed coconut oil on your back." "We sang about California and being young," agreed Dean Torrence. "They seemed to go together. In the Sixties everyone wanted to go to California, or so it seemed, and it was the time of the youth movement, too. Our records, of course, were directed to the young; they were obviously teenage songs. Who else would be hanging out at the beach or driving hot rods around?" "Lyrics," continued Torrence, "don't mean shit. I'm talking about the kind of music we do, not the kind Bob Dylan or someone else does." As Jan and Dean promoted "Surf City," folk singers in New York City such as Bob Dylan were singing about another America where African Americans protested and died for their civil rights.

5

Bob Dylan and the New Frontier

"There's other things in this world besides love and sex that're important."

Bob Dylan

Early on a Saturday night in April 1961, a 20-year-old singer carrying an oversized guitar case walked into a dimly lit folk club, Gerdes Folk City in Greenwich Village, New York City. He was dressed casually: worn brown shoes, blue jeans, and a black wool jacket covering a plain yellow turtleneck sweater. A jumble of rumpled hair crowned his head, which was topped by a black corduroy Huck Finn cap. He pressed his lips together tightly and glanced at the tables of patrons, who sipped espresso and seemed to be arguing feverishly about current events. The singer looked serious and exhibited a nervousness that a friend had earlier tried to calm with four jiggers of Jim Beam bourbon. He slowly mounted the stage, opened his guitar case, and carefully took out an old, nicked, six-string acoustic guitar, which he treated like an old friend. He fixed a wire harmonica holder around his neck and pushed a harmonica into place. As the singer stood alone on stage, motionless, a hush descended upon the coffeehouse.

The audience, mostly white middle-class college students, many of them attending nearby New York University, politely applauded the singer. For a moment the scene appeared to epitomize Eisenhower gentility and McCarthy repression: boys with closely cropped hair, button-down shirts, corduroy slacks, Hush Puppy shoes, and cardigans; and rosy-cheeked girls dressed in long skirts, bulky knit sweaters, and low-heeled shoes who favored long, straight, well-groomed hair.

The singer shattered the genteel atmosphere when he began to strum a chord and sing. He was young Bob Dylan, who had just recently arrived in New York City to sing songs of social protest.

Many college-age youths raptly listened to Bob Dylan deliver his hymns of social protest. As civil rights marchers protested in Birmingham and as President John F. Kennedy announced plans for a New Frontier, they heard the stirring message of Bob Dylan, who leveled his guitar at racism and the hypocrisy of corporate America. By 1963, the first baby boomers had entered college and were starting to become aware of the world around them.

Songs of Protest

The foundation for sixties protest music was laid at the turn of the century by the International Workers of the World (IWW). Members of the group, known as Wobblies, first penned protest songs in the United States as part of their drive to achieve equality for American workers. While marching in demonstrations, the radical unionists sang from the *Little Red Songbook*, first published in 1909 at Spokane, Washington, and compiled by organizers Ralph Chaplin and the legendary Joe Hill, a Swedish immigrant who was later executed in Utah for his political beliefs. The Wobblies adopted as their anthem Chaplin's "Solidarity Forever," a protest song set to the music of the "Battle Hymn of the Republic": "They have taken untold millions that they never toiled to earn/ But without our brain and muscle not a single wheel can turn/ We can break their haughty power, gain our freedom when we learn/ That the Union makes us strong/ Solidarity forever!"

Woody Guthrie continued the legacy of the protest song after federal and state authorities raided and closed IWW offices during the Red Scare that followed World War I. Born in July 1912 to a poor family in Okemah, Oklahoma, Woodrow Wilson Guthrie left home at 16 and drifted through the Southwest during his teens, working as a newsboy, a sign painter, spittoon washer, and farm laborer. While visiting his uncle Jeff Guthrie in Tampa, Texas, in 1929, the young Woody learned to play guitar. The youth played on street corners and continued to work odd jobs until 1937, when he became a singing act and the host for a program on the Los Angeles radio station KFVD, on which he read radical newspapers over the air. Within two more years, he moved to New York City and began writing a daily column for the Communist *People's Daily World* and the *Daily Worker*. In 1940, Guthrie recorded for folklorist Alan Lomax, who taped the singer for the Library of Congress and who a year later would do the same with Muddy Waters.

After a two-year stint in the merchant marine during World War

II, Guthrie returned to New York City, where he penned many of his 1000 songs which included "This Land Is Your Land," "Tom Joad," "Billy the Kid," and "Pastures of Plenty." "I don't sing any songs about the nine divorces of some millionaire play gal or the ten wives of some screwball," he later explained. "I've just not got the time to sing those kinds of songs and I wouldn't sing them if they paid me ten thousand dollars a week. I sing the songs of the people that do all of the little jobs and the mean and dirty hard work in the world and of their wants and their hopes and their plans for a decent life." The motto emblazoned on his guitar summed up his message: "This Machine Kills Fascists."

Pete Seeger joined Woody Guthrie, roaming the countryside to sing songs to the American worker. Born on May 3, 1919, in New York to a musical family, Seeger quit Harvard University in 1938 and worked with John and Alan Lomax. In 1940, he founded the Almanac Singers with Guthrie, Lee Hayes, and Millard Lampell, who for two years crisscrossed the nation on an informal tour. After serving in World War II Seeger formed a musician's union, People's Songs, Inc., which attracted 3000 members, including Woody Guthrie. Seeger formed the Weavers with Lee Hayes, Ronnie Gilbert, and Fred Hellerman; they debuted at the Village Vanguard in late 1949 and popularized folk songs such as "On Top of Old Smokey" and "Good Night Irene," Guthrie's "So Long, It's Been Good to Know You" and Seeger's own "If I Had a Hammer." "Like the Almanac singers," recalled Seeger, "the Weavers also hoped to sing for peace and civil rights."

93

Bob Dylan, at his first recording session
Photo by Joe Alper, Frank Driggs Collection

Protest singers such as Seeger fell into disrepute during the McCarthyite witch hunt. During the fifties until his Senate censure in late 1954, Senator Joseph McCarthy of Wisconsin doggedly pursued Communist sympathizers. He progressively accused more and more public figures of Communist tendencies, eventually creating a hysterical, crisis atmosphere throughout the nation. The Wisconsin Senator criticized politically minded entertainers such as Woody Guthrie and Pete Seeger, who were blackballed by the networks and the recording industry. "In the summer of 1950," remembered Seeger, " 'Goodnight Irene' [by the Weavers] was selling two million copies. It was the biggest hit record since the end of World War II. We were offered a coast-to-coast network TV program sponsored by Van Camp's Pork and Beans, half an hour a week. The contract came in, we signed it." Unexpectedly, continued the folk singer, "the next day, when they were supposed to sign, an outfit called the Red Channels came out with an attack on us. Called us 'commie fellow-travelers,' and Van Camp's never signed the contract. The jobs started vanishing, and pretty soon we were down to singing at Daffy's Bar and Grill on the outskirts of Cleveland."

The Folk Revival

Folk music reappeared around 1960, when the number of college students increased. In 1954, 3 million students attended college in schools across the country; six years later, almost 4 million studied within the ivy halls.

These college-age youths searched for an alternative to the popular, romanticized hit singles of Don Kirshner's songwriters, who composed for the young teen market. "Today," observed *Look* in early 1961, "the 15-to-20-year-olds, especially those in college, are showing their musical curiosity in ways that don't appear on single-record popularity charts." A few issues later, the magazine reported, "Weary of the more and more juvenile level of 'pop' music, frustrated by the dearth of good Broadway show tunes, and slightly befuddled by the growing complexity of jazz, [college students were] ready to turn solidly folknik."

The Kingston Trio started the folk revival. Formed in 1957 by three college students, Bob Shane, Nick Reynolds, and Dave Guard, the Trio scored a number-one hit in 1958 with "Tom Dooley," a song written by North Carolina banjo player Frank Proffitt. The threesome, following with a series of successful albums for Capitol Records, which in four years grossed $40 million, surpassed Frank Sinatra as Capitol's number-one moneymaker. By June 1960, *Time* called the "rockless, roll less and rich" trio the "hottest group in U.S. popular music."

The Kingston Trio projected a safe, corporate image. "They are 'sincere' without being 'serious,' " reported singer Will Holt about the Trio in 1961. "They are the kids who sing Saturday nights at fraternity house parties, and the audience gets the comfortable feeling that anyone can do it." Pictures in the national magazines featuring the well-

The Kingston Trio, 1960
Frank Driggs Collection

groomed, well-dressed Trio at poolside with their wives further promoted the image of stability.

The wholesome Trio profited from their success. In 1962, the
threesome averaged $10,000 per concert in a large hall, earned near-
ly $300,000 in record sales, and grossed $1.7 million in total earnings.
Marketed by manager Frank Werber—who, according to *Business
Week*, proved "there's a small fortune to be coined from the folksong
craze"—the group established Kingston Trio Inc., a ten-company investment firm that owned an office building in San Francisco, a land-
development concern, a restaurant, a concert-promotion agency, and
a group of music-publishing companies. "When we fight nowadays,"
one of the Kingston Trio told *Time* in 1960, "it's mostly about business—what to invest in."

The commercial success of the Kingston Trio encouraged other
apolitical, clean-cut folkies to form singing groups. In 1959, 36-year-old
Lou Gottlieb, who earned a Ph.D. in musicology from UCLA; actor and
University of Chicago graduate Alex Hassilev; and 29-year-old Glenn
Yarbrough began to sing as the Limeliters. Within a year the group
commanded $4000 a week for their performances and recorded a top-

selling album of traditional French, Portuguese, and English folk songs. "If the button-down, scrubbed-looking, youthful Kingston Trio are the undergraduates of big-time U.S. folksinging," *Time* reported in June 1961, "the Limeliters are the faculty."

The next year, ten folksters banded together into the blatantly commercial New Christy Minstrels. "When I chose our people," explained founder Randy Sparks, "I made it a point to shy away from questionable people. I looked for the All-American boy or girl who had no political complaints and no sexual problems anyone would be interested in." The "sporty, clean New Christy Minstrels," reported *Time*, offered "a bland mix of broad harmonies, familiar tunes, corny humor and just enough of the folk music spirit to cash in on the most avid adult record buyer." The group sold over 100,000 copies of its first album and in 1963 hit the Top 20 with "Green Green." In 1964, Sparks sold his interest in the group for $2.5 million.

Pete Seeger at the 1964 Newport Folk Festival
Photo by Joe Alper, Frank Driggs Collection

The commercial folk boom ironically led to the rediscovery of traditional folk. "Commercialization has actually helped folk music," claimed Pete Seeger in 1963. "It revived interest in it in the cities where it had almost died. Country interest never really stopped. Now, there are kids all over the nation plinking their banjos, and folk music is a living, vibrant thing again." College-age youths began to listen to Seeger, the re-formed Weavers, the spiritual singing of Odetta, and Jean Ritchie, who sang Appalachian folk tales to her own accompaniment on the dulcimer. They became interested in the spirited bluegrass style of such guitar pickers as Bill Monroe, Doc Watson, and Earl Taylor, and discovered the electric blues of Muddy Waters, John Lee Hooker, and Howlin' Wolf.

By the early 1960s, folk music in all its varied forms had become a craze. "Like, I mean, it's not esoteric anymore," gushed Israel Young, head of Greenwich Village's Folklore Center, in late 1961. Coffeehouses began to open in Boston, Chicago, Minneapolis, Denver, and San Francisco. Folk fans could sip mocha java and listen to minstrels at The Know Where in Joliet, Illinois, The Fourth Shadow in Fort Wayne, Indiana; the Jolly Coachman in Council Bluffs, Iowa; and The Third Man and The Crooked Ear in Omaha, Nebraska. College-age folk fans, having more money than young teens, abandoned 45-rpm hit singles for long-playing albums of their favorite groups, which helped double sales of LPs from 1956 to 1961. Beginning in April 1963, 11 million folk fans watched "Hootenanny," a nationally broadcast, Saturday-night television show which each week took viewers to a folk concert on a different campus. They bought hootenanny sweat shirts, played hootenanny pinball games, read hootenanny magazines, and even watched the feature film *Hootenanny Hoot*. "Yesterday, it was the esoteric kick of history buffs and music scholars. Today, it's show business," *Look* told its readers in 1963. "With a hoot and a holler, folk music has taken over from coffeehouse to campus to prime-time television."

Civil Rights on a New Frontier

The growing clamor of African-Americans for civil rights coincided with and shaped the burgeoning folk music scene. On February 1, 1960, four African-American students from the Agricultural and Technical College in Greensboro, North Carolina, entered a variety store, made several purchases, and sat down at the lunch counter reserved for whites to order coffee. Although refused service and told to leave, the students remained at the counter until the store closed. This tactic of passive resistance, the sit-in, attracted national attention to the civil rights movement and for the first time challenged segregation in privately owned facilities.

Sit-ins spread to other cities. On October 19, 1960, a group of African-Americans marched into the all-white Magnolia Room of Rich's Department Store in Atlanta and refused to leave. Leader Martin Luther King, Jr., was sentenced to four months of hard labor in Reidsville State

Prison for his part in the incident. As some African-Americans argued in the *Atlanta Constitution*, "We do not intend to wait placidly for those rights which are already legally and morally ours to be meted out to us one at a time."

The next year, sit-ins, picketing, and boycotts ended segregation in restaurants and at beaches. In Oklahoma City, Savannah, Atlanta, Louisville, and Norfolk, African-Americans used sit-ins to desegregate lunch counters and restaurants. In Chicago, passive resistance opened a beach that had previously been available to whites only. A weekend sit-in around the courthouse square in Monroe, North Carolina, successfully ended segregation in city facilities.

In 1961, civil rights demonstrators employed a new tactic, the freedom ride. In May, the Congress of Racial Equality (CORE), an interracial direct-action group founded in 1942, boarded members on buses in the North and sent them on "freedom rides" into the South to challenge the segregation of interstate travel facilities. Despite the warnings of federal officials to Alabama Governor John Patterson, the riders were brutally attacked by white racists in Anniston, Birmingham, and Montgomery, Alabama. When they arrived in the segregated bus terminal in Jackson, Mississippi, more than 300 of the "freedom riders," mostly college students, ministers, and professors, were arrested and jailed.

Trouble exploded next in Albany, Georgia. On December 10, 1961, youths in the Student Non-Violent Coordinating Committee (SNCC) walked into the all-white lobby of the Albany railway station, sat down, and waited until local authorities arrested them on charges of disorderly conduct. The next week, Martin Luther King, Jr., head of the Southern Christian Leadership, traveled to Albany and led 700 civil rights adherents in a march to protest the arrest of the students. After authorities arrested King, African-Americans in Albany began to boycott the local bus system, which relied heavily upon African-American riders. Within 40 days they successfully forced the bus company to cease operations.

The demand for civil rights among African-Americans escalated, turning violent in 1963. On April 3, protesters in Birmingham, Alabama, marched for fair employment and desegregation, led by Martin Luther King, Jr., and Fred Shuttlesworth, president of the Alabama Christian Movement for Human Rights. The demonstrators slowly increased in numbers, reaching more than 3000 in a month. On May 3, the marchers were assaulted by police, who unleashed dogs, wielded electric cattle prods, and used fire hoses to disperse them and achieve an uneasy peace. A week later, when racists bombed the house of a demonstrator and an African-American-owned motel, African-Americans spilled out into the streets and confronted police, pelting them with bricks and bottles. By May 12, when the violence ended, they had wrecked dozens of automobiles, burned six small stores, and gutted a two-story apartment building. The riot in Birmingham quickly spread to other cities such as Tallahassee, Nashville, and Cambridge, Maryland.

Racist-inspired violence erupted in June. That month, racists in Jackson, Mississippi, ambushed and killed Medgar Evers, the Mississippi field secretary of the National Association for the Advancement of Colored People (NAACP) near his home. Police in Danville, Virginia, arrested 347 protesters and injured 40 others when they turned fire hoses on the crowd. Racists shot and killed white civil rights crusader William Moore, who was walking near Attalla, Alabama, with a sign demanding equal rights. They pelted with rocks and herded into jail ten freedom riders who attempted to continue Moore's march. By early July 1963, authorities had arrested almost 14,000 civil rights advocates, who participated in 758 demonstrations in 11 states.

On August 28, 1963, 200,000 white and African-American civil rights partisans converged on Washington, D.C. They marched to the steps of the Lincoln Memorial to listen to ten civil rights leaders, including Martin Luther King, Jr. "I have a dream," intoned King, "that one day this nation will rise up and live out the true meaning of its creed, 'we hold these truths to be self-evident that all men are created equal.' . . . I have a dream," King continued in a mounting fervor, "that one day on the red hills of Georgia the sons of former slaves and the sons of former slave owners will be able to sit down together at the table of brotherhood. I have a dream that one day even the state of Mississippi, a state sweltering with the heat of injustice, sweltering with the heat of oppression, will be transformed into an oasis of freedom and justice."

President John F. Kennedy, elected in 1960, offered civil rights crusaders hope that King's dream could become reality. The young, energetic Kennedy assured the nation that the United States was approaching a "new frontier . . . a frontier of unknown opportunities and perils—a frontier of unfulfilled hopes and threats" that was "not a set of promises—it is a set of challenges. It sums up, not what I intend to offer the American people, but what I intend to ask of them." In his inaugural speech, the President specifically focused on "human rights to which this nation has always been committed and to which we are committed today at home."

Kennedy supported the demand for equal rights. On September 20, 1962, as part of an ongoing effort to desegregate public schools, Kennedy sent federal troops to the University of Mississippi in Oxford, at which James Meredith, an African-American air force veteran, attempted to enroll. When resisted by state troops mobilized by Governor Ross Barnett, Kennedy federalized the Mississippi national guard and on national television appealed to the students at the university to accept desegregation. After a racist-inspired riot left two dead, the president ordered a guard of U.S. marshalls to protect James Meredith, who began to attend classes.

In June 1963, the President sent federal troops to the University of Alabama to safeguard two new African-American enrollees, Vivian Malone and James Hood. He ordered federal marshalls to dislodge Alabama Governor George Wallace, who physically positioned himself in the front doorway of a university building and denounced "this illegal

Sixties idealism reflected in Kennedy for President campaign button

and unwarranted action of the Central Government." In a televised broadcast after the Wallace incident, Kennedy told the nation that the civil rights question was "a moral issue . . . as old as the Scriptures and . . . as clear as the American Constitution." He committed his administration to the proposition "that race has no place in American life or law."

Kennedy took further action the same year. The protests for civil rights, he declared, "have so increased the cries for equality that no city or state or legislative body can prudently choose to ignore them." The President proposed wide-reaching civil rights legislation to guarantee equal access to all public facilities, to attack employment discrimination based on race, and to empower the Attorney General to file suit on behalf of individuals whose civil rights had been violated.

Many college students pledged their energies to the new frontier of racial equality. They perceived Kennedy, the youngest elected president in U.S. history, as an energetic visionary who stood in sharp contrast to the grandfatherly Dwight Eisenhower. College-age youth felt an affinity to the Harvard-educated president, who surrounded himself with academics such as Harvard professor Arthur Schlesinger, Jr., and in his inaugural address told a national audience that "the torch has been passed to a new generation of Americans."

College students devoted themselves to Kennedy's program for civil rights. "This generation of college students has begun to react against being treated like adolescents," reasoned a writer in a 1961 issue of *The New Republic*. "They have been willing to associate themselves with nonconformist movements, despite warnings by parents and teachers that such activities will endanger their personal as well as their job security." Driven by a Kennedy-inspired idealism, college students became freedom riders, marched for desegregation, and gathered in Washington, D.C., to demand equality.

Student civil rights activism led to one of the first major campus protests, the free speech movement. As they returned to school in fall 1964, students at the University of California at Berkeley discovered that the tables that had been reserved for the distribution of political leaflets had been banned. "We knew at the time that it was aimed at the civil rights movement and at progressive organizations and at those of us interested in the peace movement and civil rights, mainly civil rights," recalled Jackie Goldberg, who participated in the subsequent protests. When authorities arrested CORE activist Jack Weinberg, who ignored the new policy and would coin the phrase "Don't trust anyone over thirty," the Berkeley students began a nearly four-month protest. Sparked by Mario Savio, a senior who had participated in civil rights activities in Mississippi and headed the Campus Friends of SNCC, the students occupied campus buildings and eventually found faculty support for their free speech demands. Students, uniting for their rights at Berkeley, had been mobilized by the struggle for African-American civil rights.

Bob Dylan: The Music of Protest

The convergence of the civil rights movement and folk music on the college campuses led to the mercurial rise of Bob Dylan and his brand of protest folk music. Born on May 24, 1941, to the owner of a hardware store in Hibbing, Minnesota, Robert Allen Zimmerman grew up

Bob Dylan
The Daily of the University of Washington

near the Mesabi copper range. Being Jewish in an area that, in his words, "had a certain prejudice against Jews," Dylan felt isolated. As a high school girlfriend of Dylan's, Echo Star Helstrom, later confided: "The other kids, they wanted to throw stones at anybody different. And Bob was different. He felt he didn't fit in, not in Hibbing." "I see things that other people don't see," Dylan told a reporter from *The Saturday Evening Post*. "I feel things that other people don't feel. It's terrible. They laugh. I felt like that my whole life. . . . I don't even know if I'm normal."

To cope with the isolation, Dylan turned to music. He first listened to "Hank Williams one or two years before he died. And that sort of introduced me to the guitar." As with thousands of other youths at the time, Dylan "late at night used to listen to Muddy Waters, John Lee Hooker, Jimmy Reed, and Howlin' Wolf blastin' in from Shreveport. It was a radio show that lasted all night. I used to stay up until two, three o'clock in the morning."

Bob Dylan, a fan of both country and R & B, almost naturally embraced the new music of rock-and-roll. When *Rock Around the Clock* showed in Hibbing, Dylan shouted to a friend outside the theater, "Hey, that's our music! That's written for us." He began to idolize Little Richard and then Elvis Presley and "saw Buddy Holly two or three nights before he died. I'll never forget the image of seeing Buddy Holly on the bandstand. And he died—it must have been a week after that. It was unbelievable." By his freshmen year in high school, Dylan formed "a couple of bands," including the Golden Chords, which played rock-and-roll at local functions.

Dylan turned to folk music when it reached the Midwest. "I heard a record—the Kingston Trio or Odetta or someone like that," he remembered, "and I sort of got into folk music. Rock and roll was pretty much finished. And I traded my stuff for a Martin [acoustic guitar] that they don't sell anymore." In 1959, he began to perform traditional folk music and bluegrass in coffeehouses around the University of Minnesota under the name of Dillon and then Dylan.

Bob Dylan encountered his most pervasive influence while in Minneapolis. As he told it, "I heard Woody Guthrie. And when I heard Woody Guthrie, that was it, it was all over. . . . He really struck me as an independent character. But no one ever talked about him. So I went through all his records I could find and picked all that up by any means I could. . . . Woody was my god," declared the young singer. In December 1960, he traveled from Minnesota to New York City and frequently visited the dying Guthrie at a state hospital in nearby New Jersey. Dylan's first album, recorded in late 1961 for $402, included a song dedicated to Woody.

In Greenwich Village, at such clubs as Gerdes Folk City, the Gaslight Coffeehouse, and the Village Gate, Dylan began to sing his own songs of social protest. Remembered Terri Thal, the manager of several folk acts who was then married to folk guitarist Dave Van Ronk: "He was beginning to think about and talk about people who were being trod upon [by 1961]. Not in any class way, but he hated people who were taking people. He had a full conception of people who were being taken, and he did read the newspapers, and that's what came through in 'Talkin' Bear Mountain' and 'Talkin' New York,' " both in the Guthrie-style of talking blues.

Some observers suggested that Suze Rotolo, Dylan's girlfriend, influenced him. "Dylan's girlfriend at the time, Suze Rotolo, worked as a secretary for the civil rights group CORE and probably caused Dylan to write 'The Ballad of Emmett Till,' " remarked Thal. Recalled someone then in the Village, "Suze came along and she wanted him to go Pete Seeger's way. She wanted Bobby to be involved in civil rights and all the radical causes Seeger was involved in. . . . She influenced Bobby considerably, that way." By 1962, Dylan had become friends with such civil rights activists as James Forman, Bernice Johnson, and Cordell Reagon of the Student Non-Violent Coordinating Committee and joined Broadside, a loose-knit group founded by Pete Seeger and fellow folksters Agnes Cunningham and Gordon Friesen to encourage young folk singers to compose topical songs.

Composing songs about current social issues such as civil rights rather than singing traditional or commercialized folk, Dylan politicized sixties folk music with his second album, *Freewheelin'*. The album, released in May 1963, had on its cover a picture of Suze Rotolo and Dylan, arm in arm, walking down a wind-swept New York City street on a gray winter day. It featured "Blowin' in the Wind," which became an anthem for the civil rights movement. "The idea came to me that you were betrayed by your silence," Dylan told some friends about the song. "That all of us in America who didn't speak out were betrayed by our silence. Betrayed by the silence of the people in power. They refuse to look at what's happening. And the others, they ride the subway and read the *Times*, but they don't understand. They don't know. They don't even care, that's the worst of it." Dylan told of the ordeal of James Meredith at the University of Mississippi in "Oxford Town"; composed "Hard Rain's A-Gonna Fall" about the Cuban missile crisis, which occurred in October 1962; penned "Talkin' World War Three Blues," a humorous but somber picture of life after a nuclear holocaust; and blasted government leaders in the vitriolic "Masters of War." At the time, the singer felt that "there's other things in this world besides love and sex that're important, too. People shouldn't turn their backs on them just because they ain't pretty to look at. How is the world ever going to get better if we're afraid to look at these things?"

Dylan continued to pen protest songs for his next album, *The Times They Are A-Changin'*, released in February 1964. Besides the title song, which became a battle cry of the emerging social revolution, he chronicled the struggle for civil rights in "The Lonesome Death of Hattie Carroll" and wrote about the murder of civil rights leader Medgar Evers in "A Pawn in Their Game." John Hammond, the record executive who signed Dylan to Columbia Records in 1961, believed that the singer "was thinking and talking about injustice and social problems.

Bobby really wanted to change things. He was uptight about the whole setup in America, the alienation of kids from their parents, the false values. From my leftist point of view, he was just superb, and it was real."

Dylan reinforced his politicized music by a number of public demonstrations. On May 12, 1963, he refused to perform on "The Ed Sullivan Show" when CBS censors banned him from singing "Talkin' John Birch Society Blues." On July 6, he gave a concert outside Greenwood, Mississippi, with Pete Seeger to promote African-American voter registration initiated by the Student Non-Violent Coordinating Committee. Later in the month he appeared on a local New York television program dealing with "freedom singers." In August, Dylan marched on Washington, D.C. for equal rights with Martin Luther King, Jr.

Bob Dylan began to serve as the focal point for a community of protest singers. Eric Andersen, known for his "Violets of Dawn," felt "the whole scene was generating a lot of vibes, and Dylan had the heaviest vibes of them all. Dylan was sowing the seeds of the decade." To Joan Baez, herself active in the protest movement, "Bobby Dylan says what a lot of people my age feel but cannot say."

Joan Baez

Joan Baez was Bob Dylan's female counterpart in folk protest. The daughter of a Mexican-born physicist and a Scotch-Irish mother, the dark-skinned Baez faced racial discrimination at an early age. As a girl in Clarence Center, New York, a town of 800 people, she felt that "as far as the [townspeople] knew we were Niggers."

Baez moved with her family to Boston, where, during the late 1950s, she began to perform traditional folk songs in coffeehouses around Harvard, such as Club 47 and Tulla's Coffee Grinder. In 1959, Baez debuted to 13,000 people at the first Newport Folk Festival. "A star was born," wrote Robert Shelton in *The New York Times* after the performance, "a young soprano with a thrilling lush vibrato and fervid and well-controlled projection." Baez continued to attract a following, selling out a Carnegie Hall performance two months in advance. By 1962, *Time* referred to Joan "as the most gifted of the newcomers to the folk scene" and featured her on the cover of its November 23 issue.

The singer, though composing few of her own songs, took a decidedly political stance. She sang such topical songs as the anti-war "Strangest Dream" and a parody of the House Un-American Activities Committee, which ceaselessly tracked supposed Communist sympathizers. The singer refused to appear on ABC's "Hootenanny" when the show blacklisted Pete Seeger and rejected more than $100,000 in concert dates during a single year because, as she told *Time*, "folk music depends on intent. If someone desires to make money, I don't call it folk music." In 1963, Baez demonstrated in Birmingham for desegregation and in August marched on Washington, D.C. "I feel very strongly about things," Joan told *Look* in 1963. "Like murdering babies with

Joan Baez, ca. mid 1960s
Frank Driggs Collection

fallout and murdering spirits with segregation. I love to sing and, by some quirk, people like to hear me. I cannot divide things. They are all part of me."

The Singer-Activists

Other folk singers followed the path of protest. Texas-born Phil Ochs, the son of a Jewish army physician, attended Ohio State University, where he won his first guitar by betting on John Kennedy in the hotly contested 1960 presidential election. A year later he composed his first song, "The Ballad of the Cuban Invasion," about the American invasion of Cuba at the Bay of Pigs, and joined a radical singing group called the Sundowners or, sometimes, the Singing Socialists, with roommate Jim Glover, who later became half of the pop duo Jim and Jean. In 1962, Ochs dropped out of Ohio State over censorship of the school paper and journeyed to New York City to start his folk-protest career in earnest. According to Phil, he attended the 1963 Newport Folk Festival "with the Freedom Singers, Dylan, Baez, the songwriters' workshop, where the topical song suddenly became the thing. It moved from the background to the foreground in just one weekend."

Ochs, looking for a forum to propagate his radical ideals, churned out protest songs dealing with the issues of the day. His first album, *All the News That's Fit to Sing*, released by Elektra in April 1964, included "Thresher," "Too Many Martyrs," "The Ballad of William Worthy," "Talking Cuban Crisis," and "Talking Vietnam." Said Ochs: "I was writing about Vietnam in 1962, way before the first anti-war marches. I was writing about it at a point where the media were really full of shit, where they were just turning the other way as Vietnam was being built." Subsequent albums delivered other protest hymns, such as "The Ballad of the AMA," "Freedom Riders," "Ballad of Oxford, Mississippi," "Draft Dodger Rag," and "I Ain't Marching Anymore."

Phil Ochs backed his words with action. In 1964, when he heard that the bodies of three murdered civil rights workers had been found buried under an earthen dam, he headed for Mississippi. Ochs later traveled to Hazard, Kentucky, to help striking miners engaged in a bloody struggle with mine owners who were trying to bypass provisions of the Mine Safety Act. Phil's song "No Christmas in Kentucky" became a battle cry among the workers. When Phil and folksinger Tom Paxton played a benefit for the miners, members of the John Birch Society and the Fighting American Nationalists picketed the concert with placards that read "Agrarian Reformers Go Home."

Tom Paxton raised his voice in protest in other instances. Born in Chicago, a young Paxton traveled to Oklahoma with his family and then served a stint in the army. In the early 1960s, he moved to New York City, where he became radicalized and joined the folk protest circle centered around Bob Dylan. In 1964, he landed a recording contract with Elektra and followed the lead of Dylan, offering a series of protest songs in *Ramblin' Boy*. The next year he recorded one of his most political albums, *Ain't That News*, which included "Lyndon Johnson Told the Nation," "Buy a Gun for Your Son," "We Didn't Know," and "Ain't That News." Explained Paxton about the title song: "When the poor (again, with the help of the students) are making the first hesitant steps toward organization; when Negroes, disenfranchised for years, are lining up by the thousands to register to vote; when mass demonstrations and teach-ins protest this government's foreign policy; when after the long sleep of the Eisenhower years you find heated dialogues and demonstrations throughout the country—that's news."

Dylan's Disenchantment

The folk protest movement began to fragment in late 1963 after the assassination of President John Kennedy. On November 22, in Dallas, a rifleman shot and killed the President, who was riding in a motorcade with his wife, Jackie, and Texas Governor John Connelly and his wife. The assassination produced shock and then horror throughout the nation, which mourned a president who had symbolized energy, action, and optimism.

Folk musicians felt especially disillusioned by the assassination. Phil Ochs sensed "a definite flowering-out of positive feelings when John Kennedy became president. The civil rights movement was giving off positive vibrations. There was a great feeling of reform, that things could be changed, that the government cared, that an innovator could come in. . . . Things looked incredibly promising. Then came the Bay of Pigs, the beginnings of Vietnam and the assassination. It ruined the dream. November 22, 1963, was a mortal wound the country has not yet been able to recover from."

Dylan experienced the same pain and confusion over Kennedy's death. As folk singer Eric Andersen told it, "You can't separate Dylan from history in the sense of what was going down, the way he reacted to a chain of events. The first being Kennedy's death; I think that got him out of politics. . . . Kennedy, he was sort of like the shadow of the flight . . . and then that bird got shot out of the sky and everyone was exposed, naked to all the frightening elements, the truth of the country. It had flown, that force had lost out. And people were depressed."

Dylan, though depressed over the Kennedy assassination, started to become more commercially successful. The national press began to notice Dylan during the early 1960s. In 1962, *Newsweek* tagged him "the newest rage" in folk music, and *Time* sarcastically mentioned that Bob Dylan delivered "his songs in a studied nasal that has just the right clothespin-on-the-nose honesty to appeal to those who most deeply care." The next year, the influential folk magazine *Little Sandy Review* called him "our finest contemporary folk songwriter."

Bob Dylan attracted national prominence after he signed with manager Albert Grossman, who was a major impetus in the folk revival. In 1957, Grossman opened one of the first folk clubs, The Gate of Horn, in Chicago; two years later he helped George Wein launch the first Newport Folk Festival. In 1960, he met folk singer Peter Yarrow, whom he signed to a management contract. Grossman introduced Yarrow to onetime Broadway singer Mary Travers and stand-up comic Paul Stookey, who began to perform as Peter, Paul and Mary.

The folk trio, managed by Grossman, hit the charts in May 1962 with "Lemon Tree" and five months later cracked the Top 10 with Pete Seeger's "If I Had a Hammer," which brought folk protest to a national audience. In 1963, the trio received from their manager a Bob Dylan song, "Blowin' in the Wind," which reached number two on the singles chart and lifted its composer into the national spotlight.

After gaining national exposure, and in the wake of the Kennedy assassination, Dylan started to become somewhat disillusioned with political activism. "I agree with everything that's happening," he told writer Nat Hentoff over dinner in October 1964, "but I'm not part of no Movement. If I was, I wouldn't be able to do anything else but be in 'the Movement.' I just can't sit around and have people make rules for me. . . . Those [protest] records I already made," said Dylan, referring to his first three albums, "I'll stand behind them but some of that was jumping on the scene to be heard and a lot of it was because I didn't see anybody else doing that kind of thing. Now a lot of people are doing finger-pointing songs. You know—pointing at the things that are wrong. Me, I don't want to write for people anymore. You know—be a spokesman." Dylan began to criticize Joan Baez for her involvement with the Institute for the Study of Nonviolence at Carmel, California, established to "root out violence in ourselves and in the world." By 1965, Dylan abruptly informed a *Newsweek* reporter that "I've never written a political song. Songs can't save the world. I've gone through

Simon and Garfunkel
The Daily of the University of Washington

all that. When you don't like something, you gotta learn to just not need that something."

In place of social protest, Dylan crafted complex, personal and sometimes cryptic songs. "I have to make a new song out of what *I* know and out of what *I'm* feeling," he told Nat Hentoff. "I once wrote about Emmett Till in the first person, pretending that I was him. From now on, I want to write what's inside me." *Another Side of Bob Dylan*, recorded in the summer of 1964, featured such nonpolitical poetry as "Chimes of Freedom" and repudiated the composer's folk protest in "My Back Pages." "I think it is very, very destructive music," complained Joan Baez at the time about Dylan's new orientation. "I think he doesn't want to be responsible for anybody, including himself."

Dylan's next album, *Bringing It All Back Home*, released in early 1965, abandoned folk protest for an electrified rock. It included a rock-and-roll rhythm section and highlighted such bitter, dark songs as "Subterranean Homesick Blues," "She Belongs to Me," "Maggie's Farm," "Gates of Eden," and "It's All Right Ma (I'm Only Bleeding)." His next LP, *Highway 61 Revisited*, also released in 1965, included the impressionistic, beat-inspired poetry of "Desolation Row," "Queen Jane Approximately," "Ballad of a Thin Man," and "Like a Rolling Stone."

On July 25, 1965, at the Newport Folk Festival, Dylan unveiled his electric sound and his new brand of songwriting to the folk community. Behind the stage, some of the folk performers tried to prevent Dylan from playing his new music. "On one side you had Pete Seeger, [concert organizer] George Wein, the old guard," remembered Paul Rothchild, who mixed the Dylan set. "Pete is backstage, pacifist Pete, with an ax saying, 'I'm going to cut the fucking cables if that act goes onstage.'" When Dylan did begin to play, the hard-core folk audience heartily booed their former leader. "I wouldn't mind so much if he sang just one song about the war," lamented Irwin Silber, the editor of the radical folk magazine, *Sing Out!*

Though ridiculed by old-time folksters, Dylan secured a national audience with the electric sound. He snagged the number-two spot with "Like a Rolling Stone," his first hit single. He also first hit the Top 10 with *Bringing It All Back Home*, and neared the top of the chart with *Highway 61 Revisited*. In 1966, the singer again cracked the Top 10 with *Blonde on Blonde*. Dylan had become a commercial success with a sound that would inspire a folk-rock boom.

Folk-Rock

Many groups added vocal harmonies to Dylan's electrified folk sound and sometimes used his songs to create what critics termed folk-rock. The Byrds, probably the premier folk-rockers, were formed in 1964 by Roger McGuinn, who had backed the Limeliters and the Chad Mitchell Trio. Besides McGuinn, the group consisted of bassist Chris Hillman, drummer Michael Clarke, and guitarist Gene Clark, who had been a member of the New Christy Minstrels and had met the other member of the group, David Crosby, at the Troubadour Club in Los Angeles on a hootenanny night. In 1965, after obtaining a test pressing of Dylan's "Mr. Tambourine Man," they hit the top of the charts with a version of the song which featured bouncy vocal harmonies and a 12-string guitar. The group followed with electrified, harmony-rich versions of Dylan's "Spanish Harlem Incident," "All I Really Want to Do," and "Chimes of Freedom" as well as "Turn, Turn, Turn," a song adapted by Pete Seeger from the Book of Ecclesiastes.

Other groups became successful with the folk-rock formula of electrified renditions of Dylan songs sung in harmony. In 1965, the ebullient Turtles, a band that had switched from surf music to folk the year before, hit the Top 10 with "It Ain't Me Babe." The same year, a husband-wife team, Sonny and Cher, released the million-selling, Dylan-sounding "I Got You Babe." Cher, a former backup singer for the Ronettes, scored a solo hit with Dylan's "All I Really Want to Do."

Paul Simon and Art Garfunkel were two high school friends who in 1957 had attracted notice as Tom and Jerry with "Hey Schoolgirl" and had appeared on "American Bandstand." In 1964, after being influenced by the folk boom, they reemerged with a collegiate image and an album of soft harmonies, *Wednesday Morning, 3 A.M.*, that showcased Dylan's "Don't Think Twice" and Simon's composition, "Sounds of Silence," which the next year became a number-one hit when Tom Wilson, Dylan's producer at the time, remixed the track by adding drums, percussion, and electric guitar.

Mimicking Dylan by wearing a denim cap and using a racked harmonica, Donovan Leitch of Scotland became the British answer to Dylan. In 1964, Donovan began performing folk music in clubs throughout the United Kingdom. The next year he landed a spot on the British television show "Ready, Steady, Go!," on which he appeared with a guitar that had the Woody Guthrie-style message "this guitar kills." Elkan Allen, the producer of the show, "knew immediately that I would be to the European youth what Bob Dylan was to America, the European Bob Dylan," recalled Donovan. After the television show, Donovan hit the British singles chart with the acoustic "Catch the Wind," which bore an obvious resemblance to the Dylan title, "Blowin' in the Wind." In 1966, amid the folk-rock boom, Donovan scored his first American success with the electrified sound of the chart-topping "Sunshine Superman" and "Mellow Yellow."

The Lovin' Spoonful, which in the mid-1960s hit the Top 10 with "Do You Believe in Magic?," "You Didn't Have to Be So Nice," "Daydream," and "Summer in the City," also attributed their sound to Bob Dylan. Dylan, insisted John Sebastian—who had backed several folk groups in Greenwich Village before forming the Spoonful—acted as "a force on our music, just like the 'Star Spangled Banner.' We all heard it." By the end of 1965, various folk-rockers had recorded 48 different Dylan songs, most of them concerned with topics other than protest. According to *Newsweek*, "healthy, cheap, moral or venal, folk rock is what's happening at this moment in the dissonant echo chamber of pop culture."

The folk-rock explosion, epitomized by the Byrds, also exhibited an influence from across the Atlantic. "I did feel that the real folk scene was in the Village," remembered Roger McGuinn. "But the Beatles came out and changed the whole game for me. I saw a definite niche, a place where the two of them blended together. If you took Lennon and Dylan and mixed them together, that was something that hadn't been done." Though believing that "Dylan was real and the Beatles were plastic," McGuinn grafted the bouncy, jangling harmonies of the mop-tops from Liverpool onto Dylanesque folk. As with a few other folk-rockers, the Byrds reflected the pervasive influence of the Beatles, who were conquering America and changing the sound of rock-and-roll.

The Lovin' Spoonful, ca. 1965; lead singer/songwriter
John Sebastian is second from the top

6

The British Invasion of America

"We were just the spokesmen for a generation."

Paul McCartney

Friday, February 7, 1964, at the Kennedy International Airport, New York, New York. Outside, a mass of screaming teenagers covered the rooftop on one of the airport wings. The crowd, mostly pubescent girls, had been waiting for more than eight hours in the frosty winter air. They considered themselves lucky: Only those with special passes had been permitted on the roof, patrolled by dozens of uniformed security police.

Inside the terminal, huddled around the gate that admitted incoming passengers from London, more than 9,000 teenaged girls adorned with bouffant hairdos, oversized jewelry, and their mothers' makeup shoved, clawed, and pushed each other in a mad attempt to get to the arrival entrance. They were separated from their goal only by a thin white nylon rope and a few airport guards. As the minutes passed slowly and the intensity mounted, the crowd was comforted by a voice from a transistor radio: "It is now 6:30 A.M. Beatle time. They left London 30 minutes ago. They're out over the Atlantic Ocean heading for New York. The temperature is 32 Beatle degrees."

Four of the passengers on Pan American flight 101 felt uneasy. "We did all feel a bit sick," remembered one. "Going to the States was a big step. People said just because we were popular in Britain, why

The Beatles, ca. 1964. From left to right:
Paul McCartney (bass), George Harrison (guitar),
Ringo Starr (drums), John Lennon (guitar)
Frank Driggs Collection

should we be there?" Asked another: "America's got everything, George, so why should they want us?" A third: "I was worrying about my hair as well. I'd washed it, but when it had dried, it had gone up a bit." The fourth, the oldest and the leader of the group, sat silent and motionless in his seat.

As the plane neared its destination, a few wild screams from the airport broke the tense silence. Then an entire chorus of cries from girls on the rooftop alerted the crowd inside of the arrival. In a few moments, the frenzied wails of pent-up teenage passion sent tremors throughout Kennedy International, increasing at a deafening rate. The girls started to half chant, half sing, "We love you Beatles, oh yes we do."

The plane landed safely and reached the hangar. Scurrying attendants pushed a platform toward the jet, the door swung open, and passengers started to descend the steps. Employees of Capitol Records shoved Beatle kits complete with wigs, autographed photos, and a button with the message "I Like the Beatles" at them. At last, four young Englishmen, who sported buttoned-down, Edwardian suits from Pierre Cardin and mushroom-shaped haircuts, walked out. After almost 150 years, the British had again invaded the United States; this time they would emerge as the victors. The Beatles had arrived in America.

The four lads from Liverpool—John, Paul, George, and Ringo—dashed toward a chauffeured airport limousine. They leapt in the car, locked the doors, and rode toward the terminal, assaulted by hundreds of girls who hurled themselves at the slow-moving automobile, clinging to the hood, the roof, and the sides. As they inched away, the foursome saw, pressed against the windows, the contorted faces of teenaged fans who tried to catch a glimpse of their heroes before they were pulled away by other admirers.

The foursome broke loose from the crowd and headed toward the airport complex. After a short press conference the Beatles jumped back into the limousine and sped down the Van Wyck Expressway, reaching Manhattan about an hour and a half later. Though swarmed by hundreds of fans when the car stopped at New York's plush Plaza Hotel, the Beatles managed to pry the doors open and somehow make it into the hotel lobby, where they were escorted to a twelfth-floor room. There they discovered three screaming girls in the bathtub and called maid service for help. Throughout the night and the next few days, the Beatles were protected by armed guards from ingenious girls who climbed the fire escapes and from conspiring groups of teens who checked in at the hotel, using the names of their well-to-do parents to penetrate the twelfth floor. Outside, the boys heard fans keep a 24-hour vigil by chanting "We want the Beatles, we want the Beatles."

On Sunday night the new idols from across the Atlantic came into full view. Late in 1963, Ed Sullivan, the square-faced, stocky show-business impresario, had witnessed a near riot at the London airport where more than 15,000 screaming fans descended upon the terminal, delaying the Queen and Prime Minister Sir Alec Douglas-Home in order to welcome the Beatles back from a trip abroad. Impressed, Sullivan told *The New York Times*, "I made up my mind that this was the same sort of mass hit hysteria that had characterized the Elvis Presley days." He hurriedly located Brian Epstein, the dapper, brilliant manager of the group, and for less than $20,000 booked the Beatles for three appearances on his show.

Hysterical Beatles fans, 1964
Seattle Times

On February 9, 1964, Sullivan showcased the Beatles. Seven hundred twenty-eight wild teenagers packed into the studio from which the Sullivan show was broadcast. They had battled 50,000 others for tickets to the show that featured the Beatles. When Sullivan introduced the foursome—" . . . and now, the Beeeatles!"—the room erupted. Girls with checkered skirts and Macy's blouses let out primal screams and pulled their hair, thrusting themselves toward the front of the stage or leaning perilously over the balcony. Some simply fainted. Few noticed that one of the microphones had gone dead. All eyes fastened on Paul bobbing back and forth as he played a left-handed bass guitar; Ringo, smiling as he brushed the drumskins; John, yelling the lyrics over the din; and a rather dour flu-striken George, the youngest, skinniest member of the group, just looking down at the neck of his lead guitar. The screaming intensified. Explained one girl in the crowd: "You really do believe they can see you and just you alone, when they're up on stage. That's why you scream, so they'll notice you. I always felt John could see me. It was like a dream. Just me and John together and no one else." The show, ending amid the wails, had been extremely successful. It had been witnessed by more than 73 million people across the country, more than 60 percent of all television viewers.

From New York City, the Beatles rode the King George train to Washington, D.C. On Wednesday, February 11, at 3:09 P.M., amid a storm that dropped ten inches of snow, they arrived in the nation's capital. The band emerged from the train, hurriedly made their way down a platform "behind a wedge of Washington's finest," and reached the main concourse of Union Station. "For hours," *The Washington Post* read, "teenagers had been drifting into Union Station—many of them from National Airport, where the Beatles before the show had been scheduled to arrive. . . . In the concourse, the teenagers, perhaps 2,000 strong, lined the barriers, breathed on the glass, hung through the bars, even climbed the gates." The Beatles, heads down in combat fashion, snaked through the crowd with the help of the police, who pushed and shoved the oncoming torrent of fans. Screamed one girl to the police as they dragged away her friend, "You can't throw her out, she's president of the Beatles Fan Club." Finally John, Paul, Ringo, and George broke through the crowd and leapt into a waiting limousine. They sped toward the Washington Coliseum, which was jammed with 8092 wild-eyed teens. "From the moment the Beatles were led to the stage by a phalanx of policemen," the *Post* informed its readers, "the din was almost unbearable." Reporter Leroy Aarons compared the noise to "being downwind from a jet during takeoff." During the performance frantic, distraught girls mercilessly began to pelt their heroes with jelly beans. Explained George: "It was terrible. They hurt. They don't have soft jelly babies in America but hard jellybeans like bullets. Some newspaper had dug out the old joke, which we'd all forgotten about, when John had once said I'd eaten all his jelly babies."

From Washington the Beatles flew to Miami, where they were greeted by four bathing beauties, a four-mile-long traffic jam, and 7000 screaming teens who shattered 23 windows and a plate glass door in a tumultuous attempt to touch their idols. The group played for a raucous audience in Miami, then headed toward New York City, where they upstaged the President. In an article entitled "LBJ Ignored as New York Crowds Chase Beatles," *Billboard* reported that "President Lyndon B. Johnson visited here late last week, but the arrival was overshadowed by the Beatles invasion. Few were aware of the President's presence in their midst, but no one could miss the fact that Britain's Beatles had descended upon the town. Radio, TV, and all other communication media were filled with Beatle clamor. At Kennedy Airport here, Beatle greeters began lining up at 4 A.M. Friday to await the group's arrival this afternoon."

By the time the Beatles left New York for London on February 16, the entire nation had become aware of Beatlemania. Headlines in the staid *Billboard* told the story: "The U.S. Rocks and Reels from Beatles Invasion"; "Chicago Flips Wig, Beatles and Otherwise"; "New York City Crawling with Beatlemania"; and "Beatle Binge in Los Angeles." In nine days during the Beatles' brief visit, Americans had bought more than 2 million Beatles records and more than $2.5 million worth of Beatles-related goods. They purchased blue and white Beatles hats; Beatles T-shirts and beach shirts; Beatles tight-fitting pants; Beatles pajamas and three-button tennis shirts; Beatles cookies; Beatles egg cups; Beatles rings, pendants, and bracelets; a pink plastic Beatles guitar with pictures of the four lads stamped on it; a plethora of Beatles dolls including inflatable figurines, six-inch-tall hard rubber likenesses, painted wood dolls that bobbed their heads when moved, and a cake decoration in the form of the Beatles. Others snapped up Beatles nightshirts, countless Beatles publications, Beatles ice-cream sandwiches covered with a foil Beatles wrapper, Beatles soft drinks, and Beatles wigs, which Lowell Toy Company churned out at the rate of 15,000 a day. Selteab (Beatles spelled backwards)—the American arm of the Beatles manufacturing company, NEMS—even planned for a Beatles motor scooter and a Beatles car.

The Mods, the Rockers, and the Skiffle Craze

Beatlemania had its genesis in a wartime and postwar baby boom and an economic depression that spawned gangs of British working-class youths. As with the United States, England experienced a baby boom immediately during and after World War II. "That was the Bulge, that was England's Bulge," Pete Townshend, the lead guitarist for The Who, told a reporter. "All the war babies, all the old soldiers coming back from the war and screwing until they were blue in the face—this was the result. Thousands and thousands of kids, too many kids, not enough teachers, not enough parents." As in the United States, by the late 1950s and early 1960s many baby boomers had become teenagers ready for rock-and-roll.

At the same time, England faced economic hardships. Crippled by the war, it continued to enforce wartime rationing until 1954 and tried to rebuild with little help from wartime allies. "World War Two went on there for another nine years after it finished everywhere else," recalled Keith Richards of the Rolling Stones. "I remember London, huge areas of rubble and grass growing."

During the mid- and late 1950s, many British teens, unlike their American counterparts, faced hard times upon finishing school at 15 or 16. By March 1964 Harold Wilson, a Labour Party leader from Liverpool and later Prime Minister, regarded "as deserving of the utmost censure and condemnation a system of society which, year in, year out . . . cannot provide employment for its school-leavers." British youths felt especially directionless due to the change in English conscription laws. The draft "ended," remembered Ringo Starr, "and so at 18 you weren't regimented. Everyone was wondering what to do."

Idle working-class teens began to form rival gangs: the Rockers and the Mods. The Rockers, modeling themselves after the tough Teddy Boys of the 1950s, wore black leather jackets, tight-fitting pants, and pointed boots or suede shoes. They greased back their hair in a pompadour style and sometimes put on sunglasses in beatnik fashion, roaring down the streets on motorcycles.

The Modernists, shortened to Mods, favored "teenage Italian-style clothes," according to Townshend, himself a Mod. They had "short hair, money enough to buy a real smart suit, good shoes, good shirts; you had to be able to dance like a madman. You had to be in possession of plenty of pills all the time and always be pilled up [especially with Drynamil, an amphetamine commonly known as a "purple heart"]. You had to have a scooter covered in lamps. You had to have like an army anorak to wear." The Mods sometimes adopted different fashions weekly. "One outfit might be 12 quid, a week's wages, and the next fucking week you'd have to change the whole lot," recalled Townshend. As with the Rockers, the Mods "were nothing. They were the lowest, they were England's lowest common denominators. Not only were they young, they were also lower-class young," added the guitarist. "Most Mods were lower-class garbagemen, you know, with enough money to buy himself Sunday best."

The gang experience fostered a sense of belonging among British youths. Pete Townshend knew "the feeling of what it's like to be a Mod among two million Mods and it's incredible. It's like being—suddenly you're the only white man in the Apollo [Theater in Harlem]. Someone comes up and touches you and you become black. It's like that moment, that incredible feeling of being part of something which is really much bigger than race and much bigger than—it was impetus. It covered everybody, everybody looked the same, and everybody acted the same and everybody wanted to be the same. It was the first move I have ever seen in the history of youth towards unity, towards unity of thought, unity of drive and unity of motive. . . . "Any kid," said Townshend, "however ugly or however fucked up, if he had the right haircut and the right clothes and the right motorbike, he was a Mod. He was a Mod!"

The Mods and the Rockers, each group bound by a common appearance, fought one another for dominance. During the Easter weekend of 1964 at Clacton-on-Sea, Essex, a few hundred "young scooter riders" from the eastern and northeastern parts of London attacked motorcycle gangs of Rockers. According to D. H. Moody, chairman of the

Urban District Council, "they insulted passers-by, lay in the middle of the road to stop traffic, jumped onto cars and destroyed and damaged property. The girls were almost as bad and [one witness] had seen five of them try to knock a child off his bicycle." "At one stage," reported the *London Times*, "there was almost a battle on the seafront with missiles of all descriptions being thrown." The police intervened and arrested more than a hundred rioters, who the *Times* called a "collection of uncivilized youths with no respect for persons, property, or the comfort of other people." Explaining the incident, Labour's chief front bench spokesman, Fred Willey, observed that the "general complaint of those who took part was that there was nothing for them to do. They came from housing estates with far too few social amenities and were expected to spend their time in amusement arcades. . . . The present government regarded working-class adolescents as fair game for blatant exploitation by commercial interests."

On May 17, 1964, trouble broke out in the Kent resort of Margate and at Brighton. More than 800 Mods, arriving "on scooters bristling with headlights and badges," fought 200 leather-jacketed Rockers. The *Daily Express* painted a terrifying picture: "There was dad asleep in a deck chair and mum making sandcastles with the children when the 1964 boys took over the beaches at Margate and Brighton yesterday and smeared the traditional scene with more bloodshed and violence." Fumed Dr. George Simpson, Margate Court Chairman, "these long-haired, mentally unstable petty little sawdust Caesars seem to find courage, like rats, by hunting only in packs." By Tuesday, May 18, when the clashes subsided, "at least 40 youths had been arrested," the *Daily Mirror* informed its readers. "And there was blood on the sand."

Many of these warring youths, having time and lacking direction, turned to music. "My opinion why music suddenly shot out of England in the sixties is that we were the first generation that didn't get regimented and didn't go into the army," explained Beatles drummer Ringo Starr. "Music was a way out. We all wanted to leave. Everyone wanted to fly. Music was my way. Back then every street had a band. You could hear it all over. Everyone was playing, and mostly it sounded real bad, but we were playing. We all picked up guitars and drums and filled our time with music." "Had not the government stopped the draft," echoed Dave Clark, "there would have been no Dave Clark 5, no Beatles, no Stones."

Skiffle, a mixture of Dixieland jazz and country blues, first attracted British youths. The music originated from British Dixieland, or traditional jazz, which reached its height of popularity with a group that included trombonist Chris Barber, banjo and guitar player Tony "Lonnie" Donegan, and Harold Pendelton, co-owner of the Marquee Club with Chris Barber. "We discovered that our trumpet player, Ken Coyler, had a weak lip which gave out on him, so he needed an occasional rest," remembered Pendelton. "As a solution Chris [Barber] devised a little four piece band within his band to perform as a novelty respite while Ken's lips recovered. This little band was composed of a crude guitar, a homemade base, a suitcase that was played with whisk brooms and a washboard strummed with thimbles. Chris called it his skiffle group. He got the name from having read about the rent parties that used to be given in poor, Negro quarters to raise money—that blacks of New Orleans called them skiffle groups."

Soon Barber's novelty skiffle act became more popular than his traditional jazz band and engendered an accessible, participatory musical style. According to Barber, "the way Lonnie [Donegan] did it was a way that anyone could join in with, and they did it with homemade guitars, tea chest and broom handle string bass and all this stuff. Just singing any kind of song." In 1956, Lonnie Donegan climbed the charts with skiffle versions of two Leadbelly songs, "Rock Island Line" and "John Henry," which started a skiffle craze in Britain among poor youths who could start bands with homemade instruments and little musical schooling. "Skiffle bands sprung up everywhere because the kids didn't have to learn how to play difficult instruments like the trombone or trumpet or clarinet. Anybody could skiffle." "Out of this skiffle craze," added Pendelton, "the new rock groups like the Beatles began to emerge. The Beatles began as a skiffle group."

The Early Beatles

The four rowdy Rockers from Liverpool, who banded together as the Beatles during the skiffle craze, changed rock-and-roll history. Formed in 1959, the Quarrymen, as they were first called, then Johnny and the Moondogs, the Silver Beatles, and finally just the Beatles, started their musical careers as a skiffle band in the Cavern Club of Liverpool. The next year they traveled to Hamburg, Germany, to back up singer Tony Sheridan who helped the group on its first record, "My Bonnie," released in 1961. A year later, the Beatles had become the rage of England; by 1964 they had become worldwide celebrities.

The Beatles came from working-class families. Abandoned by his father and mother, John Winston Lennon grew up with his aunt Mimi and as a boy joined a Rocker gang that "went in for things like shoplifting and pulling girls' knickers down." Paul McCartney, the son of a cotton salesman, lived in a half house: "They were such small, diddy houses, with bare bricks inside," he later reminisced. The youngest of the Beatles, George Harrison, was the son of a bus driver and began an apprenticeship as an electrician at the age of 16. Drummer Ringo Starr, born Richard Starkey, told a reporter that his family had "always been just ordinary, poor working class." When her husband deserted the family, Ringo's mother worked as a barmaid to support her child. At 15, Ringo landed a job as a messenger boy for the British Railways.

The four Liverpool youths adopted a Rocker image. To his aunt, Lennon seemed to be "a real Teddy boy." "I wasn't really a Ted, just a Rocker," Lennon insisted. "I was imitating Teds, pretending to be one. I was never a real one, with chains and real gangs. If I'd met a proper Ted, I'd have been shit-scared." Paul spent hours styling his pompadoured hair and choosing the clothes that fit Rocker fashion. Worried that his son would "turn out a Teddy boy," Jim McCartney "said over and over again that [Paul] wasn't going to have tight trousers. But he just wore me down." George Harrison "used to go to school with his school cap sitting high on top his hair. And very tight trousers," remembered his mother. "Unknown to me, he'd run them up on my machine to make them even tighter. I bought him a brand new pair once and the first thing he did was to tighten them. When his dad found out, he told him to unpick them at once. 'I can't Dad,' he said. 'I've cut the pieces off.' George always had an answer." As a band the Beatles affected a Rocker image, wearing black-and-white cowboy shirts with white tassels dangling from the pockets, leather jackets, and pointed cowboy boots.

The quasi-Western attire indicated a major musical influence on the Beatles: American rockabilly. Although first drawn to music through skiffle and covering such Chuck Berry tunes as "Rock and Roll Music" and "Roll Over Beethoven," the early Beatles modeled their sound after Elvis Presley. "Nothing really affected me until Elvis," John Lennon remembered. "I had no idea about doing music as a way of life until rock 'n' roll hit me. It was *Rock Around the Clock*, I think. I enjoyed Bill Haley, but I wasn't overwhelmed by him. It wasn't until 'Heartbreak Hotel' that I really got into it." McCartney felt that Presley "was the biggest kick. Every time I felt low I just put on Elvis and I'd feel great, beautiful. I'd no idea how records were made and it was just magic. 'All Shook Up'! Oh, it was beautiful." "Elvis changed my life," added Ringo Starr. "He was the first teenager in my life. Johnnie Ray, Frankie Laine and Bill Haley were my early heroes, around '54. But they were always a bit like me dad. Elvis was the first real lad who came out. The kid. He totally blew me away, I loved him so." When Malcolm Evans, later a road manager for the Beatles, first heard the group at the Cavern Club, he felt that they "sounded a bit like Elvis."

The Beatles idolized other rockabilly stars as well. In 1959, as a Silver Beatle, George Harrison changed his name to Carl Harrison after one of his heroes, Carl Perkins. On tour with Perkins in 1964, John Lennon told the rockabilly star, "We've got all your records! We slowed 'em down from 45 to 33 [to learn them]." After telling the Beatles that they sounded "a lot like the old Sun Records," remembered Perkins, John jumped off the couch, put "both arms around me and kissed me on the jaw." At another point in their early years, the foursome called themselves the Foreverly Brothers in honor of the Everly Brothers. *Variety* spotted the influence years later. "Malarkey," read one story. "The Beatles are dishing up a rock and roll style that was current in this country ten years ago and that is still typical of such groups as the Everly Brothers." The name the group eventually adopted reflected the rockabilly connection. As John told a reporter, "I was looking for a name like the Crickets [Buddy Holly's band] that meant two things. From Cricket I went to Beatles. . . . When you said it, people thought of crawly things; when you read it, it was beat music."

The Beatles' passion for rockabilly may have come from the popularity of country music in Liverpool. Years later, Ringo Starr unabashedly gushed that "Hank Williams was my hero. . . . At one point," he noted, "Liverpool was the capital of country 'n' western music in England."

Manager Brian Epstein

This Rocker band, playing an English brand of rockabilly influenced by R & B and skiffle music, became famous through the efforts of Brian Epstein. Epstein, born in September 1934 into a wealthy family, was raised in a five-bedroom house in Childwall, one of Liverpool's most exclusive residential areas. He began a successful career as a salesman in two of his father's stores: a furniture shop and the North End Music Enterprises. "I enjoyed selling, watching people relax and show trust in me," he explained. "It was pleasant to see the wary look dissolve and people begin to think there were good things ahead for them and I would be the provider." After expanding his father's record retailing business, Epstein turned his attention to the Beatles, a group he had heard about in one of his music stores. As he told it, "I suppose it was all part of getting bored with simply selling records. I was looking for a new hobby. The Beatles at the same time, though I didn't know it and perhaps they didn't either, were also getting a bit bored with Liverpool." In 1961, Brian Epstein became the manager of the Beatles, getting a 25 percent share of their net revenues.

To make the band more palatable to the general public, Epstein changed their Rocker image. When he first saw them at the Cavern Club, he thought "they were a scruffy crowd in leather." The Beatles "were not very tidy and not very clean. They smoked as they played and they ate and talked and pretended to hit each other." Brian tried to "clean our image up," John Lennon later remarked. "He said our look wasn't right. We'd never get past the door at a good place. We just used to dress how we liked, on and off stage. He talked us into the suit scene." Said Epstein himself: "First I got them into trousers and sweaters and eventually into suits." Besides changing their appearance, said Pete Best, the Beatles' drummer before Ringo joined the group, the manager forced the band to "work out a proper program, playing our best numbers each time, not just the ones we felt like playing." After Epstein had finished molding the four Liver-pudlians, noticed Malcolm Evans, "the image of the Beatles was so good and nice."

To sell the band, Epstein brought in other professionals from the music business. After being rejected by nearly every British label, he approached George Martin, an executive with the Parlophone branch of the Electrical Music Industry (EMI), who on September 11, 1962, recorded the Beatles' first British release, "Love Me Do" and "P.S. I Love You." Epstein, who "didn't know how you promoted a record," enlisted the services of Tony Barrow, a publicity man for Decca Records. By May 1963, the manager had set up the machinery to make the Beatles a national sensation.

The Toppermost of the Poppermost

As with most working-class youths, the Beatles initially wanted money and fame. Scarred by the insecurity of his childhood, John "wanted to be popular. I wanted to be the leader. It seemed more attractive than just being one of the toffees." "All I wanted was women, money, and clothes," Paul later confessed. In discussing his financial future with Paul, George said that he "felt he was going to make a lot of it [money]. He was going to buy a house and a swimming pool, then he'd buy a bus for his father." As a group, the Fab Four dreamed of stardom. In 1961, remembered George, "we still used to send up the idea of getting to the top. When things were a real drag and nothing happening, we used to go through this routine: John would shout, 'Where are we going, fellas?' We'd shout back, 'To the Top, Johnny.' Then he would shout, 'What Top?' 'To the Toppermost of the Poppermost, Johnny!' "

The Beatles soon achieved their goal. They first became well known in Liverpool. By late 1962, remembered Maureen Cox, Ringo's first wife, admirers "used to hang around the Cavern all day long, just on the off chance of seeing them. They'd come out of the lunch time session and just stand outside all afternoon, queuing up for the evening show. . . . It was terrible, the mad screams when they came on. They went potty." News spread quickly. More than 5000 squealing teens mobbed a Beatles performance and caused a riot in Manchester. At Newcastle-upon-Tyne, more than 4000 diehards lined up in front of a concert hall at 3 A.M. to secure tickets for an evening Beatles show. Dr. F. R. C. Casson, a psychologist who tried to explain the phenomenon for the readers of the *London Times*, likened "Beatlemania to the frenzied dancing and shouting of voodoo worshippers and the howls and bodily writhing of converts among primitive evangelical sects in the southern states of America. . . . Beat music," Dr. Casson said, "has a rhythmic stimulation on the brain. A similar result of rhythmic stimulation is seen in some types of epileptic fit which may be caused by rapidly flickering light."

On October 13, 1963, the band gained national exposure when they performed at the London Palladium. More than 15 million television viewers watched thousands of young Londoners claw at each other to get into the Beatles concert. "From that day on," insisted press agent Tony Barrow, "everything has changed. My job has never been the same again. From spending six months ringing up newspapers and getting no, I now had every national reporter and feature writer chasing *me*." Within two more weeks, on November 4, the Beatles performed for the Queen at the Royal Variety Performance and solidified their reputation. Following the heavy-set singer Sophie Tucker, they elicited screams and moans with "Till There Was You," "Twist and Shout," and "She Loves You." During one number, John asked the audience to clap. "Those upstairs, just rattle your jewelry," he added, looking up toward the royal box. The following Sunday, 26 million Britons witnessed the escapade while sitting in front of their television sets.

The Beatles in 1967 making a promotional film for the single "Hello, Gooodbye"
Frank Driggs Collection

By December 1963, manufacturers started to offer Beatles products—one firm in Peckham selling Beatles sweaters "designed specially for Beatles people by a leading British manufacturer with a top-quality, two-tone Beatles badge." The Beatles fan club swelled to more than 800,000 members, and the foursome sold a million copies of two singles which featured "I Want to Hold Your Hand" and "She Loves You." The band's first British album, *Please Please Me*, topped the British charts for more than six months. By the end of 1963, the Fab Four had sold 11 million records and $18 million worth of Beatles goods.

British public opinion responded favorably to the Beatles. The *Daily Mirror* argued that "you have to be a real sour square not to love the nutty, noisy, happy, handsome Beatles." From a different political perspective, *The Daily Worker* of the British Communist Party commented that the "Mersey sound is the voice of 80,000 crumbling houses and 30,000 people on the dole." Although Conservative politician Edward Heath first criticized the Beatles' language as "unrecognizable as the Queen's English," he later told an interviewer: "Who could have forecast only a year ago that the Beatles would prove the salvation of the corduroy industry" as thousands emulated the band in its trouser style. Prime Minister Sir Alec Douglas-Home called the group "our best export" and "a useful contribution to the balance of payments." Even the Queen complimented the Beatles. "So young, fresh, and vital," she cooed.

Amid such praise, Brian Epstein began to question his marketing tactics. He feared overexposure: "At first sight the endless discussion in the newspapers of the Beatles' habits, clothes, and views was exciting. They liked it at first and so did I. It was good for business. But finally it became an anxiety. How long could they maintain public interest without rationing either personal appearances or newspaper coverage? By a stringent watch on their bookings and press contacts we just averted saturation point. But it was very close. Other artists have been destroyed by this very thing."

The band members started to doubt the value of stardom as they began to pay the price of success. Ringo Starr complained about the loss of friendships and the diminishing control he exercised over his own life. "There were so many groups in Liverpool at one time that we often used to play just for each other, sitting in on each other's sessions, or just listening. It was a community on its own, just made up of groups." But when the Beatles became popular nationally, "it broke all the community up. People start hating each other." Moreover, Ringo felt slighted when George Martin replaced him with a session drummer on "P.S. I Love You." "Nobody said anything. What could the others say, or me? We were just lads, being pushed around. You know what I mean. They were so big, the London record company and all that. We just did what we were told." At about the same time, John believed that the band had relinquished too much control. In Liverpool, he later told an interviewer, the Beatles "felt embarrassed in our suits and being very clean. We were worried that our friends might think we'd sold out—which we had, in a way."

The Beatles Invade America

Despite their doubts, the Beatles prepared for even greater success in America. Epstein paved the way for the British invasion, convincing Capitol Records to spend $50,000 on a "crash publicity program." The company plastered 5 million "The Beatles Are Coming" stickers on buildings, fences, and telephone poles in every state and printed a million copies of a four-page tabloid about the Fab Four. Capitol executives pressed one million units of a promotional, seven-inch Beatles interview record, which gave radio listeners the impression that the Beatles had personally contacted every disc jockey in the country. They also convinced many of the major weekly publications to run stories on the British foursome before their arrival: *Time* covered the group in its November 15, 1963, issue; *Newsweek* did so three days later; and on January 31, 1964, *Life* published a color spread entitled, "Here Come The Beatles." By February 7, 1964, Brown Meggs, director of eastern operations for Capitol Records, told *The New York Times* that "I have been on full-time Beatles duty since—the date is indelibly imprinted on my mind—January 6 when I returned from vacation. All this came at once, everything happened in a tremendously concentrated period. I'm awfully tired, but Beatles only come once in a decade, if that." Voyle Gilmore, a vice-president of Capitol, summed up the efforts of his company: "There was a lot of hype."

Radio also plugged the Beatles. During February 1964, one record executive in a company that had no Beatles releases complained that "stations are playing our records like spot commercials between Beatles tunes." "What sells records is radio," explained Brown Meggs of Capitol. "The Beatles got unbelievable radio play. There wasn't a single market in the country in which airplay wasn't simply stupendous."

When the Beatles arrived in New York City on February 7, 1964, Beatlemania had swept the United States. Entering the charts at number 83, by February 1 "I Want to Hold Your Hand" had replaced Bobby Vinton's "There! I've Said It Again" in the number-one slot. The song remained in the top position for seven weeks. The third week of February 1964, contended *Billboard*, "was the week that was the Beatles'. First in the platter polls, first in the press, first in police protection, and the first in the hearts of New York teenagers who upset the mechanics of John F. Kennedy Airport, the Plaza, a CBS-TV studio, Penn Station, and Carnegie Hall ever since the foursome arrived from London."

Some adults disapproved of the new rage. After the Sullivan show, the *Herald Tribune* called the Beatles "75% publicity, 20% haircut and 5% lilting lament." To the *Daily News*, "the Presleyan gyrations and caterwauling were but lukewarm dandelion tea compared to the 100-proof elixir served up by the Beatles." Disregarding his personal ban on Sunday television viewing, evangelist Billy Graham watched the Beatles on "The Ed Sullivan Show" and believed that the performance revealed "all the symptoms of the uncertainty of the times and the confusion about us." Ray Block, orchestra leader on the Sullivan program, prophesied that the band "wouldn't last longer than a year," and actor Noel Coward said: "I've met them. Delightful lads. Absolutely no talent." Concert critic Louis Biancolli summed up the adverse reaction to the Beatles: "Their effect is like mass hypnosis followed by mass nightmare. I never heard anything like what went around me. I've read about the bacchantes and corybantes in wild Greek rites screaming insensately. They were antique squares compared to these teenage maenads."

Most media commentators, however, welcomed the clean-cut, well-tailored Beatles and their aristocratic manager. *Time* wrote that "the boys are the very spirit of good clean fun. They look like shaggy Peter Pans, with their mushroom haircuts and high white shirt collars, and onstage they clown around endlessly." The 1964 *Yearbook* of *World Book Encyclopedia* singled out the Beatles' "rambunctious and irreverent sense of fun" and the *Yearbook* of *Collier's Encyclopedia* likened the foursome to "Little Lord Fauntleroys."

Newsweek probably best captured the majority opinion when it labeled the Beatles "a band of evangelists. And the gospel is fun. They shout, they stomp, they jump for joy and their audiences respond in a way that makes an old-time revival meeting seem like a wake. . . . The Beatles appeal to the positive, not negative. They give kids a chance to let off steam and adults a chance to let off disapproval. They have even evolved a peculiar sort of sexless appeal: cute and safe. The most they ask is: 'I Want to Hold Your Hand.' " The fun-loving Beatles seemed a perfect antidote to the pessimism that had engulfed America after John F. Kennedy's death a few months earlier.

The "cute and safe" Beatles, appealing to a vast audience, scored fantastic successes in America. Shortly after their tour of the United States, John Lennon released his book *In His Own Write*, which nudged

Ian Fleming's latest James Bond thriller from the top of the bestseller list and won Lennon an invitation to the prestigious Foyles Literary Lunch on Shakespeare's four-hundredth birthday. Some compared the book to James Joyce's classic *Finnegans Wake*. Almost simultaneously, the Beatles released a full-length motion picture, *A Hard Day's Night*. "The idea was to make it as quickly as possible and get it out before their popularity faded," admitted director Richard Lester. The timing was superb. Even historian and JFK speechwriter Arthur Schlesinger, Jr., lauded the movie as "the astonishment of the month" by a band which embodied the "timeless essence of the adolescent effort to deal with the absurdities of an adult world." During its first six weeks, the film earned $5.6 million in rental fees.

In August 1965, the Beatles returned to the States for another tour. The second American tour included a stint at New York's Shea Stadium, where the Fab Four lured 55,000 rabid fans and grossed $304,000—"the greatest gross ever in the history of show business" up to that time, according to promoter Sid Bernstein.

In Seattle, a typical explosion of mayhem erupted over the second coming of the Beatles. When the foursome arrived in town, they faced screaming, clawing teenagers. Escorted by a police motorcade, the band immediately sped to Room 272 of the seaside Edgewater Inn, which had been secured with barbed wire and sawhorse barricades. While in their room, Ringo, George, Paul, and John sorted through the hundreds of letters from their fans, ate a few of the cookies and cakes that Beatles diehards had baked, and fished from a window that overlooked Elliot Bay.

The Beatles finally emerged from the hotel into the damp Seattle air that night, when they ran from the Edgewater Inn lobby and jumped into a limousine bound for the Seattle Coliseum. Marty Murphy, a 25-year-old switchboard operator at the Edgewater Inn, rode with the Beatles, dragged into the car by Brian Epstein, who desperately needed help with two terrified Beatles secretaries. According to her account, "the limousine started moving. Now I could understand why the Beatles had looked so scared when they arrived. When we got to the barricade, I have never been so frightened in my life. These children had their faces pressed up against the car, all bent out of shape. They were crying, screaming, 'Touch me! Touch me!' They were saying that to me, and they didn't even know who I was. Finally, the limousine got to the Coliseum." When the Beatles leapt onstage and started to play, remembered police officer Noreen Skagen, "I only sort of heard the music; the screaming was just too loud. The Beatles themselves looked very tense, pale, scared. . . . We had to have a regular flying wedge with our then-TAC squad to bring them into the Coliseum and onstage. The entire audience charged the stage when the Beatles were ready to leave. We were constantly dragging hysterical youngsters who had gone berserk. Back then, it wasn't a matter of drugs or alcohol. It was hysteria. The girls were in love. They would say, 'I have to talk to them! You don't understand!' "

After the performance, the police bundled the Fab Four in blankets, put them on stretchers and carried them through the crowd to a Red Cross van, which escaped the wild hordes who demanded their heroes. About the entire episode the *Seattle Times* wrote: "Seattle seethed with uncontrollable hysteria, terrifying noise and danger in a real-life nightmare last night. This was the Beatles' show. For 30 incredible minutes, those in the jam-packed Seattle Center Coliseum had the feeling of being sealed in a crazed capsule pitching through the chasms of space." A similar hysteria gripped other cities on the Beatles' tour, which by the end of 1965 had reaped more than $56 million.

The intensity and magnitude of Beatlemania in America at least partly can be attributed to the postwar baby boom. In 1964, millions of pubescent and prepubescent Beatlemaniacs were part of the more than 43 million youths who had been born between 1947 and 1957. They searched for an identity and collectively latched onto the Beatles as a symbol of unity. As one Beatles fan told a reporter as she stood vigil in 1964 outside a hotel where her heroes resided, "I'm here because everyone else is here." Though youths had idolized Elvis Presley, the mass hysteria of Beatlemania could only have occurred during the mid-sixties when the majority of baby boomers had become old enough to become interested in music. "We were just the spokesmen for a generation," explained Paul McCartney.

The Mersey Beat

In the mid-1960s, the Beatles who had conquered the American music market by appealing to the baby-boom generation paved the way for other British groups, some of them linked to Brian Epstein. "The biggest thing the Beatles did was to open the American market to all British artists," contended British promoter Arthur Howes, who planned the early Beatles tours of England. "Nobody had ever been able to get in before the Beatles. They alone did it. I had brought over lots of American stars, but nobody had gone over there." By February 1964, *Variety* told its readers, "Britannia ruled the airwaves." "The advent of the [Beatles] now has shattered the steady, day-to-day domination of made-in-America music here and abroad." During 1964, British rock bands sold more than $76 million worth of records in the United States.

Some of the British groups had grown up with the Beatles in Liverpool. Gerry Marsden, a truck driver who was a neighbor of the Beatles, in 1959 formed a band called the Pacemakers. Under the watchful eye of manager Brian Epstein, who signed the group in June 1962, Gerry and the Pacemakers established a following at the Cavern Club in Liverpool, frequently playing on the same bill as the Beatles. In 1963, they climbed to the top of the British charts with a song written for the Beatles, "How Do You Do It?" and followed with the chart-toppers, "I Like It" and "You'll Never Walk Alone," ending the successful year with an appearance on the British television show, "Saturday Night at the London Palladium." In May 1964, Gerry and the Pacemakers debuted

The Hollies; Graham Nash in center
Frank Driggs Collection

in America on "The Ed Sullivan Show," which helped promote the group's best-selling U.S. single, "Don't Let the Sun Catch You Crying." They capped their career in 1965 by starring in the movie *Ferry Across the Mersey* with a hit single of the same name.

Members of another Epstein act, Billy J. Kramer and the Dakotas, rose from their working-class backgrounds to stardom. Billy J. Kramer (a.k.a. William Ashton), a worker for the British Railways, originally sang with a group called the Coasters, but teamed with a Manchester combo, the Dakotas, on the advice of Epstein, who signed the Liverpudlian in late 1962. Observed *The Big Beat*, an English fanzine: "The marriage of the zing singing of Billy J. to the true-beat accompaniment of the Daks has proven a brilliant stroke on the part of Epstein. These boys just have to step onto the stage and the fans go wild!" Though not having "the greatest voice in the world," according to producer George Martin, Billy J. Kramer hit the charts in June 1963 with "Do You Want to Know a Secret?," a track from the Beatles' first album, and the same month toured the United Kingdom with the Beatles. Two months later, he followed with the chart-topper "Bad to Me," a song written by John Lennon specifically for Kramer. The group hit the British Top Ten with two Lennon/McCartney originals, "I'll Keep You Satisfied" and "From a Window" and in mid-1964 broke into the American market with "Little Children."

The Searchers, another Liverpool group, rode the crest of the Beatles' success. Formed in 1961 and named after a John Wayne movie, the group began performing regularly at such Liverpool clubs as the Cavern, the Casbah, and the Hot Spot, eventually becoming the house

Herman's Hermits, ca. 1965. Peter Noone, right center, on lead vocal
Frank Driggs Collection

The Dave Clark Five filming an appearance on the "Ed Sullivan Show"; Clark is on the drums
Frank Driggs Collection

band at the Iron Door. "We copied such people as Buddy Holly, Eddie Cochran, and Gene Vincent," related John McNally, one of the founders of the band. In August 1963, they topped the British singles chart with a remake of the Drifters' "Sweets for My Sweet." After an April 1964 appearance on "The Ed Sullivan Show" and amid Beatlemania, the Searchers scaled the American charts with their bestselling record, a remake of "Needles and Pins."

Together with the Beatles, the Searchers, Gerry and the Pacemakers, and Billy J. Kramer delivered the Liverpool "Mersey sound." Alexis Korner, British blues innovator, found that "there was a certain brashness about the Liverpool music, which stamped it almost immediately—they played it the way they speak English, you know! You could definitely tell a Liverpool group. The Mersey sound was basically a guitar sound: lead guitar, rhythm guitar, bass guitar, and drums was the basic Liverpool setup."

Groups from other parts of Great Britain invaded America with a sound similar to the Mersey beat. From Manchester, a dingy, smoke-stacked industrial center much like Liverpool, came Freddie Garrity and the Dreamers. Quitting his job as a milkman, Freddie and his Dreamers hit the British charts in 1963 with "If You Gotta Make a Fool of Somebody," "I'm Telling You Now," and "You Were Made for Me," becoming popular on English television for their comic act. In February 1964, the band appeared on the American television programs "Hullabaloo" and "Shindig," which promoted "Do the Freddie."

In early 1965, Wayne Fontana and the Mindbenders, another amalgam of Manchester youths, scored a hit with "The Game of Love." Fontana (a.k.a. Glyn Geoffrey Ellis), a former telephone engineering apprentice, took his stage name from his record company and named the group after a horror film that was then playing in a local theater. Besides their 1965 hit, the Mindbenders charted with a sequel, "A Groovy Kind of Love."

The Hollies proved to be more long-lasting than most other Manchester beat bands. The group was started by Graham Nash and singer-guitarist Allan Clarke, who first met in grammar school and later became the Two Teens. After a few name changes, including the Guytones and the Deltas, the duo added three other members in 1962 and labeled themselves the Hollies after their musical hero, Buddy Holly. "We were Buddy Holly crazy," recalled Nash, who, as with other Merseybeats, was influenced by such rockabillys as the Everly Brothers. Signed by EMI producer Ron Richards who saw them perform at the Cavern Club in Liverpool, the band first hit the British Top 10 in early 1964 with "Stay" and followed with the Top 10 "Just One Look," "Here I Go Again," "Yes I Will," "I'm Alive," and the Beatles' "If I Need Someone." In 1966, during a tour of America, they worked fans to a frenzy at New York City's Paramount Theater and on such television shows as "Shindig," "Hullabaloo," and "The Smothers Brothers Show," charting that year with "Bus Stop."

Herman's Hermits, another Manchester band, capitalized on the beat music craze. Formed in 1963 by front man Peter Noone, the band was signed to EMI Columbia by producer Mickie Most, who noticed the facial resemblance of Noone to John F. Kennedy. The next year, the group charted on both sides of the Atlantic with "I'm Into Something Good" which featured Noone backed by such session musicians as Jimmy Page and John Paul Jones, later of Led Zeppelin. In 1965, they followed with a string of upbeat hits which included "Silhouettes," "Mrs. Brown You've Got a Lovely Daughter," "Just a Little Bit Better," and a revival of the British music hall tune, "I'm Henry the Eighth, I Am."

The Dave Clark Five, from the Tottenham section of London, initially posed the most serious threat to the commercial dominance of the Beatles. Teaming together to raise money for Dave Clark's rugby team, in 1964 the Five toured America, appearing on "The Ed Sullivan Show." "Within the course of seven days we were household names and ended up having five records on the charts at once," explained

The Monkees, 1966. From left to right: Davey Jones, Peter Tork, Mickey Dolenz, Mike Nesmith

Clark, who, like the Beatles, had been inspired by "Little Richard, Elvis Presley, Fats Domino, all those great rockers." The DC5 hit the charts on both sides of the Atlantic with "Glad All Over," "Bits and Pieces," "Can't You See That She's Mine," and "Because." The liner notes on their American debut album predicted that "the Tottenham sound of the Dave Clark Five is on its way towards overthrowing the reign of the Beatles in this country." In 1965, they copied the Fab Four by releasing a film, *Catch Us If You Can*. The band also charted with "Over and Over" and "I Like It Like That." All told, the group sold 50 million records, placing eight singles in the Top 10.

The Monkees

Two American producers took advantage of the Mersey-beat craze by creating the Monkees, a prefabricated American version of the Beatles. Observing the success of Richard Lester's Beatles film, *A Hard Day's Night*, Bob Rafelson and Bert Schneider—the son of then president of Columbia Pictures, Abe Schneider—formed Raybert Productions. They placed an ad in the major Hollywood trade papers for "four insane boys, age 17–21, want spirited Ben Frank's types" for "acting roles in new TV series." In a month, the duo auditioned 437 hopefuls, including folk rocker Stephen Stills and mass murderer Charles Manson.

The producers picked four photogenic, energetic, largely inexperienced applicants: Robert Michael Nesmith, an unknown folk singer; Mickey Dolenz, who as a child had played Corky in the TV children's series, *Circus Boy*, and more recently had played in a California garage band; Greenwich Village folk singer Peter Thorkelson, shortened to Tork; and David Jones, the most experienced of the four, who had appeared on Broadway as the Artful Dodger in *Oliver*, had played a drug-crazed husband on the TV program *Ben Casey*, and had released an album of pop songs, some of which he performed on the same "Ed Sullivan Show" on which the Beatles had debuted.

In late 1965, Rafelson and Schneider secured $225,000 from Jackie Cooper, the former child actor who headed the television subsidiary of Columbia Pictures, for a pilot TV series. "It all went great," Rafelson told *Time*. "NBC bought the series 24 hours after it saw the pilot and sold it to two sponsors 72 hours later."

The producers quickly began to groom their new product. They hired underground film director James Frawley to provide intensive acting lessons for the group. "At first they were embarrassed, they were stiff and they were a little raw," Frawley told *Saturday Evening Post*. "We would roll over on the floor, sometimes, and do animals. 'You're a crab. Talk the way a giraffe would talk. Deal with an elephant. Now, talk the way a teapot would talk.' It was like a training period to free them physically, to start to use their bodies in a new way."

Rafelson and Schneider also shaped the Monkees musically. As well as enlisting the help of the songwriting team of Tommy Boyce and Bobby Hart, they approached former Brill Building music publisher Don Kirshner, the music president of Columbia Pictures/Screen Gems TV and its new record label, Colgems. "The boys didn't relate," explained Kirshner at the time. "I was looking for a driving, exciting, frantic young sound. There was no sound to the Monkees." Having little time to develop and record 22 songs for an album and five TV shows, he "brought in Goffin and King, Mann and Weil, Sedaka and Greenfield, the Tokens and Neil Diamond and created songs for the group. On most of the records I did with the Monkees, Carole King and Neil Diamond would sing background" and studio musicians such as Glen Campbell, Leon Russell, and James Burton would play the instruments. "The music had nothing to do with us," complained Michael Nesmith.

Though prefabricated, the look and sound of the Monkees started to sell. The group hit the top of the charts with their debut, "Last Train to Clarksville," and their follow-up, "I'm a Believer," which sold 10 million copies. In 1966 and 1967, the Monkees scored with four number-one albums. After their network debut on September 12, 1966, the group attracted 10 million viewers every Monday night for their television program, received 5000 fan letters a day and sold over $20 million in Monkees merchandise, including shirts, slacks, raincoats, sweaters, comic books, trading and playing cards, dolls, lunch boxes, stuffed animals, games, hats, bubblegum, shoes, charms, guitars, and puppets. "We're advertisers," enthused Mickey Dolenz. "We're selling a product. We're selling Monkees."

The successful Monkees had been patterned after the Beatles. Before releasing the Monkees debut LP, the band's label spent $100,000 on an ad campaign that involved 76 advance men who distributed thousands of posters proclaiming "The Monkees Are Coming" and provided preview records to 6,000 disc jockeys. The name of the group had been calculatedly misspelled, as had the Beatles, and the first Monkees single included several "no-no-no" choruses to substitute for the Beatles' "yeah-yeah-yeah." The group's management even published a *Monkees Monthly* magazine similar to the many fanzines dealing with the Beatles such as *Beat Monthly* and *Beatles Monthly*. "The teens have bought the Monkees," a Raybert official proclaimed in early 1967. "They're the American Beatles." *Newsweek* called the band members "direct videological descendants of the Beatles"; *Time* in early 1967 commented that "less than a year ago, a team of wily promoters ran the Beatles through a Xerox machine and came up with the Monkees."

The British Blues Invasion and the Rolling Stones

English groups playing American electric blues also became popular during the British invasion. The British fascination with American blues started with Chris Barber's band. When the British Musicians Union ended the ban on American musicians in 1956, Barber and his bandmates began to invite American blues performers to England. "Chris Barber and I had started to bring American musicians to play with our band," remembered Harold Pendelton. "Muddy Waters came out on stage [in 1958] and played an electric guitar. This was the first electric guitar anyone in Britain had ever seen. . . . When we opened the Marquee Club in 1960, skiffle was on the way out so we were able to occasionally feature a rhythm and blues group."

The Rolling Stones, ca. 1965. From left to right: Bill Wyman, Charlie Watts, Keith Richards, Mick Jagger, Brian Jones
Frank Driggs Collection

Alexis Korner and Cyril Davies, two members of the Chris Barber band, helped popularize American blues among British youths. "Alexis and Cyril Davies were the only ones really playing blues in London at that time," remembered Rolling Stones drummer Charlie Watts, who originally played with Korner and Davies. "Cyril was a great harmonica player; he made a couple of very good records—'Country Line Special' was one. He and Alexis got together while Alexis was playing with Chris Barber, who had one of the biggest trad bands." By 1962, the two formed Blues Incorporated and landed a regular Saturday night job at the Ealing Club, which attracted such youths as Keith Richards, Mick Jagger, and Brian Jones, who occasionally performed with Korner and Davies.

As the Rolling Stones, Richards and his companions would take Chicago blues to youths like themselves on both sides of the Atlantic. "The Stones were the first people into the blues in England, Alexis Korner and Cyril Davies were, but the Stones were the first ones who were young, you know," recalled Giorgio Gomelsky, the first manager of the Stones.

The Rolling Stones, like the Beatles, had an interest in American rockabilly. Mick Jagger "had been singing with some rock and roll bands, doing Buddy Holly," guitarist Keith Richards remembered. "Buddy Holly was in England as solid as Elvis. Everything that came out was a record smash number one. By about '58, it was either Elvis or Buddy Holly." Richards himself was "really listening to what was coming over the Atlantic. The ones that were hitting hard were Little Richard, and Presley, and Jerry Lee Lewis." He "was Rockin' away, avoidin' the bicycle chains and razors in those dance halls." When *Blackboard Jungle,* with the music of Bill Haley and the Comets, showed in London, Richards found that "people were saying 'Did ya hear that music, man?' Because in England we had never heard anything: The BBC controls it and won't play that sort of music. But everybody our age stood up for that music and the hell with the BBC."

Members of the Rolling Stones soon began to uncover the blues roots of rockabilly. Keith Richards heard "Broonzy first. . . . Then I started to discover Robert Johnson and those cats." The multi-instrumentalist Brian Jones, initially the impetus behind the group, one day heard "Elmore James, and the earth seemed to shudder on its axis. . . . The blues was real. We only had to persuade people to listen to the music, and they couldn't help but be turned on to all those great old blues cats." When Jones saw Muddy Waters perform, recalled Jones's friend Richard Hattrell, "it was as if Brian had found his mission in life. He got himself electrified and he never stopped practicing." Mick Jagger, who started out by singing in a band called Little Boy Blue and the Blue Boys, similarly "was crazy over Chuck Berry, Bo Diddley, Muddy Waters, and Fats Domino, not knowing what it meant, just that it was beautiful."

One day in London, recalled Richards, "I get on this train one morning and there's Jagger—and under his arm he has four or five albums. . . . He's got Chuck Berry, Little Walter, Muddy Waters." The two talked about their mutual passion for R & B and in a few weeks, with a friend, Dick Taylor, formed a band called the Glimmer Twins, which laid "down some of this Chuck Berry and Little Walter stuff. No drummer or anything, just two guitars and a little amplifier." Remarked Dick Taylor: "We'd sit around and listen to Mick's records, and then our little skiffle group would try to imitate what we were hearing."

In mid-1963, Keith Richards, Mick Jagger, and Brian Jones, together with Dick Taylor and drummer Tony Chapman, formed the Rolling Stones, moving into a run-down apartment in the downtrodden district of King's Road. They debuted on July 12 at the Marquee Club in London as a replacement for Blues Incorporated. By the end of the year Charlie Watts replaced Chapman as drummer and bassist Bill Wyman joined when Taylor quit to form a blues-driven band, The Pretty Things, solidifying a lineup that would remain intact for nearly 30 years. "We wanted to sell records for Jimmy Reed, Muddy, John Lee Hooker," explained Keith Richards. "We were disciples—if we could turn people on to that, then that was enough. That was the total original aim."

The material chosen by the early Stones indicated their Chicago blues orientation. For their first single, recorded in March 1963, they covered Chuck Berry's "Come On" and Muddy Waters's "I Wanna Be Loved." Their first American album, *England's Newest Hitmakers*, included Slim Harpo's "I'm a Kingbee," "Carol" by Chuck Berry, Willie Dixon's "I Just Wanna Make Love to You," and Jimmy Reed's "Honest I Do." Subsequent albums exposed teenaged record buyers to such R & B classics as "You Can't Catch Me" and "Talkin' About You" (Chuck Berry), "Little Red Rooster" (Willie Dixon), "Mona" (Bo Diddley), and "Look What You've Done" (Muddy Waters). The Stones recorded many of these cuts at the Chess studio in Chicago. "Chuck Berry wandered in while we were recording 'Down the Road Apiece,' " a wide-eyed Bill Wyman told a reporter from *New Musical Express*, "and he said to us: 'Wow, you guys are really getting it on.' Muddy Waters was also there." Even the name of the band—the Rolling Stones—came from a tune penned by Muddy Waters, and in April 1963 the *Record Mirror* characterized the Stones as "genuine R and B. As the trad scene gradually subsides, promoters of all kinds of teen-beat entertainments heave a long sigh of relief that they have found something to take its place. It's rhythm and blues . . . and at the Station Hotel, Kew Road, the hip kids throw themselves around to the new jungle music like they never did in the more restrained days of trad. And the combo they writhe and twist to is called the Rolling Stones."

The Stones Turn Raunchy

Andrew Logg Oldham, an ex-publicity man for the Beatles who became manager of the Stones on May 3, 1963, helped propel the blues-based group to fame by creating a raunchy, crude, offensive image that contrasted sharply with the reputation of the Beatles. At first the band appeared like most other British invasion bands. When performing on the British television show "Thank Your Lucky Stars" in June 1963, the Stones wore checkered suits. "You have to make some compromises," Oldham instructed the group, sounding like his one-time boss, Brian Epstein. "Just to get started in this business you have to compromise a bit." As Keith Richards later told it, the manager "tried to tidy us up. . . . There are photographs of us in the suits he put us in, those dog-toothed checked suits with the black velvet collars."

Oldham quickly changed his strategy and manufactured an opposite to the neat, smiling Beatles. "The overall hustle I invented for the Stones was to establish them as a raunchy, gamy, unpredictable bunch of undesirables. I decided that since the Beatles had already usurped the clean-cut choirboy image with synchronized jackets, I should take the Stones down the opposite road. Rejecting matching clothing was one step, emphasizing their long hair and unclean appearance was another, and inciting the press to write about them, using catchy phrases that I had coined, was yet another. . . . I wanted to establish that the Stones were threatening, uncouth and animalistic." "It was perfect, just perfect," Oldham told Jagger after a press conference at which the Stones had given flippant and insulting replies to journalists. "They're going to plaster your pictures and your terrible, terrible statements all over the papers. Those dirty Rolling Stones, that's what you are. The opposite of those nice little chaps, the Beatles. . . . We're gonna make you famous."

To refine the image, Oldham engineered a few changes. He downgraded piano player Ian Stewart to roadie. "Well, he just doesn't look the part, and six is too many for [fans] to remember the faces in the picture," Oldham told Richards at the time. The manager shaved a few years off the ages of each Stone in their official biography, making them teens again. He then convinced his label, London Records, to blitz the media. Read one ad in *Billboard*, "They're great! They're outrageous! They're rebels! They sell! They're England's *hottest*."

The rest of the media soon picked up the cue. In 1964, *Melody Maker* carried an article headlined "Would You Let Your Daughter Go Out with a Rolling Stone?" and described the band as "symbols of rebellion . . . against the boss, the clock, and the clean-shirt-a-day routine." The Stones, it continued, looked like "five indolent morons, who give one the feeling that they really enjoy wallowing in a swill-tub of their own repulsiveness." *New Musical Express* labeled the group as "the caveman-like quintet." In 1964, *Time* interviewed Keith Richards, who told the magazine that he hoped "to be sitting in a country house with four Rolls-Royces and spitting at everyone."

Success

The raunchy Rolling Stones soon achieved success in England. In September 1963, they reached number 21 on the British chart with a remake of Chuck Berry's "Come On." The same year, Oldham introduced the Stones to the Beatles, who gave the group the song "I Wanna Be Your Man," which stopped on the British chart at number 12. In March 1964, the Stones remade Buddy Holly's "Not Fade Away" in a Bo Diddley beat which reached number three. By May the group got 100,000 advance orders for their first British album, which topped the chart on its release.

The Stones initially had more difficulty in the United States. During their first tour of the United States, which started in June 1964, the Stones received scant notice. They first appeared on a segment of "Hollywood Palace" that happened to be hosted by crooner Dean Martin. After the Stones chugged through their versions of "I Just Want to Make Love to You" and "Not Fade Away," a twisted-faced Martin, eyes rolling upward, asked the audience, "Aren't they great?" He continued: "They're off to England to have a hair-pulling contest with the Beatles. . . . Their hair is not that long—it's just smaller foreheads and higher eyebrows." When a trampolinist finished his act, Martin added: "That's the father of the Rolling Stones. He's been trying to kill himself ever since." To a distraught Brian Jones, Dean Martin "was just a symbol of the whole tour for us."

On the remaining dates of the tour, the band mostly played to empty seats. In San Antonio, Texas, the crowd clamored for an encore by a trained monkey rather than one by the Rolling Stones. "We all wanted to pack up and come home," confessed Bill Wyman. The colorful Keith Richards remembered "Nebraska, we really felt like a sore pimple in Omaha. On top of that, the first time we arrived there, the only people to meet us off the plane were twelve motorcycle cops who insisted on doing this motorcade thing right through town. And nobody in Omaha had ever heard of us. We thought, 'Wow, we've made it. We must be heavy.' And we get to the Auditorium and there's 600 people there in a 15,000-seat hall."

The Stones conquered America on their second tour, which began on October 23, 1964 and featured a spot on "The Ed Sullivan Show." During the 1950s and 1960s, Ed Sullivan provided the means for teens across the United States to hear rock-and-roll. He had helped promote Elvis Presley, fostered Beatlemania, and had provided the springboard for such British invasion groups as Gerry and the Pacemakers, the Searchers, and the Dave Clark Five. Enthused Dave Clark: "The power of the man [Sullivan] and his show was unbelievable."

On the Ed Sullivan program of October 25, 1964, American teens were introduced to the Stones as a raunchy, hip alternative to the Beatles. Publicly, the host proclaimed: "I promise you they'll never be back on our show. . . . Frankly, I didn't see the Rolling Stones until the day before the broadcast. They were recommended by my scouts in England. I was shocked when I saw them. It took me seventeen years to build this show; I'm not going to have it destroyed in a matter of weeks." Privately, remembered Mick Jagger, "Ed told us it was the wildest, most enthusiastic audience he'd seen any artist get in the history of his show. Got a message a few days later saying: 'Received hundreds of letters from parents complaining about you, but thousands from teenagers saying how much they enjoyed your performance.' " Sullivan invited the Stones for a return engagement on May 2, 1965.

A critical American press also helped publicize the Rolling Stones. *Newsweek* pegged the Stones as a "leering quintet" obsessed with pornographic lyrics. *Time* magazine printed the letter of one concerned woman, who wrote: "We like the Beatles because they have rhythm, enthusiasm, and a good sound. After listening to the groans, pants, and frankly dirty words of the Rolling Stones and a few other sick groups, one begins to wonder where they dig up a DJ to play such garbage."

Such adult criticism of the band predictably pushed rebellious American teenagers into the Stones' camp. Beatle George Harrison noticed that "it's become the in thing for adults to say the Beatles are good or the Beatles are funny, it's in for adults to like us. So the real hip kids—or the kids who think they are—have gone off us. The in thing for those kids now is to be a Stones fan, because their parents can't stand the Rolling Stones."

Throughout the remaining dates of their second American tour in 1964, the Stones played to enthusiastic crowds. Keith Richards at the time felt an "energy building up as you go around the country. You find it winding tighter and tighter, until one day you get out halfway through the first number and the whole place is full of chicks screaming. We'd walk into some of these places and it was like they had the Battle of the Crimea going on—people gasping, tits hanging out, chicks choking, nurses running around. . . . There was a period of six months in England we couldn't play ballrooms anymore because we never got through more than three or four songs every night," added Richards. "Chaos. Police and too many people in the places fainting. They used to tell us, 'There's not a dry seat in the cinema.' And the bigger it got, America and Australia and everywhere it's exactly the same number." "There sure as hell weren't any empty seats this time," added Ian Stewart, who now traveled with the band as a roadie. "Wherever we went, it was bedlam."

The Stones ensured success with a new, less-blues-dominated sound. "I was convinced they couldn't make it as a top group by just playing old rhythm and blues tunes," recalled Andrew Logg Oldham. "We had all witnessed with our own eyes and ears how easy Lennon and McCartney had knocked off 'I Wanna Be Your Man' and I felt that Mick and Keith could do the same for us once they got the hang of it."

Encouraged by Oldham, Richards and Jagger pushed aside the versatile Brian Jones and began to concentrate on their own material, which combined pop conventions with Chicago-style blues. In their first three albums, Jagger told interviewer Ed Rudy, the Stones found "that American songs are better for ourselves. The songs that Keith and I write . . . we give to other people. They're mostly ballads." By their fourth LP, *Out of Our Heads*, which was recorded in mid-1965, the band moved toward the R & B-influenced hard rock sound of the rebellious, chart-topping "Satisfaction" which, according to Mick Jagger, dealt

Pete Townshend of The Who
Courtesy MCA/Chris Stamp

with "my frustration with everything. Simple teenage aggression." With the 1966 *Aftermath*, Jagger-Richards compositions such as the murky incantations of "Paint It Black" and the misogynist venom of "Under My Thumb" and "Stupid Girl" had almost totally replaced R & B covers. By the end of the year, the Rolling Stones vied with the Beatles for the rock-and-roll crown.

The Who

The Who made a similar transition from the blues to their own compositions. As with many other British invasion bands, The Who initially played Chicago blues. As the Detours, the band covered American blues songs such as Jimmy Reed's "Big Boss Man," Bo Diddley's "I'm a Man," and Willie Dixon's "I Just Wanna Make Love to You." The group, changing their name to the High Numbers, reworked bluesman Slim Harpo's "Got Love If You Want It" for their first single.

Pete Meaden, a freelance publicist who had worked with Andrew Logg Oldham, first managed and reshaped the R & B cover band. To distinguish the leather-clad boys from other blues cover bands in Britain, Meaden created a Mod image for the group. "I had this dream of getting a group together that would be the focus, the entertainers for the Mods; a group that would actually be the same people onstage as the guys in the audience. . . . an actual representation of the people," remembered the manager. "Our Mod image was engineered by our first manager, a very bright boy named Peter Meaden," recounted singer Roger Daltrey. "At the time in England, 90 percent of the bands resembled either the Rolling Stones or the Beatles. If anything, we were similar to the Stones. . . . The Mod look was very clean-cut, Ivy League, fashion conscious, which was exactly opposite from the Stones."

The band quickly adopted the clean-cut Mod style. "The original idea was for Roger [Daltrey] to dress up as a sharp top Mod: a face and the rest of the band to be in T-shirts and Levi's, boxing boots and the current 'in' clothes of a typical street Mod: a ticket," remarked Richard Barnes, an early confidant of the band. "Pete Meaden introduced the Who to the very hub of this exclusive group. He took them to the Scene Club in Ham Yard in London's Soho. This dark, dirty dingy basement not far from Piccadilly Circus was the 'in' place. Top Mods would check each other out and dance or stand around looking cool until about 4 o'clock in the morning," recalled Barnes. Guitarist Pete Townshend even "practiced the complicated steps to the two main Mod dances, the 'block' and the 'bang.' He rehearsed the Mod way of walking and tried to pick up the correct way of standing around."

In 1964, Meaden promoted the reworked blues single of the High Numbers as a Mod anthem. He titled the song "I'm the Face," a reference to a sharply dressed Mod. His press release called the record "the *first authentic* Mod record, a hip, tailored-for-teens R & B-oriented shuffle rocker . . . with a kick in every catchphrase for the kids of the fast-moving crowd . . . to cause an immediate rapport between the High Numbers and the thousands of young people like themselves. In a nutshell—they are the people." In the summer of the same year, Meaden negotiated with filmmakers Kit Lambert and Chris Stamp, the brother of actor Terence Stamp, to feature group in a film about the Mods.

After working on the film, the band fired Meaden and hired as managers Lambert and Stamp, who reinforced the Mod image of the group. On the advice of their new managers, recalled drummer Keith Moon, the band members went "to Carnaby Street with more money than we'd ever seen in our lives, like a hundred quid each. . . . We weren't into clothes, we were into music. Kit thought we should identify more with our audience. Coats slashed five inches at the side. Four wasn't enough. Six was too much. Five was just right." The band returned with garb that would become their trademark: bull's-eye T-shirts; and pants, shirts, and jackets cut from the British flag. The group renamed themselves The Who and played for 16 consecutive Tuesdays at the new London Marquee Club, a Mod hangout owned by Ziggy Jackson.

To complete the reshaping of The Who, Pete Townshend began to write original material for the band on the advice of the managers. He first penned "I Can't Explain." Though "Roger in particular wanted the band to be a blues based band and thought that 'I Can't Explain' was too pop sounding," according to Richard Barnes, Townshend followed with "Anyhow, Anyway, Anywhere." As his third song, he wrote "My Generation," which became the battle cry of the Mods. "That's my generation, that's how the song 'My Generation' happened, because of the Mods," Townshend explained.

The members of The Who grew up in the same working-class neighborhoods as other London Mods. Roger Daltrey, lead singer and organizer of the group at the age of 15, Townshend, and bassist John Entwistle were raised in Shepherd's Bush, a dilapidated suburb of West London. Before The Who gained notoriety, band members worked as manual laborers—Daltrey for five years as a sheet metal worker, and Townshend and Entwistle at various odd jobs. Keith Moon, the ebullient madman of The Who, who met an untimely death in 1978, grew up in Wembley and joined the band when he wandered into the Oldfield Hotel one day to listen to their show. Noticeable by his "dyed ginger hair and a ginger cord suit," Moon asked the band if he could play with them during one number. In the words of the drummer, "they said go ahead and I got behind this other guy's drums and did one song— 'Road Runner.' I'd several drinks to get me courage up and when I got onstage I went arrgggGhhhh on the drums, broke the bass drum pedal and two skins, and got off. I figured that was it. I was scared to death. Afterwards I was sitting at the bar and Pete came over. He said: 'You . . . come 'ere.' I said, mild as you please: 'Yes yes?' And Roger, who was the spokesman then, said: 'What are you doing next Monday?' I said: 'Nothing.' I was working during the day, selling plaster. He said: 'You'll have to give up work . . . there's this gig on Monday. If you want to come, we'll pick you up in the van.' I said: 'Right.' And that was it."

The Who's sound captured the anger and rebelliousness of the English Mods. Roger Daltrey screamed the lyrics of a song, backed by Townshend's crashing chords, the thumping bass of Entwistle, and Moon's propulsive drumming. Townshend, who wrote most of the band's material, felt that The Who's brand of rock-and-roll "is a single impetus and it's a single force which threatens a lot of crap which is around at the moment in the middle class and in the middle-aged politics or philosophy." Townshend's guitar-smashing antics and Moon's destruction of his drum kit accentuated the rebellious spirit of the band. Though reaching the height of their popularity during the late 1960s with the rock opera *Tommy*, the R & B-influenced group became the most popular band among British Mods. "The groups that you liked when you were a Mod were The Who," bragged Pete Townshend. "That's the story of why I dig the Mods, man, because we were Mods and that's how we happened."

The Blues Onslaught

Other British bands, enamored with Chicago blues, gained the allegiance of British and American teens. The Yardbirds were convinced of the power of the blues by the Rolling Stones. Around 1963, singer Keith Relf and drummer Jim McCarty "went to see the Rolling Stones because they started playing in Richmond, which was quite near . . . and we gradually listened to more of this R & B stuff, got more records," recollected McCarty. That year, McCarty's band, which included guitarists Chris Dreja and Top Topham, merged with Relf and bassist Paul Samwell-Smith, both of whom "wanted to play more R & B like Jimmy Reed, Howlin' Wolf and Chuck Berry."

The Yardbirds first performed as a backup band for Cyril Davies and in 1963 replaced the Rolling Stones as the house band at the Crawdaddy club, owned by the first manager of the Stones, Giorgio Gomelsky. They debuted on record with a cover of Chicago bluesman Billy Boy Arnold's "I Wish You Would" and first charted with Don & Bob's R & B standard, "Good Morning Little School Girl." On a December 1963 tour of England booked by Gomelsky, the band backed Sonny Boy Williamson. "A lot of the basis of our act was rearranged rhythm and blues," commented Dreja.

The Yardbirds featured a series of guitar wizards steeped in the blues. When lead guitarist Top Topham left for college in 1963, the band hired blues purist Eric Clapton, who "grew up loving black music." Clapton left the group in 1965 when he felt that the hit, "For Your Love," sounded too pop, and the band added the more rockabilly-influenced Jeff Beck. "We still played the blues—Jeff could play a great blues—but at the same time we were always looking to something new, something fresh," remarked McCarty. In 1966, Jimmy Page, who would later help invent heavy metal blues with Led Zeppelin, joined the group. By 1968, when they disbanded, the Yardbirds had scored blues-inspired hits in Britain and America with "I'm a Man," "Heart Full of Soul," "Shapes of Things," and "Over Under Sideways Down."

From the Muswell Hill region of London, a northern working-class suburb, came the Kinks. The band was formed in 1963 by R & B enthusiasts Ray and Dave Davies, Peter Quaife, and Mick Avory, who had briefly played with the Rolling Stones. In 1964, they unsuccessfully debuted with Little Richard's "Long Tall Sally." By September of the same year, the group topped the charts with "You Really Got Me," which almost defined power-chord rock. Dave Davies explained to *Melody Maker* that the distinctive sound originated because at that time "I was never a very good guitarist . . . so I used to experiment with sounds. I had a very small amplifier which distorted badly." The Kinks followed with the crunching "You Really Got Me" and "All Day and All of the Night" before turning toward a softer, music hall style. Although charting in America, the group met disaster when U. S. authorities instituted a four-year ban on them for unprofessional conduct after their first American tour in June 1965.

Spencer Davis, a teacher and blues enthusiast, formed another R & B-based band. In August 1963, he joined with drummer Peter York and the Winwood brothers, Steve and Muff, to start the Spencer Davis Group, which debuted with a remake of John Lee Hooker's "Dimples." "We were really heavily into the blues, blues singers and blues writers," remembered Davis. "Basically what we used to do was more or less copy—or do our own arrangements of—blues and rhythm 'n' blues records, which at the time were fairly unheard of," agreed Steve Winwood. Within two years, added Winwood, "we had an idea that we no longer wanted to actually copy, [we wanted] to write; we felt we could contribute ourselves toward the material." From 1965 to 1967, the band scored with their own blues-based compositions such as "Gimmie Some Lovin'," "Somebody Help Me," and "When I Come Home."

In 1962, Manfred Mann (a.k.a. Michael Lubowitz) teamed with Mike Hugg to become the Mann-Hugg Blues Brothers. After being greeted by wild receptions at the London Marquee Club, the duo added three more members to emerge as Manfred Mann and the Manfreds or, in the United States, as just Manfred Mann. In 1964, the band scored with "5-4-3-2-1," the theme of the popular British rock television show, "Ready, Steady, Go!," and topped the charts with a remake of the Exciters' "Do Wah Diddy Diddy." The band subsequently covered such R & B standards as Muddy Waters's "Got My Mojo Working," "Smokestack Lightning" by Howlin' Wolf, and Willie Dixon's "I'm Your Hoochie Coochie Man."

The Animals, a group of poor youths from a mining town in northern England who were named for their wild stage behavior, played a convincing brand of British R & B. In 1962, jazz organist Alan Price joined with lead guitarist Hilton Valentine, bassist Bryan "Chas" Chandler, drummer John Steel, and Eric Burdon, who had become captivated by Chicago blues after witnessing a Muddy Waters performance. Price was pushed in the direction of rhythm and blues by the new musicians, especially Burdon, who, according to New Musical Express, had "written out hundreds of lyrics by artists like Mose Allison and Chuck Berry. On the first page he had written the word Blues in his own blood. He had cut his finger especially for it." During their first two years, the Animals attracted a following at the Club-a-Go-Go in their hometown of Newcastle-on-Tyne. Price remembered that "we used to play everything from the blues to Chico Hamilton, and it used to swing like the clappers." After moving to London in 1964, the band reworked the folk blues "The House of the Rising Sun" into a million-selling hit. They then revived John Lee Hooker's "Boom Boom" and "I'm Mad Again," and Sam Cooke's "Bring It on Home to Me," and in the fall of 1964 triumphantly toured the United States.

George Ivan Morrison and his group, Them, were equally dedicated to American R & B. Raised in Ulster by parents who were blues and jazz enthusiasts, Van Morrison grew up listening to John Lee Hooker, Muddy Waters, Leadbelly, and Sonny Boy Williamson. At 15, he dropped out of school to join a band called the Monarchs, which headlined at the R & B Club in Belfast. In 1965, Morrison formed the group Them, which charted with "Baby, Please Don't Go" and "Here Comes the Night," and recorded "Gloria." Though hardly cracking the charts with "Gloria," which Morrison attributed to "listening to all those old blues records," the band defined a sound which would be emulated by thousands of garage bands in the United States during the next few years.

The British blues invasion of America provided notoriety for some blues pioneers. "We still have mostly Negro adults at our gigs," remarked B. B. King in 1966, but "I've noticed in the last year or so I've had a lot [more] of the white kids come than ever before." Muddy Waters noticed the same trend: "The Rolling Stones came out named after my song, you know, and recorded 'Just Make Love to Me' and the next thing I knew [white youths] were out there. And that's how people in the States really got to know who Muddy Waters was." In the mid-1960s, the sounds of Chicago blues ironically had been introduced to American youths by British bands. Soon the music of another group of African-Americans in Detroit would also become known to white teens.

The Animals, ca. 1965. Lead vocalist Eric Burdon is second from left
Frank Driggs Collection

7

Motown: The Sound of Integration

"This organization is built on love."

Berry Gordy

"This organization is built on love," 35-year-old Berry Gordy, the founder of Motown Productions, told *Newsweek* in early 1965. "We're dealing with feeling and truth."

Gordy, sounding much like Martin Luther King, Jr., created a music empire that exemplified the peaceful integration advocated by King and reflected the progress of the civil rights movement. The African-American-owned-and-operated Motown was established a year before the first sit-in demonstration and achieved moderate success during the civil rights strife of the early 1960s. The Detroit-based company, using the assembly-line techniques of the nearby auto factories, became a major force in popular music from late 1964 to 1967, when civil rights partisans won a series of significant legislative victories. At a time when the civil rights of African-Americans began to be recognized, Motown became the first African-American-owned label that consistently and successfully groomed, packaged, marketed, and sold the music of African-American youths to the white American masses.

Motown: The Early Years

Berry Gordy started his career in the music industry as a producer and songwriter. Born in Detroit in 1929, Gordy became interested in song-writing as a youth. "I did other things," he remembered. "I was a plasterer for a while in my father's business, took a job on an automobile assembly line. But I always wrote songs." In 1957, Gordy had his first success with the song "Reet Petite," which was recorded by Detroit-born Jackie Wilson, who had at one time replaced Clyde McPhatter as the lead singer of the Dominoes. The next year he penned the million-selling "Lonely Teardrops" for Wilson and established the Jobete Music Publishing Company. At the same time Gordy began to produce such records as the Miracles' "Got a Job" and "You," Eddie Holland's first single, and Brian Holland's "Shock."

In 1959, the same year that Don Kirshner started Aldon Music, Berry Gordy borrowed $800 from his family, rented an eight-room house at 2648 West Grand Boulevard, and founded the Motown Record Corporation, which would issue records under a variety of labels. "If I ever get this house and get it paid for," Gordy told his sister Esther at the time, "I'll have it made. I'll live upstairs, I'll have my offices down in the front part, and I'll have a studio out back where I can make demonstration records or masters to sell to record companies."

Gordy initially recorded rhythm-and-blues artists on Tamla Records. He signed Mabel John, the gospel-trained sister of blues singer Little Willie John, who described herself as "basically a blues singer." Gordy scored a minor hit with the first Tamla release, R & B singer Marv Johnson's "Come to Me," and later in his first year of operation co-wrote and released "Money," which was recorded by Barrett Strong and climbed to the number-two position on the R & B chart. In September 1959, the Motown founder recorded "Bad Girl" by young William "Smokey" Robinson and the Detroit-born Miracles, which reached number 93 on the pop charts with the help of national distribution by Chess Records.

Gordy became convinced by Smokey Robinson that Motown should distribute its own records. "When I started," Gordy told *Black Enterprise*, "we licensed our singles to other companies such as United Artists. Smokey Robinson gave me the idea to go national with my own product; my attorneys and other people said it was madness, that I shouldn't do it because a hit would throw me into bankruptcy since [we were] undercapitalized." In 1960, Gordy co-wrote and distributed "Shop Around" by Smokey Robinson and the Miracles, which hit the top of the charts and established Motown as an important independent company.

Throughout the next four years, Berry Gordy continued to produce hits by capitalizing on the girl-group craze. In 1959, 16-year-old Mary Wells, who had written a song for Jackie Wilson, approached the Motown founder. Unable to write music, she sang the song to Gordy, who immediately signed the teenager and released her version of "Bye

Martha (Reeves, far right)
and the Vandellas, ca. 1963

Bye Baby," which hit the Top 10 on the R & B chart in 1960. Two years later, Wells teamed with Smokey Robinson, who by now wrote and produced for Tamla and hit with "The One Who Really Loves You," "You Beat Me to the Punch," and "Two Lovers." The next year she recorded "Laughing Boy" and "Your Old Stand By." In 1964, Wells topped the pop charts with "My Guy."

Gordy also charted with the Marvelettes. "We were discovered at a talent show in Inkster [Michigan]," recalled Wanda Young, who founded the group with Gladys Horton. "One of our teachers arranged an audition for us with Motown, even though we didn't even win the contest. This was around 1961 and there were five of us then." The group signed with the label and released "Please Mr. Postman," written by Marvelette Georgeanna Dobbins, which became Motown's first number-one hit. The next year the Marvelettes hit the charts with "Playboy," "Beachwood 4-5789," "Someday, Someway," and "Strange I Know." In November 1962, the group toured the South in a bus and five cars as part of the first Motortown Revue and, according to Katherine Anderson of the Marvelettes, "did what we could to play for integrated audiences."

Berry Gordy, encouraged by his success with the Marvelettes, recorded another group of girls from Detroit, Martha and the Vandellas. Martha Reeves, influenced by gospel shouter Clara Ward and jazz singer Billie Holiday, joined with Annette Sterling, Rosalind Ashford, and Gloria Williamson to sing as the Del-Phis while in high school and recorded the unsuccessful "I'll Let You Know" for Chess. In 1961, Reeves accepted a job at Motown as a secretary and by 1962 convinced the company to record her group. The persistent trio sang backup vocals on a number of Motown hits, including "Hitch Hike" and "Stubborn Kind of Fellow" by Marvin Gaye, a romantic balladeer who had sung in the doo-wop group the Moonglows and in 1961 had joined Motown. In 1963, amid the girl-group explosion, Martha and the Vandellas hit the charts with "Come and Get These Memories" and followed with the million-selling "Heat Wave" and "Quicksand." The next year they recorded the memorable "Dancing in the Street," which neared the top of the pop charts, and along with hits by Mary Wells and the Marvelettes, identified Motown as a major source of the girl-group sound.

Civil Rights in the Great Society

The civil rights movement, which began in the 1950s and escalated during the early 1960s, resulted in significant achievements in 1964 and 1965 that would coincide with the Motown heyday.

On July 2, 1964, Congress passed the most sweeping civil rights legislation since the Civil War. The Civil Rights Act established a sixth-grade education as a minimum voting requirement and empowered the attorney general to protect the voting rights of all citizens. It forbade discrimination in such public places as restaurants, hotels, bathrooms and libraries, created an Equal Employment Opportunity Commission and a Community Relations Service to help communities solve racially based problems, banned discrimination in federally funded programs, and authorized technical and financial aid for school desegregation. Also in 1964, Congress ratified the Twenty-fourth Amendment to the U.S. Constitution, which outlawed the poll tax in federal elections.

Congress enacted the Voting Rights Act the next year after violence erupted in Selma, Alabama. Early in 1965, Sheriff James G. Clark forcibly resisted a voter-registration drive in Dallas County, Alabama, where no African-Americans had voted in years. He collected a posse wielding whips, clubs, and canisters of tear gas to disperse peaceful demonstrators, two of whom were murdered. Martin Luther King, Jr., and 3200 equal-rights partisans, protected by the Alabama National Guard, marched 50 miles from Selma to Montgomery to protest the blatant discrimination and violence. "No tide of racism can stop us," King exhorted 25,000 listeners in Montgomery after the completion of his five-day march.

Disturbed by the events in Selma, President Lyndon Johnson proposed greater voting safeguards for African-Americans and, in the words of the civil rights anthem, promised Congress that "we shall overcome." Congress complied with a law that banned the unfair literacy tests used in the South to disenfranchise African-Americans and authorized the attorney general to dispatch federal examiners to register voters in areas where local examiners discriminated on the basis of color. By the end of the year, nearly 250,000 African-Americans registered to vote for the first time.

President Lyndon Johnson also promised a Great Society "where the city of man served not only the needs of the body and the demands of commerce but the desire for beauty and the hunger for community." He encouraged America to ask "not only how much, but how good; not only how to create wealth, but how to use it; not only how fast we are going, but where we are headed."

To achieve his dream, Johnson pushed through Congress a series of bills designed to eradicate economic inequality. In 1964, Congress passed the Economic Opportunity Act, which declared a "war on poverty." It created the Office of Economic Opportunity, which included a Job Corps for high school dropouts; a Neighborhood Youth Corps for unemployed teens; the Volunteers in Service to America (VISTA), which was a domestic version of the Kennedy-established Peace Corps; a Head Start Program for disadvantaged children; and the Upward Bound Program, which prepared the poor to attend college.

The same year, Congress enacted the Criminal Justice Act, which provided the indigent with adequate legal representation. It passed the Food Stamp Act to provide groceries to needy families and ratified the Housing Act, which authorized $1 billion for urban renewal of the inner cities. Congress also agreed to cut taxes by $11.5 billion in two years, which Lyndon Johnson called "the single most important step that we have taken."

In 1965, Congress continued to legislate reforms. It passed the Elementary and Secondary Education Act, which earmarked more than $1.3 billion for the improvement of school districts that had desegregated. Congress also created Medicare, which provided medical and hospital insurance to the aged. Coupled with civil rights legislation, the new laws of the Great Society provided African-Americans with hope for a better future and seemed to be a giant step toward realizing the dream of Martin Luther King, Jr.

The Sound of Integration

In 1964, Berry Gordy assembled the parts of a music machine to create a distinctive Motown sound, which reflected and furthered the integration of African-Americans into white America. Gordy had always supported the peaceful integrationist program of Martin Luther King, Jr., who once had paid a brief visit to the Motown offices. In 1963, he had released a recorded version of King's "I Have a Dream" speech, delivered on the steps of the Lincoln Memorial at the end of the march on Washington, D.C. and another album of King's speeches, "Great March to Freedom." "Motown was a very strong backer of Martin Luther King's total program," asserted Motown producer Mickey Stevenson. "Berry felt that our job in Detroit was to make blacks aware of their culture, of the problems and some of the ways out of the problems. We'd showcase our artists to young kids at the Graystone Ballroom and it gave us a chance to get the youngsters off the street and see what our image was about . . . inspiring them a little to maybe live up to that imagery. Motown was a tremendous avenue of escape and hope." "I saw Motown much like the world Dr. King was fighting for," explained Gordy, "with people of different races and religions, working together harmoniously for a common goal."

Gordy, the son of an African-American entrepreneur who hoped for the upward mobility of African-Americans, specially groomed and cultivated streetwise teens from Detroit to make them acceptable to mainstream America. In 1964, he hired Maxine Powell, who formerly had operated a finishing and modeling school, to prep his performers. "The singers were raw," remembered Powell. "They were from the streets, and like most of us who came out of the [housing] projects, they were a little crude: Some were backward, some were arrogant. They had potential, but they were not unlike their friends in the ghetto. I always thought of our artists as diamonds in the rough who needed polishing. We were training them for Buckingham Palace and the White House, so I had my work cut out for me."

Powell tried to transform the Motown artists into polished professionals. "Many of them had abusive tones of voice, so I had to teach them how to speak in a nonthreatening manner," she explained. "Many of them slouched, so I had to show them what posture meant. Some were temperamental and moody; I would lecture them about their attitude. . . . I chose which clothes were best for them as well. We used to call them 'uniforms,' and before we had them specially made, I would have to choose outfits that would complement all of the people in a group, which wasn't easy. As far as makeup, I worked with all of the girls on wigs, nails, and that sort of thing. And on stage technique, I taught them little things like never turning their backs to an audience, never protruding their buttocks onstage, never opening their mouths too wide to sing, how to be well-rounded professionals." She also taught them the art of the inoffensive interview. "I had to force these lessons," Powell concluded. "The youngsters often had to be pushed and shoved."

A few months after adding Maxine Powell to the staff, Berry Gordy hired choreographer Cholly Atkins. Atkins, a well-known dancer in the 1930s and 1940s who had performed in the Cotton Club and the Savoy Ballroom, tried to teach the Motown groups to move gracefully. "What I was really trying to do with them was to teach them physical drama, which most of them had no respect for," he said. "My method for the Motown artists was that I always wanted them coming from someplace and going to someplace." Within a year, boasted Atkins, "we had the best-looking artists in the record business."

Atkins worked with Maurice King, who served as the executive musical director. King, who had arranged shows at Detroit's Flame Show Bar for years and had worked with such jazz artists as Billie Holiday and Dinah Washington, taught the Motown acts about stage patter. "My rehearsals were conducted like a class, a noninterrupted class," he recalled.

By the mid-1960s, Berry Gordy had assembled a Motown team that could take poor African-American youths from Detroit and teach

Marvin Gaye, ca. 1964

them to talk, walk, dress, and dance like successful debutantes and debonair gentlemen. "I'm sure that blacks were wearing tuxedos, top hats, wigs and eyelashes before Berry Gordy came along but not with the popular music we were recording, and not for the same reasons," observed one Motown staffer. "We really wanted young blacks to understand that you do not have to look like you came out of the ghetto in order to be somebody other blacks and even whites would respect when you made it big. They'll believe you had a rough childhood; you don't have to prove it to them by looking like hell."

Berry Gordy combined the polished image of the Motown acts with a gospel-based music that could appeal to the American mainstream. "Blues and R & B always had a funky look to it back in those days, and we at Motown felt that we should have a look that the mothers and fathers would want their children to follow. We wanted to kill the imagery of liquor and drugs and how some people thought it pertained to R & B," explained Motown producer Mickey Stevenson. "I did not like blues songs when choosing material for our artists, and Berry agreed with that," continued Stevenson. "We enjoyed John Lee Hooker and B. B. King just as much as the next guy, but we would reject anything that had a strong blues sound to it."

In place of blues and R & B, Gordy favored a distinctive music grounded by an insistent, pounding rhythm section, punctuated by horns and tambourines and featuring shrill, echo-laden vocals that bounced back and forth in the call-and-response of gospel. Building upon his experience with the girl-group sound, he produced a full sound both reminiscent and expanding upon Phil Spector's wall of sound. Aiming for the mass pop market, Gordy called the music "The Sound of Young America" and affixed a huge sign over the Motown studio that read "Hitsville U.S.A."

The Supremes on the Assembly Line

The Supremes fulfilled Berry Gordy's dream of a polished African-American act that sang gospel-based pop to both African-Americans and whites. Born in Detroit and meeting in the low-income Brewster housing project, Diana Ross, Mary Wilson, Florence Ballard, and Betty McGlown began singing together in high school, "when groups were becoming very popular with teenagers," recalled Wilson. They sang as the Primettes at sock hops and in 1960 won first prize at the Detroit/Windsor Freedom Festival talent contest. Late that year, after pestering Motown staffers for a few months, the group—which included Barbara Martin, who replaced Betty Travis—signed to Motown and on the advice of Berry Gordy changed their name. "One day I was working at my desk," recalled Motown songwriter Janie Bradford, "and Berry came up to me and said, 'I'm changing the name of this group called the Primettes, four giggly little girls. Come up with a name.' So I thought it over and came up with three names, put them in a hat on little slips of paper. Florence picked the Supremes."

The newly signed act had little success initially. In December 1960, the Supremes recorded "I Want a Guy," which attracted so little attention that Barbara Martin quit the group. During the next three years, the group recorded more than 40 songs, of which only 12 were released and met with limited success.

Around 1964, when Mary Wells left the company, Motown began to polish the Supremes. It sent the girls to Maxine Powell, who taught them proper etiquette and attire. "We spent only about six months working with Mrs. Powell, but anything we learned would be incorporated the same day," recalled Mary Wilson. "We would be out eating something, and if one of us accidentally picked up her chicken with her fingers, the other two would say, 'remember what Mrs. Powell said.'" The company also provided the group with lessons from music director Maurice King and choreographer Cholly Atkins.

The Supremes, groomed by the Motown organization, scaled the charts in 1964. After cracking the Top 30 with "When the Love Light Starts Shining Through His Eyes," the group recorded "Where Did Our Love Go," which was released just 15 days after the passage of the momentous Civil Rights Act; by the end of the year it topped both the pop and R & B charts. On December 24, 1964, the Supremes made their first of 20 appearances on "The Ed Sullivan Show," which had introduced both Elvis Presley and the Beatles to the American public. The Supremes, appearing in sleek, light blue chandelier gowns, embodied

The original Supremes; Diana Ross is at the top, ca. 1964

the Motown image of the slick, cultivated African-American entertainer and became overnight pop stars.

Berry Gordy, using methods practiced in the Detroit auto factories, ensured the continued success of the Supremes by assembling the parts of a hit-making machine that included standardized songwriting, an in-house rhythm section, a quality control process, selective promotion, and a family atmosphere reminiscent of the paternalism fostered by Henry Ford in his auto plant during the early twentieth century. "I worked in the Ford factory before I came in the [record] business, and I saw how each person did a different thing," Gordy reasoned. "And I said, 'Why can't we do that with the creative process?' It was just an idea of coming in one door one day and going out the other door and having all these things done."

The songwriting team of Brian Holland, Lamont Dozier, and Eddie Holland, joining forces in 1962, perfected the formula of success that they discovered with their composition "Where Did Our Love Go." From late 1964 to 1967, they wrote a series of number-one hits for the Supremes which rivaled the chart success of the Beatles and included "Baby Love," "Come See About Me," "Stop! In the Name of Love," "Back in My Arms Again," "I Hear a Symphony," "You Can't Hurry Love," "You Keep Me Hangin' On," and "Love Is Here and Now You're Gone." "When 'Where Did Our Love Go' hit for the Supremes," remembered Lamont Dozier, "we knew we had stumbled onto a sound. You'll notice that we patterned 'Baby Love' and 'Come See About Me' right after the first hit. In fact, all the Supremes' big hits were really children of 'Where Did Our Love Go' "

The different singles also sounded remarkably similar because of the in-house rhythm section known as the Funk Brothers who played on most of the Supremes' recording sessions. In 1964, Earl Van Dyke, a former be-bop jazz pianist who had toured with R & B singer Lloyd Price, became the leader of the studio band. He played with drummer Benny Benjamin and bassist James Jamerson, who had backed Jackie Wilson and the Miracles. Together with a few other musicians who joined them occasionally in the studio, the Funk Brothers provided the trademark percussive beat of the Motown sound.

Berry Gordy attempted to maintain the consistent quality of Motown material by conducting weekly meetings that scrutinized possible releases. "The quality control meetings on Fridays were real intense," remarked Motown songwriter Ron Miller. "All of the writers, producers, and many of the executives gathered in Berry's office, and he would play everyone's songs. And then he went around to everyone there and asked them for their opinion. It was brutal."

Berry Gordy carefully promoted the songs that were released through means that kept the slick Motown image intact. Besides spots on "The Ed Sullivan Show," he snagged appearances for the Supremes on such mainstream television programs as "The Dean Martin Show," "The Tonight Show," "Hollywood Palace," a special presented by African-American crooner Sammy Davis, Jr., and the Orange Bowl Parade. For concerts, Gordy favored such posh settings as the Copacabana in New York, which hosted the Supremes in July 1965; the Yale University prom of 1965, which featured jazz great Duke Ellington and the Supremes; and exclusive Las Vegas hotels such as the Flamingo, where the Supremes performed in 1967. He even asked established entertainers such as Sammy Davis, Jr., and Broadway star Carol Channing to write the liner notes for Supremes' albums.

Gordy retained control of the successful group by creating a family atmosphere at the company. In 1965, like a watchful father, he limited each Supreme to a $100 weekly allowance and funneled the remainder of their $300,000 profit for the year into a joint bank account. The Motown owner refused to allow the girls to date and, to fend off possible suitors, gave each girl a diamond ring. "They're Christmas presents from Gordy," Florence Ballard told *Newsweek* about her ring in 1965. "Someone saw mine the other week," chimed Mary Wilson. "He said, 'Oh, you're engaged.' I said, 'Yeah. To Motown.' " "You have to be very strict with young artists," asserted Berry Gordy, sounding like a stern father. "That instills discipline."

The Motown Stable

Berry Gordy's paternal, production-line approach produced other successful performers such as the Temptations. In 1957, the 15-year-old, Detroit-raised Otis Williams started a street-corner doo-wop group with a few friends, including Elbridge Bryant. Two years later he invited teenager Melvin Franklin to join and named the group the Elegants,

The Temptations, ca. 1964
Frank Driggs Collection

then the Questions, and finally the Distants, who released "Come On" on Warwick Records. Later in 1959, on the advice of local Detroit promoter Milton Jenkins, the group added Eddie Kendricks and Paul Williams and renamed themselves the Primes.

In 1960, between sets at a local club, Williams walked into the bathroom and met Berry Gordy, who complimented the group and eventually signed them to Motown by the end of the year. Renamed the Temptations when signed by Gordy, from 1960 to 1964 the group released several singles, which met only moderate success.

Berry Gordy shaped the Temptations into the Motown image and placed them on the charts by 1964. He replaced their processed hair styles with carefully cropped Afros, discarded their casual clothes for top hats and tails, inserted such standards as "Old Man River" into their repertoire, and added the precise choreography of Motown dance master Cholly Atkins to their stage show.

When David Ruffin replaced Elbridge Bryant, the refurbished Temptations recorded the Smokey Robinson composition, "My Girl," an answer to the Mary Wells hit "My Guy" that topped both the pop and R & B charts in early 1965. The group remained on the charts with a series of songs including "Since I Lost My Baby" and "Get Ready" by Smokey Robinson, and "Ain't Too Proud To Beg," "Beauty Is Only Skin Deep," and "(I Know) I'm Losing You," all by Eddie Holland and Norman Whitfield who, with Robinson and the Holland-Dozier-Holland team, formed the legendary Motown songwriting-production crew.

This Motown team revived the careers of other former doo-woppers, the Four Tops. The group, Levi Stubbs, Renaldo Benson, Lawrence Payton, and Abdul Fakir, grew up together in Detroit during the late 1940s; in 1954 they banded together as the Four Aims, which released "Kiss Me Baby" in 1956 on Chess Records. The vocal group began to back jazz vocalist Billy Eckstine and in 1960 signed with Columbia and recorded the unsuccessful "Ain't That Love." In 1962, they signed with Riverside Records and recorded "When Are You," which also failed to chart. "We were working," recalled Abdul Fakir, "perfecting our craft and just out there hustling. Guess you could say were we getting ready for the Chairman."

Chairman Berry Gordy signed the group in 1963, dressed them in tuxedos, and within a year paired them with the songwriting team of Holland-Dozier-Holland, who wrote "Baby I Need Your Loving," a smooth, gospel-flavored composition that hit the number-11 slot on the pop charts. Gordy continued to provide the Four Tops with Holland-Dozier-Holland material, including the number-one pop hits "I Can't Help Myself" and "Reach Out I'll Be There" and other chartbusters such as "Shake Me, Wake Me (When It's Over)," "Standing in the Shadows of Love," and "It's the Same Old Song." As with the Supremes and the Temptations, the Four Tops benefited from the Motown finishing school, the dance classes, the music direction, and the promotion to become a slick, popular act that appealed to both white and African-American audiences.

During the mid-1960s, Berry Gordy had established a music empire that included eight record labels, a management service, and a publishing company and grossed millions of dollars a year. From 1964 through 1967, Motown placed 14 number-one pop singles, 20 number-one singles on the R & B charts, 46 more Top 15 pop singles, and 75 other Top 15 R & B records. In 1966 alone, 75 percent of all Motown releases hit the charts. "It is no coincidence," observed a British newspaper columnist in 1965 amid a Motown tour of England, "that while 10,000 Negroes are marching for their civil rights in Alabama, the Tamla-Motown star is on the ascendent." Berry Gordy, putting into action the program of peaceful integration, had created one of the most commercially successful African-American-owned enterprises and certainly the most successful African-American-owned record company.

In 1967, the Motown empire began to decline. A few days before a scheduled performance by the Supremes at the Hollywood Bowl in April, Berry Gordy fired Florence Ballard, who had become jealous of the increasingly prominent position of Diana Ross, and replaced her with Cindy Birdsong. In July 1968, he discharged David Ruffin of the Temptations and substituted Dennis Edwards. Gordy quarreled about royalty rates with the songwriting-production team of Holland-Dozier-Holland, who in 1968 quit the company and filed suit against Motown. When the inner cities exploded in rage and thousands of young college students took to the streets to protest the war in Vietnam, the Motown machine had begun to slow down.

8

Acid Rock

"We have a private revolution going on."
**A handbill distributed from the Blue Unicorn,
a coffeehouse in the Haight**

"Everybody's relaxing and not afraid to speak out and not afraid not to wear a tie to work," asserted Marty Balin, one of the founders of the Jefferson Airplane, which took off in San Francisco during the mid-1960s. "The one word I can think of is love, even though that sounds like a cliché, but that's where it's at, it's uninhibited, coming out emotion. It's like the twenties. The twenties were really a start and at the end of it, they had all these great creative different things come out of it. I really feel it's the same. It's the most moving generation since the twenties. In creativity. And out of this are going to come many wonderful artists and people and thinkers. Even the philosophy of the day is being changed by what's happening now."

Speak out, love, creatively, moving generation, uninhibited, happening now became the bywords of a new era. In the wake of the British invasion, thousands of middle-class, college-educated youths clustered around San Francisco Bay to demonstrate to the country, and eventually to the world, that love could replace war, sharing could replace greed, and community could supersede the individual. These San Francisco visionaries strove for nothing less than a total transformation of

America, which they demanded immediately. As Jim Morrison, lead singer of the Doors, screamed: "We want the world, and we want it *now.*"

A new hybrid of rock-and-roll reflected and helped propagate the new culture. Named after a strange new drug, LSD, acid rock broadcast the word of hippiedom from the epicenter, San Francisco, to the hinterlands. Unlike the working-class British invaders who used music to entertain, the West Coast bands such as the Jefferson Airplane, the Grateful Dead, Quicksilver Messenger Service, and countless others (1500 by one count) led the youth movement that consciously withdrew from America's nine-to-five, workaholic society and tried to create an alternative community built upon love. From 1965 to 1967, the vanguard of rock-and-roll had a mission.

The Beats

The social upheaval of hippiedom had its origins with the Beats, who had wandered from their homes in New York City to San Francisco's North Beach more than a decade earlier. In 1951, Jack Kerouac, the Columbia University football-star-turned-writer, planted the seeds of the Beat Generation when he bummed around the country with the ever-energetic, ever-adventuresome Neal Cassady and told of their travels in his book *On the Road*. The same year, poet Lawrence Ferlinghetti left New York for San Francisco because "it was the only place in the country where you could get decent wine cheap." Two years later he opened the prime beatnik haunt in North Beach, City Lights Bookstore. Also in 1953, Allen Ginsberg migrated to San Francisco on the advice of his friend Neal Cassady. Two years later he organized the first public appearance of the Beat Generation—a poetry reading advertised as "Six Poets at the Six Gallery," at which he premiered his controversial poem, "Howl," which the San Francisco Police Department first declared obscene, then banned and confiscated. In 1957, Kerouac finally published *On the Road*, to the critical acclaim of *The New York Times*.

The Beats formulated a countercultural philosophy based upon tenets of Eastern religion. Their metaphorical name—Beat—suggested the quest for beatitude that could be discovered in Zen Buddhism. It also referred to the patron saints of the movement, the drifters, who shed the trappings of institutional society and gathered in places such as New York City's Bowery. Although appearing "beat down" and downtrodden to "straights," the bums symbolized the freedom that the avant-garde so dearly cherished. As one writer put it, the beatniks "chased the unwashed American dream." Finally, the term alluded to the beat of jazz, especially the be-bop of such artists as Charlie Parker and Dizzy Gillespie and the cool jazz of Miles Davis, Lennie Tristano, and Gerry Mulligan, who were considered cultural heroes by the Beat writers.

Congregating in San Francisco and New York City's Greenwich Village, these countercultural literati lambasted traditional American

Poet Allen Ginsberg: a bridge between the Beats and the Hippies
The Daily of the University of Washington

values. In his once-banned *Naked Lunch* (1959), William S. Burroughs, the literary genius who had inherited the Burroughs adding-machine fortune, wove together powerful, graphic images of a decaying society: "Smell of chili houses and dank overcoats and atrophied testicles . . . A heaving sea of air hammers in the purple brown dusk tainted with rotten metal smell of sewer gas." Ginsberg penned such anti-establishment poems as "America" (1956) which blasted racism against African-Americans and Native Americans and criticized the Army and the "sixteen hours a day" work ethic. "America I've given you all and now I'm nothing," the poem began. "I'm sick of your insane demands."

In place of traditional bourgeois values, the Beats preached a cultural relativism. "We love everything," explained Kerouac. "Billy Graham, the Big Ten, Rock and Roll, Zen, apple pie, Eisenhower—we dig it all." Believing no value to be absolute, the Beats felt that morality depended upon the individual. As one Beat argued, "I stay cool, far out, alone. When I flip it's over something *I* feel, only me."

Such an ethos led to experimentation with sex and drugs, especially marijuana and amphetamines, which Kerouac mentioned in *Dharma Bums* and Ginsberg glorified in his poetry. "They had no interest in building a greater America, in fighting Communism, in working at a career to buy hundred-dollar suits and dresses, color television sets, a house in the suburbs, or a flight to Paris," observed writer Burton Wolfe. "In fact, they laughed at those goals. Some brew, a few joints, a sympathetic partner in the sack, a walk in the park, an afternoon of lying in the sun on the beach, a hitchhike trip to Mexico—this was all there was."

The Fugs performing at the
Fillmore East, 1969
Photo © Raeanne Rubenstein

The anti-institutional values of the Beats led to an adverse reaction from more traditional quarters. Right-wing FBI director J. Edgar Hoover, turning literary critic in 1959, reviewed Lawrence Ferlinghetti's poem "Tentative Description of a Dinner Given to Promote the Impeachment of President Eisenhower," concluding "it appears that Ferlinghetti may possibly be a mental case." A month later, the Alcoholic Beverages Commission declared North Beach a "problem area" and refused to issue any more liquor licenses. Other, more violent critics bombed the women's rest room at the Co-Existence Bagel Shop, a favorite gathering spot for the San Francisco Beats which, along with The Place, closed down shortly thereafter. By the end of 1959 Eric Nord, one of the most visible West Coast Beat writers, told a courtroom that "the Beat Generation is dead. I don't go to North Beach anymore."

The Reemergence of the Beats: The New York Connection

Some of the Beats reappeared on the cultural scene to parent the psychedelic movement during the mid-1960s. On the East Coast, at St. Mark's Place in Greenwich Village in 1965, Beat poets Tuli Kupferberg, Ken Weaver, and Ed Sanders, the editor of *Fuck You: A Magazine of the Arts*, started the Fugs. "We used to read at the Metro, on Second Avenue," recalled Kupferberg. "After the readings, we'd go to the Dom, on St. Mark's Place . . . where lots of young people would go. The jukebox had Beatles and Stones albums on it, and some of the kids would dance. Once they started, the other paper-assed intellectuals tried to get up and dance, too. And Ed Sanders got the idea it might be good to try to combine some of our poetry with rock music."

The band caricatured American society, in the process using the verse of William Blake in "How Sweet I Roamed from Field to Field" and the prose of William S. Burroughs in "Virgin Forest." Allen Ginsberg described the countercultural message of the group in the liner notes on the Fugs' second album, released in 1966. "The United States is split down the middle," he contended. "On one side are everybody who make love with their eyes open, maybe smoke pot and maybe take LSD and look inside their heads to find the Self-God Walt Whitman prophesied for America. . . . Who's on the other side? People who think we are *bad*. . . . Yogis and Beatles say there is no other side. 'We can get along.' Can we? NOW sings Sanders and the Fugs come camping and screaming along, out in the open where every ear can hear the soul politics ecstasy message—They've put it in Front. . . . The Fugs came to tell the truth that was only dreamy till they opened their mouths for Whitmanic orgy yawp. Group Grope, Dirty Old Man, Skin Flowers and Frenzy! Teenagers rise up and understand. When they scream 'Kill for Peace' they're announcing publicly the madness of our white-haired crazy governments." The poet concluded: "The Bible says that when Christ comes back, 'every eye shall see.' Now every ear can hear, and when the Fugs break thru the monopoly blockade and their image is broadcast on National Television, every kid in America and most white-haired old suffering men will turn them on with Relief at last and every eye shall see."

The Velvet Underground drew inspiration from the same Beat source. In 1964, at a party in New York City, songwriter Lou Reed met John Cale, who had been performing with an avant-garde classical ensemble, and decided to form a band. "When I first met Lou, we were interested in the same things," recalled Cale. "We both needed a vehicle. Lou needed one to carry out his lyrical ideas and I needed one to carry out my musical ideas." They enlisted the help of guitarist Sterling Morrison and drummer Angus MacLise, who the next year was replaced by Maureen Tucker, to begin playing as the Primitives at local clubs.

Avant-garde artist Andy Warhol helped the band achieve notoriety. After meeting Reed and Cale through mutual friends in 1965, Warhol agreed to manage the group, adding Hungarian chanteuse Nico. He showcased the band, named the Velvet Underground after a pornographic novel, at his Factory and added them to his multimedia extravaganza, the Exploding Plastic Inevitable. "He was the catalyst," remarked Reed about Warhol years later.

Reed, who wrote the lyrics for the band, derived his ideas from Beat sources. The songwriter, who had studied at Syracuse University with Beat poet Delmore Schwartz, crafted songs that dealt with the down-and-out themes of Beat fiction—heroin addiction in "I'm Waiting for the Man" and the rushing "Heroin," and cocaine in "Run, Run, Run." In one Velvet album, Reed led the listener through the adventures of a girl named Candy, who roamed the cultural underground assisted by her junkie boyfriend. The sexual and drug-related themes of the Velvet

Underground, Reed later mentioned, were "only taboo on records. Let's keep that in mind. Movies, plays, books, it's all there. You read Ginsberg, you read Burroughs."

The Haight-Ashbury Scene

The Beats resurfaced in San Francisco to inspire the hippies, as *San Francisco Examiner* writer Michael Fallon first called them in September 1965. At the first hippie gathering, held at Longshoremen's Hall near Fishermen's Wharf on October 16, 1965, wrote journalist Ralph Gleason, "long lines of dancers snaked through the crowd for hours holding hands. Free-form improvisation ('self-expression') was everywhere. The clothes were a blast. Like a giant costume party." Amid the revelry whirled a long-haired, bearded Allen Ginsberg.

Three weeks later, on November 6, Allen Ginsberg appeared at the Appeal, a benefit rock concert for the San Francisco Mime Troupe, an avant-garde theater group managed by Bill Graham. He brought his Beat friends, the Fugs, who flew in from New York for the event, mingling with hundreds of free-minded participants who lived in the surrounding Haight-Ashbury district near San Francisco State College. At the end of the evening, Ginsberg chanted as the Hashbury hippies cleaned the Mime Troupe loft.

For three days in late January 1966, Beat writer Ken Kesey, author of *One Flew Over the Cuckoo's Nest* (1962), and his band of free spirits known as the Merry Pranksters, hosted the Trips Festival, which attracted more than 6600 people. For the event they enlisted the services of the Grateful Dead and Big Brother and the Holding Company; set up five movie screens, on which they projected a mind-boggling combination of colors and shapes; and spiked the punch with a little LSD, a concoction that became known as the Kool-Aid acid test. At the festivities, Kesey stalked the floor dressed in a space helmet and a jumpsuit and periodically composed free-form poetry on an overhead projector. Eyewitness Ralph Gleason saw one man "bandaged all over, with only his eyes peeking out through dark glasses, carrying a crutch and wearing a sign: 'You're in the Pepsi generation and I'm a pimply freak.' Another long-haired exotic dressed in a modified Hell's Angels' leather jerkin that had 'Under Ass Wizard Mojo Indian Fighter' stenciled on his back. Several varieties of Lawrence of Arabia costumes wandered through." At one point Neal Cassady, the Beat High Priest who had appeared in Kerouac's *On the Road* as Dean Moriarty and had inspired the Indian in Kesey's *Cuckoo's Nest*, "stood for a while upstairs and then swung out and over the back of the balcony railing, scaring everyone who saw him, as they expected him to slip and fall to the floor." Cassady would reappear at countless Grateful Dead concerts to deliver amazing free-associational monologues as preludes to the performances. He also sat at the helm of the psychedelic bus that took Kesey and the Merry Pranksters on a symbolic trip across the country that later inspired the Beatles' Magical Mystery Tour.

Neal Cassady especially influenced the Grateful Dead, the premier psychedelic band. "There's no experience in my life yet that equals riding with Cassady in like a '56 Plymouth or a Cadillac through San Francisco or from San Jose to Santa Rosa," remembered Jerry Garcia, lead guitarist for the Dead. "He was the ultimate *something*—the ultimate person as art." "When I fell in with Ken Kesey and Neal Cassady, it seemed like home sweet home to me," added Bob Weir, another Dead guitarist. "We picked up a lot from those guys. Particularly from Cassady."

Other Beats helped organize the "First Human Be-In," which took place in Golden Gate Park Stadium on January 14, 1967. Allen Ginsberg, painter Michael Bowen, playwright Michael McClure, and poets Lenore Kandal and Gary Snyder helped stage the multicolored community gathering, which attracted 20,000 people on an unseasonably warm day. Early in the morning Ginsberg and Snyder opened the proceedings by conducting an ancient Hindu blessing ritual, the *dakshina*, around the Polo Field to ensure its suitability for the coming pilgrimage. Throughout the day hippies danced on the grass to the sounds of the Grateful Dead, the Jefferson Airplane, and Quicksilver Messenger Service. "The costumes were a designer's dream, a wild polyglot mixture of Mod, Paladin, Ringling Brothers, Cochise and Hell's Angels' Formal," wrote Ralph Gleason in the *San Francisco Chronicle*. "The poets read. Allen Ginsberg (who may yet be elected president) chanted and Gary Snyder sat on the stage and joined in. Bells rang and balloons floated in the air. A man went around handing out oranges and there were sandwiches and candy and cookies. No one was selling anything." The celebration ended when Gary Snyder blew on a conch shell, the ritual instrument of the Yamabushi sect of Japanese Buddhism, and Allen Ginsberg led a chant of "Om Shri Maitreya" to the Coming Buddha of Love.

When news of these remarkable events spread to the burgeoning ranks of college-aged baby boomers, the psychedelic ranks in San Francisco began to swell. "Like, wow! There was an explosion," remarked Jay Thelin, co-owner with his brother Ron of the Psychedelic Shop, which served as the briefing center for hippie initiates to the city. "People began coming in from all over and our little information shop became sort of a clubhouse for dropouts and, well, we just let it happen, that's all." By 1967, 50,000 hippies resided in or near the Haight-Ashbury district of San Francisco.

The Hippie Culture

Many who flocked to the Haight were baby boomers who had grown up in educated, middle-class homes. Most of the hippies, wrote journalist Hunter Thompson, who lived in San Francisco at the time, "were white and voluntarily poor. Their backgrounds were largely middle class; many had gone to college." According to a report by a San Francisco State sociologist, H. Taylor Buckner, 96 percent of the Haight hippies were between the ages of 16 and 30; 68 percent had attended college for a time; and 44 percent had a father who had earned a college degree.

The hippies, like the Beats, criticized the bourgeois values with which they had been raised. "The standard thing is to feel in the gut that middle-class values are all wrong," remarked one hippie. "It's the system itself that is corrupt," added another. "Capitalism, communism, whatever it is. These are phony labels. There is no capitalism or communism. Only dictators telling people what to do." The hippies, remarked Peter Cohan of the Haight, "are the fruit of the middle class and they are telling the middle class they don't like what has been given them."

The hippies, raised in an age of relative affluence, attacked the materialistic American culture that had been formed and embraced by their Depression-bred parents. "I have no possessions," remarked Joyce Ann Francisco of the *San Francisco Oracle*, the preeminent psychedelic newspaper published by Ron Thelin in the Haight. "Money is beautiful only when it is flowing. When it piles up it's a hangup." "I could have a job selling real estate in Tahoe for $400 a week anytime, but that isn't what I want," agreed Jay Thelin of the Psychedelic Shop. The residents of the Haight, noticed historian Arnold Toynbee when he toured the District during spring 1967, "repudiate the affluent way of life in which making money is the object of life and work. They reject their parents' way of life as uncompromisingly as Saint Francis rejected the rich cloth merchants' way of life of his father in Assisi."

Many hippies challenged other dominant values. Morning Glory, a long-haired, 22-year-old hippie, felt that the "human body is a beautiful thing. It should be displayed. I want people to see what I look like, and I want to see what they look like without a bunch of clothes covering them up. Nude, everybody is in the same bag, the same economic class."

Such a freewheeling attitude toward nudity, coupled with the use of the birth control pill by more than 6 million women in 1966, a decade after its introduction to the general public, led to a rejection of sexual taboos. As early as 1965, Haight residents started the Sexual Freedom League to confront traditional standards concerning sex. Within two years, hundreds of youths engaged in premarital sex with many partners, continuing a trend that had intensified with the Beats. "The 60s will be called the decade of the orgasmic preoccupation," predicted Dr. William Masters, the director of the Institute for Sex Research at Indiana University. "Young people are far more tolerant and permissive regarding sex."

To distinguish themselves from, and many times to antagonize, the middle-class American mainstream, male hippies generally wore their hair long. "As for bad vibrations emanating from my follicles, I say great," wrote James Simon Kunen in the *Strawberry Statement*. "I want the cops to sneer and the old ladies to swear and the businessmen to worry."

By challenging authority, the hippies hoped to create an atmosphere that engendered freedom of individual expression. "We have a private revolution going on," read a handbill distributed by the Blue Unicorn, a coffeehouse in the Haight. "A revolution of individuality and diversity that can only be private."

The hippies turned to mind-expanding drugs to enhance their individual potentials. Most rolled marijuana or the more expensive hashish into joints or smoked the weed Indian-style in pipes. In 1965, Haight residents organized the Legalize Marijuana movement (LEMER), which held meetings at the Blue Unicorn. By the end of the decade, more than 96 percent of the hippies in the Haight had smoked marijuana and more than 10 million youths across the nation had tried the drug.

Another drug, the hallucinogen LSD (lysergic acid diethylamide), defined the hippie experience. Discovered in Switzerland in April 1943 and legal in the United States until October 6, 1966, "acid" fragmented everyday perception into a multitude of melting shapes and vibrant colors. "The first thing you notice is an incredible enhancement of sensory awareness," related Timothy Leary, the ex-Harvard professor who edited the *Psychedelic Review*, organized the LSD-based League for Spiritual Discovery, and became the most visible popularizer and high priest of acid. "Take the sense of sight. LSD vision is to normal vision as normal vision is to the picture of a badly tuned television set. Under LSD, it's as though you have microscopes up to your eyes, in which you see jewel-like, radiant details of anything your eye falls upon. . . . The organ of the Corti in your inner ear becomes a trembling membrane seething with tattoos of sound waves. The vibrations seem to penetrate deep inside you, swell and burst there. . . . You not only hear but *see* the music emerging from the speaker system like dancing particles, like squirming curls of toothpaste."

Timothy Leary contended that the drug experience resulted in altered, introspective states that expanded individual consciousness. In September 1966, comfortably lying on a mattress in his headquarters, a 64-room mansion in Millbrook, New York, about 35 miles from Woodstock, he outlined the various states of consciousness to *Playboy:* "The lowest level of consciousness is sleep—or stupor, which is produced by narcotics, barbiturates and our national stuporfactant, alcohol. The second level of consciousness is the conventional wakeful state, in which awareness is hooked to conventional symbols: flags, dollar signs, job titles, brand names, party affiliations and the like. . . . In order to reach [the third level], you have to have something that will turn *off* the symbols and open up your billions of sensory cameras to the billions of impulses that are hitting them. The chemical that opens the door to this level has been well known for centuries. . . . It is marijuana. . . . But we must bid a sad farewell to the sensory level of consciousness and go on to the fourth level, which I call the cellular level. It is well known that the stronger psychedelics such as mescaline and LSD take you *beyond* the senses into a world of cellular awareness. During an LSD session, enormous clusters of cells are turned on, and consciousness whirls into eerie panoramas for which we have no words or concepts." Leary advised readers to "turn on, tune in and drop out."

Many heeded Leary's advice. "Grass and LSD are the most important factors in the community," remarked Jay Thelin. "You should acquaint yourself with all of the consciousness-expanding drugs. I turn on every Sunday with acid, and I smoke grass everyday, working continuously with an expanding consciousness." "The only way to understand," agreed Gabe Katz of the *San Francisco Oracle*, "is to turn on. The chemicals are essential. Without them you can ask a million questions and write a million words and never get it." On October 6, 1966, when legislation outlawing LSD took effect, hundreds of residents in the Haight staged a Love Pageant to assert the "inalienable rights" of "freedom of the body, the pursuit of joy, and the expansion of consciousness." In 1966, an official from the Food and Drug Administration estimated that more than 10 percent of all college students had ingested LSD and more than 90 percent of youths in the Haight had taken the drug. Many of the hippies had obtained LSD from chemist Augustus Owsley Stanley III, the grandson of Senator A. Owsley Stanley of Kentucky, who had produced and distributed an estimated 15 million acid tabs and sometimes dispensed them free at events such as the Trips Festival.

With their newfound consciousness, the hippies embraced the beliefs of past, less technology-driven civilizations, real or imagined, to create a counterculture. Some followed the example of the Beats by looking for salvation in the mysteries of the Orient. One San Francisco free spirit expounded that "society feeds us machines, technology, computers and we answer with primitivism: the I Ching, the Tibetan Book of the Dead, Buddhism, Taoism. The greatest truths lie in the ancient cultures. Modern civilization is out of balance with nature." Many hippies adopted the teachings of Zen popularizer Alan Watts, and some joined Hare Krishna when in January 1967 the International Society for Krishna Consciousness moved to the Haight and Allen Ginsberg declared that a Hare Krishna mantra "brings a state of ecstasy."

Attempting to recapture a lost innocence, some tried to recreate the popular image of the noble American Indian. They slipped into moccasins and sported fringed deerskin jackets, headbands, feathers, and colorful beads. Many hippies painted their faces and bodies for festive occasions, as did Native Americans for ceremonies. In September 1965, the Committee Theater in the Haight staged a multimedia extravaganza, "America Needs Indians," and a few months later took their show to the acid tests. In January 1967, organizers of the Human Be-In in Golden Gate Park called the event a "Pow Wow" and a "Gathering of Tribes," advertising it with a poster that pictured a Plains Indian on horseback clutching a blanket in one hand and an electric guitar in the other. The *San Francisco Oracle* philosophized that "the white-eye who once annihilated the buffalo must now, in an action-reacted, be saved from slaughtering himself by the Indian incarnate."

Timothy Leary: the guru of LSD
The Daily of the University of Washington

Even though most Native Americans such as Robert Costo, president of the American Indian Historical Society, believed that the hippies practiced a "certain insidious exploitation of the Indian which is the worst of all," residents of the Haight created a cult of tribalism. "For one of the yearly Tribal Stomp dances at the Avalon, we gave everyone a little leather thong with a little Indian bell and a long white turkey feather tied to it," recalled Chet Helms, manager of the dance hall. "I can't tell you how effective that thematic favor was. It made everyone a member of the tribe."

Some, adhering to the notion of tribalism, banded together in communal living arrangements. At Drop City near Trinidad, Colorado, 22 midwestern hippies built and lived in geodesic domes constructed from automobile hoods. Roughly 40 miles from San Francisco near ebastopol, more than 50 hippies communally farmed the 31-acre Morningstar Ranch. Morningstar founder Lou Gottlieb, who held a Ph.D. in musicology and had played in the folk group the Limeliters, envisioned the Ranch as "an alternative for those who can't make it in the straight society and don't want to. . . . This sort of thing could be a beautiful alternative for people who are technologically unemployable and for other people it would be a retreat where they could come and re-create, I mean really re-create themselves. I can see ten Morningstars in every state, where people from straight society would come to live for a while in the 'alternative society,' a whole different culture based on non-competition." In the Haight itself, reported a San Francisco State sociologist, more than 25 percent of the hippies lived with ten or more people.

Some hippies, believing in a noncompetitive, tribalistic society, shared their resources with others. The Diggers, most of them former members of the San Francisco Mime Troupe who named themselves after a seventeenth-century society of English agricultural altruists, provided free food, shelter, and transportation to needy hippies in the Haight-Ashbury district. A Digger leaflet distributed at the October 1966 Love Pageant advertised "free food, everyday, free food, it's free because it's yours." The Prunes in Cleveland, the Brothers in Seattle, and the Berkeley Provos followed the Digger example.

Even the shopkeepers in the Haight exhibited a community spirit. On November 23, 1966, the *San Francisco Examiner* told its readers that "the hip purveyors of painting, poetry, handcrafted leather and jewelry along Haight Street, having been blackballed by the Haight Merchants' Association, have formed their own Haight Street Merchants' Association, HIP for short." Once organized, HIP established a job cooperative to cope with the incoming hippies and provided free legal advice. Psychedelic Shop owners Jay and Ron Thelin additionally devoted over a third of their shop's floor space to a "calm center," where hippies could meditate, rap, or sleep.

The hippies cultivated personal appearances that reflected the elements of their counterculture. In 1966, Janis Joplin, lead singer for Big Brother and the Holding Company, described Haight fashion in a letter to her family. "The girls are, of course, young and beautiful looking with long straight hair. The beatnik look, I call it, is definitely in. Pants, sandals, capes of all kinds, far-out handmade jewelry, or loose-fitting dresses and sandals. . . . The boys are the real peacocks," observed the singer about the colorful, acid-inspired male attire. "All hair at least Beatle length. And very ultramod dress—boots, *always* boots, tight low pants in houndstooth check, stripes, even polka dots! Very fancy shirts—prints, very loud, high collars, Tom Jones full sleeves. Fancy print ties, Bob Dylan caps. Really too much. . . . The younger girls," added Joplin, "wear very tight bell-bottoms cut very low around the hips and short tops—bare midriffs," which reflected the ongoing sexual revolution and contributed to the doubling of the sales of Levi Strauss jeans from 1963 to 1966. The hippies had created a fashion that exemplified a counterculture influenced by the Beats, accessed by LSD, and based upon a loose-knit community of individuals who focused upon self-expression.

By the mid-1960s, hundreds of newspapers were established to promulgate the countercultural ethos. In 1964, Art Kunkin started the *Los Angeles Free Press*, an underground newspaper modeled after the *Village Voice* in New York. In late 1966, the *San Francisco Oracle* published the first of 13 issues, unveiling a non-news, art-oriented format and a psychedelic look of vibrant, random colors and swirling typefaces perfected by hip artist Rick Griffin. "Our philosophy at the time was that newspapers are a lie," remembered *Oracle* editor Allen Cohen. "We were going to make the newspaper format a joke that would show everyone that newspapers were destroying sensibilities, causing paranoia and fear. We were going to fill our newspaper with art, philosophy, poetry and attend to this change of consciousness that was happening in the Haight-Ashbury and, we hoped, the world." The *Oracle* staff wanted to "serve as vehicles for the forces that were emerging." By 1967, when the Underground Press Syndicate (UPS) was founded, five other major underground tabloids printed stories about sex, drugs, and revolution: *The East Village Other; The Paper* in East Lansing, Michigan; the *Berkeley Barb*; the *Seed* in Chicago; and the *Fifth Estate* in Detroit. Two years later, more than 500 underground newspapers printed stories about the counterculture that reached nearly a million readers.

Acid Rock: The Trip Begins

A legion of rock bands, playing what became known as acid rock, stood in the vanguard of the movement for cultural change. The *San Francisco Oracle* defined rock music as a "regenerative and revolutionary art, offering us our first real hope for the future (indeed, for the present) since August 6, 1945." "Rock and roll," announced *Rolling Stone*, which had been established in 1967 by Berkeley dropout and budding journalist Jann Wenner and well-known music critic Ralph Gleason, "is more than just music. It is the energy center of the new culture and the youth revolution. . . . Rock and roll is the *only* way in which the vast but formless power of youth is structured," the magazine concluded. Even handbills distributed to promote the Trips Festival in January 1966 hinted that "maybe this is the ROCK REVOLUTION."

Not surprisingly, psychedelic music had its basis in Dylanesque folk. "I began as a folk musician. I went to New York and I heard Dylan when he was at Gerdes. And I was very impressed by, I don't know what it was, his youth I guess, his exuberance," mentioned Marty Balin (a.k.a. Martyn Buchwald), who had played in the Los Angeles folk group the Town Criers. "So I decided to come up here and started up here [San Francisco]. I went through a million different guys and then I saw Paul [Kantner]. He was walking into a folk club [The Drinking Gourd]. I just saw him, and I said, 'That's the guy.' I just knew it. He had a twelve-string and a banjo and he had his hair down to here and an old cap." The duo asked a few other musicians to join their band and then, according to lead guitarist Jorma Kaukonen, the group was "thinking of names, trying to think of some sort of name that would imply a whole different way of looking at things." They settled on the Jefferson Airplane.

The Grateful Dead, another major exponent of acid rock, grew from folk roots. "When the whole folk music thing started, I got caught up into that," remembered Jerry Garcia. "When Joan Baez's first record came out I heard it and I heard her finger picking the guitar, I'd never heard anything like it before so I got into that and I started getting into country music, into old-time white music. Mostly white spiritual stuff, white instrumental music and I got into finger style, the folk-music-festival scene, the whole thing. And I was very heavy into that for a long time and I sort of employed a scholarly approach and even went through the South with tape recorders and stuff recording bluegrass bands. I spent about three years playing bluegrass banjo, that was my big thing and I almost forgot how to play the guitar during that period of time. And then I got into a jug band, we got a jug band going and I took up the guitar again and from the jug band it was right into rock and roll. . . . I was sort of a beatnik guitar player. . . . Bob Weir, who plays rhythm," continued Garcia, "did the whole folk-blues coffeehouse thing. That was his thing. And he also played jug and kazoo in the jug band [Mother McCree's Uptown Jug Champions] when we were playing. And he's a student, you might say. His musical leader was Jorma [Kaukonen]." Concluded Garcia: "Like here on the West Coast, the guys that are into rock 'n' roll music have mostly come up like I have . . . like me and Jorma for example . . . up through folk music." In early 1965, folkies Garcia and Weir joined with blues enthusiast Ron "Pig Pen" McKernan, drummer Bill Kreutzmann, and bassist Phil Lesch to form the band The Warlocks, which was renamed the Grateful Dead later that year.

Other acid rockers rose through the ranks of folk. Peter Albin, the impetus behind Big Brother and the Holding Company, had organized folk concerts during the early 1960s with his brother, Rodney. David Freiberg, the unofficial leader of Quicksilver Messenger Service, learned guitar in 1963 amidst the folk craze, and one-time fellow band member, drummer Dino Valenti, had worked for several years as a folk singer in Greenwich Village, writing the classic "Hey Joe." In 1964, Country Joe McDonald "came to become a folksinger with the beatniks in San Francisco" and formed a jug band with Barry Melton, a friend of Peter Albin, shortly before he teamed up with the Fish to deliver his politically minded brand of psychedelic rock. Likewise, lead guitarist Robby Kreiger of the Doors—which formed in late 1965 with Kreiger, fellow Psychedelic Ranger John Densmore on drums, singer Jim Morrison, and organist Ray Manzarek—had started a jug band during his stay at the University of California at Santa Barbara.

Unlike the acoustic strummings of early Bob Dylan, the acid rockers amplified their message to glass-shattering levels. Jerry Garcia thought of it as "a sensory overload . . . It's very loud." The San Francisco bands also favored extended guitar solos and distorted guitar feedback and added some blues riffs, a dash of country-western, and traces of Indian ragas to create the heralded San Francisco sound.

Rock-and-Roll Revolution

The new sound came from middle-class youths. Grace Slick, the daughter of a Chicago investment banker, attended the exclusive Finch College where, in her words, she became a "regular suburban preppy." Fellow Airplane member Jorma Kaukonen was the son of a foreign service official and graduated from the University of California, Santa Clara; Airplane drummer Spencer Dryden had moved to Hollywood with his father, an assistant film director. Jim Morrison, the son of a rear admiral, had enrolled in the Theater Arts Department at UCLA, where he met keyboardist Ray Manzarek. John Cipollina, the guitarist for Quicksilver Messenger Service, had become interested in music through his mother, a concert pianist, and his godfather, Jose Iturbi, a well-known classical pianist. Peter Albin of Big Brother and the Holding Company grew up in suburban San Francisco, the son of a magazine editor-illustrator.

These middle-class youths wanted to overturn the social order in which they had been raised. Jim Morrison, characterized as a "post-beat writer influenced by Ginsberg and Kerouac" by fellow-Door Ray Manzarek, professed an interest "in anything about revolt, disorder, chaos. It seemed to me to be the road toward freedom—external revolt is a way to bring about internal freedom. . . . When I sing my songs in public," he told The New York Times, "that's a dramatic act, but not just acting as in theater, but a social act, real action." As he sang in one song, he hoped to "break on through to the other side." Grace Slick of the Jefferson Airplane hoped for "a whole turnaround of values." Chet Helms, the transplanted Texan who opened the Avalon Ballroom in the Haight because he "liked to dance" and who became the manager of Big Brother and the Holding Company, "was very interested in the scene's potential for revolution. For turning things upside down, for changing values."

As with the hippies in general, the psychedelic rockers challenged restrictive middle-class values, especially those dealing with sex. The Fugs, always forthright, belted out "Boobs Alot," "Group Grope," and "Dirty Old Man." Their name itself raised the eyebrows of the sexually inhibited. Reveling in the same theme, the Doors hit the charts with "Love Me Two Times," "Hello I Love You," "Love Her Madly," and their biggest hit, "Light My Fire." Morrison, who characterized himself as an "erotic politician," faced legal charges when he supposedly exposed himself on stage in Florida. The outspoken Grace Slick, who delivered such songs as "Somebody to Love," confessed that "it doesn't matter what the lyrics say, or who sings them. They're all the same. They say, 'Be free—free in love, free in sex.' " "The stage is our bed and the audience is our broad," added Marty Balin of the Airplane. "We're not entertaining, we're making love."

Many psychedelic bands renounced the competitive, corporate structure of American society in general and of the recording industry in particular. Jerry Garcia of the Grateful Dead resented "being just an-

Poster for a Jefferson Airplane show at the Fillmore

other face in a corporate personality. There isn't even a Warner 'brother' to talk to. The music business and the Grateful Dead are in two different orbits, two different universes." The Dead, added Stephen Stills of Buffalo Springfield and later of Crosby, Stills and Nash, "were the first people, I don't know whether it was acid or what, to come to that realization where they really didn't give a shit whether they made it or not." "The record companies sell rock and roll records like they sell refrigerators," complained Paul Kantner of the Jefferson Airplane. "They don't care about the people who make rock or what they're all about as human beings any more than they care about the people who make refrigerators." Max Weiss, owner of Fantasy Records in the Bay area, characterized the San Francisco bands as "good but a little crazy. They are absolutely non-commercial."

Opposed to a faceless commercialism, bands such as the Grateful Dead and the Airplane began to stage free concerts. "We don't do what the system says—make single hits, take big gigs, do the success number," Dead manager Rock Scully told an interviewer. "The summer of '67, when all the other groups were making it, we were playing free in the park, man, trying to cool the Haight-Ashbury." "The first thing that really hit me hard was the Grateful Dead were playing a lot of gigs for nothing," Eric Clapton, a former Yardbirds guitarist, remembered of his first visit to San Francisco. "That very much moved me. I've never heard of anyone doing that before. That really is one of the finest steps that anyone has taken in music yet, aside from musical strides. I guess that sums it up, what I think about San Francisco, what the Grateful Dead are doing. There is this incredible thing that the musical people seem to have toward their audience: they want to give."

The emphasis upon sharing determined the role of band members. David Getz, drummer for Big Brother and the Holding Company, remembered that "the whole philosophy of the psychedelic scene was to consciously avoid making anyone the star, focusing more on the interaction between the audience and the band, and trying to create something together. That's how the energy happened."

Most San Francisco bands felt a camaraderie with one another. "All of the bands were very close," remembered Mickey Hart of the Grateful Dead. "The Quicksilver and the Grateful Dead and Big Brother and the Airplane. We were like sister bands. We'd be over at each other's houses, see each other all day long, party at night. There were no hassles about who was going to open the show or close the show. It seemed like when we played with one of our sister bands, our compadres, we always played a little better for each other."

The cooperative feeling within bands sometimes extended to their own living arrangements. The members of the Grateful Dead lived communally in the Haight district at 710 Ashbury Street. Quicksilver Messenger Service roomed together in a house near the Dead headquarters. For a time, the Jefferson Airplane lived together in the Haight at 2400 Fulton Street.

Many acid rockers discovered the cooperative alternative to a competitive society through LSD. "Along came LSD and that was the end of that whole world. The whole world just went kablooey," related Jerry Garcia. "It changed everything, you know, it was just—ah, first of all, for me personally, it freed me, you know, the effect was that it freed me because I suddenly realized that my little attempt at having a straight life and doing that was really a fiction and just wasn't going to work out."

As well as showing the hollowness of self-centered mainstream values, acid helped Garcia realize the existence of more interconnected social relationships. "To get really high is to forget yourself," he asserted. "And to forget yourself is to see everything else. And to see everything else is to become an understanding molecule in evolution, a conscious tool in the universe."

As the avenue to understanding a new social order, mind-expanding drugs became the centerpiece of acid rock. They inspired the names of many West Coast bands: the Loading Zone, Morning Glory, the Weeds, the Seeds, and the Doors, the last name taken from a phrase of poet William Blake quoted by Aldous Huxley in a book about a mescaline experience, *The Doors of Perception*.

Many San Francisco bands extolled psychedelic drugs in their songs. The Jefferson Airplane delivered the Haight-Ashbury anthem, "White Rabbit": "One pill makes you larger and one pill makes you small, and the ones that mother gives you don't do anything at all. Go ask Alice when she's ten feet tall," sang Grace Slick while the Airplane churned out a sinister, electric drone in the background. She continued: "When the men on the chessboard get up and tell you where to go. You just had some kind of mushroom and your mind is moving low. Go ask Alice, I think she'll know." Then Slick launched into her piercing vibrato: "When logic and proportion have fallen softly dead, and the white knight's talking backwards and the red queen's lost her head, remember what the dormouse said, FEED YOUR HEAD, FEED YOUR HEAD." By 1969, a distraught Art Linkletter, whose daughter had overdosed on LSD, charged that at least half of all rock songs were "concerned with secret messages to teenagers to drop out, turn on, and groove with chemicals." A year later, Vice-President Spiro Agnew complained that much of "rock music glorified drug use."

Drugs defined the purpose of some psychedelic bands. According to Jerry Garcia, "the Grateful Dead is not for cranking out rock and roll, it's not for going out and doing concerts or any of that stuff, I think it's to get high."

Light shows at dances in the Haight simulated the LSD experience. The projection of light through liquid pigments in motion to create ever-changing expressionistic light shows had been discovered in 1952 by San Francisco State professor Seymour Locks as he prepared for a national conference of art educators. Through the efforts of beatnik art student Elias Romero, who witnessed some of Locks's first shows, hipsters such as Bill Ham, Anthony Martin, and Ben Van Meter learned the craft and adapted it to the hippie subculture. By 1966, dances in the

Haight—normally held in Chet Helm's Avalon Ballroom or the Fillmore Theater, rented by ex-Mime Troupe manager Bill Graham—featured light shows of melting colors, which mimicked an LSD experience.

The poster art advertising the gatherings consisted of the same swirling designs. Based upon the style of early twentieth-century artist Alfred Roller, the posters featured thick, distorted letters that melted together against a bright, solid-color background. They were crafted by self-taught Haight artists such as Wes Wilson, Stan Mouse (a.k.a. Miller), Alton Kelley, Victor Moscoso, Greg Irons, and Rick Griffin, who also designed album covers for the Grateful Dead and Big Brother and the Holding Company.

Bill Graham, a politically minded, 35-year-old émigré who had changed his name from Wolfgang Grajonca, organized the psychedelic groundswell in San Francisco. In 1965, after staging two benefit concerts as the manager of the San Francisco Mime Troupe, Graham decided to concentrate his efforts on the concert scene, coordinating the Trips Festival for Ken Kesey and his Merry Pranksters. By March 1966, Graham had secured a three-year lease on the Fillmore which, like the Avalon Ballroom, became a popular dance hall in the Haight. He also began to manage the Fillmore house band, the Jefferson Airplane and, later, the Grateful Dead. Although never "a great fan of high volume rock and roll, and a lot of it was nonsensical to me," Graham took pride in his organizational abilities. "I was always, 'Well, I took your ticket and you came here expecting something, and I want you to have that,' " he recalled. "I want the food to be hot and the drinks to be cold." "Bill Graham was the star of the sixties," asserted Marty Balin of the Airplane. "In the beginning there was great talent, but there were no sound systems. No microphones. Graham came along and changed it. He made the performers a stage. He was what Alan Freed was to the fifties."

The acid-inspired music, organized locally by Graham, reached youths across the country through airplay on FM radio. Not produced for the Top 40 play list of AM radio, the meandering psychedelic sounds first aired on the freewheeling San Francisco station KMPX on the programs of such disc jockeys as Larry Miller and Tom Donahue. "Somewhere in the dim misty days of yore, some radio station statistician decided that regardless of chronological age, the average mental age of the audience was twelve and a half, and Top 40 AM radio aimed its message directly at the lowest common denominator," sniped Donahue. "The disc jockeys have become robots performing their inanities at the direction of programmers who had succeeded in totally squeezing blips and bleeps and happy, oh yes, always happy sounding cretins who are poured from a bottle every three hours." To eradicate the "rotting corpse stinking up the airwaves," the San Francisco jockey used FM radio to air songs that lasted more than three minutes, began to spin entire albums, discontinued the breakneck delivery of Top 40 disc jockeys, and played songs by the new groups of the Bay area. When confronted by an unhappy owner and a strike at KMPX, Donahue and

The Doors
Courtesy of Elektra/Asylum Records

his staff took their hip format to KSAN, which poster artist Alton Kelley described as a "community drum." Soon FM stations in other parts of the country began to adopt Donahue's format and broadcast psychedelia across the airwaves.

Promoted by FM radio, acid rock started to scale the charts. In June 1967, the Jefferson Airplane, the first Haight band signed by a major label, hit number three with *Surrealistic Pillow*, an album that involved Jerry Garcia as musical advisor and showcased vocalist Grace Slick, who had replaced original singer Signe Anderson. The same year the Grateful Dead cracked the charts with its self-named debut LP. By the next year, Quicksilver Messenger Service charted with its first album. The Doors, probably the best-selling West Coast band, in early 1967 neared the top of the charts with its self-named debut album and later the same year hit the Top 5 with *Strange Days*. They also scored on the singles chart with "People Are Strange," "Love Me Two Times," and "Touch Me," as well as the chart-topping "Light My Fire" and "Hello, I Love You."

Other bands jumped on the psychedelic bandwagon. In 1967, the lovable, mop-topped Beatles released two albums: *Magical Mystery Tour*, a concept album and movie modeled after Ken Kesey's travels in his psychedelic bus, and *Sgt. Pepper's Lonely Hearts Club Band*, which included the cryptic "Lucy in the Sky with Diamonds," LSD for short.

Later that year, the bubbly Paul McCartney admitted that he had taken LSD. The Beatles began to study transcendental meditation with Maharishi Mahesh Yogi, and George and Pattie Harrison, wearing heart-shaped granny glasses and paisley frocks, took a ceremonial tour of the Haight district. The same year, the Rolling Stones released *Their Satanic Majesties' Request*, a psychedelic album featuring a three-dimensional cover, and Mick Jagger joined the Beatles in transcendental meditation. Eric Burdon of the Animals, after abandoning the blues for psychedelia, told *Melody Maker*, "It wasn't me singing. It was someone trying to be an American Negro. I look back and see how stupid I was." Adorned in vibrantly colored shirts and love beads, Burdon sang such odes to hippiedom as "San Franciscan Nights" and "Monterey." Even Dick Clark changed with the times to mastermind a movie, *The Love Children*, which starred a young Jack Nicholson and featured music by such psychedelic bands as the Seeds and the Strawberry Alarm Clock.

By 1967, acid rock had spread to youths throughout the country. Philadelphia hippies danced at the Electric Factory. The counterculture heard acid rock at the Tea Party Ballroom in Boston, at the Kinetic Playground in Chicago, and at the Grand Ballroom in Detroit. In New York, hippies went to the Electric Circus and the Fillmore East, which Bill Graham had designed as an East Coast alternative to the San Francisco original. Acid rock had become a national phenomenon.

The Decline and Fall of Hippiedom

The counterculture had a short-lived heyday, falling victim to its own drug-based logic. Many hippies, initially using drugs to increase awareness and open alternative realities, became wasted addicts. As some youths repeatedly tried to delve deeper and deeper into their own consciousnesses with LSD, they became isolated and detached from their own bodies. In the street vernacular, these hippies "burned out." Others became hooked on drugs that seemed to promise freedom. By 1967, many Haight residents had become methedrine or "speed" addicts who, according to Dr. Ellis D. ("LSD") Sox, the San Francisco public health director, cost the city $35,000 a month for treatment. "You had a lot of people talking to posts," remembered Travis Rivers, then owner of the Print Mint, which sold psychedelic posters in the Haight. "They were ripping one another off, because it costs a lot of money once you get strung out on speed."

Some of the major figures in the Haight drug culture fell prey to the guns of gangland. On August 3, 1967, John Kent Carter, a dealer known as "Shob," was found murdered, his arms hacked off at the elbows. Three days later, William "Superspade" Thomas ended up in a sleeping bag with a bullet through his head at the bottom of a cliff in Marin County.

The saga of Skip Spence provides a moving testimony to the perils of drug experimentation. Alexander ("Skip") Spence was the original drummer for the Jefferson Airplane, composing "Blues from an

The Jefferson Airplane, ca. 1965; lead
singer Grace Slick, front right
Photo by Herb Greene, courtesy RCA Records

Airplane." When he quit the Airplane to form the path-breaking psychedelic band Moby Grape, he began to overindulge in psyche-delics. Confided Skip: "Acid was like heaven, a moment of God, in-spiring, tragic. I must have taken it a hundred times, a thousand times." One day, Spence reached too high. He woke up in a hospital: "An over-dose where I died and was brought back to life." Today the scraggly, unwashed ex-rock star lives in San Jose, where he spends his seven-dollar-a-day allowance from the state. At night, when he does not confine himself to the psychiatric ward of the San Jose hospital, Spence stays alone in a dingy, rundown room in Maas Hotel. Sometimes he speaks to Joan of Arc. Once in a while he is visited by Clark Kent, who the drummer/guitarist finds to be "civilized, decent and a genius." And on a few thick, intense, San Jose summer nights, Spence meets his "master," who materializes with startling revelations. Says Spence, delivering his own autobiography, "I'm a derelict. I'm a world savior. I am drugs. I am rock and roll."

A deterministic psychedelic world view, unlocked by mind-expanding drugs, made hippiedom susceptible to cooptation. Most hippies, like Jerry Garcia, considered themselves "conscious tools of the universe" who were directed by "cosmic forces" that bound disparate individuals and events into a logical pattern. They believed in an almost preordained "flow" that would sweep everyone into a psychedelic community.

Businessmen, more interested in individual gain than universal cooperation, began to exploit the counterculture. During the first months of 1967, more than 20 shops opened their doors in the Haight-Ashbury district to accommodate the tourist traffic. The Pall Mall Lounge began to market "love burgers," and one store began to sell hippie costumes to weekenders—scraggly wigs for $85 and beards for $125. Even the Greyhound Bus Company started a "Hippie Hop" in San Francisco, advertised as "the only foreign tour within the continental limits of the United States." "Haight Street is no longer fun," complained Tsvi Strauch, an original hippie proprietor in the Haight. "Many of us are getting away from it because of all the plastic hippies and tourists that are fouling up the whole scene. They've made a mess of it."

On October 4, 1967, Jay Thelin closed the Psychedelic Shop, a hub of the Bay area counterculture, and posted a sign on the front door: "Be Free—Nebraska Needs You More." Two days later a procession of original hippies in the Haight district loaded a coffin full of beads, peace signs, flowers, and other symbols of their lifestyle and publicly burned it, announcing the "death of hippie, loyal son of media." The same day, the Fugs coordinated a similar procession in the East Village, memorializing the hippie culture. "The tourist buses started coming through. Then they [hippies] left," summarized one Haight resident. "The kids went out to the country. Bolinas, Santa Rosa, Healdsburg, Auburn, Santa Cruz. Basically, they all left the city and it became a very different situation. More drugs came in and it was an angrier crowd. There were some homicides in the Haight-Ashbury. A lot of rapes, many of them unreported, came down. Essentially, there was a dissipation of the environment."

Even acid rock, the music of the counterculture, became subsumed by the recording industry. Though complaining about the corporate structure of the music industry, the psychedelic rockers readily signed contracts with the major record labels that marketed the psychedelic sound. "We found we couldn't sell the Grateful Dead's records in a traditional manner," said Joe Smith, at the time president of Warner-Reprise. "You couldn't take your ad in *Billboard* and sell a record that way. . . . The packaging was important. The cult was important. Free concerts where you handed out fruits and nuts were important" as well as exposure on the underground club circuit, the campuses, and FM radio. Gil Frieson, then vice-president of A & M Records, assembled a Standard American Promotional Package—"billboards on Sunset Strip and Broadway, full-page advertising in the underground press, the trades, and various other outlets; radio spots and a promotional tour

The Grateful Dead, ca. mid 1970s.
Jerry Garcia is third from the left
Frank Driggs Collection

with all expenses paid by the label." "It's funny, the group out there on the stage preaching a revolutionary message, but to get the message to the people, you gotta do it in the establishment way," complained Bill Siddons, manager of the Doors.

By late 1967, acid rock and the counterculture it exemplified had been drawn into the competitive society it attacked. "When the Summer of Love happened, that was it," recalled Bill Thompson, a manager of the Jefferson Airplane. "It had all started happening in the summer of 1965 and it was over by the summer of 1967." The psychedelic baby boomers, armed with flowers and a hopeful spirit, would soon confront the M-1 rifles of National Guardsmen, who would turn the brightly colored hopes of hippiedom into a dark nightmare of war-torn campuses.

9

Fire from the Streets

"Soul is sass, man."

Claude Brown

Four o'clock on a muggy, steamy Sunday morning in Detroit, July 22, 1967. A crowd of young African-Americans clustered around a pack of police squad cars on Twelfth Street, the heart of the city's West Side ghetto. As the African-Americans pressed against one another to get a better view of the action, blue-shirted, white-faced policemen herded 74 captives into paddy wagons. The arrested African-Americans had been accused of drinking liquor after hours at the United Community League for Civic Action, which also offered sermons on the spreading gospel of Black Power. After finishing their job, the policemen jumped into the squad cars, revved the engines, and started to move out of the area. Someone in the crowd flung a full wine bottle through the air, shattering the windshield of Tenth Precinct Sergeant Arthur Howison's Ford. Howison slammed on the brakes and leapt into the street. He was pelted first by a few stones and then by a barrage of rocks and bottles. The police officer ducked back into the car and sped off, followed by the angry mob.

The crowd multiplied as it made its way down Twelfth Street until it had grown to 3000 agitated men, women, and youths. Someone grabbed a brick from the pavement and hurled it through the window of a grocery store. People swarmed toward the jagged opening. They poked out the rest of the glass in the window frame with sticks, jumped into the store, and began gathering armloads of meat, bread, and canned goods. One man struggled with an entire side of beef. "I've always wanted to be a butcher," he told an onlooker.

Around daybreak, some teens overturned a line of garbage cans and set the trash on fire. Another man threw a homemade firebomb into a shoe store that already had been sacked. Summer breezes fanned the flames, which spread to adjoining buildings. Within a few hours, columns of fire engulfed East Detroit and spread across Woodward Avenue into the west part of the city. Williams's Drug Store and Lou's Men's Wear, along with hundreds of other buildings, disappeared in flames. "It looks like 1945 in Berlin," reported a dejected Mayor Jerome Cavanaugh.

Rioting and looting continued for the next four days. Enraged African-Americans ravaged thousands of stores, searching for food, clothing, furniture, and liquor. They only spared storefronts that had been marked "Soul Brother" or "Afro All the Way." Fires set by the rioters gutted 14 square miles of Detroit, causing an estimated $500 million in damage. "Man, this is crazy," one older African-American told *Newsweek*. "We're burnin' our own houses up. Where these poor people going to live now?" "This is madness," echoed another homeowner. "Why do they have to burn our houses? That's not right. Goddamn. And there's not a house burning in Grosse Point [a white, middle-class suburb of Detroit]. This has got to stop." But other African-Americans in the Motor City, unemployed and confined to dilapidated slums, were impatient for the reforms promised by the Civil Rights Act of 1964 and predicted more trouble. Said one 22-year-old youth: "We're tired of being second-class. We've been asking too long. Now it's time to take. This thing ain't over. It's just beginning."

The authorities responded to the rioting with armed force. During the first day of troubles, Mayor Cavanaugh unleashed his 4000-man police force on the ghetto. When police proved inadequate, Michigan Governor George Romney mobilized 7300 state troopers and National Guardsmen armed with tear gas, grenade launchers, M-1 rifles, submachine guns, M-48 tanks, and Huey helicopters. "I'm gonna shoot anything that moves and is black," vowed one young guardsman. The next day, President Lyndon Johnson airlifted Task Force Detroit, a 4700-man paratrooper unit commanded by Lieutenant General John L. Throckmorton, who had served as a deputy to General William Westmoreland in Vietnam. All told, a 16,000-man army marched into Detroit to quell the tumult. The city had become an armed camp divided into war zones, cordoned off by barbed wire, and patrolled by helmeted troops in khakis.

After the fires had been stamped out and the smoke had cleared, the authorities counted 42 dead, 2250 injured, and 5557 arrested. Most of the casualties were African-American men. On national television President Johnson pleaded that the "violence must be stopped—quickly, finally, and permanently. There are no victors in the aftermath of violence. . . . We have endured a week such as no nation should live through: a time of violence and tragedy."

Incited by Black Power activists such as H. Rap Brown, who threatened, "If America don't come around, we're going to burn America down," disgruntled African-Americans rioted in other urban areas. Trouble occurred in such Michigan cities as Pontiac, Saginaw, Flint, Grand Rapids, Albion, and Kalamazoo. During the last days of July looters sacked stores in the African-American neighborhoods of Phoenix, Hartford, Passaic, Poughkeepsie, and South Bend. The next month, four nights of violence ripped Milwaukee, leaving four dead and more than a hundred injured. African-Americans in nearby Chicago took to the streets, and riots scarred Providence and Wichita. By the end of August, race riots had torn apart more than 70 cities and had left a trail of 86 dead, thousands injured, and blocks of charred rubble. One government report estimated that 41 percent of the cities with populations of more than 100,000 had experienced racial violence. The press called it the "long hot summer."

On April 4, 1968, the murder of African-American leader Dr. Martin Luther King, Jr., triggered another wave of violence. "When White America killed Dr. King," sneered African-American militant Stokely Carmichael, "she declared war on us. . . . We have to retaliate for the deaths of our leaders. The executions of those deaths are going to be in the streets." Carmichael proved to be prophetic. A few hours after the King assassination, Washington, D.C., burst into flames. As described by *Newsweek*, the more than 700 fires in the national capital, the worst conflagration in the city since the British burned it during the War of 1812, "made Washington look like the besieged capital of a banana republic, with helmeted combat troops, bayoneted rifles at the ready guarding the White House, and a light machine-gun post defending the steps of the Capitol." President Lyndon Johnson activated more than 15,000 troops—more than twice the size of the U.S. garrison that defended Khe Sanh in Vietnam—to quiet the disorders. In three days of rioting, the death toll reached ten and property damage exceeded $13.3 million.

Other African-American-populated urban areas exploded after receiving news of the King assassination. In Kansas City six rioters died and 65 were injured. Chicago's riot, quelled by 5000 federal troops and 6700 National Guardsmen, left 11 dead, 91 injured, and miles of burned-out buildings. By the end of the week 168 cities had erupted into violence, 5117 fires had been started, about 2000 shops had been ransacked, $40 million worth of property had been destroyed, and 46 people, mostly African-Americans, had died. It took almost 73,000 Army and National Guard troops to quell the disturbances. In 1967 and 1968, many African-Americans had dramatically reasserted their collective identity, an identity born in slavery and shaped by a century of discrimination. They called their reclaimed identity *soul*.

Ray Charles in full evening regalia, ca. mid 1950s
Photo courtesy Atlantic Records

Soul Music

Soul music reflected the militant search for an African-American identity. The term *soul* had been used by African-Americans during the fifties to suggest the essence of being an African-American in the United States. Jazz musicians had soul: In 1957, horn man Lou Donaldson recorded *Swing and Soul*; the next year saxophone great John Coltrane released *Soultrane*; trombonist Bennie Green cut *Soul Stirring* (1958) and *Hornful of Soul* (1959); trumpeter Blue Mitchell played *Blue Soul* (1959); and saxophonist Johnny Griffin led a *Big Soul-Band* (1960). During the early sixties, Eldridge Cleaver noted in *Soul on Ice* that many referred to jazz as "soul music."

Around 1965, as the African-American ghettos of Watts and Harlem erupted in violence, many African-Americans started to equate soul with the struggle to reassert African-American dignity in the face of continued discrimination. "Soul is sass, man," wrote Claude Brown, author of *Manchild in the Promised Land*. "Soul is arrogance. Soul is walkin' down the street in a way that says, 'This is me, muhfuh.' . . . Soul is that uninhibited, no, *extremely* uninhibited self-expression that goes into practically every Negro endeavor. That's soul. And there's a swagger in it, man." Music writer Arnold Shaw came to the same conclusion in *The World of Soul*: "Soul is black, not blue, sass, anger and rage. It is not just feeling but conviction. Not just intensity but involvement. A force as well as a style, an accolade as well as identification. It is an expressive explosiveness, ignited by a people's discovery of self-pride, power and potential for growth." Emphasizing the value of their culture, African-Americans began to refer to chitterlings, collard greens, black-eyed peas, candied yams, and sweet potato pie as soul food. Fellow African-Americans became soul brothers and soul sisters, and rhythm and blues became soul music.

Some of the "soul" performers had been involved in R & B long before it underwent a name change. James Brown, "Soul Brother Number One," released his first record, "Please, Please, Please," with his Famous Flames in 1956. Two years later he scaled the R & B chart with "Try Me," and in 1960 reworked the Five Royales' "Think" for a hit.

By 1963, when he recorded the now legendary album *Live at the Apollo*, Brown had perfected a stunning stage act complete with a back-up band and vocal group known as the James Brown Revue. In a typical performance, the singer leapt on stage wearing skin-tight black pants, a half-unbuttoned, dark-blue satin shirt, and a purple cape. Without missing a beat, his head jerking to the music, he suddenly jumped into the air, landed in a perfect split, and bounced back to his feet. Before the audience recovered, Brown was snaking across the floor or twirling in midair.

Ray Charles, considered to be the "Genius of Soul" during the mid-sixties, initially gained fame in R & B. Born Ray Charles Robinson in 1930, Charles traveled from his hometown of Albany, Georgia, to Seattle in 1947 to play cocktail-swing piano in the Nat King Cole style at such venues as the Elks Club, the Rocking Chair, and the Black and Tan. In 1949, on Swingtime Records, he cut his first disc, "Confession Blues," and two years later followed with the R & B hit "Baby, Let Me Hold Your Hand." During the next few years he toured with blues growler Lowell Fulson, R & B singer Ruth Brown, African-American comic Moms Mabley, and Eddie "Guitar Slim" Jones. In 1952, Atlantic Records, a leading company in the R & B field, bought Ray's contract from Swingtime for $2500. During late 1953 in New Orleans, remembered then Atlantic vice-president Jerry Wexler, Atlantic president Ahmet Ertegun and Wexler "ran into Ray at Cosimo's famous small studio, and Ray asked us to please do a session with him. . . . This was the landmark session because it had Ray Charles originals, Ray Charles arrangements, a Ray Charles band." The session produced the single "Don't You Know." The singer-pianist quickly followed with "I've Got a Woman," one of his most notable hits. During the rest of the fifties, he scored repeatedly. In 1955, he hit with "Blackjack," "Come Back," "Fool for You," "Greenbacks," and "This Girl of Mine"; "Drown in My Own Tears," "Hallelujah, I Love Her So," "Lonely Avenue," and "Mary Ann" the next year; and in 1959 with "Right Time" and "What'd I Say." By the turn of the decade Ray Charles had firmly established himself as a major figure in R & B.

Wilson Pickett, although not as prominent in the fifties as Ray Charles, had roots in early R & B. One day in 1959, as Pickett lounged

James Brown
Seattle Times

188

Aretha Franklin recording in 1961
Frank Driggs Collection

on his porch strumming a guitar and singing, Willie Scorefield, a member of the R & B group the Falcons, happened to pass by. According to Pickett, Scorefield walked up to him and said, " 'Man, you got a good voice,' and invited me to come to the next rehearsal. That's when I found I could sing rhythm and blues." In 1962, Pickett wrote and recorded with the Falcons the hit "I Found a Love."

Otis Redding, recognized as "The King of Soul" by some, initially drew his inspiration from Little Richard. In an unlikely success story that took place in late 1962, Redding drove some friends, Johnny Jenkins and the Pinetoppers, to the Stax studio in Memphis for a recording session. "They had 30 minutes left in the studio and I asked if I could do a song," remembered Redding, who had recorded some unsuccessful Little Richard-sounding songs for the Confederate label. "He did one of those heh, heh, baby things," recalled Stax president Jim Stewart. "It was just like Little Richard. I told them the world didn't need another Little Richard. Then someone suggested he do a slow one. He did 'These Arms of Mine.' " Impressed by the song, Stewart signed Redding and released "These Arms of Mine," which hit the R & B chart in early 1963. In 1964, Redding cut *Pain in My Heart*, a mixture of Little Richard screamers and Sam Cooke-type ballads.

Most soul artists, as with R & B performers of the fifties, started their careers in the church. Wilson Pickett had sung in small-town gospel groups before he joined the Falcons; he described his own style as "a gospel melody, not nothing pretty, a funky groove with lines that mean something." Eddie Floyd, who in 1966 hit with "Knock on Wood," had helped start the Falcons, which had begun as a gospel group and drifted toward R & B by the time Pickett joined. Solomon Burke had worked as a boy preacher, had been a broadcaster on the religious show "Solomon's Temple," and had soloed in his family's own Philadelphia church, The House of God for All People. Before turning to secular music in 1955, he had debuted with the single, "Christmas Presents from Heaven." Percy Sledge had sung with his cousin's gospel group, the Singing Clouds. Garnet Mimms, who charted in 1963 with "Cry Baby," had sung with the Philadelphia gospel groups the Norfolk Four and the Evening Star Quartet. As youngsters, both Sam Moore and Dave Prater, later teaming up as Sam and Dave, had joined Baptist choirs and in their teens had toured with gospel groups.

Otis Redding had learned about music in the church. The son of a minister, he had sung in the Mount Ivy Baptist Church choir as a young boy. "Otis and I were very close," remembered Katie Webster, who played piano for Redding. "It was a spiritual thing. Both our fathers were ministers, and we would read the Bible together." James Brown had played organ and drums during the forties for various gospel outfits. "I sang gospel in prison," recalled the singer. "Once I got out I joined Sarah Byrd's group, the Gospel Starlighters, and it was here I got acquainted with her brother Bobby," who became a Famous Flame when Brown switched to secular music in 1954.

Ray Charles' music reflected his religious upbringing. He changed the Pilgrim Travelers' "I've Got a New Home" to "Lonely Avenue," shortened "Nobody But You, Lord" to "Nobody But You," changed the gospel standard "This Little Light of Mine" to "This Little Girl of Mine," and exulted in gospel screams in "Hallelujah, I Love Her So." "Now I'd been singing spirituals since I was three and I'd been singing the blues for just as long," explained Charles. "So what could be more natural than to combine them? It didn't take any thinking, didn't take any calculating. All the sounds were there, right at the top of my head." Added bluesman Big Bill Broonzy about Ray Charles, "He's cryin', sanctified. He's mixing the blues with the spirituals. He should be singing in a church."

Aretha Franklin, the five-feet-five-inch dynamo dubbed "Lady Soul," had a direct connection to the church. Her father, the Reverend Clarence L. Franklin, served as the pastor of Detroit's 4500-member New Bethel Baptist Church and recorded more than 70 albums of fiery, blues-drenched sermons. Two white-uniformed nurses commonly stood guard at the aisles of New Bethel Baptist to aid parishioners who were overcome by the emotionally draining message of the minister. As a youth, Aretha came into contact with such gospel greats as James Cleveland and Mahalia Jackson, and at a funeral of an aunt she witnessed Clara Ward belt out a powerful rendition of "Peace in the Valley." At that moment, the minister's daughter later recollected, "I wanted to become a singer." Aretha began to learn gospel from James Cleveland: "He showed me some real nice chords and I liked his deep, deep sound. There's a whole lot of earthiness in the way he sings, and what he was feelin', I was feelin', but I just didn't know how to put it across. The more I watched him, the more I got out of it." Soon Aretha joined a family-organized traveling gospel troupe, in which she premiered until signing with Columbia Records. The soul of Aretha Franklin had matured in the church.

Atlantic Records distributed most of the gospel-based R & B, which would become known as soul music. The company had been established in 1947 by Ahmet and Nesuhi Ertegun, sons of the Turkish ambassador to the United States. Avid jazz and blues record collectors, they auctioned 15,000 78-rpm discs to start Atlantic Records with fellow record collector Herb Abramson, who had helped cofound the National and Jubilee labels. In 1949, Atlantic scored its first hit with the R & B song "Drinking Wine, Spo-Dee-O Dee," by Stick McGee. During the next 15 years, Atlantic produced a variety of jazz and R & B artists, hitting the R & B charts with such performers as former Drifter Clyde McPhatter, Big Joe Turner ("Shake, Rattle and Roll"), La Vern Baker ("Tweedle Dee"), Chuck Willis ("C.C. Rider"), and Ray Charles.

Building upon their success with Ray Charles, who as early as 1959 had been promoted as a "soul brother" by the company, Atlantic began to produce more soul acts. In 1960, the Erteguns signed Solomon Burke, who in 1965 topped the R & B chart with "Got to Get You Off My Mind." The year that Burke scaled the chart, Atlantic Records lured Wilson Pickett from the Double LL label. For the next two years Atlantic had success with Pickett, who charted with "In the Midnight Hour," "634-5789," "Land of a Thousand Dances," and "Mustang Sally." Percy Sledge, the Alabama farm boy who had chopped cotton as a youth, joined the Atlantic stable and in 1966 topped the singles chart with "When a Man Loves a Woman."

Atlantic also distributed the music of artists on Stax Records. In 1958, the brother-sister team of Jim Stewart and Estelle Axton started the Memphis-based Satellite Records and recording studio, which they renamed Stax three years later. The new label initially recorded local talent such as African-American disc jockey Rufus Thomas and his daughter, Carla, who in late 1960 hit the national chart with "Gee Whiz."

They followed with other African-American artists such as William Bell. "We just didn't sit down and say, 'We're going on with the black music,' " mentioned Stewart. "Once we had the success with Rufus and Carla it was as though we cut off a whole part of our lives that had existed previously. We never looked back from there." In 1960, on the strength of their success with Carla Thomas, Stax signed an agreement with Atlantic, which agreed to distribute all Stax product.

Stax gave artists who recorded at the Stax studio on McLemore Avenue a distinctive sound, which was created by the Stax house band, Booker T. and the MG's. The band originally consisted of several high school friends, including Packy Axton, Estelle's son. By 1962, the band had solidified into a racially integrated rhythm section: keyboardist Booker T. Jones; drummer Al Jackson, Jr.; guitarist Steve Cropper, who drew his inspiration from 5 Royales guitarist Lowman Pauling; and bassist Lewis Steinberg, who in 1964 was replaced by Donald "Duck" Dunn. The band, which in 1962 hit with its own "Green Onions," played with the Memphis Horns, anchored by Andrew Love and Wayne Jackson, to back virtually every artist who recorded at Stax, including Wilson Pickett, Aretha Franklin, Percy Sledge, Otis Redding, and Sam and Dave.

Sam and Dave, the "Double Dynamite" soul duo from Miami, were discovered by Atlantic vice-president Jerry Wexler, who agreed to let the duo record for Stax. In 1966, they hit with "You Don't Know Like I Know," "Said I Wasn't Going to Tell Nobody," "You Got Me Hummin'," and their trademark, "Hold On, I'm Coming."

The gospel-based rhythm and blues, primarily recorded by Atlantic and Stax, became known as soul music during the mid-sixties, when many African-Americans discovered a sense of self-esteem. In 1965, station WOL in Washington, D.C., attracting primarily African-American listeners, began to call itself "soul radio," local disc jockey Fred Correy labeled himself "Soulfinger," and Soul magazine began publication. In 1965 and 1966, Otis Redding perfected his style with Soul Album, Dictionary of Soul, and Otis Blue (Otis Redding Sings Soul), the last including the hit "Respect."

Around the same time, James Brown began to perfect a new style called funk and became part of the soul contingent. From 1954, when he began to sing secular music, to his breakthrough Live at the Apollo album nine years later, Brown sang a mixture of gospel and spirited blues. In late 1964, with the single "Out Of Sight," Brown unveiled a new style that featured bursts of dominant, repeating, overpowering rhythm accented by phrase-shouting vocals and the staccato punchy sound of horns. The next year the singer refined the funk style with "Papa's Got a Brand New Bag," which hit the national Top 10, topped the R & B chart, and sold a million copies. Later in the year he released the equally successful funk single "I Got You (I Feel Good)."

As Brown shifted from more traditional R & B to funk, he recalled, "I got the name 'Soul Brother Number One.' The word 'soul' by this time meant a lot of things—in music and out. It was about the roots of black music, and it was a kind of pride thing, too, being proud of yourself and your people. Soul music and the civil rights movement went hand in hand, sort of grew up together."

During 1965 and 1966, amid the civil rights movement, African-Americans supported soul acts. Otis Redding broke attendance records at shows in Harlem and Watts, and in 1966 grossed $250,000 on a month-long rhythm and blues tour. He earned enough money to start Jotis Records, signing Arthur Conley, who in late 1966 hit the charts with "Sweet Soul Music." James Brown bought a bright red Sting Ray, a fleet of Cadillacs, and a wardrobe of 150 suits and 80 pairs of shoes with the money he had amassed from the sale of records to an audience which, except for the crossover interest in his *Live at the Apollo* album, consisted almost exclusively of African-Americans. During the mid-sixties, while white youths listened to the Beatles, acid rock, or British bands such as the Rolling Stones who based their style on American R & B, African-Americans took pride in a gritty soul sound performed by fellow African-Americans. "It's SOUL, man, SOUL," exclaimed African-American disc jockey Magnificent Montague in *Billboard*. "Now what is soul? It's the last to be hired, the first to be fired, brown all year-round, sit-in-the-back-of-the-bus feeling. You've got to live with us or you don't have it. The Black Brothers are the mainstay of our pop music today. Artists like John Lee Hooker, Otis Redding and others are heavy soul—one thing our English friends can't imitate."

Black Soul in White America

The inner-city explosions during the late 1960s made many Americans, especially those raised during the civil rights era, more aware of and interested in African-American culture. Though causing a white backlash in some quarters, the 1967 riots in Detroit allowed many whites to better understand the plight of African-Americans. Discrimination "hurts them real bad. I'd probably be rioting right with them," a Texas salesman told *Time* magazine. "It degrades [the African-American] which no one likes. Therefore it is natural [for them] to fight back," echoed a California truck driver. Mrs. Margaret Lamb, a widow from Owensboro, Kentucky, told *Time*: "It makes you wonder that they do as good as they do the way people treat them sometimes. You see things that make you wonder why they put up with it."

Sympathizing with African-Americans, many young whites tried to adopt an African-American outlook. Radicalized students, protesting the war in Vietnam, embraced the ideology of militant Black Power groups such as the Black Panthers, who in late 1966 formed in Oakland, a few miles from the Berkeley campus. "We had captured the imagination of the white radical left in this country to a point that its whole identification became connected with what the Black Panther Party was doing, how it was personifying things," boasted Panther cofounder Bobby Seale. The students also successfully lobbied for ethnic studies classes, which fostered a greater awareness of the contributions of

African-Americans to such fields as history, psychology, literature, and anthropology.

White youths also started to buy soul records. The year "1967 saw the greatest emergence of the blues in recent pop history. It was the year in which rhythm and blues became the music of the charts and the year in which 'soul' became the popular music of America," exclaimed Jon Landau, rock writer and later manager of Bruce Springsteen.

African-American soul crossed over into white America with Aretha Franklin. In 1960, Aretha signed with John Hammond, the talent scout for Columbia Records, who had discovered Count Basie, Benny Goodman, and Bob Dylan. Mitch Miller, the Columbia executive who had assailed rock during the fifties, gave her voice lessons, hooked her up with Bob Mersey, the musical arranger for pop singer Barbara Streisand, and assigned her such dated material as the show tune "If Ever I Would Leave You," and Al Jolson's "Rock-A-Bye My Baby With a Dixie Melody." By 1966, a dissatisfied Aretha had found only moderate success and was in debt to Columbia.

Late in 1966, when her contract with Columbia expired, Jerry Wexler of Atlantic Records signed the singer. As Wexler told it, "One day, I happened to be in Muscle Shoals doing a Wilson Pickett session, and I got a call from [a friend] in Philadelphia. All she said was 'Call this number, *now!*' It was Aretha. I had never spoken to her, but I called her and that was it."

Within a few months Aretha recorded for Atlantic *I Never Loved a Man the Way I Love You*, which included the single "Respect." "Respect," an R & B hit for Otis Redding two years earlier, took on an added importance in 1967. The song, belted out by the Detroit native Aretha Franklin, hit the streets as the ghetto of the Motor City exploded into flames. To whites, it seemed to epitomize the renewed self-pride that African-Americans had discovered. The chart-topping song sold more than 1 million copies in ten months and brought African-American soul into white America. The album reached number two on the chart.

Aretha continued to achieve crossover success. During the next two years she charted with the million-selling singles, "(You Make Me Feel Like a) Natural Woman," "(Sweet Sweet Baby) Since You've Been Gone," "Baby, I Love You," and "Chain of Fools," and hit the Top 5 with the albums *Aretha: Lady Soul*, *Aretha Now*, and *Aretha Arrives*. In 1968, Franklin won the Best Female Vocalist of the Year award, and Detroit Mayor Jerome Cavanaugh declared Aretha Franklin Day. *Ebony* magazine characterized the summer of 1967 as "'Retha, Rap [Brown], and Revolt." In July 1968, Aretha solidified her reputation among whites as the soul spokeswoman with her rendition of "Think," which ended with the singer crying, "Oh, Freedom, Freedom, Freedom, ya, Freeeeeedom."

Other soul singers began to attract greater mainstream interest after the rioting. In 1967, Wilson Pickett hit the Top 10 with a remake of Dyke and the Blazers' "Funky Broadway" and spent eight weeks on the album chart with *The Best of Wilson Pickett*. Sam and Dave scored

Sam and Dave, ca. mid 1960s
Photo collection Joyce Moore

a crossover hit with the number-two "Soul Man." In 1968, James Brown reached the Top 10 with "Say It Loud—I'm Black and I'm Proud." Otis Redding, who had died in December 1967 when his twin-engine Beechcraft plane plunged into an icy lake outside Madison, Wisconsin, won posthumous accolades for the chart-topping "Dock of the Bay." The King of Soul, who had received little attention from the white audience during his lifetime until he electrified youths at the 1967 Monterey Pop Festival, hit the Top 5 with the album *Dock of the Bay*.

Atlantic Records, which had produced many of the soul artists, began to reap financial rewards. In July 1967, *Time* calculated that "Manhattan-based Atlantic, with such singers as Aretha, Wilson Pickett and Sam and Dave, can now sell more records in a week (1,300,000) than it did in six months in 1950." Remarked Jerry Wexler in 1968: "The young white audience now digs soul the way the black does." Soul had become the music of white America.

10

Militant Blues on Campus

"The pop scene has become a roaring, pulsating paradox of sound—the white man singing the black blues."

Time magazine

Young college students took to the streets to protest the war in Vietnam as race riots swept across urban America. As the decade came to a close, the hopeful mood of psychedelia changed to a somber resolve and then a dark depression. During the late sixties, young rock-and-rollers listened to desperate, loud blues that reflected the times.

Campus Unrest

The disturbances on campus were a reaction to the war in Vietnam. Late in 1961, the first combat troops arrived in Vietnam. Worried about the threat of communism in Southeast Asia, American officials slowly increased the U.S. commitment in Vietnam. In 1965, through the Gulf of Tonkin Resolution, the number of American troops skyrocketed from 23,000 to 184,000. By 1968, the United States had sent 542,000 troops to the war-torn country.

Small groups of youths, clustered in major universities such as Berkeley, started to protest the war. In April 1967, in New York's Central Park, more than 100,000 demonstrators gathered for the Spring

Mobilization to End the War in Vietnam. On the same day 75,000 San Francisco protesters came together for the same purpose. Others started a draft-resistance movement to "urge that other young men join us in noncooperation with the Selective Service System."

Many of the initial protests—such as the October 21, 1967 levitating of the Pentagon—were conducted in a hippie spirit. The Pentagon protest was organized by Abbie Hoffman, a civil rights organizer, and his friend Jerry Rubin, head of the Youth International Party (Yippie) which, according to its leader, "merged New Left politics with a psychedelic lifestyle. Our lifestyle—acid, long hair, freaky clothes, pot, rock music, sex—is the Revolution. Our very existence mocks America. The old order is dying." On October 21, Hoffman and Rubin, who had spoken at the Human Be-In, banded together with Allen Ginsberg, Ed Sanders of the Fugs, and others to levitate the Pentagon. Standing outside the building with 150,000 co-conspirators, the leaders chanted "in the name of the lives of the dead soldiers in Vietnam who were killed because of a bad karma, in the name of the Tyrone Power pound cake society in the sky, out demon out, out demon out." Unsuccessful in their attempt, the exorcising demonstrators were dispersed by the police, who arrested 647 protesters. "We wanted to be stoned, wasted, and free," asserted Ray Mongo, cofounder of the Liberation News Service, who had been arrested at the event. "We were proud of being individuals."

In 1968, student protests against the war became more serious and violent, driving a wedge between the hippies and radicals. After the Viet Cong had launched their Tet offensive and the United States had stepped up aerial bombardment and defoliation efforts, students at Columbia University occupied university buildings to protest the war. "Columbia was seen as part of a power structure linked to the same forces that were waging war in Vietnam," contended Allen Young of the Liberation News Service. "We viewed the disruption of university life as a necessary step. For life to go on as usual in the face of the horror of the Vietnam War was unacceptable and immoral."

In early May 1968, at 2:30 A.M., 1000 New York City policemen approached the Morningside Heights campus of Columbia University. They moved onto the campus in police vans and squad cars, sealed off the entrances to the university and, on orders from Police Commissioner Howard Leary, marched toward five buildings that had been occupied by student rebels to protest the university's affiliation with the Institute for Defense Analysis. As they began to dislodge student militants, the police encountered resistance. At Fayerweather Hall, they clubbed and kicked angry students and bystanding newsmen such as columnist Walter Winchell. By mid-morning, the police had dispersed the students from the buildings, arresting 698 and injuring 120. To noted anthropologist Margaret Mead, who had taught at Columbia for 48 years, the police action signaled "the end of an epoch."

The protest at Columbia sparked trouble at other colleges and universities. More than 500 students at Princeton demonstrated in

Student protest on campus
The Daily of the University of Washington

support of students at Columbia. At Stony Brook, 50 student militants staged a 17-hour sit-in to express their sympathy. More than 200 Temple University students picketed university buildings in the wake of the Columbia protests. By the middle of June, as the inner cities burst into violence, a National Students Association report estimated that almost 40,000 students engaged in 221 major demonstrations at 101 colleges and universities.

In August, student dissent intensified at the National Democratic Convention in Chicago, where the ineffectiveness of the flower-power approach became evident. To protest the war in Vietnam, 10,000 young, peaceful reformers traveled to the Windy City for the opening of the convention on August 26. They were organized by David Dellinger of the National Mobilization Committee to End the War in Vietnam, Tom Hayden and Rennie Davis, cofounders of the Students for a Democratic Society (SDS), and Jerry Rubin of the Yippies, who the year before had won 22 percent of the vote in the Berkeley mayoral race on a platform that included the legalization of marijuana. In the summer of 1968, Rubin announced that "the Democratic Party is dying. While it dies, we will celebrate the Festival of Life. Come to Chicago! We are the politics of the future. . . . Join us in Chicago in August for an international festival of youth, music and theater," he continued. The Yippies promised "making love in the parks . . . singing, laughing, printing newspapers, making a mock convention, and celebrating the birth of FREE AMERICA in our own time."

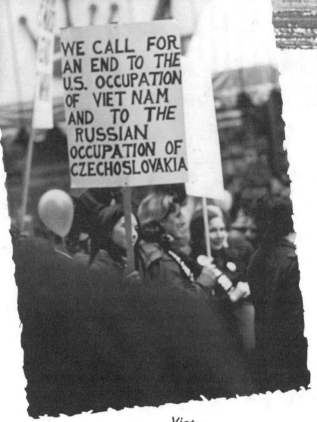

Vietnam protest demonstration
The Daily of the University of Washington

As hopeful student militants flooded into Chicago armed with backpacks and flowers, Chicago Mayor Richard Daley readied the city for battle. The mayor, who the previous year had recommended that looters be maimed and arsonists be killed during a race riot, heavily barricaded the Amphitheater, the site of the convention. He activated 6000 National Guardsmen; requested and received 6000 federal troops armed with bazookas, barbed wire, and tanks, and placed 12,000 Chicago policemen on 12-hour shifts. After encountering stiff resistance from the organized students, Daley planned a strategy of confrontation which, according to the subsequent *Walker Report*, created a "police riot." When the Democrats left on August 29, Daley's police force had injured 198 and arrested 641 protesters. Violence at the Chicago convention, and the subsequent trial of eight protest leaders, labeled by *Rolling Stone* as the "trial of the new culture," radicalized many hip students who had once believed in the power of example. "I saw the power of flowers wilt, first by gas, then when the guy next to me—a hardened street hippie out of *A Clockwork Orange*—lobbed a trash can through the windshield of a trapped squad car," remembered Abe Peck of the psychedelic Chicago underground paper *Seed*.

Events at Columbia University and the Chicago convention changed the mood of students from a hope-filled ebullience to a dark, protective aggression. "The scene has changed," wrote Steve Dreyer in the Austin *Rag*, "as people realized that you can't build a 'community' of beautiful people in a rotten, capitalist society. And it occurred with Columbia and Chicago—with the death (and cooptation) of 'do your own thing' with the beginning of the revolutionary consciousness." "Nobody wanted to know about communal living in the country, about organic food," agreed Steve Diamond of the Liberation News Service. "It was 'Be in the city, in the streets fighting the man.' " In January 1969, *The Rat*, an underground newspaper in New York City, told its readers that "the revolution has come. It's time to pick up your gun."

In 1969, campus violence escalated. In May, 3000 students at the University of California, Berkeley, tried to remove a chain that university officials had roped around a grassy lot known as People's Park. Ronald Reagan, then governor of California, calling the action "a deliberate and planned attempt at confrontation," activated 2000 National Guardsmen who gassed the unsuspecting students from a helicopter and with birdshot killed one onlooker, wounded 30 protesters, and arrested 800 others. Even *Time* magazine called the reaction a "crushing repression."

More of the 7 million university students across the country marched in protest. In 1969, disturbances occurred at state universities in Maryland, Delaware, and Minnesota. Students faced the police in major confrontations at San Francisco State, Duke University, Queens College in New York, Dartmouth College, and even at Harvard University, the bastion of academic respectability. At the University of Wisconsin at Madison, students protested the war in Vietnam by building 435 crosses which they planted in rows on the lawn of the main administration building. The organizer of the demonstration wanted to show that "students really are faced with death." By the end of 1969, millions of students had taken to the streets, and more than 100,000 of the militants had banded together in 350 chapters of the radical Students for a Democratic Society (SDS).

Radicalized to a large extent by the war in Vietnam and the establishment of the first lottery drawing to draft men into the armed forces since 1942, the militant American youths became interested in a hard-edged rock. Rather than the folk-based, airy, acid rock, they began to listen to the angry, slashing, piercing blues of British and American guitar heroes. Faced with police clubs and tear gas, they turned to the music of an oppressed race. "The blues are bigger now than ever—ten times bigger," John Lee Hooker noticed in late 1968. "You know why it's bigger? Because all the college kids are digging it now. Ten years back the blues was just in a certain area, it was the blues lovers only. But nowadays all the kids are digging the blues—the college kids."

The Psychedelic Blues

Jimi Hendrix, a poor, half African-American, half Native American from a broken home in Seattle, reflected the desperate mood of late-sixties youth through a psychedelic blues. On the cover of his 1967 debut album, *Are You Experienced?*, Hendrix and his band appeared to be the quintessential flower children. Hendrix wore bright yellow hip-huggers and a white vest over a red, pink, and yellow paisley shirt which had two openings around the chest that let two red eyeballs peek out. Around his neck Hendrix sported a vibrant orange, tufted scarf. Bass player Noel Redding favored a double-breasted, yellow felt sport coat with flowers emblazoned on it; and drummer Mitch Mitchell had white-and-blue-striped trousers, a yellow scarf, and a white, red, and yellow tie-dyed shirt. The group stood against a backdrop of blood-red trees.

Hendrix and the Experience also freely experimented with drugs. "I fully admit that drugs controlled our music," Noel Redding later admitted. "Whether it was true or not, we felt we had to be stoned to play properly. Good dope equalled good music." Hendrix, identifying with the drug culture of the sixties, used such titles as "Are You Experienced?" and "Stone Free" for two songs on the British issue of his first album.

Despite his hippie trappings, Jimi Hendrix unleashed gut-wrenching electric blues. The young Hendrix had listened to such Chicago blues greats as Muddy Waters, Howlin' Wolf, and Elmore James. After being discharged as a paratrooper from the 101st Airborne Division in 1961, he and fellow paratrooper Billy Cox began to play around Nashville, backing such blues acts as Nappy Brown, Slim Harpo, and Ironing Board Sam. For the next three years he backed such R & B performers as Little Richard, James Brown, Jackie Wilson, and B. B. King. In 1964, Hendrix relocated to New York City, where he performed with the Isley Brothers and soul singer Curtis Knight.

In late 1966, Hendrix formed the Experience and amazed European audiences with an act modeled on such former employers as Little Richard and James Brown. At the Paris Olympia he twisted, rolled, shook, and writhed in perfect time to every half-note of his thunderous electric blues. During the next few months, the guitarist staged similar shows for spectators at Stockholm's Tivoli, the Sports Arena in Copenhagen, and the Saville Theater in London.

Hendrix delivered a loud, angry electric blues that characterized the violence of the era. Using various electronic devices such as the wah-wah pedal, the fuzz box, and feedback at almost deafening levels, the guitarist pioneered a harsh, thrashing style of electric blues. Explained Hendrix of the sound: "Lots of young people now feel they're not getting a fair deal. So they revert to something loud, harsh, almost verging on violence; if they didn't go to a concert, they might be going to a riot." "He revolutionized the blues," contended Billy Cox, who played with the guitarist in the Band of Gypsys in 1970. "He took it to another level." The titles Hendrix gave to his songs reflected the desperation of the times. For his 1967 debut he penned "Manic Depression," "I Don't Live Today," and "Purple Haze."

Hendrix also exemplified the militant era through his stage show. At the 1967 Monterey Pop Festival, where he first attracted American acclaim, he finished his set with a thrashing, tortured version of the Troggs' "Wild Thing." As the last notes of the song blasted the audi-

Jimi Hendrix and The Moving Sidewalks, whose members included ZZ Top guitarist Billy Gibbons
Courtesy of Alan Douglas and Warner Brothers Records

ence from a column of nine amplifiers and 18 speakers, Hendrix ceremonially doused his guitar with lighter fluid and set it on fire. "The Experience's destruction is inevitable rather than accidental, the surfacing of a violent streak," commented *Newsweek*, "the spontaneous and impulsive violence of the young."

Other paisleyed guitar heroes hit the American scene to sing the blues. Though appearing on stage in eye-boggling outfits, Cream played a driving, electric blues-based music. The trio—Eric Clapton, Jack Bruce, and Ginger Baker—had individually started out in various blues units: Drummer Ginger Baker had been a member of Blues Incorporated and had powered the Graham Bond Organization; Jack Bruce had played his six-string bass with Baker in Blues Incorporated and the Graham Bond Organization, leaving to join John Mayall and Manfred Mann; and Clapton, idolizing Muddy Waters and Little Walter, had perfected a piercing guitar sound in the Yardbirds and John Mayall's Bluesbreakers before joining Cream. In June 1966, Ginger Baker approached Clapton about forming a group which, upon the guitarist's suggestion, included Jack Bruce on bass and vocals.

Like Hendrix, Cream delivered a high-volume, jazz-tinged version of the electric blues. They first released the album *Fresh Cream*, which included Muddy Waters's "Rollin' and Tumblin'," "I'm So Glad" by Skip James, and "Four Until Late" by legendary blues man Robert Johnson. In late 1967, the group followed with *Disraeli Gears*, their U.S. breakthrough, which contained several blues-based originals such as "World of Pain" and "Blue Condition." After hearing the album, Rose Clapp, Clapton's grandmother who had raised him, felt that Eric had "always been a lonely boy and his music still gives me that feeling about him."

Said the guitarist about his music: "Rock is like a battery that must always go back to the blues to get recharged." After attending a May 1968 concert on the band's final tour, Ian Whitcomb wrote in the *Los Angeles Times* about "great cataleptic hunks cut from the aged blues and pummeled out, slit up, reshaped, thoroughly examined by the violent guitars and drums."

Jeff Beck, another guitar hero who had formerly played with the Yardbirds, produced a hard-edged blues. After splitting from the Yardbirds in 1967, Beck formed his own group, which included blues shouter Rod Stewart. The guitarist, though dressed in paisley shirts and bell-bottomed, multicolored pants, reworked such blues standards as Willie Dixon's "You Shook Me" and "I Ain't Superstitious" in a tumultuous, shattering style. He characterized his second LP, *Beck-Ola*, a collection of blues-drenched originals and rock standards such as "All Shook Up," as "heavy music."

Alvin Lee, the blues fanatic who fronted Ten Years After, produced a loud, aggressive electric blues. He first drew attention to his guitar mastery when he backed John Lee Hooker at the Marquee Club in London. In 1965, he formed the blues-oriented Jaybirds with bass player Leo Lyons and drummer Ric Lee. A year later, the band added Chick Churchill on keyboards and changed their name to Ten Years After. In 1967, the band released their first LP which, though on the cover featuring psychedelic art and a blurred picture of the band in paisley-print shirts, delivered biting renditions of such blues as Sonny Boy Williamson's "Help Me" and Willie Dixon's "Spoonful." The group developed their blues style on such albums as the 1969 *Ssssh* and *Cricklewood Green*, released the next year, both of which reached the Top 20.

Janis Joplin, propelled to stardom amid the hippie craze, sang the blues. In 1963, she and Chet Helms, the future owner of the Avalon Ballroom, hitchhiked from her home in Port Arthur, Texas, to San Francisco to sing in various North Beach folk clubs such as the Coffee Gallery, sometimes backed by Jorma Kaukonen, who later would help start the Jefferson Airplane. Joplin returned home but in 1966 drifted back to San Francisco, joining Big Brother and the Holding Company, which she transformed from one of the original psychedelic bands into a blues unit that showcased her razor-sharp cries of anguish. As with so many young American blues artists of the late sixties, Joplin first surprised the rock-and-roll world at the 1967 Monterey Pop Festival. The next year, the first Big Brother album which featured Joplin, *Cheap Thrills*, reached the million-dollar mark in sales within a few months, and her reputation started to grow.

As *Cheap Thrills* scaled the charts, Joplin began to shed her psychedelic backdrop. In September 1968, she dumped her one-time psychedelic band to assemble the Kosmic Blues Band, which charted with *I Got Dem Ol' Kozmic Blues Again Mama!* In May 1970, she hired the rock-blues outfit, the Full-Tilt Boogie Band, which hit the top of the charts the next year with *Pearl*. On a visit to Philadelphia in August 1970, she bought a headstone for the unmarked grave of blues great Bessie

Eric Clapton
Courtesy of Warner Brothers Records

Smith, probably Joplin's greatest influence. Despite the raves of journalists and her financial success, Joplin continued to feel the blues.
"Someday," she confided to an interviewer, "I'm going to write a song
about making love to 25,000 people in a concert and then going to my
room alone."

The MC5 also made the transition from psychedelia to an aggressive, radicalized blues. Formed by five high school friends in Detroit in 1964, the Motor City Five took off in 1966 while attending Wayne
State University, where they met their manager, John Sinclair. According to drummer Dennis Thompson, "Sinclair was in charge of the beatnik community then; he was the head man. Basically [vocalist Rob] Tyn-
er, [guitarist Wayne] Kramer and [guitarist Fred "Sonic"] Smith realized
it would be a good thing to get in line with John, because John was a
powerful figure in the beatnik community. This was the same time as
things were happening in Frisco, and we were getting vibrations from
Big Brother, the Grateful Dead, bands that were forming out there. It
was like, 'Hey, let's get something happening back here' " in Detroit.

As with their counterparts in San Francisco, the MC5 lived and
worked in a communal atmosphere. They roomed together above the
office of the underground newspaper *Fifth Estate*. Believing in cooperation, the band started "trans-love energies" which guitarist Wayne
Kramer described as "a communal association that provided all the services that we, as a band, needed. . . . It was like a multicultural collective with a lot of marijuana smoke and LSD thrown in." Though playing
a James Brown-type, free-jazz-influenced, blues-based music, the MC5

Jeff Beck of the Yardbirds
Courtesy of Cam Garrett/S.C.V.D. Studio

**Janis Joplin belting
out the blues**
The Daily of the University of Washington

adopted as a "three-point program" the slogan "dope, rock 'n' roll and fucking in the streets."

During the late sixties, the MC5 became radicalized. According to Kramer, they expanded their three-point program "into a ten-point program that got more overtly political, like Free Economy, Free All Political Prisoners and the rest of the agenda of the day." The MC5 Social and Athletic fan club became the White Panther Party, and the band played to the rioters at the 1968 National Democratic convention. By 1969, asserted manager John Sinclair, the group was "totally committed to the revolution, as the revolution is totally committed to driving people out of their separate shells and into each other's arms."

In 1969, the MC5 released their first album, *Kick Out the Jams*, which included such songs as "Motor City Is Burning." To open the album, they enlisted the services of Brother J.C. Crawford, who delivered one of the most rousing, gospel-sounding exhortations in rock history: "Brothers and sisters, I want to see a sea of hands out there, let me see a sea of hands. I want everybody to kick up some noise. I want to hear some revolution out there, brothers, I want to hear a little revolution!" The crowd, clapping when Crawford had begun, became more agitated. "Brothers and sisters, the time has come for each and every one of you to decide whether you are going to be the problem or whether you are going to be the solution," he continued, using a Black Panther slogan. "You must choose, brothers, you must choose. It takes five seconds, five seconds of decision, five seconds to realize your purpose here on the planet. It takes just five seconds to realize that it's time to *move*, it's time to *get down with it*. Brothers, it's time to testify, and I want to know, are you ready to testify? *Are you ready?*" screamed Crawford to a wild crowd that was jumping on the auditorium chairs. "I give you a testimonial—the MC5." The band launched into a near-deafening version of a hard-edged blues called "Rambling Rose."

Creedence Clearwater Revival, although marketed as a psychedelic band on their first two album covers, also infused the blues with a political message. In his San Francisco home during the beat era, amid the stirrings of hippiedom, bandleader John Fogerty listened to the records of Muddy Waters, Howlin' Wolf, Elvis Presley, and Carl Perkins. By 1959, he joined with his brother Tom and high school classmates Stu Cook and Doug "Cosmo" Clifford in bands called the Blue Velvets, the Golliwogs, and finally Creedence Clearwater Revival. The band, mixing Chicago electric blues with early rockabilly into a driving concoction that Fogerty labeled "swamp music," covered such rhythm and blues classics as "I Put a Spell on You" by Screaming Jay Hawkins and Little Richard's "Good Golly Miss Molly." It repeatedly scored hits with a string of originals such as "Proud Mary," "Born on the Bayou," "Green River," "Bad Moon Rising," and "Down on the Corner."

During the late sixties, Fogerty increasingly turned to social commentary. He penned such antiwar songs as "Effigy," "Fortunate Son," and "Who'll Stop the Rain," which mirrored the sentiments of young Americans who feared being drafted and sent to the unpopular and escalating war in Vietnam. "Some folks are born, made to wave the flag, ooh, they're red, white and blue," sang the gravelly voiced Fogerty in "Fortunate Son." "When the band plays 'Hail to the Chief,' they point the cannon at you. Some folks inherit star-spangled eyes, ooh, send you off to war, and when you ask them how much should we give, the only answer's more, more. It ain't me, it ain't me, I ain't no military son. It ain't me, it ain't me, I ain't no fortunate one."

Heavy Metal

Some young British rockers, reflecting the militant mood of the times, delivered a loud, explosive blues unfettered by psychedelia to produce a sound that critics termed "heavy metal." Led Zeppelin, an outfit led by Jimmy Page, stood at the vanguard of the heavy metal blues. Page, a poor youth from the London working class, had played brilliant session guitar for the Rolling Stones, the Kinks, and The Who before joining the Yardbirds. After the Yardbirds disbanded in June 1968, he enlisted the help of session bassist John Paul Jones, drummer John Bonham, and vocalist Robert Plant, who had earned the moniker "wild man of the blues from the Black Country" for his work with such groups as the Delta Blues Band and the Crawling King Snakes. The foursome toured briefly in Scandinavia as the New Yardbirds before changing their name to Led Zeppelin.

In 1968, Led Zeppelin entered the studio to record their blues-based debut. "I've never been so turned on in my life," recalled Robert Plant of the 15-hour recording session. "Although we were all steeped in blues and R & B, we found out in the first hour and a half that we had our own identity." On the album they unveiled a slashing, amplified blues, including Willie Dixon's "You Shook Me" and "I Can't Quit You Baby," and a reworked version of Howlin' Wolf's "How Many More Years," called "How Many More Times." By early 1969, Led Zeppelin had hit the Top 10 in Britain and the United States with the album, and later in the year hit the top of the charts with their second effort, which featured their signature "Whole Lotta Love." The next year, the group topped the charts with *Led Zeppelin 3*, becoming the top rock act in the world.

Black Sabbath perfected the loud, aggressive blues that characterized heavy metal. Formed in 1967 as Earth by four Birmingham toughs, the band changed its name to Black Sabbath two years later on the advice of its manager and pounded out a hard-driving, militant sound on its 1970 debut. "I don't profess to be a messiah of slum people," insisted vocalist John ("Ozzy") Osbourne, "but I was a back-street kid, and that little demon is still in there, shoving the hot coal in. The aggression I play is the aggression I know. And it's obviously aggression a lot of people have." The group recorded such songs as "War Pigs" and "Iron Man" on the album *Paranoid* (1970), which embodied the destructive tendencies and the antiwar sentiment of the era.

The band fastened upon a preoccupation with demons and a hell-

Led Zeppelin, ca. 1969
Frank Driggs Collection

ish otherworld that had tormented many Delta blues men such as Robert Johnson, who had recorded "Me and the Devil Blues." They titled their first single "Evil Woman" and followed with "Electric Funeral" and "Sabbath, Bloody Sabbath." "If we come across doomy and evil, it's just the way we feel," contended guitarist Tony Iommi.

Deep Purple turned to heavy metal midway in its career. Funded in 1967 by two London businessmen, the band began to chart with a series of remakes such as Joe South's "Hush" and Neil Diamond's "Kentucky Woman." In 1969, they recorded a *Concerto for Group and Orchestra* with the Royal Philharmonic Orchestra. After *Concerto* failed to sell in the United States, guitarist Richie Blackmore began to dominate the band, which banged out a series of heavy metal classics such as *Fireball* (1971), *Machine Head* (1972), and *Made in Japan* (1973).

The Rebirth of the Blues

The militant, dark mood that fostered heavy metal led to a late-sixties electric blues revival. Young white blues performers raised in the American South began to gain popularity. Johnny Winter, raised in Beaumont, Texas, had played the blues for years before attracting national attention. After starting a number of blues-rock outfits with his brother, Edgar, Winter traveled to Louisiana and then to Chicago, where he backed local blues greats. He returned to Texas, played the Georgia-

Florida blues circuit, and produced a demo tape that included such blues standards as Howlin' Wolf's "Forty-Four," "Help Me" by Sonny Boy Williamson, and Muddy Waters's "Rolling and Tumblin'."

Winter began to reap the rewards of his efforts. In a 1968 *Rolling Stone* review of the Texas blues scene, the guitarist was referred to as "a hundred-and-thirty-pound cross-eyed albino with long, fleecy hair, playing some of the gutsiest fluid blues guitar you have ever heard." A few weeks later Winter was signed by East Coast club owner Steve Paul, who had rushed to Houston after reading the article. In 1969, Johnny Winter debuted on Columbia Records with an electric blues album that hit the Top 25. "I'd been put down for years for singing the blues and suddenly everyone liked me and wanted to hear me," shrugged Winter in 1969.

ZZ Top followed the path of their fellow Texan. In the early 1960s, guitarist Billy Gibbons listened to "all the Little Richard stuff, Larry Williams's 'Short Fat Fanny,' Jimmy Reed, T-Bone Walker, B. B. King, the usual line-up of R & B stars." In 1967, he formed a psychedelic band, The Moving Sidewalks, which had a minor hit with "99th Floor," and in June 1968 opened for Jimi Hendrix. After The Moving Sidewalks disbanded in 1969, Gibbons joined with bassist Dusty Hill and drummer Frank Beard, die-hard blues rockers, who had played together in American Blues, to form ZZ Top.

ZZ Top, ca. mid 1970s
Frank Driggs Collection

The Steve Miller Band
The Daily of the University of Washington

The struggling ZZ Top found inspiration in Johnny Winter. "Johnny Winter certainly deserves mention in this conversation because he led the way for so many with his blues guitar interpretations," Billy Gibbons told an interviewer. "We were immediately able to grasp the music through Johnny's performances in Beaumont and elsewhere. The way he did it was something; he ripped it up." Added Dusty Hill: "Johnny and also Edgar jammed with Frank and me in Houston clubs way back when we had blue hair for our old band, American Blues."

ZZ Top signed to London Records and in 1970 released their first LP, a collection of blues rockers and reworked gospel songs. They toured the South constantly, developing a cult following that supported their second LP. By 1973, when they released the Top 10 album *Tres Hombres*, the band had become one of the most successful touring blues bands. "We have not only been fans of the blues for a long time," remarked Billy Gibbons, "but we've really tried to study and deliver it with some kind of forceful feeling."

Steve Miller offered another brand of Texas blues. As a youth he met T-Bone Walker, who provided him with "my basic lead phrasing." In 1961, after backing Jimmy Reed in a Dallas bar, Miller traveled from his Texas home with friend Boz Scaggs to the University of Wisconsin in Madison, where they formed a white blues group, the Ardells. In 1964, he migrated to Chicago, where he backed blues greats Howlin'

Wolf, Muddy Waters, and James Cotton and organized a blues band with Barry Goldberg. "Texas and then Chicago," Miller told a reporter, "where I spent some time learning Chicago blues and by the time I got to San Francisco [in 1966] I realized I had picked up a whole lot of Chicago blues."

In San Francisco the guitarist formed the Steve Miller Blues Band, which sounded, in the words of a reviewer, like "huge sheets of steel violently shaken." In 1968, after appearing at the Monterey Pop Festival and backing Chuck Berry on his *Live at the Fillmore* album, the band signed with Capitol Records and released *Children of the Future*. The next year Miller won critical approval and commercial success with *Sailor*.

Canned Heat, a Los Angeles blues band named after the blues song "Canned Heat Mama," also began to attract fans by the end of the sixties. Brought together in 1965 by singer Bob ("The Bear") Hite and guitarist Alan Wilson, Canned Heat initially had trouble finding work. "Nobody would hire us because we were blues," complained Hite, who in the sixties rabidly collected more than 70,000 blues records. In 1968, after the group performed at the Monterey Pop Festival, the band began to gain recognition. They signed to Liberty Records and hit the charts with the single "On the Road Again." The next year, the group neared the Top 10 with the single "Going Up the Country." In 1971, after a series of successful, blues-drenched LPs, Canned Heat recorded an album with one of their idols, John Lee Hooker.

The Allman Brothers delivered electric blues from the Deep South. In 1965, brothers Duane and Gregg Allman, raised in Florida, played as the Allman Joys, recording a commercially unsuccessful version of Willie Dixon's "Spoonful." Two years later they moved to Los Angeles and signed with Liberty Records as Hourglass. After two LPs, Hourglass disbanded and Duane moved to Muscle Shoals, Alabama, providing background guitar for Wilson Pickett, Aretha Franklin, and Percy Sledge.

In 1969, Duane Allman formed a new band with brother Gregg, Dickey Betts on second guitar, Berry Oakley on bass, and drummers Butch Trucks and Jaimoe Johanson. "Duane and Gregg were students of the urban blues," recalled Betts. "Their thing was like a real honest, truthful chilling delivery of that music, whereas Oakley and I may have been influenced by the blues and were students of it, but we were more innovative. We would try to take a blues tune and, instead of respecting the sacredness of it, we would go *sideways* with it. . . . So when we all came together," concluded the guitarist, "we gave each other a new foundation." In 1970, the Allman Brothers released their unique electric blues on a debut album, which sold well in the South. They backed Jimi Hendrix and B. B. King at the Atlanta Pop Festival and released a second album that reached the Top 40. A year later, when the band released the commercially successful *Live at the Fillmore East*, it had become the spearhead of what critics termed southern rock, paving the way for bands such as Lynyrd Skynyrd and the Marshall Tucker Band. At the turn of the decade, with such bands as the Allman Brothers, reported *Time* magazine, "the pop scene has become a roaring, pulsating paradox of sound—the white man singing the black blues."

Woodstock and the End of an Era

The intense mood of American youths, reflected by their interest in hard-edged, high-volume electric blues, changed at the turn of the decade as the militant hope of Woodstock turned into dark fear at Altamont and Kent State. The Woodstock Music and Arts Festival in Bethel, New York, held from August 15 to 17, 1969, seemed to herald a new era. Organized by John Roberts, a young millionaire who had graduated from the University of Pennsylvania; Joel Rosenman, a Yale Law School graduate and the son of a prominent Long Island orthodontist; Mike Lang, organizer of the Miami Pops Festival; and Artier Cornfield, head of Contemporary Products at Capitol Records; the Woodstock Festival symbolized unity of purpose among the swelling ranks of youth who opposed the war in Vietnam and hoped to assert

Canned Heat at the Fillmore East, 1969
Photo © Raeanne Rubenstein

211

their own power. "Woodstock signified the coming together of all tribes," remarked Carlos Santana, the guitarist, who played a mixture of Latin rhythms and the blues to the 400,000 at the festival. "It became apparent that there were a lot of people who didn't want to go to Vietnam, who didn't see eye to eye with Nixon and none of that system, you know?"

The music at the festival reflected the anti-authoritarian attitude of late-sixties youth. Though including a motley assortment of sounds from such folk rockers as Melanie to psychedelic bands such as the Grateful Dead and the Jefferson Airplane, Woodstock featured performances by Country Joe and Jimi Hendrix. Dressed in an army fatigue shirt and jeans, Country Joe McDonald took the stage at Woodstock without his band. "I get kind of mystical about my solo performance at Woodstock," remembered McDonald. "I was hanging around, and I was just filling time, singing a few country and western songs and folk songs. Then I did the [anti-Vietnam war song,] "Feel-Like-I'm-Fixing-To-Die-Rag"—the F-U-C-K cheer—the rest is history. From the first response to 'Give me an F', when they all stopped talking and looked at me and yelled, F, I knew there was no turning back."

Jimi Hendrix appeared near the end of the festival. Taking the stage with a group of musicians called the Electric Sky Church, he launched into a powerful version of "The Star Spangled Banner" which featured screaming-rockets and exploding-bomb guitar effects and sounded like a heaving, wounded monster about to die. In his rendition of the national anthem, Hendrix captured the militant outlook sixties youth held toward the government.

The festival at Altamont Speedway near San Francisco, held in December 1969, dashed the sense of power that Woodstock had engendered among many youth. Drawn by a free concert staged by the Rolling Stones, who wanted to repeat their successful Hyde Park performance, more than 300,000 fans flocked to the site. During the event, hundreds required treatment for drug overdoses, including one youth who jumped off a freeway overpass after ingesting some LSD. Horrified, powerless spectators watched the San Francisco contingent of the Hell's Angels motorcycle gang, hired to keep order in exchange for $500 worth of beer, stab to death an 18-year-old African-American from Berkeley, one of four deaths at the concert. "Altamont was the end of the sixties," contended Bill Thompson, manager of the Jefferson Airplane. "It was December 1969, and that was the end. Of the whole feeling."

Events at Kent State University in May 1970 destroyed any remaining feeling of militant power that existed among sixties youth after Altamont. After President Richard Nixon had announced that American troops had been sent into Cambodia, students at Kent State University in northeastern Ohio took to the streets. On May 2, they hurled bottles at police cars, smashed store windows, and doused trees with gasoline, setting them on fire. The next day, protesters firebombed the one-story ROTC building on the Kent State campus.

The authorities responded swiftly and decisively to the disruptions. Mayor Leroy Satrom asked Ohio Governor James Rhodes to activate the National Guard. Rhodes, who described the students as "worse than the 'brownshirt' and Communist element . . . the worst type of people that we harbor in America," responded with 900 troops armed with M-1 rifles, submachine guns, and canisters of tear gas. On the third day of troubles, guardsmen chased a mob of students to a knoll near Taylor Hall. Suddenly, without warning, 16 National Guardsmen each knelt on one knee and leveled their guns at the crowd. Asserted journalism professor Charles Brill, who witnessed the action: "They all waited and they all pointed their rifles at the same time. It looked like a firing squad." The soldiers pumped 35 rounds from their M-1 rifles into the protesters standing 75 feet away. "It's about time we showed the bastards who's in charge," sneered one guardsman. The gunfire killed four students and wounded ten others. "My God! My God! They're killing us," screamed one Kent State freshman.

The murders at Kent State caused an immediate reaction in colleges and universities across the nation. Students sacked the treasurer's office at the University of South Carolina; they bombed the ROTC buildings at the universities of Utah and Idaho; and 124 students were arrested in a fight with state troopers at the University of Colorado. Protesters occupied the ROTC building at the University of Nebraska, and a half-million-dollar fire blazed at Colorado State. Three weeks of rioting ravaged the Berkeley campus; and in rioting at the University of Maryland state troopers injured 138 and arrested 200. Students at the University of Wisconsin, chanting, "We're gonna open up a second front in Madison," took over the Army Mathematics Research Center and were responsible for at least 20 major firebombings. More than 75,000 students marched on Washington, D.C., gathering in front of the White House, and more than 200 colleges and universities shut down for at least one day, most for the rest of the academic year. In May and June 1970, over 508 protests rocked college campuses.

After initial outbursts of violence, a sense of helplessness enveloped many American youths. Said one youth at the post-Kent State demonstration in Washington, D.C.: "The people here understand that we are surrounded by fully armed troops and that if we start anything, we'd be destroyed." "I thought that the war was just escalating, was never going to stop, that Nixon was absolutely crazed, that these people had taken over everything, that the Movement didn't have a chance," recalled Cheryl McCall of the underground newspaper *South End*. "They had put up with us protesting, marching in the streets, but now they were just going to kill us." For the first time in a decade, rebellious youths who had hoped for a better world felt that they had reached a dead end.

During the next few months, shocking news of the deaths of several prominent rock figures deepened the hopeless mood of youth. Jimi Hendrix passed away on September 18, 1970, a victim of complications from an overdose of sleeping pills. On September 3, Al Wilson, lead guitarist for Canned Heat, died of a drug overdose. Only a few weeks later, on October 4, at the Landmark Hotel in Hollywood, authorities confirmed the death of Janis Joplin from an overdose of heroin. On July 3, 1971, Jim Morrison of the Doors died of a heart attack in a bathtub in Paris. By the beginning of the 1970s, many youths who only a few years before had vowed to work for sweeping social change listened to the guns of Kent State and retreated to the cerebral music of jazz-rock and classical rock and the soft sounds of a nonpolitical, country-tinged folk revival.

Jimi Hendrix at Woodstock festival
Courtesy of Alan Douglas

11

Soft Sounds
of the
Seventies

"These days nobody wants to hear songs that have a message."
**Vocalist Robert Lamm
of the group Chicago**

"We know that people and movements are fallible," one college senior from American University told *Time* magazine in the early 1970s. "We're afraid to believe too much in anything or anyone."

In the aftermath of Kent State, most youths of the Woodstock generation agreed with the cautious sentiments expressed by the college senior from American University. Sent to a war in a faraway land and attacked by National Guardsmen at home, they abandoned the hope for a revolution in values and began to turn inward.

Economic conditions caused further concern. From 1969 to 1970, unemployment in the United States increased from 3.5 percent to 6.2 percent. In the same year, the buying power of the dollar declined by nearly 6 percent, and the government cut public spending and imposed credit restrictions. Throughout the country, the fear of a major recession gripped most Americans.

Music reflected the somber, conservative mood as many deserted a hard-driving rock. "The fading out of ear-numbing, mindblowing acid rock," *Time* contended in early 1971, "is related to the softening of the youth revolution. Its decline is variously viewed as a symptom of

Miles Davis, 1972
Photo by Gerry Bahl, Frank Driggs Collection

either progress toward harmony and thoughtfulness or a tragic slide from activist rage to a mode of 'enlightened apathy.' "

Rather than the pounding, loud sounds of psychedelia, the punchy rhythms of soul, or the wrenching, angry urban blues, rock became soft, serious, and introspective. Built upon the yen for experimentation fostered during the hippie era, it was fused with more respectable, established musical forms such as jazz, classical, country, and folk. During the early seventies, rock-and-roll became an apolitical, intensely personal experience.

Miles Ahead

Rock-and-roll had always been a union of diverse types of music. At its inception it had been an amalgam of electric R & B and country, first joined together by Chuck Berry, Elvis, and the rockabillies. During the mid-1960s, when Bob Dylan plugged an electric guitar cord into an amplifier, rock merged with folk for what critics called folk-rock. Later in the decade, the Rolling Stones had rediscovered Chicago blues, and African-Americans had turned gospel-based R & B into soul and funk. The psychedelic bands, experimenting in many aspects of their lives, had merged fifties rock with blues, folk, and such exotic-sounding world music as the Indian raga.

At the turn of the decade, performers continued to fuse rock with other musical forms such as jazz. Blood, Sweat and Tears spearheaded the trend toward a jazz-rock fusion. Organized by Al Kooper, a former member of the Blues Project who had been onstage when Bob Dylan first performed with an electric guitar, Blood, Sweat and Tears played a blues-based music complemented by the horns of such New York jazzmen as trumpeter Randy Brecker. In 1968, they cut their first LP, the commercially unsuccessful *The Child Is Father to the Man*. When Kooper quit in 1969, the band recruited vocalist David Clayton-Thomas, who added a pop element to the jazz rock for the top-selling *Blood, Sweat and Tears*, which included the music of jazz-great Billie Holiday. The next year, the band again topped the chart with *Blood, Sweat and Tears 3*, and in 1971 followed with the Top Ten *BS&T 4*, both featuring Clayton-Thomas on vocals and such jazz horn men as Joe Henderson and Lew Soloff.

James William Guercio, who had worked for Blood, Sweat and Tears, successfully promoted and managed another jazz-rock unit, Chicago. Formed in 1966 as Big Thing by two school friends, guitarist Terry Kath and saxophonist Walter Parazaider, the band changed its name to Chicago Transit Authority and in 1969 released a political jazz-rock album that included protest chants from the 1968 Democratic National convention. Under the guidance of manager James William Guercio, the band shortened its name to Chicago, dispensed with radical politics, and fused its sound with pop to achieve a long-standing commercial success. In 1970, they hit the Top 5 with *Chicago II*, the next year reached the number-two position with *Chicago III*, and topped the album chart in the next four years with five LPs. As with other rock acts during the early seventies, Chicago delivered an apolitical music. "These days nobody wants to hear songs that have a message" asserted vocalist and keyboardist Robert Lamm.

Carlos Santana added Latin rhythms to the jazz-rock amalgam. Born in Tijuana, Santana moved to San Francisco and, in 1966, started the Santana Blues Band. By 1968, the band had begun to incorporate different types of influences into their electric blues. "If I would go to some cat's room" remembered the guitarist about the band, "he'd be listening to Sly [Stone] and Jimi Hendrix; another guy to the Stones and the Beatles. Another guy'd be listening to Tito Puente and Mongo Santamaria. Another guy'd be listening to Miles [Davis] and [John] Coltrane. So every room that I went, to me it was like being at a university." In late 1969, the band featured Latin and jazz rhythms on the rock album *Santana*, which hit the Top 5 with the help of the band's appearance at Woodstock. The next year, as jazz-rock scaled the charts, they topped the chart with *Abraxas* and the next year did the same with *Santana III*. In 1972, the band continued their chart success with the jazzy *Caravanserai*, the sound on which Santana attributed to "Trane or Miles or Freddie Hubbard."

Pink Floyd, 1969
Photo © Raeanne Rubenstein

Donald Fagen and Walter Becker, the cofounders of Steely Dan, drew their inspiration from similar sources. "I met Walter in college and we had very similar musical interests," remembered keyboardist Fagen, who learned piano from Thelonious Monk and Red Garland records. "He was also a weenie jazz fan. . . . So we kind of combined the [rhythm and] blues thing—which was much simpler but very direct and emotional—with the jazz stuff we knew into a big mess." In 1973, the duo, helped by various session musicians, charted with their debut, *Can't Buy a Thrill*, which, according to Fagen, "used devices that I think had formerly been used only by jazz people." The next year, Steely Dan reached the Top 10 with *Pretzel Logic*, which included the hit "Rikki Don't Lose That Number." Throughout the rest of the decade, they produced three more Top 20 albums, which helped popular jazz-rock.

Jazz great Miles Davis, who had been present at the inception of bop during the mid-forties and had helped spearhead the movement toward cool jazz, provided the context for future jazz-rock experiments. In 1970, Davis blended a raw-edged, slightly dissonant sixties jazz with the electric sound of rock, emerging with *Bitches Brew*, his first chart success. "This music is new," wrote music critic and *Rolling Stone* magazine cofounder Ralph Gleason in the liner notes for the album. "It hits me like an electric shock and the word 'electric' is interesting because the music is to some degree electric music. . . . Electric music is the music of this culture and in the breaking away (not the breaking down) from previously assumed forms a new kind of music is emerging."

The album included future innovators of the fusion movement:

John McLaughlin on guitar, Joe Zawinul's electric piano on some cuts, Chick Corea's electric keyboard on others, and the soprano saxophone of Wayne Shorter. John McLaughlin, playing with the Graham Bond Organization during the early sixties and later with the Tony Williams Lifetime jazz outfit, went on to form the jazz-rock Mahavishnu Orchestra, which charted with *Birds of Fire* (1973). Zawinul and Wayne Shorter continued the fusion experiment in Weather Report, and in 1972 Chick Corea brought together Stanley Clarke, Joe Farrell, and Airto Moreira in *Return to Forever*, which hit the album chart four times during the seventies. Herbie Hancock, another pianist who had played with Miles Davis, formed Headhunters, which in 1974 placed a self-named debut and *Thrust* on the chart. These musicians, along with a number of mainstream jazz performers who adopted the new style, defined and shaped the sound of seventies jazz-rock fusion.

Classical Rock

Some British musicians merged rock with classical music, sometimes adding escapist, fantasy-laden lyrics to create a hybrid, which became popular on both sides of the Atlantic during the early seventies. Two English R & B bands, the Moody Blues and Procol Harum, became the forerunners of the classical rock movement. Formed in 1964, the Moody Blues initially delivered a high-powered British R & B, appearing with the Animals and the Rolling Stones at the Empire Pool in Wembly and backing Sonny Boy Williamson. In 1965, they topped the British chart and hit the U.S. Top 10 with "Go Now," a cover of an American R & B song by singer Bessie Banks. "At that time, there were only two bands in Birmingham playing the blues, us and the Spencer Davis Group," explained vocalist and harmonica player, Ray Thomas, a founder of the Moody Blues.

In late 1966, when bassist/singer John Lodge and guitarist Justin Hayward replaced bassist Clint Warwick and guitarist Denny Laine, who would later join Beatle Paul McCartney in Wings, the band shifted from R & B to an atmospheric, classically driven sound. In 1967, the reformed Moody Blues showcased Mike Pinder's mellotron, a keyboard capable of reproducing the sounds of violins, trumpets, cellos, and other orchestralinstruments. Using their new-found sounds, the band scaled the charts with *Days of Future Passed*, which featured the Mellotron and the London Festival Orchestra and which included the Hayward composition "Nights in White Satin." Hayward called their chart success "a little rock opera." By the turn of the decade the Moody Blues again neared the top of the chart with two albums of orchestrated rock highlighted by obscure, fantasy-filled lyrics, and in 1972 topped the chart with *Seventh Sojourn*.

Procol Harum also presaged the flowering of seventies classical rock. Beginning in 1959 as the R & B band the Paramounts, the band struggled until 1964, when they charted with a remake of the Coasters' "Poison Ivy" and were named the best British R & B group by the Rolling

Steve Howe of Yes
The Daily of the University of Washington

Stones. After guitarist Robin Trower left the Paramounts, eventually to form a Hendrix-style power trio, vocalist Gary Brooker and lyricist Keith Reid joined with classically trained organist Matthew Fisher, guitarist Ray Royer, and bassist Bobby Harrison to start Procol Harum. In 1967, the group topped the British chart and reached the U.S. Top 5 with "A Whiter Shade of Pale," a surreal poem by Reid set to music adapted from one of the movements in Bach's Suite No. 3 in D Major. After several commercially disappointing follow-ups, in 1972 Procol Harum rode the crest of classical rock with *Procol Harum in Concert with the Edmonton Symphony Orchestra*, which included an orchestral version of "Conquistador."

King Crimson, fueled by the ideas of Robert Fripp, served as a prototype for seventies classical rock. In early 1969, the band formed around Fripp, who combined classical guitar technique with screaming rock sounds. After backing the Rolling Stones at the Hyde Park Festival before 650,000 people, the group neared the top of the chart with its debut, *In the Court of the Crimson King*, which included the symphonic sounds of the Mellotron and featured mythical, escapist, fantasy-based lyrics similar to the motifs that would appear on the albums of other classical-rock bands. The next year they followed with the commercially successful *In the Wake of the Poseidon*, which included "The Devil's Triangle," based upon Gustav Holst's orchestral suite, *The Planets*, and continued their fascination with deep-sea mythology.

Banding together in June 1970 during a chance meeting in San Francisco, former King Crimson guitarist Greg Lake, classically trained pianist Keith Emerson, and drummer Carl Palmer made their debut at the 1970 Isle of Wight Festival. That year they reached the Top 20 with their first album, embellished with classical motifs and songs written by ex-King Crimson lyricist Pete Sinfield. In 1971, the trio released a live version of Moussorgsky's composition *Pictures at an Exhibition*, which reached the Top 10. The same year they hit the top of the chart in Britain and the Top 10 in the United States with *Tarkus*, which revolved around the concept of a mechanized armadillo that battled the mythical beast the Manticore. In 1974, after creating their own record label named after the Manticore, the group charted with the three-record set, *Welcome Back My Friends*, which included "Toccata" by Bach and Aaron Copland's "Rodeo." According to *Time*, the group used "classical style and technique in much the same way the Stones draw on blues."

The Electric Light Orchestra also explored the connection between rock and the classics. As The Move disbanded at the turn of the decade, guitarists Roy Wood and Jeff Lynne founded the Electric Light Orchestra. "I had the idea of ELO," explained Wood. "I thought, 'wouldn't it be great to get a band together and instead of advertising for a guitarist, advertise for a french horn player or a cellist 'cause there must be young people around that play those instruments that like rock 'n' roll."

The band first released *No Answer*, an album graced with cellos and violins. In 1973, after the departure of Wood, they enlisted the help of three former members of the London Symphony Orchestra to help with their second effort, which included their first hit, a richly orchestrated version of Chuck Berry's "Roll Over, Beethoven." In 1974, the band cracked the U. S. Top 20 with *Eldorado*, promoted as "a symphony by the Electric Light Orchestra," and included their first U. S. Top 10 hit, "Out of My Head," which showcased a 30-piece string section. "I like the *sound*," insisted Jeff Lynne. "That's all music is for me. Not for putting a message over."

Pink Floyd, a British psychedelic band formed in 1965, moved toward classical structures during the seventies. Named after country-blues duo Pink Anderson and Floyd Council, the band began by playing R & B music. By 1967, Pink Floyd had developed a psychedelic sound that featured feedback and other electronic experiments. In early 1968, when vocalist-guitarist Syd Barrett became incapacitated because of an LSD dependency, the group hired guitarist David Gilmore, who led the band to a more subtle, classically based sound evident on several atmospheric soundtracks and the albums *Atom Heart Mother* and *Meddle*. "Syd moving out meant that we had to start writing," explained bassist/vocalist Roger Waters. "In fact, his leaving made us pursue the idea of the extended epic and a more classically constructed idea of music." By their 1973 masterpiece, *Dark Side of the Moon*, which took nine painstaking months to produce and sold more than 13 million copies, Pink Floyd had perfected a Wagnerian electronic sound that provided a backdrop for epic tales of alienation, paranoia, and madness.

Yes, a band formed in 1968 during a meeting at a London businessman's drinking club, La Chasse in Soho, featured neoclassical structures and three-part harmonies. After adding guitarist Steve Howe and classically trained pianist Rick Wakeman, the group recorded the Top 5 *Fragile* (1971), their U.S. breakthrough, which contained the hit

"Roundabout." The group followed with *Close to the Edge*, consisting of three extended cuts and a four-movement title suite. By 1974, *Time* gushed over "the complex, educated sounds" of groups such as Yes. "Thus do barriers fall," the magazine concluded, "and such often enclosed worlds as rock music get a little sunshine in."

Back to the Country

Confronted by the harsh, complicated realities of an unwanted war in Vietnam and events at Kent State, some folk rockers began to move toward a country music that extolled simple living and rural traditions. "Country rock," observed *Time* in 1970, was a "turning back toward easy-rhythmed blues, folk songs and the twangy, lonely lamentations known as country music." The new musical blend, continued *Time*, was a "symptom of a general cultural reaction to the most unsettling decade that the U.S. has yet endured. The yen to escape the corrupt present by returning to the virtuous past—real or imagined—has haunted Americans, never more so than today."

Bob Dylan, the most visible protest singer of the 1960s, led youth back to the country. In 1968, Dylan began to lean toward a country sound on *John Wesley Harding*, which neared the top of the chart. In May 1969, Dylan made his country influences more obvious on the million-selling *Nashville Skyline*, recorded in the country music capital of Nashville, Tennessee. This album featured a duet with former rockabilly and country music giant Johnny Cash on "Girl from the North Country." In the same month Dylan appeared with Cash on a television special filmed at the Grand Ole Opry.

As Dylan moved toward country, the Byrds, the folk-rock group that had risen to fame on Dylan compositions, looked to country music for inspiration. Prodded by new Byrd singer-guitarist Gram Parsons, the group released *Sweetheart of the Rodeo* (1968), which included several notable country musicians such as guitarists John Hartford and Clarence White. Although achieving only moderate commercial success with their new direction, the band signaled the way back to the country and, in late 1968, Byrds Michael Clarke and Chris Hillman joined with Parsons to form the country-rock outfit the Flying Burrito Brothers.

The Band, Dylan's sometime backing group, began to achieve popularity with its country-based rock. After a stint with rockabilly singer Ronnie Hawkins, in 1965 guitarist Jaime "Robbie" Robertson, pianist Richard Manuel, drummer Levon Helm, bassist Rick Danko, and organist Garth Hudson formed their own group. Robertson and Helm backed Dylan when he first plugged in an electric guitar and after Dylan's 1965 motorcycle accident the group moved near the reclusive singer in Woodstock, New York.

The Band, as they were now called, recorded their debut at Woodstock in their large, pink-colored house; in 1968 they released *Music From Big Pink*, using several Dylan songs. The next year they hit the Top 10 with a heavily country-influenced, self-named LP, which included the hit "Up On Cripple Creek." By late 1970, the group reached the Top 5 in the United States with their third album, *Stage Fright*. The Band, wrote *Time*, perfected a rock hybrid that "comes on mainly as country music full of straight lines and sentiment."

Poco offered a similar brand of country rock. In late 1968, when the folk-rock group Buffalo Springfield splintered into the trio Crosby, Stills and Nash and a solo career for Neil Young, Springfield guitarist Richie Furay decided to form a country-rock outfit with his friend Jim Messina. "Richie and I were riding in a cab in Nashville," remembered Messina. "We talked about forming a new band that would be an extension of what we'd been doing with the Springfield, but more country and rock than folk and rock." The duo invited guitarist Rusty Young, bassist Randy Meisner, and drummer George Grantham to join Pogo, renamed Poco when the owners of the Pogo comic strip threatened legal action over use of the name. After two moderately successful efforts, in 1971 the group neared the Top 20 with *Deliverin'*, which relied heavily on such traditional country instruments as steel guitars, mandolins, and dobros. "I think the most dominating thing was the fact that we had this country sound," Furay remarked about the album. "We were pioneering the country-rock sound at this time with the introduction of the steel guitar, the high, countryish harmonies and all."

The Arizona-born Linda Ronstadt served as the focal point for several other seventies country rockers. In 1964, she moved to Los Angeles to join the folk trio the Stone Poneys. Though selling few copies of their debut, the group scored with "Different Drum (1968)" before disbanding. After two unsuccessful solo efforts, Ronstadt began to frequent the Troubadour folk club in Los Angeles, where she recruited a tour band, including guitarist Glenn Frey and drummer Don Henley.

The Band, ca. 1972
Frank Driggs Collection

The singer recorded her third solo album, which included such country-flavored songs as "I Fall to Pieces" and "Crazy Arms." In 1973, she hired as manager Peter Asher, who had started in the music business as half of the folk-rock duo Peter and Gordon.

Helped by a new manager, the singer released *Don't Cry Now*, which remained on the charts for 56 weeks. During the next five years Ronstadt recorded a number of top-selling albums that combined sensitive ballads with smooth renditions of such country and rockabilly classics as the Everly Brothers' "When Will I Be Loved," "I Can't Help It If I'm Still in Love with You" by Hank Williams, and Buddy Holly's "It's So Easy" and "That'll Be the Day."

Linda Ronstadt professed politically conservative beliefs, which had become prevalent during the early 1970s. She hoped for a "real resurgence of patriotism in this country." After campaigning for liberal candidates, the singer felt that "I really didn't know what I was talking about. Who knows who should be President and if anybody should have an interest in determining those things, shouldn't Standard Oil? I mean, they have more to gain and more to lose. If something terrible happens to Standard Oil, a lot of people will be out of jobs. You can say what you want about big multi-nationals running the country and stuff, but the fact remains that we need that, we need their services, we need jobs from them and they are in a better position to decide what's going to be good for the economic climate of the country and for the rest of the world."

Ronstadt's one-time tour band, splitting from the singer in August 1971, achieved stardom as the Eagles. By 1972, Frey and Henley had formed the Eagles with bassist Randy Meisner, who had played for Poco, and guitarist Bernie Leadon, who had backed Linda Ronstadt and had been a member of the Flying Burrito Brothers. "Glenn [Frey] said we needed to get those guys [Meisner and Leadon] because they could play the kind of country rock we were all so interested in," observed Henley. That year the group recorded their self-named debut album, which neared the Top 20 and included the hits "Take It Easy," "Peaceful Easy Feeling," and "Witchy Woman." In 1973, they recorded *Desperado*, a concept album about the mythical Old West, especially the Dalton gang and its leaders, Bill Dalton and Bill Doolin. Three years later they scored their first million-selling single, "The Best of My Love," which exemplified their trademark soft, country-influenced rock. During the rest of the seventies they released four chart-topping albums, which included such laid-back hits as "One of These Nights," "Lyin' Eyes," and "Take It to the Limit."

Jackson Browne, writing songs for the Eagles and Linda Ronstadt, epitomized the country-tinged, West Coast tunesmith of the seventies. According to the singer, he was influenced by his sister, who "was two years older than me, and she hung around with these guys who wrote songs and did a lot of civil rights stuff. I started hanging around with them and writing songs when I was 15. We gravitated toward Bob Dylan, Pete Seeger kind of stuff. This is 1964, '65.'"

Linda Ronstadt
Photo by Bonnie Lippel, courtesy of Peter Asher Management

Browne, like Dylan himself, deserted social protest for an intensely personal, country-flavored folk. After traveling to New York City, where he wrote songs recorded by the Byrds, he signed with the newly established Asylum Records. In 1972, with the help of David Crosby and country guitarist Clarence White, the singer-songwriter released his first LP, which contained the hit "Doctor My Eyes." Later in the year, to promote the album, he toured with the Eagles. As he toured, Browne hit the charts as a co-composer of the Eagles' hit "Take It Easy," which he wrote with former roommate Glenn Frey. He continued to compose hits for the Eagles, who charted with Browne's "Doolin' Dalton" and "James Dean." By the second half of the decade he hit the charts as a solo artist with three Top 5 albums of highly personal compositions. Browne called his work "the residue of my life."

With the help of Johnny Cash, Kris Kristofferson, another struggling songwriter, stepped into the country-rock spotlight at the turn of the decade. After earning a Ph.D. in English literature and serving a stint as a paratrooper in the army, in 1965 the songwriter moved to Nashville, where he worked as a janitor at CBS Records studios. Four years later Kristofferson dropped in on his idol, Johnny Cash. "One

Sunday he landed in my yard in a helicopter and brought me 'Sunday Morning Coming Down,' " remembered Cash. "That's true. He fell out of the helicopter with a beer in one hand and a tape in the other and said, 'By God, I'm gonna get a song to you one way or the other.' I said, 'Well, you just did.' "

Johnny Cash volunteered to allow the brash songwriter to appear the next week at the Newport Folk Festival during his set. At the festival "when he heard his name over the loudspeaker," recalled Cash, "it stunned him and he just stood there. June [Carter Cash, Johnny's wife] got behind him and put her high heel right on his butt and pushed him out onstage. Next day on the *New York Times* front page: 'Kris Kristofferson Steals Show at Newport.' He was on his way." By the end of the year, the new sensation placed his "Me and Bobby McGee" with country star Roger Miller, who scored a hit with the song. In 1971, amid the country-rock boom, Kristofferson approached the Top 20 with his second LP, *The Silver-Tongued Devil and I*, and two years later starred with Bob Dylan in the movie *Pat Garrett and Billy the Kid*, which led to a successful career in film.

Seventies Folk

The disintegration of the American family, coupled with the decline of political activism, gave rise to a less-country-based version of folk music that dealt with the loneliness of the single adult. During the 1970s, as the number of women in the work force doubled, many Americans, especially the baby boomers, began to divorce their partners at an increasing rate. In 1969, only three Americans in 1000 filed for divorce. Five years later 4.5 per 1000 divorced their mates. By the end of the seventies 5.3 Americans in 1000 ended their marriages; for every five Americans who married, three divorced.

Many baby boomers began to question the institution of matrimony. In one study conducted during 1971 among college students, more than 34 percent of the respondents believed that marriage was obsolete. Two years later, according to a Rutgers University student survey, 30 percent of the seniors felt that marriage was no longer a viable option.

By divorcing or not marrying, many baby boomers lived the sometimes-lonely life of the unmarried adult. By 1978, more than 1.1 million Americans lived in single households, an increase of 117 percent in a decade. To find companionship, they populated singles bars, singles resorts, and singles housing complexes.

During the early 1970s, singer-songwriters sang ballads about the emotional traumas of divorce, lost love, and loneliness in a plaintive, confessional style that had its roots in sixties folk. James Taylor, the prototype of the easygoing seventies folkster, grew up in North Carolina and spent his summers on the island of Martha's Vineyard off Cape Cod listening to the records of the Weavers, Woody Guthrie, and Pete Seeger. He began playing with friend Danny Kortchmar as a folk duo, James & Kootch, which won a local hootenanny contest. In 1966, he joined Kortchmar's band, the Flying Machine, which performed in such Greenwich Village coffeehouses as the Night Owl before disbanding a year later. Taylor, exhausted and suffering from a heroin addiction, in 1968 traveled to England, where he recorded his first LP for the Beatles-owned Apple Records. When his vinyl debut failed to chart despite background work by Paul McCartney and George Harrison, the singer returned to the United States.

Taylor rebounded from his setback. After appearing at the Newport Folk Festival, he landed a contract with Warner Brothers through manager Peter Asher. In early 1970, he recorded the album *Sweet Baby James*, which reached the Top 5 and remained on the chart for more than two years. The singer followed with *Mud Slide Slim and the Blue Horizon*, which neared the top of the charts in the United States and Britain and included the Carole King-written chart-topper "You've Got a Friend," a soft, reassuring ballad appropriate for the millions of divorced and unmarried baby boomers.

Taylor, like most of the seventies singer-songwriters, wrote and performed a collection of acoustic confessions. "I wish I weren't so self-centered or self-referred all the time with the stuff I write," he later complained, "but for some reason that's the window I utilize, hopefully in an open-ended way."

Other seventies folk artists, congregating around James Taylor, penned self-revelatory paeans of loneliness and confusion. Carole King, the Brill Building sensation of the early 1960s, became intrigued by the New York folk scene after she divorced her husband-collaborator, Gerry Goffin. She backed the Flying Machine in Greenwich Village and in 1968, with Danny Kortchmar, formed the short-lived band City.

In 1970, through the help of James Taylor, King again hit the top of the charts. That year she played piano on *Sweet Baby James* and with the encouragement of Taylor released *Writer*. At mid-year she toured with Taylor to promote the album. In October, with drummer Russ Kunkel, Kortchmar, and Taylor, Carole King began to record the chart-topping *Tapestry*, which sold more than 15 million copies and included her own version of "You've Got a Friend." Like the Taylor rendition, King's version climbed to the top of the charts. She also composed such tales of lost love as "So Far Away" and "It's Too Late."

Carly Simon had an even more intimate relationship with James Taylor. Daughter of Richard L. Simon, cofounder of Simon & Schuster publishers, Carly left the exclusive Sarah Lawrence College to perform and record as a folk duo with her sister Lucy. In 1967, after the Simon Sisters disbanded, she signed with Bob Dylan's manager, Albert Grossman, who hoped to promote her as a female Dylan, and recorded four unreleased tracks. Two years later Carly met Jac Holzman, owner of Elektra Records, who signed her to his label and in 1971 released the singer's solo debut, which reached number 30 on the album chart. She recorded her second LP, *Anticipation*, which included the top-selling single of the same name. In 1972, Carly Simon topped the charts with the single "You're So Vain" and the LP *No Secrets*, and on

Crosby, Stills and Nash
The Daily of the University of Washington

November 3 married James Taylor in her Manhattan apartment. In 1974, the husband-wife team dueted on the Top 5 single "Mockingbird."

Joni Mitchell, collaborating with a number of sixties folksters, strummed to the top of seventies folk. Born Roberta Joan Anderson, she began to play acoustic folk in her native Calgary, Canada. In 1964, she performed at the Mariposa Folk Festival and the next year, after moving to Toronto, she met and married Chuck Mitchell, who played with her as a folk duo in local coffeehouses. In 1966, Mitchell moved to Detroit, where she became a sensation on the folk scene, then began to make appearances in New York City. While in Greenwich Village, Mitchell met such folk artists as Judy Collins, who hit in 1967 with Mitchell's "Both Sides Now."

In 1967, Mitchell signed to Reprise Records and released her debut album, which was produced by ex-Byrd David Crosby and included on guitar Stephen Stills, formerly of the folk-rock band Buffalo Springfield. The next year she recorded her second LP, *Clouds*, which reached the Top 30 and earned her a Best Folk Performer award.

Mitchell, like other singer-songwriters of the era, sang about the pain of broken relationships. In 1971, enlisting the support of Stephen Stills on bass and James Taylor on guitar, who had Mitchell sing background vocals on "You've Got a Friend," she recorded the album *Blue*, featuring such tales of lost love as "The Last Time I Saw Richard," "This Flight Tonight," and the title song. "When I think of Vietnam or Berkeley, I feel so helpless," Mitchell told *Time*. "I just write about what happens to me."

Joni Mitchell helped the careers of Crosby, Stills and Nash, two of whom had aided Mitchell on her debut LP. In mid-1968, after the breakup of the folk-rock group Buffalo Springfield, Stephen Stills began to practice with ex-Byrd David Crosby (a.k.a. David Van Courtland) and Graham Nash, formerly of the Hollies. A year later the folk rockers released a self-titled album featuring a blend of floating harmonies and acoustic guitars. As their album slowly scaled the charts, the group asked ex-Buffalo Springfield guitarist Neil Young to join; in May 1970 they released *Déjà Vu*, which topped the charts and included their best-selling single, Joni Mitchell's "Woodstock."

In late 1970, amid a tour, the foursome disbanded due to internal tensions and splintered into four successful solo acts. David Crosby, backed by Joni Mitchell, neared the Top 10 with *If I Could Only Remember My Name* (1971). Stephen Stills, studying guitar with Jimi Hendrix, released a blues-drenched solo LP that almost topped the charts, and in 1971 Graham Nash recorded his solo debut. In late 1970, Neil Young released the Top 10 *After the Goldrush* and two years later followed with the chart-topper *Harvest*, which included background help from James Taylor and Linda Ronstadt. In 1974, the group temporarily re-formed for a 30-city tour that featured their light, acoustic-backed harmonies. Crosby, Stills, Nash and Young, one of the most successful, soft folk-rock acts for a time, would soon be challenged by heavy metal excess.

12

The Era of Excess

231

"It's a very selfish decade," Tom Hayden, the cofounder of the radical Students for a Democratic Society (SDS), complained to *Newsweek* magazine in 1977. "It's all me. People who experienced profound disappointment trying to change the system are jogging and growing vegetables and concentrating on brightening their own corners of the world."

During the mid- and late seventies, Hayden's observation characterized the outlook of many former sixties radicals. One winter day in 1973, Rennie Davis, the other cofounder of SDS, closed his eyes, saw the bright light of the mythic "third eye" in his forehead, and, as he related, "suddenly I was in a place no words could describe. I felt such a peace—it humbled me and shattered all my assumptions about life." Having experienced transcendental Consciousness Four, he joined the spiritual sect of the guru Maharaj Ji and began selling life insurance for John Hancock in Denver. Four years later, Davis described his life as "light and music and vibration."

Jerry Rubin, the radical yippie who practiced his guerrilla theater of the absurd during the late 1960s, underwent a similar rebirth. In 1970,

Rubin began to question his radical beliefs and by 1977 lived in a Manhattan high-rise apartment, feasted on vitamin pills and health food, jogged regularly, and attended seminars about money consciousness. He hoped to be "as Establishment as I can possibly get."

John Sinclair, the head of the White Panther Party who exhorted MC5 fans to join the revolution, became disillusioned with radical politics after a prison term and parenthood. The "Left, man, I'm just not interested anymore," Sinclair, dressed in a suit and tie, told *Newsweek*. "You can't make a revolution if you have to make a living."

The "Me" Decade

An end to the war in Vietnam, disillusionment with politics, and a sometimes booming economy helped transform sixties radicals into seventies yuppies. The war in Vietnam, escalating steadily throughout the 1960s, ended by the early 1970s. In 1973, the United States signed a formal peace accord with North Vietnam and ended the draft, leaving behind 56,555 dead American soldiers. By 1975, the United States had withdrawn all troops and military advisors from Vietnam and Cambodia, an action that satisfied one of the last major demands of college-aged radicals.

As the war in Vietnam came to a close, Richard M. Nixon, who had first attracted national prominence for his strident, anti-Communist stance during the McCarthy hearings, was reelected to the presidency by voters in 49 of 50 states. He defeated George McGovern, the liberal senator and former college professor who had been championed by radicalized college-aged youths. Coupled with an end to the war, the reelection of Nixon deflated the rage and blunted the resolve of the college radicals. As Rennie Davis contended, "Suddenly that collective energy was gone. The war was over and Nixon had just been reelected. People just found themselves living lives—settling in, getting a job because you had to buy food and pay the rent."

A new crop of college students in the mid-1970s, the last of the baby-boom generation, focused their energies on immediate, material concerns. The students, a senior from Boston University told *Time* in late 1974, were "seeking tangible, not spiritual, returns for their investment in a university." Oriented toward financially rewarding careers, they began to enroll in business administration and engineering classes, bypassing the history, English, and philosophy courses so popular only a few years before. "The mood here is, 'I'm here for me,' " remarked senior Steve Ainsworth, editor of the *Daily Bruin* at the University of California at Los Angeles. During the seventies *Time* magazine characterized baby boomers in general as "the Self-Centered Generation."

A prospering economy throughout most of the decade allowed the baby boomers to indulge themselves. Though beset by a temporary economic downturn and inflated prices after the Vietnam War, Americans enjoyed an increased real disposable income, which during

the seventies rose 28.5 percent and allowed many baby boomers, graduating from college and entering the white-collar work force, to satis-
fy their fantasies.

Having more money to spend and raised with such gadgets as the
television, baby boomers embraced the full array of new consumer
products introduced during the 1970s. They bought pleasure boats, hair
transplants, facelifts, automatic garage door openers, and hot tubs. The
boomers acquired food processors, air-conditioned cars, snowmobiles,
and ten-speed bicycles.

Many self-indulgent boomers purchased drugs, which only a few
years earlier had been considered to be weapons to break down barriers and change the social order. "Drugs have become coopted by the
consumer society," asserted sixties LSD guru Timothy Leary in 1976.
"Drugs are now just another thing people can buy to make themselves
feel one way or another."

Though smoking marijuana had been decriminalized in such states
as Alaska and Oregon by 1975, baby boomers began to indulge in the
more expensive, ego-enhancing cocaine, the drug introduced to the
U.S. market in 1886 by John Styth Pemberton, who mixed it with caf-
feine for a syrup he called Coca-Cola. As early as 1973, more than 4.8
million Americans had sampled the drug, which *Time* magazine labeled
"tyrannical King Coke." "Why the fad?" asked the magazine. "For one
thing smoking pot has become commonplace, even passé, and some
people look for new thrills."

Some baby boomers sought excitement in their personal relationships, especially through open sexual relations. Expanding on a sixties trend, many practiced freewheeling sex. Singles, a category that
doubled to 1.3 million during the decade, spent $40 billion a year in
singles bars, resorts, and housing complexes in an effort to meet ready
partners. More than a few married boomers discussed open marriage,
engaged in wife swapping, and joined such free-sex clubs as the Sand-
stone in Los Angeles, which sought the "membership of stable couples,
young middle-class sensualists who believed that their personal relationships would be enhanced, rather than shattered, by the elimination
of sexual possessiveness."

Some homosexuals, becoming more open and vocal about their
sexual orientation, experimented with many sexual partners. In June
1969, when homosexuality remained illegal in every state except Illinois, gays at the Stonewall Inn in Greenwich Village resisted police arrest and rioted. Spurred by the protest, gays banded together in the
Gay Liberation Front and began to publish newspapers such as *Come
Out!*, which called for gay power. In December 1969, gays founded the
Gay Activist Alliance and the *Gay Activist* to highlight gender politics.
At the turn of the decade, homosexuals united through other newspapers such as *Gay Sunshine*, *Gay*, and *Gay Power*. By the late seventies,
the Institute for Sex Research discovered that 6 percent of single men
considered themselves to be homosexual, and another 5 percent had
at least one homosexual experience after the age of 19. Among single

Elton John, 1975
Frank Driggs Collection

women, 5 percent considered themselves lesbians and another 13 percent had at least one homosexual encounter as an adult.

Many of these homosexuals, especially men, practiced unrestrained sex. Though 50 percent of gay men enjoyed a steady relationship at the time of the Institute study, gay men confessed to having sex with a stranger 80 percent of the time, 30 percent admitted to "cruising" in parks, and 28 percent contended that they had sex with more than 1000 different partners. As with the heterosexual population, many gays became absorbed by their own search for pleasure.

The baby boomers, preoccupied with themselves, chased the dream of self-perfection. They aimed at "changing one's personality—remaking, remodeling, elevating, and polishing one's very self. . . . and observing, studying, and doting on it," wrote Tom Wolfe in his influential essay "The Me Decade." Some made the trek to Big Sur, California, where they paid $200 a week to attend the Esalen Institute which, in the words of Tom Wolfe, promised "lube jobs for the personality." Others flocked to Oscar Ichazo's Arica or Werner Erhard's est sessions to purge themselves through abuse and self-deprivation. A few expelled personal demons and discovered themselves through primal scream therapy. Unlike the hippies, who rapped with friends about changing the social system, the baby-boom generation in the 1970s paid money for encounter sessions that delved into the individual psyches of the participants. In their material possessions, their intimate relationships, and their self-explorations, seventies baby boomers became obsessed with their own needs and sometimes excessive desires.

Elton John

Elton John mirrored the extravagance of the era, serving as the transitional figure from the early-seventies sensitive singer to mid-seventies excessive rock star. One of the most commercially successful and atypical of the seventies acoustic solo acts, pianist John (a.k.a. Reginald Dwight) was raised in England and as a teen joined the blues group Bluesology. In 1967, he auditioned for Liberty Records and, at the suggestion of the label, teamed with songwriter Bernie Taupin. Three years later, Elton released his debut, which featured a gospel-influenced piano sound and the sensitive ballads of Taupin. Throughout the seventies he crafted five singles that became number-one hits. Between 1972 and 1975, the singer recorded six number-one albums and became the first act since the Beatles to place four albums in the Top 10 simultaneously.

Unlike the subdued seventies singer/songwriters who generally strummed their guitars with few flourishes, Elton John developed a wild stage act that included handstands on the piano and kicking over the piano bench. "I'm pretty much making up for lost time," he told an interviewer. "Not having had a real teenage life, I'm living those 13-to-19 years now. Mentally I may be 28, but somewhere half of me is still 13."

John complemented his antics with extravagant costumes. Many times he wore sequined, gaudy jumpsuits, platform shoes, and pink boas. He sported his trademark outrageous glasses, owning more than 200 pairs, including mink-lined glasses, diamond-inlaid spectacles, and a pair with 57 tiny light bulbs that spelled ELTON. "I love people who expect me to wear great, feathery costumes—and I do it," revealed the singer. "It's like an actor getting into his costume for his part. I don't really feel that part until I'm into whatever I'm going to wear." Though specializing in such sensitive ballads as "Your Song," played on an acoustic instrument during the early seventies, Elton John reflected the theatrical excess that characterized the "me" generation of the mid- and late 1970s. "With me," he confessed, "I'm very excessive. If I do it, I do it to extreme excess."

Heavy-Metal Theater

A theatrical, glittery, sometimes androgynous heavy metal, exemplified by David Bowie, epitomized seventies rock-and-roll excess. Born David Jones, a teenaged Bowie joined a number of rock outfits, including the King Bees, the Mannish Boys, and the Lower Third, all of which released unsuccessful singles. In 1966, he changed his name to avoid confusion with Davy Jones of the Monkees and the next year took mime dance

David Bowie, ca. mid 1970s
Frank Driggs Collection

236

lessons. In 1969, amid the furor over the first moon landing, Bowie released "Space Oddity," which hit the Top 5 in Britain.

Bowie began to change his image at the turn of the decade. After backing Marc Bolan, who had begun a glitter-rock craze in England as T-Rex, the singer began to affect an androgynous image, appearing in a dress publicly as well as on the album cover of *The Man Who Sold the World*. In January 1972, Bowie declared his bisexuality to the British music paper the *New Musical Express*, reflecting the seventies trend toward an openness about bisexual and homosexual orientation.

Expanding on his image, Bowie created the bisexual, space-age, glittery persona of Ziggy Stardust. On August 16, 1972, at the Rainbow Theater in London, he materialized from a cloud of dry ice, adorned by a tight-fitting, glimmering jumpsuit; high-topped, sequined hunting boots; and orange-tinted hair. "His eyebrows have vanished, replaced by finely sketched red lines. He's wearing red eyeshadow which makes him look faintly insect-like," wrote the *New Musical Express*. "The only thing that shocks now is an extreme," explained the singer about his space-age character. "Unless you do that, nobody will pay attention to you. Not for long. You have to hit them on the head."

The shocking image of Ziggy Stardust began to sell. After having only limited success with his previous albums, Bowie sold more than a million copies of *The Rise and Fall of Ziggy Stardust and the Spiders from Mars*, which featured a hard-rocking band anchored by guitarist Mick Ronson. The next year he hit the Top 10 with *Aladdin Sane* and began to chart with such previous albums as *Hunky Dory*.

The heavy-metal androgyny of Ziggy Stardust gave direction to the careers of other bands such as Mott the Hoople. Begun in 1969 as a hard-rock outfit led by singer Ian Hunter, Mott the Hoople initially released four poor-selling albums, which convinced the group to disband. On the eve of their dissolution in March 1972, they met David Bowie, a longtime fan of the group, who offered them one of his songs, "All The Young Dudes." The band, agreeing to wear nine-inch platform shoes, heavy mascara, and sequined costumes, recorded the hard-rocking song, which hit the charts in both Britain and the United States and became a gay-liberation anthem. "We were considered instant fags," remembered the heterosexual Hunter. "A lot of gays followed us around, especially in America." Mott the Hoople, reinforcing its image with such songs as "Sucker" and "One of the Boys," climbed the charts in 1974 with *The Hoople* and the next year with *Mott the Hoople—Live*.

Iggy Pop revitalized his career by following the advice of David Bowie. The young Pop, born James Osterberg, traveled from his native Michigan to Chicago, where he briefly played drums for such electric-blues artists as Junior Wells and Buddy Guy. Upon returning to Ann Arbor in 1967, he formed the Stooges, which debuted at a Halloween party and during the next three years recorded two slashing, hard-driving proto-punk LPs that failed to chart. Disconsolate, Iggy moved to Florida, where he cut lawns for a living.

In 1972, on a trip to New York, Iggy met Bowie and manager Tony

Iggy Pop
The Daily of the University of Washington

DeFries, who persuaded Pop to reform the Stooges under DeFries's management and Bowie's guidance. The Stooges, continuing their trademark live performances, unleashed wild theatrical shows. "Iggy had gone beyond performance—to the point where it was really some kind of psychodrama," observed John Sinclair, manager of the MC5. "It exceeded conventional theater. He might do *anything*. That was his act. He didn't know what he was going to do when he got up there on stage." In April 1973, Iggy and the Stooges released *Raw Power*, which showcased the thrashing guitar of James Williamson and on the cover pictured a shirtless Iggy with bleached-blond hair, heavy makeup, dark red lipstick, eyeshadow, and silver-lamé, skin-tight studded pants. Though disbanding with a year after the album's release, the Stooges served as a model for late-seventies punk, and Iggy became a collaborator with Bowie, writing "Jean Genie" for the singer.

Lou Reed also collaborated with Bowie for a new direction. After quitting the Velvet Underground in late 1970, the New Yorker went into seclusion at his parents' home in Long Island. In 1972, Reed met Velvet Underground fan David Bowie, who encouraged him to pursue a solo career. He began to perform with bleached-blond hair, makeup, and black fingernail polish. In April 1973, Reed recorded the Bowie-produced album *Transformer*, which on the cover pictured a prominent New York drag queen and included "Walk on the Wild Side," a song about a transvestite that became Reed's first pop hit. The next year he earned his first gold album with the live, hard-edged *Rock 'n' Roll Animal*.

The New York Dolls adopted the Bowie-defined image of heavy-metal androgyny. Formed in 1971 and fronted by guitarist Johnny Thunders and singer David Johansen, the group began playing locally at such clubs as the Mercer Arts Center. In 1973, they released their first album, which included such thrashing, driving, proto-punk anthems as "Personality Crisis." On the cover, done in gray and shocking pink with the band's name written in lipstick, the group posed with heavy make-up, jewelry, and ruby lipstick. Johansen, a shoulder thrust forward, stared wistfully into the mirror of his powder box. The other group members looked straight ahead, attired in six-inch-heeled boots, skin-tight leather or spandex pants, and provocative blouses.

On stage, the New York Dolls delivered a wild, extreme heavy-metal act. They "were totally outrageous. They were setting the pace," remarked rock photographer Bob Gruen. In one show that Gruen witnessed, the band appeared in "cellophane tutus with army boots. They mixed the genders. . . . The Dolls blew up more equipment than anybody because they were just over the top. They did everything to the fullest, to the maximum."

New York Dolls, ca. 1973
Frank Driggs Collection

Kiss tried to outdo the New York Dolls, their crosstown rivals. "In 1972 there was only one impressive band in New York and that was the New York Dolls," remembered Gene Simmons, the former school-teacher who started Kiss. "I was impressed mostly by their stage presence, and the fact that they didn't look like other American bands. . . . In the beginning," he added, "we were extremely jealous of the New York Dolls and we were going to do them one better."

To grab attention, the band, according to Simmons, "decided to put on bizarre makeup. I was the bat, without the black lips, wearing a sailor suit. I had no clue. [Guitarist] Paul [Stanley] had the rouge and the whiteface, very much like a pretty boy." Like cartoon characters, the face-painted group began to dress in skin-hugging, bejeweled, spandex pants; platform shoes; and black, glittering, leather shirts. Coached by ex-television producer Bill Aucion, Kiss assaulted their audiences with rockets, police lights, snow machines, smoke bombs, and levitating drum kits. By 1975, when they released the million-sell-ing albums *Dressed to Kill* and *Alive!*, the hard-rock band had become one of America's hottest acts.

Alice Cooper also delivered overtly sexual, heavy-metal rock theatrics. In 1965, members of a high school track team in Phoenix, Arizona, performed as a band in a skit for a school assembly. They de-cided to continue after their debut, calling themselves Alice Cooper, a name eventually adopted by the group's leader, Vince Furnier. Travel-ing to Los Angeles in 1968, the band met Frank Zappa, who recorded the group on the largely unnoticed *Pretties for You* and *Easy Action*.

The band began to attract more attention through sensationalist tactics. In 1971, they released the hard-rock album *Love It to Death*, which included the hit "Eighteen" and on the cover showed Cooper's thumb suggestively thrusting through a three-inch-wide ring. The next year they hit the Top 25 with *Killer*. Having more money and encour-aged by manager Shep Gordon, who felt that "people feel threatened by the sexual thing," the group attracted an even larger audience through an elaborate, degenerate show that included throwing live chickens into the crowd, axing off the heads of dolls, staging mock executions in fake electric chairs, Alice draping himself with a live boa constrictor, and beating fans over the heads with six-feet-long, inflat-ed phalluses. By 1974, when they released the Top 10 *Muscle of Love*, the band had become one of the preeminent practitioners of rock the-ater. "The thing that really turned it all around for us was when we realized that we were not into peace and love," explained Alice. "We were more sensational. We were the *National Enquirer* of rock 'n' roll."

Queen rivaled Alice Cooper in extravagance. Formed in 1971 by guitarist Brian May and drummer Roger Taylor, the band featured the vocalist Freddie Mercury (a.k.a. Bulsara), who named the band. "I'd had the idea of calling a group Queen for a long time," he asserted. "It was a very strong name, very universal and very immediate; it had a lot of visual potential." Mercury built upon the visual potential of the name, staging excessive live shows that featured smoke bombs, flash pots,

Alice Cooper
Courtesy of Warner Brothers

and androgynous costumes. Sometimes he favored dresses, tights, and black nail polish, modeling his demeanor after one of his idols, pop singer Liza Minnelli. In other shows Mercury wore leather storm-trooper outfits that emphasized the gay connotation of the band's name. *The New York Times* referred to Mercury's act as "strutting and preening, by turns campy and almost militaristic." "Of all the more theatrical rock performers, Freddie took it further than the rest," explained David Bowie, who collaborated with Mercury on the 1981 hit "Under Pressure." "He took it over the edge. And of course, I always admired a man who wears tights."

Queen produced a dramatic music equal to its theatrical stage shows. After securing a following in Britain during 1973 and 1974, the band hit the U.S. Top 5 with *A Night at the Opera* (1975), which included the operatic heavy metal of "Bohemian Rhapsody." In 1977, they neared the top of the charts with *News of the World*, featuring the militaristic thump of "We Will Rock You" and the dramatic-sounding, self-important "We Are the Champions of the World." By the end of the decade Queen had fashioned a sound and an act that reflected the escapist, extravagant "me" generation. "With the revolt long since gone out of the music," observed *Time*, "what is left is really a new kind of vaudeville or sometimes a freak show."

Funk from Outer Space

During the mid-seventies, George Clinton covered funk with heavy-metal glitter. Funk, the stripped-down gospel blues that featured an insistent rhythm, punchy horns, and repetitious, drumlike vocals, had been unveiled by James Brown. In 1964, Brown shifted from a gospel-drenched soul to a minimalistic funk on "Out of Sight" and the next year perfected his new style with "Papa's Got a Brand New Bag." After 1965, Brown completed his transition to funk when he hired musical director Alfred "Pee Wee" Ellis and such new musicians as bassist Bootsy Collins, drummer Clyde Stubblefield, saxophonist Maceo Parker, guitarist Jimmy Nolan, and trumpet player Fred Wesley. The singer charted with such funky singles as "Cold Sweat," "I Got the Feelin'," "Licking Stick, Licking Stick," "The Popcorn," "Get Up, I Feel Like Being a Sex Machine," and "Let Yourself Go." "Funk," observed bassist William "Billy Bass" Nelson, "comes from James Brown. And James Brown got it from the blues."

Sly Stone (a.k.a. Sylvester Stewart) combined funk with rock-and-roll. As a child, Stewart moved with his family from Texas to San Francisco, where he sang in gospel groups and studied trumpet. During the flowering of hippiedom, he landed jobs as a disc jockey on KDIA and as a producer for Autumn Records, where he mixed the psychedelic music of the Mojo Men and the Great Society, which included Grace Slick. In 1966, Stewart formed the racially integrated Sly and the Family Stone with his brother Freddie on guitar; his sister Rosie, who added gospel-inflected vocals; trumpeter Cynthia Robinson; his cousin, bass player Larry Graham, Jr., who had played with the Drifters; John Lee Hooker and several gospel groups; and cousins Jerry Martini on saxophone and Greg Errico on drums.

Sly and the Family Stone combined their rock and funk influences with a psychedelic sensibility to top the charts. Though flopping with their debut, the band hit with "Dance to the Music" (1968). The next year, Sly and the Family Stone topped the chart with "Everyday People," hit number two with "Hot Fun in the Summertime" and neared the Top 10 with the politically charged *Stand!*, which included "You Can Make It If You Try" and "Don't Call Me Nigger, Whitey (Don't Call Me Whitey, Nigger)." "It was just a recognition of all the racial tensions that were happening," recalled Martini. During the next two years, after an appearance at Woodstock, the group again reached the top of the charts with the funky classics "Thank You (Falettinme Be Mice Elf Again)," "Family Affair," and *There's a Riot Goin' On*. "It was Sly who first cracked the barrier between black and white rock," observed funkmaster George Clinton.

George Clinton took Sly's funk rock into the extravagant mid-seventies. In 1955, Clinton started the Parliaments, a doo-wop group that performed on the streets of New Jersey. Four years later the group relocated to Detroit, where they recorded unreleased tracks for Motown and Clinton became a staff writer for the label. In 1967, amid the soul explosion, the Parliaments finally hit the R & B singles chart with "(I Wanna) Testify."

On the road to promote the hit single, Clinton changed the direction of his band. The leader, forced to use the equipment of a rock

Sly Stone, 1969
Photo © Raeanne Rubenstein

band, "went out and bought Jimi Hendrix's *Are You Experienced?*, Cream's album, a Richie Havens record and Sly's *Whole New Thing.* I gave them to Eddie [Hazel, guitarist] and Billy [Nelson, bassist] in the band." After fusing hard rock sounds to their funky base, Clinton created a stage show similar to the onstage antics of fellow Detroiters Iggy and the Stooges. "It was like the Stooges!," Clinton remembered. "I had a head with a dick shaved onto it right down the middle with a star on one side and a moon on the other and bald all around that. I was crawling all around on the floor sticking my tongue out. We were James Brown on acid, the Temptations on acid, the Stooges."

During the seventies, Clinton solidified the funky rock sound of his band. Threatened with a lawsuit over the name Parliaments, he began to call the group Funkadelic and added such ex-James Brown sidemen as William "Bootsy" Collins, Fred Wesley, and Maceo Parker. By the mid-seventies, when he had regained the right to the Parliament name, Clinton had created a hard funk-rock amalgam with Parliament and, to some extent, with Funkadelic, which he continued as a more rock-oriented outfit. "We got Fred [Wesley] and Maceo [Parker] on the horns and Bootsy [Collins] and all that power in the bass. They had been with James Brown," recalled Clinton. "So we had the James Brown thing. And then on the other side we had doo-wop, Motown, Jimi Hendrix, rock 'n' roll white groups."

George Clinton, in tune with the times, changed his mid-seventies stage image. "By the time I got the name Parliament back, I knew the psychedelic thing was all but gone. So I went with glitter." Touring to promote his breakthrough *Mothership Connection* (1976), Clinton and his band appeared Bowie-like, garbed in leather spacesuits, gogglelike sunglasses, and jewel-studded boots. He hired Jules Fisher, who had designed overblown stage sets for David Bowie and Kiss, to create a huge spaceship that descended to the stage from a denim cap. "Black [audiences] have never experienced a really loud group, let alone all these theatrics," enthused Clinton. "You cannot make sense and be funky. We take the heaviness out of being profound." The funk-rock master had accurately gauged the rock audience, who bought millions of such Top 20 Parliament albums as *The Clones of Dr. Funkenstein* (1976), *Funkentelechy Vs. the Placebo Syndrome* (1977), and *Flash Light* (1978).

Disco

Disco, a simplified version of funk, epitomized seventies excess. It began in New York City at African-American, Latin, and gay all-night clubs, where disc jockeys played nonstop dance music with an insistent, funky, thumping beat. Gradually disco incorporated the antiseptic, rock-steady, electronic beat of such European synthesizer groups as Kraftwerk which, according to Ralf Hutter who started the group with Florian Schneider, consisted of "industrial music; not so much mental or meditative music, but rhythmically more primitive."

By the mid-1970s, disco began to appeal to self-obsessed baby boomers who yearned for center stage. "A few years ago, I went into clubs, and I realized people needed mood music," remarked Neil Bogart, then president of Casablanca Records. "They were tired of guitarists playing to their amplifiers. *They* wanted to be the stars."

Disco, unlike most rock-and-roll, allowed the participants to assume primary importance. Not involving musicians standing on stage, it centered upon the audience. "It's like an adult Disney World. We really give people a chance to get off on their fantasies," explained Steve Rubell, co-owner of one of the premier discos, Studio 54 in New York. "I think the theater atmosphere has a lot to do with it. Everybody secretly likes to be on stage and here we give them a huge space to do it all on." Discos should let "everyone feel like a star," echoed Mark Hugo, manager of a Boston disco.

The various elements of the disco culture embodied the narcissistic extravagance of the mid- and late seventies. Discothèques, *Time* told its readers in 1977, offered "a space-age world of mesmeric lighting and Neroian decor." Studio 54, once the baroque Fortune Gallo Opera House, featured theatrical lighting, flashing strobes, and more than 450 special effects, including plastic snowfalls and 85-foot backdrops. Zorine's in Chicago offered members rooms of mirrors, twisting staircases, balconies, and secret nooks. In Los Angeles, Dillion's boasted four floors, which were monitored on closed-circuit television. Pisces in Washington, D.C., was distinguished by old movie sets; 1000-gallon, shark-filled aquariums; and exotic flora.

The dancers reflected glittery opulence and freewheeling sex via their clothing. Men sported gold chains, gold rings, patent leather platform shoes, tight Italian-style pants, and unbuttoned shiny satin shirts. Women wore low-cut, backless, sequined gowns; spiked heels; long gold necklaces; and gold lamé gloves. "The new boogie bunch dress up for the occasion—with shoulders, backs, breasts and midriffs tending to be nearly bare," observed *Time*. In a disco, where the participants became the stars, remarked photographer Francesco Scavullo, "the dress becomes your dancing partner."

The dances, notably Le Freak, which was popularized in 1978 by a premier disco group, Chic, exhibited an unrestrained sexuality. The exotic dance consisted of two people spreading their legs, bending their backs backwards, and thrusting their pelvises against each other in time to the music.

Disco, first started in gay clubs, also provided a focal point for gay liberation. "The music is a symbolic call for gays to come out of the closet and dance with each other," explained Nat Freedland, director of artist relations for Fantasy Records. It allowed gays, who many times owned the prominent New York discos, as well as serving as the disc jockeys and lighting crews, to become highly visible and respected for their creative achievements.

The disco culture involved the use of drugs, especially cocaine. "Drugs?" replied Steve Rubell when asked about drug use at Studio 54. "What can I tell you? We look the other way. Anyway, so many people are taking pills these days how do I know if it's an aspirin or something else?" As one of its special effects, the New York disco displayed a man in the moon with a spoon uplifted to his nose.

The discos, trading in excess, tried to lure celebrities to their doors. Studio 54 hired socialite Carmen D'Alessio to entice her rich and famous friends to the club. "It's all the celebrities," explained Rubell. "You have to have them first. They draw business in." He successfully added Cher, actress Farrah Fawcett, actor Warren Beatty, Christina Onassis, Woody Allen, and David Bowie to the guest list. Pisces in Washington, D.C., attracted such stars as Elizabeth Taylor and actor Gregory Peck. In Los Angeles, Pip's lured actors Paul Newman, Peter Falk, and Tony Curtis, and singer Frank Sinatra. In urban discos, baby boomers rubbed shoulders with stars of the entertainment industry.

The star-studded disco became a craze near the end of the decade. In late 1977, Robert Stigwood, owner of RSO records, filmed the movie *Saturday Night Fever*, which showed the transformation of a poor, trouble-ridden, Italian teenager, played by John Travolta, into a white-suited disco star. He built the soundtrack of the film around songs written and performed by one of his groups, the Bee Gees. By 1978, the record executive had scored a major success with the movie and had sold more than 30 million copies of the soundtrack worldwide.

Discomania spread across the country in the wake of *Saturday Night Fever*. In New York, more than 1000 discos opened their doors for business. The Holiday Inn motel chain added more than 35 discos on its premises. A $100,000 disco even opened in the small town of Fennimore, Wisconsin (population: 1900). High schoolers went to disco proms and disco roller-skating rinks. One disco in Dubuque, Iowa, provided a disco wedding service complete with smoke-machine effects. Throughout the country in 1978, more than 36 million Americans danced on the floors of 20,000 discos.

Records especially made for disco, first popularized in 1975 with "Never Can Say Goodbye" by Gloria Gaynor, began to sell. The acknowledged queen of disco, Donna Summer, hit the charts in 1976 with the suggestive "Love to Love You Baby," which was punctuated by Summer's sighs and groans, and followed with a series of disco smashes. The Village People, a costumed band of actors and singers portraying stereotypes of the rugged American male, hit the charts in 1978 and 1979 with the million-selling gay anthems "Macho Man," "In the Navy," and "Y.M.C.A." Even such established artists as Rod Stewart and the Rolling Stones released disco-influenced songs. In 1978, *Billboard* categorized more than 20 percent of songs on the singles chart as disco. "Disco will be the major force in the music marketplace for some time," predicted Nat Freedland of Fantasy Records.

By the end of the decade, disco had become a lucrative business. Besides record sales, it involved such products as spandex pants, magazines such as *Discothekin'*, disco dresses slit to expose the thighs, more than 200 disco radio stations from Los Angeles to Miami, and undersized disco purses. Discos such as Studio 54 netted yearly profits of $800,000. "The profits are astronomical," enthused Steve Rubell. "Only the Mafia does better." By 1979, disco, a mirror for the excesses of the rock generation, was a $5-billion industry.

Corporate Rock

The record business, supported by the increasing number of materialistic baby boomers who had contributed to the disco industry, consolidated into a few highly profitable international companies, which dominated the marketplace. During the 1950s, American business in general started to consolidate. By 1955, the 50 largest corporations controlled 27 percent of the national market and sold more than $86 billion of manufactured goods, a figure equal to more than one fourth of the Gross National Product. The trend toward merger continued until by 1970 the market share of the 600 largest companies increased to 75 percent, and the share held by the top 200 corporations rose to over 60 percent. The 102 giants on top of the corporate pyramid, holding assets of $1 billion or more, controlled 48 percent of the market and made 53 percent of the profits.

The record industry followed the pattern of consolidation. Though influenced by a number of viable independent companies such as Chess

The Bee Gees in concert, ca. mid 1970s
Frank Driggs Collection

and Sun during the 1950s, by 1973 the record business was almost completely controlled by seven majors—CBS, Capitol, MCA, Polygram, RCA, A & M, and Warner Communications. The top four companies accounted for more than 52 percent of all record and tape sales, and the leading two—CBS and Warner-Elektra/Asylum-Atlantic—sold 38 percent of the total product manufactured by the industry.

These companies, like other American conglomerates during the decade, had interests in fields besides music. MCA owned Universal Films, various television stations, Arlington and Mount Vernon cemeteries, a bank in Colorado, and the Spencer Gifts novelty chain. RCA, the twentieth largest corporation in the country, operated NBC television and radio, owned the Hertz Rent-A-Car company, Banquet Foods, the Cushman and Wakefield real estate firm, and Random House and Alfred Knopf publishers. It also served as a prime defense contractor.

These giant corporations built rock-and-roll, which by 1975 accounted for 80 percent of all record sales, into a multi-billion-dollar enterprise. In 1950, record companies sold $189 million of product, increasing their gross revenues five years later to $277 million. By 1971, in the United States alone, the industry sold $1.7 billion in records and tapes. Two years later it grossed $2 billion, which surpassed the gross revenues of Broadway ($36 million), professional sports ($540 million), the film industry ($1.3 billion), and network television ($1 billion). By 1978, the record industry grossed about $4 billion.

Many companies posted healthy profits. In the summer quarter of 1978, MCA made a profit of more than $5.5 million, CBS cleared $48.5 million, and Warner netted $19.8 million. "Records are where the big money is in the entertainment business these days," observed *Forbes* in July 1978.

Profits came from around the world. In 1973, the companies sold $2 billion worth of records and tapes in the United States, a per capita expenditure of $9.70. That same year, they sold more than $555 million worth of records and tapes in Japan, $454 million in West Germany, $441 million in the Soviet Union, $384 million in the United Kingdom, controlled largely by the British Electrical Manufacturing Industries (EMI), and even $16 million in Poland. Per capita expenditures amounted to $7.57 in West Germany, $6.91 in the Netherlands, $7.64 in Sweden, and $5.14 in Japan. By the end of the decade the corporate rock establishment had penetrated nearly every world market to amass excessive profits in an excessive age.

Some seventies rock stars eagerly embraced the international music business. Gene Simmons of Kiss equated a "successful rock and roll band" with "a well-oiled machine. It's a good business." "Now artists are more upfront about admitting that they are interested in selling some records," observed Columbia Records talent scout Greg Geller as he compared sixties and seventies rock performers. "This is not an ivory tower age: there's some recognition that we're involved in commerce."

Some of the performers worked with the music corporations to become millionaires. For Alice Cooper, "the idea all along was to make $1 million. Otherwise the struggle wouldn't have been worth it. . . . I am the most American rock act. I have American ideals. I love money."

Many rock stars realized their financial goals. In 1973, *Forbes* estimated that at least 50 rock superstars earned and invested between $2 and $6 million a year, each musician accumulating from three to seven times more than the highest-paid executive in the United States.

Many successful seventies stars invested their earnings. The Bee Gees, one of the biggest draws of the 1970s, established their own merchandising company, which sold "things like nice T-shirts," according to Barry Gibb, who with his twin brothers Maurice and Robin started the band. "We deal in jewelry but only real gold plate. We're doing a little electronic piano with Mattel Toys that'll be available soon." They also marketed "a cute Andy Gibb doll" to promote the career of their younger brother. Alice Cooper financed such films as *Funny Lady* and *Shampoo* for tax shelters and invested in art, antiques, and tax-free municipal bonds. Ted Nugent, the guitarist who scaled the charts during the seventies with a heavy-metal sound and Neanderthal costumes, owned a mink farm and a trout operation. Said Bob Weed, the Nuge's financial manager, "All of this fits in with Ted's plan for acquiring land. Sure, we're involved in some oil and gas-lease tax shelters, but when I tell him about property, that's something he understands." Rod Stewart, the blues singer turned disco star, had a similar investment strategy. "I've always said that Rod isn't a rock star. He's a growth industry," remarked Billy Gaff, Stewart's manager. "Rod is essentially very conservative. He doesn't invest in football clubs or crazy movie- or record-financing schemes. The tax shelter scams are all a little scary, so we stick to art and real estate." By the end of the decade, rock-and-roll had become a big business dominated by millionaire rock stars. Soon it would be challenged by the rebellious music of a new generation.

13

Punk Rock and the New Generation

"You don't sing about love to people on the dole."

Johnny Rotten

"Punk is so constipated it should be called hemorrhoid rock," snapped Linda Ronstadt to an interviewer. "All that punk singers can bring to the presentations of their songs is the gesture of sexual obscenity or of impotent rage. There is a lot of caged simian gibber," wrote Anthony Burgess, author of the futuristic *A Clockwork Orange*, in a 1977 issue of *Psychology Today*. "British youth, like American and French and Upper Slobovian youth, needs a good kick in the pants and a bit of solid education." *The London Times* declared that "punk rock is the generic term for the latest musical garbage bred by our troubled culture. It features screaming, venomous, threatening rock sounds."

A new generation of rock-and-rollers centered in New York and London inspired this outrage. Most punks had been born after Elvis was inducted into the army and, in some cases, after Bob Dylan first began to sing in Greenwich Village. They had been preteens during the Vietnam War and the Woodstock festival, and had few memories of the civil rights movement and disturbances on campus. Most punk rockers had been in elementary school when the Beatles disbanded and Jimi Hendrix died. Opposed to the excessive corporate rock of the mid-1970s, they created a minimalistic, angry music that threatened their materialistic baby-boom elders. In 1977, a new generation had arisen to lay claim to a rebellious rock-and-roll heritage.

New York Punk

CBGB, a small bar in the Bowery, New York City, served as the birthplace of punk rock. Established in December 1973 by ex-U.S. Marine sergeant Hilly Kristal, the bar first catered to Bowery bums. "When I first opened it as Hilly's on the Bowery," recalled the proprietor, "I ran it for a while as a derelict bar, and bums would be lining up at eight in the morning, when I opened the doors. They would come in and fall on their faces even before they had their first drink." In a few months, Kristal changed the name of his bar to CBGB—OMFUG, which stood for "country, bluegrass, blues, and other music for uplifting gourmandizers."

In 1974, such bands as Television, influenced by the New York avant-garde of Andy Warhol, the Velvet Underground, and the free jazz improvisation of John Coltrane and Albert Ayler, began to play regularly at CBGB. Formed in late 1973, Television originally included bassist Richard Hell (a.k.a. Richard Meyers), who had traveled to New York City to "become a real sophisticated writer"; guitarist Richard Lloyd; drummer Billy Ficca; and vocalist-guitarist Tom Verlaine (a.k.a. Tom Miller), who renamed himself after the French symbolist poet. After debuting at the New York Townhouse Theater, the band convinced Andy Warhol associate Terry Ork to manage them. Through the efforts of Ork in early 1974, the group landed a permanent job at CBGB.

The Talking Heads, ca. 1977; lead singer/songwriter David Byrne, second from left
Frank Driggs Collection

Terry Ork, persuading his artist friends to hear Television, created an avant-garde scene at CBGB. "He brought in a lot of theatre and poetry people from this area, since he lived around here and knew them all," remembered Hilly Kristal. "It wasn't really so much his bookings, but because he knew so many things about theatre, film, and art, and he knew all those people. He also had the energy and he was very excited about the whole thing, and he excited me about it. I do think it's true, the whole scene wouldn't have happened without him."

The Talking Heads began to play at the burgeoning avant-garde scene. Fellow students at the Rhode Island School of Design, David Byrne, Tina Weymouth, and Chris Franz traveled to New York and in late 1974 began to play with one another as the Talking Heads, a name found in an issue of *TV Guide*. "We started rehearsing our songs, the songs I had written," remembered Byrne. "I was writing these things but I didn't know what they were for. I didn't have any plans to put a band together, but there were the songs." Living in an apartment only a few blocks from CBGB, the Talking Heads auditioned for Hilly Kristal and in May 1975 began to play at the bar. In 1977, the group invited keyboardist Jerry Harrison to play with them and released their debut album, which included the eccentric minor hit "Psycho Killer." "The Heads were great and Television were great, but on a sort of intellectual level," recalled Kristal. "The Heads were so quirky and weird that they set much of the stylistic tone. Not punk, but a transition period."

Patti Smith helped transform the avant-garde into punk rock. The daughter of a New Jersey factory worker, Smith worked in a factory herself until migrating to New York City. Once in town, she worked with artist Robert Mapplethorpe and playwright Sam Shepard and began to write a William Burroughs-Arthur Rimbaud style of poetry. She regularly read her work at the Mercer Arts Center and published two books of poetry, *Witt* and *Seventh Heaven*.

A die-hard fan of Jimi Hendrix and Jim Morrison of the Doors and a former writer for the rock magazine *Creem*, Patti Smith combined her poetry with a rock sound. In early 1971, Smith read her poetry at St. Mark's Church in New York, accompanied by guitarist/rock writer Lenny Kaye, who had assembled the sixties punk *Nuggets* compilations. By March 1974, she had invited pianist Richard Sohl to help Kaye provide an improvisational rock backdrop to her readings. "Of course it was still more of an art thing," Kaye pointed out. "It wasn't even a club circuit. We played with Television." Three months later, Smith recorded the independently produced single, "Hey Joe/Piss Factory," which convinced Sire Records to sign the fledgling group. After club dates on the West Coast, Smith added guitarist Ivan Kral and drummer Jay Dee Daugherty to form the Patti Smith Group. "As soon as we started adding Ivan Kral and then started adding Jay Dee Daugherty, we became more of a rock band," observed Lenny Kaye.

The poet adopted the vague, populist stance of the sixties. She admired "all the great sixties guys" who "had sort of a political consciousness." With her music, Smith was "determined to make us kids,

RICHARD HELL
& THE VOIDOIDS

BLANK
GENERATION

YOU MAKE ME

*Richard Hell: king of New York punk
and originator of punk fashion*
Photo by Robert Bayley, courtesy of Richard Hell and Sire Records

us fuck-ups, us ones who could never get a degree in college, whatever, have a family, or do regular stuff, prove that there's a place for us."

In early 1975, the Patti Smith Group brought attention to the
emerging scene at CBGB during a seven-week stint at the club. "What
happened was that as we played there more and more people came
down," mentioned Lenny Kaye. "CBGB became not only a place for
them to come and check us out, but it sort of got into the New York
consciousness." "Patti's stay here was one of the most memorable
seven-week periods the club ever had," added Hilly Kristal. "Clive Davis
[of Arista Records, which signed Smith in January 1975] came a number
of times and a lot of the record people came, but mostly it was newspapers and a lot of people on the periphery of theatre and the arts.
Those first dates put us on the map, at least initially."

The Patti Smith Group began to sound less and less arty. On their
1975 debut, *Horses*, the group combined rock with avant-garde poetry in such songs as "Gloria" and "Free Money." The follow-up, *Radio
Ethiopia*, similarly combined hard-driving numbers such as "Pumping
(My Heart)" and "Ask the Angels" with more freewheeling songs. By
the 1978 Top 20 release, *Easter*, the band had largely abandoned
an improvisational sound for the hard rock of "Space Monkey," "Till

Victory," and "Because the Night," co-written with Bruce Springsteen. Smith "was really the first of, I don't like the word, punks," commented Hilly Kristal.

Richard Hell helped to define the emerging punk rock. As a member of Television, Hell created a minimalist, populist image that would characterize punk rock and contrast starkly with the glittery image of David Bowie. Modeling himself after such French poets as Rimbaud, he cut his hair in a short, spiky style and wore ripped T-shirts. "My look was a sort of a strategy," explained the bassist. "I wanted it to look like do-it-yourself. Everything we were doing at the time had that element, from having ripped up clothes to not knowing how to play instruments. The whole thing was partly a reaction to the hippie stadium music. . . . I wanted the way we looked to be as expressive as the material on the stage," added Hell. "It was all of a piece. The ripped T-shirts meant that I don't give a fuck about stardom and all that or glamour and going to rock shows to see someone pretend to be perfect. The people wanted to see someone they could identify with. It was saying, 'You could be here, too.' "

Richard Hell also adopted a populist attitude in his songs. He delivered the New York punk anthem "Blank Generation," which he wrote in 1975 and recorded two years later with the Voidoids after the rock-and-roll-oriented Hell left the more improvisational Television. "To me, 'blank' is a line where you can fill in anything. It's positive," he told an interviewer. "It's the idea that you have the option of making yourself anything you want, filling in the blank. And that's something that provides a uniquely powerful sense to this generation."

The Ramones added a buzz-saw guitar attack to the populist stance and ripped T-shirt fashion of Richard Hell to complete the transition from the avant-garde to punk rock. Banding together after playing at a private party in late 1974, Johnny Cummings, Dee Dee Colvin, Jeffrey ("Joey") Hyman, and Tommy Erdelyi adopted the surname Ramone. They first performed in public at CBGB, appearing in black leather jackets, black pegged pants, torn jeans, and ripped T-shirts. "We wanted to do punk rock and decided the punks were people from the fifties like Eddie Cochran and Elvis Presley. You would always see them walking around in motorcycle jackets. We thought that was the coolest thing, to have a motorcycle jacket, to really prove you were in the groove."

The Ramones cared little for the artistic avant-garde. On one tour with the Talking Heads, remembered then manager Danny Fields, "the Ramones hated Europe. They didn't like the idea that people didn't speak English. The Talking Heads adored it. It was really yuppie chic at work. The Ramones were like Archie Bunker at the Vatican. They were not amused. They hated the food and just looked for hamburgers everywhere." On a Talking Heads-planned side trip to Stonehenge during the tour, the Ramones refused to leave the bus. "It's really nothing to see," explained Dee Dee. "It's not like going to see a castle."

The Ramones reflected their populist attitude in a thrashing sound

Joey Ramone: a CBGB original
Courtesy of Cam Garrett/S.C.V.D. Studio

borrowed from the New York Dolls. "What really kicked it off was seeing the New York Dolls in clubs around Manhattan," recalled Dee Dee Ramone. "It was so inspiring to see a bunch of young people playing rock and roll that we wanted to do it too. It took off from there." Unlike the more meandering art groups, which looked to literary and free-jazz sources, the Ramones sped through eight-song, 17-minute sets at CBGB, defining the punk sound on their first LP, which featured "Blitzkrieg Bop," "Beat on the Brat," and "Now I Wanna Sniff Some Glue." "Rock 'n' roll was a hodgepodge of Pink Floyd and ELP and all this crap," explained Joey Ramone. "So basically what we did was we stripped it right down to the bone and we disassembled it and re-assembled it and put all the excitement and fun and spirit, raw energy and raw emotion and guts and attitude back into it." "For me it was like I was an old car and I was being taken out for a ride at 100 miles an hour," said excited writer Norman Mailer after attending a Ramones concert.

The CBGB Rock Festival Showcase Auditions in mid-1975 brought international attention to the emerging New York punk scene. Featuring the Ramones, the Talking Heads, and Television, the festival attracted writers from *Rolling Stone*, *The New York Times*, the *Village Voice*, and the British rock papers *The New Musical Express*, *Sounds*, and *Melody Maker*. "The coverage of the festival started making things happen," maintained Hilly Kristal. "The record companies started coming down, mainly Sire Records, but also others."

Promoted by the British press after the Rock Festival Showcase Audition, the Ramones unveiled their thrashing sound in England. In early 1976, they released the British version of their first album, which impressed the British critics and gave some English punks direction. "I heard the Ramones' first record and I thought that it was fucking brilliant," remembered Billy Idol, who started the British punk band Generation X and was a member of the Bromley contingent that followed the Sex Pistols. "We got that first record and every song was under two minutes and it was like a revolution! . . . We were playing normal speed until we heard the Ramones," added Idol, "and because of them, [we] revved everything up. Everybody did, 'cause the Ramones really had their groove and we were still searching for ours."

On July 4, 1976, the Ramones brought their live show to British youths. They celebrated the U.S. Bicentennial by performing in London at the Roundhouse, which, contended Hilly Kristal, "started the whole thing going. All the other groups saw them and realized they could do it too." "I feel we were responsible for the whole punk revolution," asserted Joey Ramone. "We signed to Sire in 1975 and our first album came out in 1976. It came out in England about six months before it came out in America. That's sort of what inspired the English bands to start up. When we first went over there the big thing was pub rock." Though overstating his influence, Joey and the other Ramones mirrored and, to some extent, shaped the music that would explode from Britain a year later.

The Sex Pistols and British Punk

Unemployed British youths infused New York punk with a desperate anger. In 1974, the inflation rate in England stood at about 24 percent. A year later it had climbed three more points. Simultaneously, between 1974 and 1977 the unemployment rate shot up 120 percent, increasing by more than 200 percent among the young.

The Sex Pistols embodied the anger of unemployed British youths, who envisioned no future for themselves. The group began to form in 1972, when lower-class London schoolmates Paul Cook, Steve Jones, and Wally Nightingale began to play as the Swankers, attracting the attention of Malcolm McLaren, who owned a clothing shop called Too Fast To Live, Too Young To Die. The next year, Glen Matlock, an assistant in McLaren's shop, joined the band.

In early 1975, clothing store owner Malcolm McLaren traveled to

New York to manage the fashion-conscious New York Dolls. Upon his return six months later, McLaren agreed to manage the Swankers and suggested the group move Jones to guitar and dispense with Nightingale, who appeared too clean-cut. As a lead singer, he proposed Richard Hell, who in 1975 had begun to play with ex-New York Doll Johnny Thunders in the Heartbreakers. Confronted with opposition from the group over an American addition to the band, McLaren asked John Lydon, nicknamed Rotten because of his green teeth, to come to the manager's shop, renamed Sex. In August 1975, wearing an "I Hate Pink Floyd" T-shirt, Lydon successfully auditioned for the band by singing along to Alice Cooper's "School's Out," which played on the jukebox.

The Sex Pistols, reflecting the situation of most British teens, had few options other than forming a band. Johnny Rotten characterized the group as "a collection of extremely bored people. I suppose we'd come together out of desperation. There was no hope as far as any of us were concerned. This was our common bond. There was no point in looking for a normal job because that would be just too awful. There was no way out."

The desperate Sex Pistols combined the energy of the New York Dolls, Iggy Pop, and the Ramones. Playing their first show in November 1975 at St. Martin's School of Art in London, the group featured a frenzied, buzz-saw attack anchored by guitarist Steve Jones. "I'd wake up in the morning at our studio on Denmark Street," related Jones, "and play along with an Iggy Pop record and the New York Dolls' first album. I would listen to them over and over again and play guitar to them." "*Funhouse* by Iggy and the Stooges was my kind of music," agreed Johnny Rotten. "Our sound was pretty damn close to that." Sid Vicious listened to the Ramones, the New York punk band that had been influenced by the Stooges and the New York Dolls. "The Ramones were the only American band that the English punks recognized," remarked Chrissie Hynde, the singer/guitarist who followed the Sex Pistols and later founded the Pretenders. "Sid learned how to play guitar playing with the Ramones albums for two or three days. He fucking loved the Ramones!"

Besides adopting the sound of American punk, the Sex Pistols created an onstage image which at least partly derived from the Stooges and New York punk. Like Iggy Pop, they taunted, shouted, and spat at the audience, blurring the distinction between the artists and the audience. Band members appeared in ripped, graffitied shirts and pants, black boots, and leather jackets that flashed with metal studs and zippers. Like Richard Hell, they cut their hair in a short, spiky style. To reinforce their image, in February 1977 the band fired bass player Glen Matlock because, according to Rotten, "he was so clean and had that look, like he had never gone without a meal," and replaced him with Sid Vicious (a.k.a. John Ritchie), who, like Iggy, mutilated himself onstage with broken beer bottles.

The rebellious band, comprised of teenaged members unlike the

New York punks who were baby boomers in their twenties, offered this furious music to a new generation of rock-and-rollers. "The millionaire groups were singing about love and their own hangups," sneered Rotten. "That's stupid. You don't sing about love to people on the dole. We're totally against apathy of any kind. We have got to fight the entire super band system. Groups like The Who and the Stones are revolting. They have nothing to offer the kids anymore."

The Sex Pistols substituted an angry anarchism for the theatrical excess of seventies superstars. In November 1976, they recorded their first single, "Anarchy in the U.K.," which warned of impending chaos in Britain. The band next blasted royalty in "God Save the Queen," releasing the single to coincide with Queen Elizabeth's Silver Jubilee in June. The Sex Pistols followed with other songs such as "Pretty Vacant" and "Holiday in the Sun," which described the hopeless plight of many British youths. "There'll always be something to fight—apathy's the main thing," asserted Rotten. "The Pistols are presenting one alternative to apathy and if you don't like it, that's just too bad. Anarchy is self-rule and that's better than anything else." Rotten later observed, "The Pistols projected that anger, that rock-bottom working-class hate."

An outraged, threatened establishment aimed a barrage of criticism at the anarchistic Sex Pistols, reminiscent of the outcries against Elvis Presley in 1956. On April 10, 1976, the British music paper *Melody Maker* told its readers that "the Sex Pistols do as much for music as World War II did for the cause of peace." Robert Adley, a Conservative member of Parliament, called the group "a bunch of ill-mannered louts, who seem to cause offense wherever they go." One vicar of the Anglican Church, his face muscles tightened and his head raised high, planted himself outside a club where the Sex Pistols were scheduled to play, and warned concertgoers: "Keep out of there! They're the devil's children." Almost every local council in Britain banned the Pistols; publications refused to print ads publicizing the band; and in June 1976, after the release of "God Save The Queen," royalists attacked both Johnny Rotten and Paul Cook with razors, knives, and iron pipes.

The record industry offered little help to the Sex Pistols. EMI first signed the band for a £40,000 advance. After packers in the Hayes record plant refused to handle "Anarchy in the U.K.," and after drunken band members had been prodded into using profanities on the live BBC broadcast "Bill Grundy Show," the company criticized the Pistols for "aggressive behavior" and terminated the band's contract. In a ceremony outside Buckingham Palace in March 1977, A & M Records signed the Sex Pistols; six days later A & M rescinded the contract. Two months later Virgin Records offered a contract to the band and released *Never Mind the Bollocks—Here's The Sex Pistols* in England.

Despite opposition, the Sex Pistols' records topped the charts. "God Save the Queen," even though banned by British radio, sold 150,000 copies in five days and shot to the number-two spot on the chart. "Pretty Vacant" hit the number-six slot, and "Holiday in the Sun"

The Sex Pistols
The Daily of the University of Washington

reached number 8. In November 1977, the band's first and only studio album, *Never Mind the Bollocks*, topped the British charts.

Other bands such as the Clash, inspired by the Sex Pistols, joined the punk legion. After hearing the Sex Pistols at the 100 Club in London, Joe Strummer quit his pub-rock band, the 101'ers, and joined with guitarists Mick Jones and Keith Levene, bass player Paul Simonon, and drummer Terry Chimes to start the Clash. The group asked Bernie Rhodes, a regular at Malcolm McLaren's boutique, to become manager. They first performed in Sheffield in mid-1976, backing the Sex Pistols. In December 1976, they played on the Pistols' "Anarchy in the U.K." tour. The next month, after the departure of Levene and Chimes, the latter replaced by Topper Headon, the Clash signed with CBS and in April debuted with the single "White Riot." They released their first, self-named LP, which hit the Top 20 and included such punk anthems as "All the Young Punks," "I'm So Bored with the U.S.A.," "Career Opportunities," and "London's Burning." Though ignored by distributors in the United States, in 1978 the Clash followed with *Give 'Em Enough Rope*, which hit the number-two slot in Britain.

The Damned began their career backing the Sex Pistols. Formed in 1976 by Dave Vanian, Brian James, Captain Sensible, and Rat Scabies, the group first performed at the 100 Club in London, supporting the Pistols, and in December played on the "Anarchy in the U.K." tour. In March 1977, they released the first British punk album, *Damned, Damned, Damned*, which climbed to number 36 on the English charts.

Siouxie and the Banshees began as part of the Bromley Contingent, a group of fans who religiously followed the Sex Pistols. In

September 1976, at the 100 Club Festival headlined by the Pistols, Siouxie Sioux (a.k.a. Susan Dallion), Sid Vicious, Marc Pironi, and Steve Havoc (a.k.a. Steve Severin) jumped on stage and performed an extemporaneous, 20-minute punk version of "The Lord's Prayer." At the end of the year Siouxie appeared with the Sex Pistols on the British television show "Today," and late the next year the fledgling band backed Johnny Thunders in concert. In June 1978, the Banshees signed with Polydor Records and in three months released their first single, "Hong Kong Garden," which hit the number-seven spot on the British singles chart. They quickly recorded *The Scream*, which by the end of the year climbed into the British Top 15.

Generation X was started by two Bromley Contingent fans, Billy Idol (a.k.a. William Broad) and Tony James. In September 1976, the duo formed the band with Mark Laff on drums and guitarist Bob Andrews and released the single, "Your Generation," an answer to The Who's baby-boom anthem, "My Generation." Later in the same year, Generation X became the first punk band to perform at the venue The Roxy, which became a punk hangout. In March 1978, the group released their first LP, which charted at number 29 in Britain. By 1978, bands such as Generation X, the Clash, the Damned, and Siouxsie and the Banshees had followed the Pistols to create a punk movement. "The Pistols had changed the whole musical scene," recalled Rotten. "Everyone started doing it the way the Pistols did it."

The Clash, 1985
Frank Driggs Collection

Rock Against Racism

Rock Against Racism united many of the British punk bands in a fight against the racism rampant in Britain. It began after an August 14, 1976, concert in Birmingham at which a drunken Eric Clapton lectured concertgoers about Britain "becoming a black colony within ten years." "Musicians were coming out with the 'Blame the Blacks bit,' " recalled one organizer. "Bowie and Clapton were the last straws—how dare they praise Hitler or want to repatriate the race that had created the music they profitably recycled. We loved music, hated racism and thought it was about time rock and roll paid back some dues." Rock Against Racism, mentioned the organizer, tried to "fight back against the creeping power of racist ideas in popular culture" and attacked the right-wing, neo-Nazi National Front. By April 1978, the coalition had organized 56 chapters and attracted more than 80,000 adherents to an Anti-Nazi League Carnival in London headlined by the Clash.

Elvis Costello headed another Rock Against Racism benefit. The son of bandleader Ross McManus, Declan McManus played at local folk clubs under his mother's maiden name, Costello. In 1976, he signed to Stiff Records, owned by Jake Riviera, who suggested that he rename himself Elvis. In April 1977, Elvis released his vinyl debut, "Less Than Zero," a song attacking Oswald Mosley, a 1930s British fascist who inspired the organization of the National Front. Costello then recorded a ballad, "Alison," which blunted the hard-edged punk sound and became a model for the post-punk new wave. "What I really wanted to do was approach the music with the same attitude, the same attack as punk, without sacrificing all the things I liked about music—like, say, tunes," Elvis remembered. In the summer of 1978, Costello played such songs as "Less Than Zero" at a Rock Against Racism concert in Brixton.

In June 1978, the Clash, the Tom Robinson Band, and Sham 69 played to 50,000 young punks who attended a Rock Against Racism concert. Tom Robinson, who had formed his band in early 1977 and had hit the Top 10 in Britain with "2-4-6-8-Motorway," shouted to the audience that the National Front must be confronted "at school and at work." "If music can erase even a tiny fraction of the prejudice and intolerance in this world, then it's worth trying," he told an interviewer. "Through my lyrics," agreed Morgan Webster of Sham 69, "I want to show the National Front that they're fucking assholes." "We're against fascism and racism," declared Joe Strummer of the Clash. By the end of summer 1978, more than 250,000 youths had rocked against racism in 36 concerts held across England.

The Jamaican Connection: Reggae and Ska

Reggae, the music of the downtrodden in Jamaica, was championed by British punks dedicated to racial equality. It was an essential element of the Jamaican Rastafarian religion, which emerged as early as the 1930s, when the rotund American Marcus Garvey urged Jamaican blacks to return to the Ethiopian kingdom of Haile Selassie, who was considered to be the Lion of Judah. Garvey's back-to-Africa message appealed to the many unemployed Jamaicans, about 35 percent of the working-age population during the sixties, who congregated in the slums of West Kingston.

Trapped in this poverty-stricken situation, many Jamaicans adhered to Rastafarianism's coherent set of beliefs: Selassie became the prophet Prince of God, or Jah, and, after his fall, the martyred King; the Ethiopian colors—black, green, and red—were adopted as the Rasta standard; Jamaicans began to sport a plaited hair style known as dreadlocks; and in the late 1960s reggae, which combined African and indigenous Jamaican rhythms, replaced the westernized calypso to become the music of the countercultural religion. Peter Tosh, one of the fathers of reggae, explained that "reggae, the word, means 'king's music,' and I play the King's music. The King put many princes on earth, and the music is given to those who praise Him. You have to be spiritually inclined to deal with this kind of talent."

Reggae originated in the slums of the Jamaican capital. "When I came to Kingston at about 16 years of age," Tosh remembered, "I soon realized that nine out of ten singers found themselves in poverty in Trenchtown, the ghetto. It was me, Bob Marley, Bunny Livingstone, Joe Higgs, the Maytals—we'd sit around every night and just sing. At that time, me and Joe Higgs were the only ones who could play the guitar. Finally Joe Higgs helped to get us into the studio with Sir Coxsone Dodd producing, and that was the start of recording for me and Bob and Bunny." In 1964, Tosh and his friends, calling themselves the Wailers, hit the Jamaican charts with the ska-influenced "Simmer Down." Two years later they recorded another ska song, "Rude Boy," which immortalized the outlaws of Kingston's shantytown and reached the number-one spot in the former British colony.

Around 1970, the Wailers abandoned the more traditional Jamaican ska for a new music that was rooted in Rastafarianism and became known as reggae. They delivered such songs as "African Herbsman" and "Rasta Revolution." In 1973, the group released the reggae LPs *Catch a Fire* and *Burnin'*, the second including "I Shot the Sheriff," a song ironically covered by Eric Clapton. Two years later the Wailers cut *Natty Dread*, a testament to the Rastafarian culture.

The Wailers, along with other reggae groups such as Toots and the Maytals, Burning Spear, Black Uhuru, and Steel Pulse, lambasted the racism and the capitalism that Britain had imposed upon Jamaica. Burning Spear (a.k.a. Winston Rodney) used the Rastafarian dialect to express his belief that everyone should "be equal or i-qual and get an equal share. An' everyman entitled to Dem share an' should get Dem share. . . . The work is to bring the whole world together. See. That is naturality. Non-violence, less pollution, more togetherness, more industry, less institution like prisons; more schools, more hospitals. These things come through the music. And the music is those things and those things is the music." Jamaican producer Lee Perry told a reporter that reggae "denounces the very heart of the system on which much of the capitalist world is built." Not just voicing rhetoric, many reggae bands such as Bob Marley and the Wailers actively backed the government of socialist prime minister Michael Manley. At one 1976 rally for the prime minister, Marley barely escaped an assassination attempt.

Discontented British punks championed the activist reggae bands. "I was heavily into reggae," recalled Johnny Rotten. In 1976, the Clash remade Junior Murvin's reggae hit, "Police and Thieves." "You see, there wasn't enough good punk records around. So, to supplement it, we filled it out with a lot of reggae records," explained Mick Jones of the Clash. "It was like punk's chosen 'other music.'" Many British youths supported such reggae bands as Steel Pulse, Aswad, and Matumbi, who regularly played with British punks at Rock Against Racism concerts. "Everybody loved reggae music," commented Chrissie Hynde about the English punks.

Some British youths took ska—the light, happy Jamaican music that predated reggae—and fused it with the radical message and the energy of punk. "We were the first band which wanted to combine punk and reggae because we liked them both," recalled Jerry Dammers of the racially integrated Specials, one of the most influential of the new ska groups. "Both were rebel music," said fellow Special member Horace Panter. In 1979, the band borrowed £700 to record the Prince Buster ska classic "Al Capone," which was released on the group's own 2-Tone label. They followed a few months later with a debut album, produced by Elvis Costello, which cracked the British Top 5.

The Selector recorded on the Specials' 2-Tone label. Living in Coventry, as did the Specials, the racially integrated Selector delivered a politically charged version of punk-ska. Featuring the vocals of Pauline Black, the band chronicled the tense racial and political situation in Britain with singles such as "Three Minute Hero," "Too Much Pressure," and "Murder."

The English Beat, the other major seventies ska band, produced a similar sound for a similar purpose. Guitarist Dave Wakeling rediscovered ska because "it said what a terrible world this was—with a smile on its face." In 1979, the Birmingham group created its own Go Feet label and released their top-selling debut, which included "Stand Down Margaret," aimed at Prime Minister Margaret Thatcher.

The Independent Labels

Other independent labels arose to distribute the politicized punk and ska. In 1976, Rough Trade Records began pressing discs. In the words of staffer Allan Sturdy, the label hoped to "provide an alternative to the music establishment so that a record could be available that otherwise wouldn't." The 25 staffers at Rough Trade democratically made decisions about material, rejecting songs that were sexist or racist. "I wouldn't sign a band that was racist or sexist or fascist or anything like that," Rough Trade's Howie Klein told a reporter.

The Specials: two-tone originals
Courtesy of Chrysalis Records

Enforcing its standards, Rough Trade first recorded the debut LP of the politically minded Ulster band Stiff Little Fingers, which delivered such songs as "Alternative Ulster," "Suspect Device," "Law and Order," "Rough Trade," and "White Noise," the last detailing white Britain's racism toward blacks, Pakistanis, and the Irish. It featured subsequent releases by such all-female punk bands as the Slits and Girls at Our Best and the gender-integrated Delta 5, which called for both racial and sexual equality.

The new independent based its operations on cooperation with the musicians, since, as Klein commented, most "record companies are part of an anti-social movement in Western society, part of the industrial complex that enslaves people." They split profits fifty-fifty between the company and the artist, keeping the prices as low as possible and funneling business profits back into the company.

The Rough Trade ethic of do-it-yourself cooperation spread. Factory Records opened a cooperative venture in Manchester; Fast Product did the same in Edinburgh; and Graduate Records was started in Dudley. Although a few independents such as I.R.S., Virgin, and Stiff became small versions of the majors, many followed the example of the humanistic Rough Trade.

Some punk bands, though approving of the independents, signed with major labels for better distribution of their records. Tom Robinson, facing the contradiction between his leftist politics and the money-making goals of his label, asserted that one has "to use the capitalist media to reach the people. And I do feel that pop music is the way to reach people. Ideally, I'd like to be played on AM stations rather than FM stations, rather than the rarefied atmosphere. I'd rather be played in taxis, in factories, for housewives working at home." The Clash, explained vocalist Joe Strummer, "is trying to do something new, we're trying to be the greatest group in the world, and that also means the biggest. At the same time, we're trying to be radical—I mean, we never want to be *really* respectable—keep punk alive." "We realized that if we were a little more subtle, if we branched out a little, we might reach a few more people," added guitarist Mick Jones of the Clash, which had signed with CBS. "We finally saw we had been reaching the same people over and over. This way if more kids started hearing the record, maybe they'd start humming the songs, they'll read the lyrics and learn something from them."

Right-Wing Reaction

The National Front attempted to destroy such politicized bands as the Clash. In 1977, the *British Patriot*, the magazine of the National Front, warned its readers that the Clash was "the most left-wing of the contemporary groups." To diffuse their influence, it instructed National Front members to keep "an eye out for posters that advertise Clash concerts so that they may be removed from walls and boardings and reconsigned to the gutter where they will reach the most appropriate clientele."

The Clash met resistance from other fronts. During their first tour of Great Britain, police repeatedly stopped their tour bus for little or no excuse, and the band members were arrested and fined for forgetting to return hotel keys. In the United States, Epic Record executives at first refused to issue the group's debut, *The Clash* (EMI: April 1977), branding it "too crude" for American consumption. They released the album two years later in an altered form.

Other punk bands also met opposition. In July 1978, the National Front burned down two auditoriums used for Rock Against Racism shows. A year later British police stormed into the Southall Musicians Cooperative—the home of punks and reggae musicians—and wantonly smashed instruments and sound equipment. Benefit concerts for the Cooperative, organized by the Clash and Pete Townshend of The Who, generated enough money to replace the damaged goods.

Throughout the late seventies, the new Teddy Boys and the skinheads attacked punks in gangland fashion. The two groups of youth, maintained Pete Townshend, were "fascist. They despise everybody who isn't like them. It's a kind of toy fascism, fed by organized fascism; fed by Martin Webster and the National Front." In 1979, right-wing teens, organizing into the Young National Front, launched a Rock Against Communism movement to counterbalance Rock Against Racism. They also formed rock groups such as Ventz, Column 44, and Tragic Minds to disseminate such songs as "Master Race," "White Power," and "Kill the Reds."

The Decline of Punk

Businesses on both sides of the Atlantic undermined punk by selling punk style without its substance. Punks had created a minimalist fashion directly related to their aggressive attitude. "They wear with snarling pride the marks of the downtrodden," wrote Anthony Burgess. "Hair is cropped because long hair holds lice. Clothes are not patched, since patching denotes skill and a seedy desire for respectability; their gaping holes are held together with safety pins." Punk artists such as Jamie Reid, who designed the cover for the Sex Pistols' *Never Mind the Bollocks*, adapted the agitational-propaganda art form of such Russian revolutionaries as Malevich, Tatlin, and Rodchenko, creating posters characterized by sharp, piercing lines against stark backgrounds.

Business capitalized on a copy of punk fashion. As early as June 1977, *Newsweek* observed that "both Saks on Fifth Avenue and Bonwit Teller carry gold safety pins at prices up to $100, and noted British designer Zandra Rhodes recently created a collection of gowns for Bloomingdale's that incorporate stylized rips and glitter-studded safety pins—at $345 to $1,150 a gown." The June 1980 issue of *Mademoiselle* offered its readers the choice between "punk or prep" fashion in a four-page spread. Richard Hell began to lament that "punk was intended to be a whole kind of consciousness. But then it got corrupted into being simply a style or a fad."

John Lydon (a.k.a. Johnny Rotten)
Courtesy of Cam Garrett/S.C.V.D. Studio

Some seventies rock acts began to co-opt the punk image. Linda Ronstadt appeared with spiked hair on the pink-and-black album cover of *Mad Love* (1980) and covered "Alison" by Elvis Costello. Billy Joel, the piano man who topped the charts in 1977 with *The Stranger*, posed in a leather jacket and a rock in his cocked arm for the cover of his *Glass Houses* (1980). Even Cher, the folk singer turned disco queen, surfaced in full punk regalia as the lead singer of the short-lived punk/heavy-metal band, Black Rose. In 1979, Sandy Pearlman, producer of the Clash's second album, complained that "no one's really very scared of punk, especially the record companies. They've sublimated all the revolutionary tendencies this art is based on."

The aggressive British punk rock, its image being assimilated into the rock mainstream, began to abandon the buzz-saw guitar sound for different styles of music. In 1979, Tom Robinson confessed to *Melody Maker* that "after two and a half years, [punk] has become a bit tame and predictable. It's time to move on and try something fresh." He opted for the electronic pop of Sector 27. Amid a 1980 European tour, a disgusted Joe Strummer of the Clash complained to *New Musical Express* that "punk rock has just hit Europe in a big way, but it's totally worthless. . . . It's just another fashion. It's become everything it wasn't supposed to be. I was emotionally shattered." The Clash, always interested in Jamaican rhythms, moved further and further from the boisterous sound of their first album. By the triple album *Sandinista* (1980) and *Combat Rock* (1982), they sounded little like the snarling punks of 1976.

Even the Sex Pistols deserted punk rock. On January 14, 1978, after an American tour, the group was disbanded by Johnny Rotten, who felt that the band had extended rock to its outer limits. "The Pistols finished rock and roll. That was the last rock and roll band. It's all over now," he told an interviewer. "Rock and roll is shit. It's dismal. Granddad danced to it." Paul Cook and Steve Jones played briefly with Johnny Thunders before starting more pop-oriented ventures. On February 2, 1979, Sid Vicious, the archetype of the punk image, died from a drug overdose in New York City. Johnny Rotten reclaimed his original surname, Lydon, and started the "anti-rock-and-roll" band Public Image Ltd. (PiL) with ex-Clash member Keith Levene, novice bass player Jah Woble, and drummer Jim Walker. Extending the minimalistic tendencies of the punks, PiL produced a dissonant, jagged electronic sound perfected on *Metal Box* (1979). "I've grown very far away from human beings," Lydon told *Trouser Press* magazine. "I like being detached; I don't even like shaking hands. I don't like sweat. I think everyone is ugly. Faces disgust me and feet really make me reek. I think the human body's about one of the most ugly things ever created." Rather than people, the ex-Pistol found solace in "machines. Lots of buttons on record players. Knobs and gadgets, electrical equipment of any kind."

The Cure
Courtesy of Cam Garrett/S.C.V.D. Studio

The Post-Punk Explosion

Punk, though beginning to disintegrate by 1978, shattered the monopoly of corporate rock. "Imagine in your mind an ELP [Emerson, Lake and Palmer] number," suggested Joe Strummer of the Clash. "Then imagine punk rock like a blow torch sweeping across it. That to me is what punk rock did."

Punk rock paved the way for other bands that played music to a post-baby boom generation. "I did it. I did it," boasted Johnny Rotten. "I made doors open, I made it easier for up-and-coming bands. It was a Rolling Stones-type of monopoly of the entire business. Record companies would not sign new acts. I opened that up."

Some post-punk bands such as Joy Division, following the model of Rotten's PiL, delivered a chilling, dissonant, minimalistic music. In 1976, friends Peter Hook and Bernard Albrecht decided to form a band. "We were both 21 when we started and had never played an instrument before in our lives. It was straight after seeing the first Sex Pistols gig in Manchester," recalled Hook. "We thought they were so bad, but yet it was so exciting. God! We could have a go at that." A few months later Hook, Albrecht, and their friend Steven Morris met singer Ian Curtis who, according to Hook, "introduced us to Lou Reed and the Velvet Underground, to Iggy Pop and the Stooges, and the Doors."

By mid-1977, the foursome began to produce a droning, Velvet Underground-inspired sound punctuated by Curtis's gloomy lyrics. They called themselves Warsaw and, to avoid confusion with another band, renamed themselves Joy Division after the prostitute wing in a Nazi concentration camp. In June 1979, the band signed with the newly established Factory Records owned by Tony Wilson, who used his life savings to finance the group's first LP, *Unknown Pleasures*. Joy Division hit the Top 20 with the single "Love Will Tear Us Apart," and started to gain critical acclaim before Ian Curtis hanged himself in May 1980 on the eve of an American tour.

The Cure reflected the post-punk pessimism. Formed in 1976, the band debuted with the single "Killing an Arab," inspired by a passage in the Albert Camus novel *The Stranger*. In May 1979, they released their first LP, the pop-oriented *Imaginary Boys*, which reached number 44 on the British charts. The band turned to such pessimistic themes as "The Funeral Party" and "The Drowning Man" on such subsequent albums as *17 Seconds* and *Faith*. In 1982, the Cure released the downbeat classic *Pornography*, which reflected the deep pessimism of some post-punk bands. "I suppose doing an album like *Pornography* and coming to those depths and coming out of it proves that something can come out of nothing," observed singer-lyricist Robert Smith after the band had returned to a pop sound in the mid-1980s.

Some punks such as the Police offered a bright, pop alternative to post-punk depression. In January 1977, Stewart Copeland and Gordon Sumner, nicknamed Sting because he often wore a black-and-yellow jersey, met at a jazz club and began rehearsing with guitarist Henri Padovani. The next month the trio released the punk single "Fall Out," and in March toured with Johnny Thunders and the Heartbreakers. "All I could see in punk was a very direct, simple image of power and energy," recalled Sting, who had been enamored with jazz as a youth. "I could relate to that. I could easily ally myself with that, and forget about changes, chords with flatted fifths, forget all that."

The Police quickly changed musical direction. They replaced Padovani with guitarist Andy Summers and in 1978 released the single "Roxanne," which blended the energy of punk with a reggae-influenced, jazz-tinged sound. "I'm an opportunist," admitted Sting. "I saw this vacuum between punk, which was unschooled, and the horrible corporate rock on the other side. I saw this thing in the middle that was clean and simple. That's what 'Roxanne' is; it's so simple and bare. It's not the energy of *Never Mind the Bollocks*, nor is it corporate rock. It's right in between them."

The new pop sound of the Police led to superstardom. The album *Outlandos D'Amour* (1978), which included "Roxanne," hit the Top 10 on the British chart. "Message in a Bottle" and "Walking on the Moon," singles from the band's second album, both topped the U.K. chart. In 1980, *Zenyatta Mondatta* hit the top of the British chart and became the group's first Top 10 effort in the United States. The next year, *Ghost in the Machine* climbed to number two in America and again topped the chart in England, yielding such hits as "Every Little Thing She Does Is Magic" and "Spirits in the Material World." *Synchronicity* provided the band with its first number-one album on both sides of the Atlantic, making the Police a pop phenomenon. "I don't think pop music is a pejorative term," Sting told an interviewer in 1987. "I want to be proud of being a pop singer when I turn 40."

Billy Idol channeled his punk energy into a bouncy pop. After quitting Generation X in 1981, the singer hired ex-Kiss manager Bill Aucoin and recorded such pop songs as "White Wedding," "Hot in the City," and "Love Calling," which fused the persistent beat of punk with snappy melodies. In 1983, he released the Top 10 album *Rebel Yell*, and followed in 1986 with the million-selling *Whiplash Smile*.

Chrissie Hynde hit the charts with a combination of hard-edged punk and soul. After attending Kent State University in Ohio, she journeyed to London, where she modeled, sold leather handbags, and wrote for the rock paper *New Musical Express*. In 1974, Hynde worked part time for Malcolm McLaren in his clothing shop Sex; two years later she tried unsuccessfully to form a band with guitarist Mick Jones, who had just joined the Clash. Hynde then briefly played guitar for the Malcolm McLaren-managed band Masters of the Backside, which eventually became the Damned.

The Police
Courtesy of Cam Garrett/S.C.V.D. Studio

In 1978, Chrissie Hynde formed the Pretenders with bassist Pete Farndon, James Honeyman-Scott on guitar, and Martin Chambers on drums. During the next three years the band released two top-selling albums, which expanded the sound of punk by infusing it with elements of soul. "I didn't quite fit into the London punk scene because I'd been listening to too many Bobby Womack albums," Hynde insisted.

Adam Ant, born Stuart Goddard, transformed punk energy into pop hits. In 1977, after leaving Hornsey Art College, he formed a punk band named the Ants, which recorded a series of unsuccessful singles. Two years later he hired as manager Malcolm McLaren, who encouraged the Ants to split from Adam and form Bow Wow Wow with Annabella Lwin.

Adam Ant, deserted by McLaren, began to adopt a different image. He abandoned the ripped T-shirts and safety pins of punk for foppish scarves; embroidered, double-breasted jackets; skin-tight leather pants; and sashes. Enlisting the help of ex-Siouxie and the Banshees guitarist Marco Pironi, he formed a pop version of the Ants, which featured an upbeat, drum-based sound. From 1980 to 1983, Adam and his Ants hit the chart with the albums *Kings of the Wild Frontier, Prince Charming*, and *Friend or Foe*, which were promoted by videos of the photogenic group. In 1985, Adam disbanded the group, deciding to concentrate exclusively on his acting career. Adam Ant had been transformed from an angry punk into a video star who became popular on an American music channel that would change the direction of rock during the early 1980s.

14

I Want My MTV

"Video will be the way to keep time with the future."
Time magazine

"Increasingly, and perhaps irreversibly, audiences for American mainstream music will depend, even insist, on each song being a full audiovisual confrontation," observed Time in 1983. "Why should sound alone be enough when sight is only as far away as the TV set or the video machine? . . . Video," concluded the magazine, "will be the way to keep time with the future."

MTV, a music television channel established only two years earlier, was the subject of the *Time* article. During the early 1980s, MTV began to replace radio among a generation of teens, born during the 1960s, who had no personal recollection of Elvis, the Beatles, or Vietnam and sought their own musical identity. It helped create the visual rock of Duran Duran and pop metal and played a major role in the Michael Jackson mania. In the 1980s, MTV designed and delivered rock to the TV generation.

MTV and the Video Age

Americans of the 1980s became obsessed with a video technology that had first been introduced to the mass market with the television set. They continued to buy television sets until, by the end of the decade, 98.2 percent of all American households watched television, most had

273

at least two sets, and 85 percent owned a color TV. Americans also purchased compact video recorder-players, first mass marketed in 1976 by the Victor Co. of Japan (JVC). In 1981, Americans purchased 1.3 million units, a 69 percent increase from the previous year. By 1989, more than 97 million Americans owned JVC-manufactured VCRs. In 1990, Americans bought more than 200 million prerecorded tapes and 280 million blank videocassettes for use with their machines.

In 1981, Americans spent $9.2 billion on video products. Four years later they purchased more than $15 billion in video hardware and accessories. By the end of the decade most American consumers had become part of the expanding video culture.

American teenagers who had been raised on television were especially susceptible to the video craze. The post-baby boomers on the average watched television from three to four hours a day. By the time of high school graduation, they had spent more time watching commercial television than sitting in the classroom. In a 1981 survey of eighth graders, the youths named TV personalities as their top-ten role models. The post-baby boomers even stared at television sets in their schools, which, by the 1980s, became increasingly equipped with instructional TV.

American teenagers of the 1980s, accustomed to the television screen at home and at school, became entranced by video games. They first began to play Space Invaders at the turn of the decade. By 1981, the TV generation dropped more than 25 billion quarters into video game machines at local arcades, which grossed more than the combined television revenues of baseball, football, and basketball and more than the combined income of all the casinos in the country. Teens, mostly male, spent an average of $4.30 a week on coin-operated video games; in 1981 they spent the equivalent of 75,000 years playing Pac-Man, Asteroids, Space Invaders, and other video games. By the early eighties they also began to play video games at home. In 1982, the Atari Corporation, owned by Warner Communications, grossed about $1.3 billion in home video game console and cartridge sales. By that year more than 8 percent of all households owned home video games.

Warner Communications applied video technology to the pop music field. Aided by the advent of stereo TV and the deregulation of the airwaves, which encouraged the growth of cable television, Warner and American Express invested $20 million to launch Music Television (MTV) on August 1, 1981. They broadcast a nonstop format of three-minute video clips, focusing primarily on Warner artists, which initially appeared on 300 cable outlets in 2.5 million homes.

Music Television, headed by 28-year-old Robert Pittman, targeted its programming to the under-25-year-old generation, which had been neglected by radio. "Where is the Woodstock generation? They're all old and bald," Pittman told *Time*. Recycling the 1960s ad campaign for the once-popular breakfast cereal Maypo into "I Want My MTV," he stalked the "TV babies," who seldom read newspapers, books, or even the rock press.

The New Romantics

MTV attracted the TV generation with young, visually exciting bands from the dance clubs of England. Started as a reaction to the austerity of punk, English dance clubs such as The Blitz in Covent Garden provided working-class youths with escapist entertainment. "Most kids who actually live there are sick of the street," contended Gary Kemp, the founder and guitarist of Spandau Ballet, a prominent dance club band. "They take it for granted, because that is where they live, and they don't know anything better. . . . They want to be in a club with great lights, and look really good and pick up girls."

Like its American counterpart, English disco focused on a fashion-conscious audience. "Discos are always parties because you have to make your own visual entertainment," commented Kemp. "The most important thing in a club is the people, not the music they listen to. You become the most important person. You become the visual aspect of the evening, rather than the band." Discos, he continued, appealed to "people who like being looked at—that's why dancing is so important, and why people try and beat each other at dancing. It's also why clothes are so important."

Ultravox, ca. 1978
Frank Driggs Collection

Gary Kemp traced the excessive concern over fashion to British culture. "The attitude behind it has always been there; mods, skinheads and the soul kids—just kids who want to dress smart and enjoy themselves," he told *Trouser Press* magazine. "My dad was a Teddy Boy and my older cousin was a mod. I guess it's hereditary."

The music played at the clubs, a combination of the steady disco beat and atmospheric sounds of the electronic synthesizer, originated with such groups as Roxy Music. Formed in early 1971 by singer Brian Ferry and named after the popular chain of Roxy cinemas in England, the band wore stylish, sometimes flamboyant costumes designed by the futuristic Anthony Price. One member of the group, wrote *Music Scene*, "has been seen traveling the Underground wearing heavily applied brown eye shadow, thick mascara, lipstick, black glitter beads, pearly nail varnish, and violent purple streaks in his blonde hair."

Roxy Music, unlike most glam rockers of the 1970s who delivered hard rock, featured the synthesizer of Brian Eno, who added an almost ethereal element to the music. The band released its debut, self-named album in 1972; it reached the Top 10 in Britain and included the smash British single "Virginia Plain." The next year Roxy Music refined its distinctive style with *For Your Pleasure*, which contained such synthesizer-based songs as "Do the Strand," "Editions of You," and "In Every Dream Home a Heartache."

Brian Eno, who shaped the unique Roxy sound, left the group in 1973 to, in his words, "pursue a partially defined direction—probably involving further investigations into bioelectronics, snake guitar, the human voice, and lizard girls." The band replaced him with the teenage multi-instrumentalist Eddie Jobson and began to deliver a quieter, smoother sound that showcased Brian Ferry's vocals. By 1975, just as the band scored its first U.S. hit single, "Love Is the Drug," Roxy Music disbanded.

Ultravox continued the tradition of Roxy Music and became the direct precursor of the New Romantic movement. Brought together in 1976 by John Foxx, who had dabbled in tapes and synthesizers while in school, the extravagantly bedecked band recorded two albums of straightforward rockers punctuated by the violin and keyboards of Billy Currie. In 1978, the band added the synthesizer of Chris Cross and enlisted the help of producer Conny Plank, who had worked with such experimental electronic groups as Can and Kraftwerk. That year they released *Systems of Romance*, which offered listeners a sparse, crystalline, electronic sound that defined electro-pop, New Romantic music.

When John Foxx left Ultravox in December 1979, keyboardist Billy Currie joined fashion-conscious Steve Strange, synthesizer player Midge Ure, and members of a group called Magazine to form Visage. As with Ultravox, the band emphasized outrageous fashion. "Fashion," commented Steve Strange, "has been missing from the scene since the early seventies with Bowie and Roxy, so what we're part of is just an upsurge in fashion."

Gary Numan and synthesizer
Courtesy of Cam Garrett/S.C.V.D. Studio

Visage expanded the Ultravox sound, featuring two synthesizers and guitars supported by a heavy, repetitious drumbeat. "We were trying to get away from the obvious disco sound," explained Strange. "I messed around with synthesizers and found sounds which were really different from the traditional guitar and bass. We wanted to create a danceable beat, I know you can do that with drums and a bass but it was a new sound that we wanted to use."

Gary Numan popularized the sound of electro-pop that Ultravox and Visage had developed. Born Gary Webb in 1958 and taking his pseudonym from the Yellow Pages, Numan first played in the punk-influenced Tubeway Army. He soon abandoned the guitar for the synthesizer, donned futuristic outfits, and on May 4, 1979, released the synthesizer dance number, "Are 'Friends' Electric." Two weeks later Numan and his band, which included Billy Currie, appeared on the British television show "Top of the Pops," and by the end of July the single and the album *Replicas* hit the top of the British charts. "Gary Numan just released 'Are "Friends" Electric' when everyone thought synthesizer bands were just junk or something or that anyone who used a synthesizer was just a bit of a joke," remembered Midge Ure. "At the time it was very unfashionable but six months later because of Gary Numan it became very fashionable to be a synthesizer band."

The ease of mastering the synthesizer contributed to its popularity. "In some ways it's quite strange that synthesizers were so hated in the punk era," remarked Andy McClusky of the successful electro-pop band Orchestral Manoeuvres in the Dark, which formed in 1980. "They're the ideal punk instrument if you believe in the ethic of 'anybody can do it.' Someone who's been playing synth for ten minutes can easily sound as good as someone who's been playing for years, provided the ideas are there." "We couldn't hardly play at all then; we can't play very well now," confessed Andy Fletcher in 1982, a year after his all-synthesizer band, Depeche Mode, was formed. "In pop music nowadays you don't need technical ability, you need ideas and the ability to write songs. That's the main thing."

By the beginning of the 1980s, portable synthesizers had become relatively inexpensive. Unlike the cumbersome, sometimes stationary Moog models of the previous decade, easy-to-handle portables could be purchased for as little as $100 to $300.

The electro-pop sound of the synthesizer, easily attainable and affordable, embodied the digital, push-button eighties. "Not a day goes by when you don't press a button, whether it's for a cup of coffee or to turn on the stereo or video," observed David Ball of the two-man synthesizer group Soft Cell, which came together in 1981. "People are so surrounded now by electronics, of course there's electronic music."

MTU Goes Electro-Pop

MTV, searching for videos of new bands to air on its 24-hour-a-day format, promoted the electro-pop of such fashion-obsessed New Romantics as Duran Duran. Begun in 1978 as a duo and named after a character in the science fiction movie *Barbarella*, by 1981 the group had become a fivesome that featured an airy-sounding synthesizer, the insistent drumbeat of disco, and a pop sensibility for what keyboard player Nick Rhodes dubbed "entertainment music." The group achieved notoriety with its first, self-named album and the subsequent *Rio* (1982) and *Arena* (1984) through the imaginative use of videos on MTV. "Videos are incredibly important for us," asserted Rhodes. "It's a way of expressing a song in visuals. It gives another dimension. . . . MTV," added the keyboardist, "was instrumental in breaking us in America." Norman Sammick, senior vice-president of Warner Communications, put it more succinctly: "I think Duran Duran owes its life to MTV."

The music channel helped other electro-pop bands such as the Human League reach the record-buying American public. The group, formed in Sheffield in 1977, first produced icy, dense electronic music modeled after such European outfits as Kraftwerk. In 1980, founder Philip Oakley disbanded the Human League because of its reliance on taped music during concerts, and with Philip Wright and four new members re-formed the band. The next year, the revamped Human League hired producer Martin Rushent, who infused the band's synthesizer-based music with a toe-tapping, pop sensibility. "I wanted to make a pop electronic album," remembered Rushent. "Not a DAF or a Kraftwerk, but something that was accessible to everybody. The Human League just walked through the door at the right time." The producer replaced the traditional keyboard synthesizer with a Roland Microcomposer sequencer, added the flawless beat of a drum machine and in 1982 produced *Dare*, which included the singles "Don't You Want Me" and "Love Action (I Believe in Love)." After MTV placed "Don't You Want Me" in heavy rotation, the song became a number-one single and the album hit the number-three position on the chart.

MTV lifted other wildly garbed, British electro-pop bands up the American charts. Through repeated showings of selected videos, it successfully promoted the London quintet Spandau Ballet, which hit the Top 10 with "True" (1983). Soft Cell scored with a remake of the obscure soul song "Tainted Love" (1983), and A Flock of Seagulls hit with "I Ran (So Far Away)" (1982). MTV also marketed Depeche Mode, which had the dance smash "Just Can't Get Enough," and the Thompson Twins' "In the Name of Love."

MTV refurbished the career of David Bowie, the seventies icon who had helped lay the groundwork for electro-pop. Bowie, the king of

Duran Duran
Courtesy of Capitol Records

glitter rock who served as a model of fashion for the foppish New Romantics, began to abandon a hard, guitar-based rock sound for the synthesizer around 1976, when he released a collection of techno-pop songs, *Station to Station*. The next year he began a three-album collaboration with synthesizer wunderkind Brian Eno, who produced a sometimes-fragile, sometimes-dense synthesizer sound that he had pioneered as a member of Roxy Music. In 1983, at the height of the New Romantic success, the ever-visual Bowie recorded *Let's Dance*, which, with the help of MTV and a world tour, neared the top of the American chart.

By 1983, the electro-pop sound, largely introduced to America by videos on MTV, had swept across the United States. It dominated the charts, filtered into mainstream pop, and captivated the TV generation. Pursuing this new sound, devotees bought an unprecedented number of synthesizers in place of guitars, which declined in sales by 37 percent in one year. MTV, created in the decade of technology, had sold a visually interesting, electro-pop dance music to a generation raised on glitter rock, disco, and television.

The increase in viewers indicated the success of MTV. Initially broadcast to 2.5 million households in late 1981, by 1983 the music channel reached more than 17 million homes on 2000 cable affiliates. The average MTV viewer was 23 years old and watched the network an hour a day on weekdays and 90 minutes on weekends. "They're watching it," said MTV vice-president Les Garland in early 1983, "not in front of their homework, not as background. They're watching it."

MTV, attracting the under-25-year-old bracket, appealed to many corporate sponsors that manufactured products for the youth market. "MTV is very attractive," asserted Joseph Ostrow, executive vice-president of the ad agency Young & Rubicam. "It allows you to target very discreetly to a particular segment of the population. For youth-oriented companies that's terrific." "We are a company that believes in specialized entertainment," agreed John Lack, executive vice-president of Warner Amex, when his company started the network, "and if you are a Budweiser or Kawasaki motorcycles or Pepsi-Cola, you want our audience." During its first year of operation MTV convinced more than 100 companies such as Budweiser to spend $1500 for a 30-second spot and grossed $20 million. By 1984, revenues had jumped to $73 million.

Music Television provided a needed boost to a radio-dependent American record industry that had peaked in 1978 with gross revenues of roughly $4 billion and then the next year had sharply declined. The network created a style of music for a new generation, which radio had neglected. "Groups are chalking up huge sales on songs [through MTV] that have never been played on radio," boasted Les Garland. In 1983, *Billboard* estimated that exposure of mostly new bands on MTV resulted in sales increases of 15 to 20 percent. "We were there for the industry," explained John Lack. "We found we could help a business in trouble and it's worked, and they've responded. Ask anyone at CBS or RCA or Arista."

MTV and Michaelmania

MTV continued to support the American recording industry by promoting a Motown-style revival, which followed naturally from electro-pop. Though using new technology, the New Romantics created a disco-like dance music that had its foundation in the slick, fashionable Motown. As a youth Steve Strange of Visage "used to go to these Northern soul clubs," which featured Motown-type bands. "Our direction came from the soul/disco/dance side, not rock," agreed Gary Kemp of Spandau Ballet, which in 1983 abandoned synthesizers for the Motown sound. The electro-pop band Soft Cell first hit the charts with the soul ballad "Tainted Love," and in 1982 scored with a remake of the Supremes' classic, "Where Did Our Love Go?"

As the synthesizer craze began to fade in 1982, MTV capitalized on the renewed interest in Motown by airing videos of former Motown star Michael Jackson. Growing up in Gary, Indiana, during the 1960s, Jackson and his siblings Tito, Jermaine, Jackie, and Marlon practiced songs and dance steps at home. "When I found out that my kids were interested in becoming entertainers, I really went to work with them," recalled father Joe Jackson. "I rehearsed them about three years before I turned them loose. That's practically every day for at least two or three hours. When the other kids would be out on the street playing games, my boys were in the house working—trying to learn how to be something in life."

Under the tutelage of Joe Jackson, the boys entered and won talent contests in Indiana and Illinois and played at such Chicago clubs as the High Chaparral and the Guys and Gals Club. "This was on weekends," remembered the elder Jackson. "I had a Volkswagen bus and I bought a big luggage rack and put it on the top and had everybody on the inside of the bus."

Joe Jackson approached Motown about his family musical act. In 1967, he "sent Berry Gordy a tape. They kept it about three months and then sent it back." Two years later the persistent father convinced Gordy to sign the Jackson 5, who had impressed Diana Ross when she performed on the same bill as the boys in 1968 at a civic Soul Weekend in Gary.

Berry Gordy, following his formula for success, began to groom the boys. "We provide total guidance," a Motown vice-president explained to *Time*. "We provide their material, set their basic sound and work out the choreographic routines." The company gave special attention to the ten-year-old Michael, who was taught to mimic James Brown's frenzied dancing and the romantic pleadings of Smokey Robinson. In late 1969, Motown featured Michael on the first Jackson 5 release, "I Want You Back," which by January 1970 hit the number-one slot on the singles chart and sold more than 2 million copies. "We're labeling it soul-bubblegum," declared Berry Gordy.

The Jackson 5 became the last major recording act signed by Motown. They followed their first hit with 13 consecutive Top 20 singles, including the number-one hits "ABC," "The Love You Save," and "I'll Be There." By 1976, when they left Motown, the Jackson 5 had received a commendation from Congress for their "contribution to American youth," served as the characters of a Saturday morning network television cartoon show, and had become the most successful African-American pop vocal group, selling more than 100 million records worldwide.

The Jackson 5, Gordy's crossover dream, appealed to all races, genders, and ages. "The Jackson music," stated Joe Jackson, "is a type of music that the young kids like, and as you know, the older people like, too. It's music to send a message to all the people whether they're black or white. It's music for rejoicing, whether you're black or white. It's for the whole world."

In early 1976, the Jackson 5 left the Motown stable, changed their name to the Jacksons, and signed with Epic. Using the songwriting team of Kenny Gamble and Leon Huff, the group continued to churn out hits, including "Enjoy Yourself" and "Lovely One." Later they wrote their own material.

Michael Jackson enjoyed a successful solo career as well. As the popular lead singer of the Jackson 5 at Motown, in 1971 and 1972 he hit the chart with the Top 10 singles "Got To Be There," a reworking of "Rockin' Robin," and "Ben." In 1978, he played the scarecrow in the movie *The Wiz*, an all-African-American version of *The Wizard of Oz* starring Diana Ross. While filming the movie, Jackson met producer Quincy Jones, who arranged the music for the soundtrack. The next year, assisted by Jones, Jackson recorded *Off the Wall*, which sold 8 million copies and included the hit singles "Don't Stop 'Til You Get Enough," "Rock with You," "Off the Wall," and "She's Out of My Life."

In 1982, Jackson again teamed with Quincy Jones on *Thriller*. Trying to appeal to both African-American and white audiences, he chose as the first single "This Girl Is Mine," a duet with former Beatle Paul McCartney, a choice that ensured a wide audience. He then released "Beat It," which included an Eddie Van Halen guitar solo that assured play on rock radio stations. To further disseminate his product, Jackson filmed slick videos of some songs on the album.

Video provided an ideal medium for Jackson, who had been trained in the Motown school. "Rock videos have transformed the music industry, providing a showcase for Jackson in much the same way as musical comedy did for Fred Astaire in the 1930s," *Maclean's*, the Canadian counterpart to *Time* magazine, told its readers in 1984. "Videos have revived the demand for old fashion entertainment skills, an ideal situation for Jackson who has been perfecting his act from the age of five."

First encouraged by the Motown, the singer perfected dazzling choreography, unlike most other rock acts. Gene Kelly, the popular dancer of the 1940s, raved about Jackson's "native histrionic wit. He knows when to stop and then flash out like a bolt of lightning." "I think he's terrific," enthused Bob Fosse, the director-choreographer who became known for his work on the movie *Cabaret*, and the

The Jackson 5, Michael Jackson (center), ca. 1970
Frank Driggs Collection

Broadway smash *Pippin*. "Clean, neat, fast with a sensuality that comes through. . . . It's the style. That's what Michael Jackson has." Even Fred Astaire, probably the best-known dancer in American history, complimented Jackson: "My Lord, he is a wonderful mover."

MTV, criticized for only airing videos of white artists, played the visually stunning, expertly choreographed Jackson videos and helped to create Michaelmania. Though Jackson's records had always sold well, *Thriller* began to sell at an amazing rate after it was promoted on MTV. At the height of the mania it sold a million copies every four days. It stayed on the Japanese charts for 65 weeks, sold on the black market in the Soviet Union, and even topped the charts in South Africa. "Jackson, you might say, bridges the apartheid gap," observed one record executive.

Crazed fans around the globe began to snap up Michael Jackson paraphernalia. They bought posters, buttons, and T-shirts, which most rock acts sold by the 1980s. Michael Jackson fanatics also purchased *Thriller* caps, key chains, duffel bags, bubblegum cards, an 11-inch Michael Jackson doll that could be twisted into various dance poses, and replicas of the single white sequined glove that Jackson wore onstage. They even bought a video that chronicled the making of the video for the song "Thriller."

When the mania subsided in early 1985, Jackson had achieved singular success. He had released seven of the ten songs on the album as singles; they all reached the Top 10. The 25-year-old singer had sold 40 million copies of *Thriller* worldwide, topped the U.S. charts in both

1983 and 1984, and won 150 gold and platinum awards as well as a record-breaking eight Grammy awards. "Jackson," asserted *Time* in March 1984, "is the biggest thing since the Beatles. He is the hottest single phenomenon since Elvis Presley."

Michael Jackson, the most important rock star of the early 1980s, epitomized the growing conservatism in America. He did not smoke, drink, or take drugs. He even refused to utter the word *funky*, preferring *jelly* instead. A devout adherent to the Jehovah's Witnesses, the singer attended meetings at a Kingdom Hall four times a week and regularly fasted on weekends. "Such pop superstars as Elvis Presley, Bob Dylan or the Beatles have traditionally posed a sexual or political challenge to the status quo," contended *Maclean's* magazine, "but Michael Jackson is by contrast an establishment figure, perfectly in tune with the conservative America of Ronald Reagan." In 1984, Jackson received a public service award from the President, a former forties actor, who himself had become one of the most popular presidents through his use of video.

Jackson amassed a fortune from his success. By the end of 1984, he had earned more than $30 million from the sale of *Thriller* and grossed another $50 million from the burgeoning industry of Michael Jackson products. The singer increased his personal net worth to $75 million in 1985, becoming one of the richest men in America.

The Jackson Legacy

The success of Michael Jackson paved the way for other soul-pop artists, including such British bands as Culture Club, which merged the English concern for fashion with a Motown-influenced sound to climb the charts. Formed in 1981 by singer Boy George (a.k.a. George O'Dowd), bassist Mikey Craig, and drummer Jon Moss, the group dressed in outlandish costumes. "I used to dress up from the age of 13 or 14, and George is the same," related Mikey Craig. "Dressing up in different styles and going to the clubs is a big thrill for kids. You follow the fashion changes and get caught up in it."

The extravagantly bedecked, video-ready Culture Club played, in the words of Boy George, "imitation soul." In 1982, they released the soul-pop album, *Kissing to Be Clever*, which included the warm, bouncy, Top 10 "Do You Really Want to Hurt Me," "Time (Clock of My Heart)," and "I'll Tumble 4 Ya." Scaling the charts on the coattails of Jackson's *Thriller* the next year, the group produced number-two *Colour by Numbers*, which employed signature Motown riffs. " 'Plagiarism' is one of my favorite words," admitted Boy George. "Culture Club is the most sincere form of plagiarism in modern music—we just do it better than most."

The Eurythmics also scored with an updated Motown sound. Formed in 1980 by Dave Stewart and the photogenic, classically trained Annie Lennox, the duo first recorded electronic experimental music on the unsuccessful *In the Garden*. During the next two years they released five singles which also failed to chart.

The Eurythmics, Dave Stewart and Annie Lennox, ca. 1983
Frank Driggs Collection

Amid Michaelmania in 1983, the twosome earned international acclaim for *Sweet Dreams (Are Made of This)*, which featured the sultry,
Motown-influenced vocals of Lennox over the insistent beat of a drum
machine. "I identify my vocal style very much with black soul music,"
explained Lennox at the time. "Not with blues, but with 60s soul. It really struck a chord in me, and I can't get away from that." "What she
really loved was Tamla/Motown material," chimed Stewart. In the next
two years the duo followed with the Top 10, soul-tinged *Touch* and *Be
Yourself Tonight*.

Wham!, another sharply dressed duo from Britain, hit the charts
with African-American-inspired dance music. Wham!'s Andrew Ridgeley and George Michael (a.k.a. Georgios Panayiotou) met as young
teens and frequented local clubs, dancing to the soundtrack of *Saturday Night Fever*. In 1982, the two friends formed Wham! and scaled the
British charts with a series of singles, including "Young Guns" and "Bad

Madonna, ca. 1987
Frank Driggs Collection

Boys." In 1984, amid the furor over Michael Jackson, Michael and Ridgeley released a second album, *Make It Big*, which, after being promoted through videos aired on MTV, yielded three number-one singles: "Wake Me Up Before You Go-Go," "Careless Whisper," and "Everything She Wants." When Wham! disbanded in 1986, George Michael continued to offer spunky dance hits on the chart-topping *Faith* (1987), which yielded four number-one singles. "The big shame about modern black music is that, to a degree, anybody can pick up a machine and make a funk record," noted Michael. "It's a shame I can do it," he joked.

On the other side of the Atlantic, Madonna combined a decadent sex appeal with African-American dance rhythms to attain stardom. Born of Italian-American parents in Detroit in 1959, Madonna Louise Ciccone won a dance scholarship to the University of Michigan. After her freshmen year she left school to pursue a career as a dancer in New York City. After briefly studying at the Alvin Ailey Dance Theater, she moved to Paris, where she began to dance with the revue of disco star Patrick Hernandez. In 1979, Madonna formed a band with drummer Steve Bray; the next year she gave a tape of the band to Mark Kamins, a disco disc jockey, who helped Madonna land a record contract with Sire.

In 1983, Madonna released her first record, which presented the singer's breathy vocals over a disco beat. Propelled by videos of songs on the album that accentuated her sexually aggressive, Marilyn Monroe-like image, including her trademark attire of lacewear and religious-oriented jewelry, she became a minor hit. The next year Madonna attained national stardom with the number-one *Like a Virgin*, a dance album that included the hook-laden singles "Material Girl," "Like a Virgin," and "Dress You Up," and on its cover pictured Madonna in a flimsy lace bodice cinched by a belt that carried the inscription, "Boy Toy." By 1986, Madonna had sold more than 9 million copies of her first two albums, hit the top of the charts a second time with *True Blue*, and, based upon her initial exposure through MTV, snagged a leading role in the feature-length movie *Desperately Seeking Susan*.

The success of Michael Jackson's brand of Motown dance music also helped the careers of African-American soul-pop performers. "It inspired black artists not to look at themselves in a limited way," noted producer Quincy Jones. "Before Michael, those kinds of sales had never happened for a black artist. Michael did it. He did it for the first time."

Motown artist Lionel Richie followed Jackson to the top of the charts. In 1968, Richie joined with five other freshmen at the African-American Tuskegee Institute in Tuskegee, Alabama, to form the Commodores, a name randomly picked from the dictionary. Three years later the band signed with Motown; for two years they served as the opening act for the Jackson 5. In 1974, the Commodores recorded their first album, *Machine Gun*, characterized by a raw, sharp-edged sound. After two more albums, Lionel Richie convinced the group to record his softer, soul-pop ballads such as "Three Times a Lady" and "Sail On," which hit the top of the singles chart. In 1982, the Motown performer released his first solo album, which contained the chart-topping single "Truly." In the midst of Michaelmania, he recorded *Can't Slow Down*, which, with the help of MTV, hit the top of the charts and transformed Lionel Richie into *Billboard's* Top Artist of 1984.

MTV helped the youngest member of the Jackson family. In 1982, before the success of *Thriller*, Janet Jackson released a self-named debut, which barely cracked the Top 75. She followed with the even less successful *Dream Street*. In 1986, promoted by a series of videos and amid the Motown-influenced craze that had been created by her brother, Janet Jackson hit the top of the chart with *Control* and three years later duplicated her feat with *Janet Jackson's Rhythm Nation 1814*. "Janet's a video artist," reasoned Roger Davies, who managed the singer.

Whitney Houston achieved similar success through video. The daughter of Cissy Houston, who had anchored the Aretha Franklin backup group, the Sweet Inspirations, Whitney began performing professionally with her mother at the age of 15. Three years later she signed with Arista Records, which, as Motown had done with its young talent, groomed the young singer. By 1984, Houston had appeared as a model in *Glamour, Cosmopolitan, Seventeen*, and other fashion magazines and had backed dozens of artists in the studio, including Jermaine Jackson on "Take Good Care of My Heart."

In 1985, Houston recorded her first album, which featured upbeat ballads in the Motown tradition. As the first two singles from the LP climbed the chart, she filmed a video of "How Will I Know," which, according to Peter Baron, Arista's associate director of video production and promotion, "helped build her image. She's become a superstar in a year." The singer had three consecutive number-one singles and sold 14 million copies of the album, the biggest-selling debut in history. In 1987, Houston recorded a follow-up, *Whitney*, which shot to the number-one spot and yielded four chart-topping singles.

Prince grafted rock guitars and overtly sexual lyrics onto a soul-pop sound for an innovative hybrid of the Michael Jackson formula for success. Born in Minneapolis to a bandleader father, Prince Rogers Nelson taught himself piano, guitar, and drums by the age of 14 and began to play a mixture of rock and soul. "I never grew up in one particular culture," Prince related. "I'm not a punk, but I'm not an R & B artist either—because I'm a middle-class kid from Minnesota, which is very much white America."

During the late 1970s, Prince met Minneapolis ad man Chris Moon, who suggested sexually explicit lyrics. "It was amazing to see," recalled Moon. "Here was this very quiet kid, but once he'd discovered the notion of sex as a vehicle for his writing, it was as if a door unlocked for him." In 1978, Prince signed with Warner Brothers and recorded *For You*, which included the suggestive "Soft and Wet." The next year he hit the top of the R & B charts with "I Wanna Be Your Lover" and in 1980 recorded the widely covered "When You Were Mine" on *Dirty Mind*.

In 1982, after only moderate commercial success with his recordings, Prince released *1999* and filmed a video of the song "Little Red Corvette," one of the first clips by an African-American artist aired on the music channel, which lifted the single to the Top 10. Through constant promotion by MTV, Prince sold 14 million copies of *Purple Rain* (1984), the soundtrack for the movie of the same name, which won an Oscar and a Grammy award. In 1985, Prince followed with the number-one *Around the World in a Day*. Like other African-American and white soul-pop artists in the wake of the mania over Michael Jackson, Prince had attained international stardom through video.

Pop Goes the Metal

MTV ensured its preeminent place among the cable networks during the decade by creating a craze for pop metal bands. As it had done with electro-pop and soul-pop, the music channel delivered a visually exciting, largely inoffensive heavy metal to the post-baby boomers.

Van Halen served as the archetype for the metal bands of the 1980s. Sons of a jazz musician, Alex and Eddie Van Halen grew up in the Netherlands, where they received extensive classical music training. In 1965, they moved with their family to California, where they discovered and began to play rock-and-roll. In 1974, the Van Halen brothers joined with bassist Michael Anthony and singer David Lee Roth to form a band, which for three years performed at such Los Angeles bars as Gazzari's on Sunset Strip.

The members of Van Halen each contributed a different element to their unique sound. "I think the only true rocker of the bunch is Al," related guitarist Eddie Van Halen. "He's the only one who listens to AC/DC and all that kind of stuff. Dave will walk in with a disco tape and I'll walk in with my progressive tapes and Mike walks in with his Disneyland stuff." At home, Eddie preferred the "progressive stuff" and "a lot of Chopin, piano. Very little rock and roll."

Van Halen, ca. 1980, with lead singer David Lee Roth (second from left)
Frank Driggs Collection

Unlike the blues-rooted heavy metal artists of the late 1960s and early 1970s, the eclectic Van Halen presented a more polished, smooth sound. The band favored a variety of tempos; rapid-fire, arpeggio guitar solos much shorter than the extended guitar breaks of the original heavy-metal groups; fast-paced, light bass lines; and periodic harmonies that reinforced the hooks in the songs. In addition, Van Halen featured frequent falsetto screams by the photogenic, acrobatic David Lee Roth, who added a wry sense of humor to the lyrics. "Van Halen is entertainment," contended singer Roth. "Van Halen is entertainment delivered at maximum impact, but it's entertainment."

In 1976, the band recorded a demo tape financed by Gene Simmons of Kiss, who spotted them at the Starwood club in Los Angeles. A year later they signed a contract with Warner Brothers and in early 1978 released their first album, which hit the Top 20 and sold more than 2 million copies. Van Halen followed with four Top 10 albums, the last of which, *Diver Down* (1982), reached the number-three slot. After Eddie Van Halen received mass notoriety for his guitar work on Michael Jackson's "Beat It," the band neared the top of the chart with *1984*, receiving constant support from MTV.

Def Leppard perfected the pop metal that Van Halen had originated. Raised in the factory town of Sheffield in the midlands of England, Joe Elliott, guitarists Steve Clark and Pete Willis, and bass player Rick Savage worked in blue-collar jobs before founding the band. They drew their inspiration from a combination of heavy metal and pop. "We always loved the heavy bands of the early seventies, obviously Zeppelin, Uriah Heep, Deep Purple even, but other than that we also were very influenced by what was happening in the pop charts," related bassist Rick Savage. "I suppose if you analyzed it, it was some sort of cross between the two forms. . . . We always want to have that commercial aspect that's pleasing on the ear, while the 17-year-olds can still get off on the power of it," added the bass player.

In 1981, after two commercially unsuccessful releases, the band joined with producer Robert ("Mutt") Lange, who began to help Def Leppard refine their pop-metal sound. "I heard those vocal harmonies and thought, 'Wow, an English band doing that stuff,' " remembered Lange. "Since they had the looks and they had the riffs I knew that with me as an extra member, so to speak, we could pull the songs together." The group released the Lange-produced *High and Dry*, which entered the U.S. Top 40.

By 1983, after Phil Collen replaced guitarist Willis, who became disgusted with the more popular direction of the band, Def Leppard had perfected its sound. The group featured tight vocal harmonies and dramatic guitar work accentuated by Lange's production. Joe Elliott called the sound "nice, youthful melodic rock 'n' roll."

The band members penned catchy, unobtrusive lyrics. "Because the whole idea of Def Leppard is escapism," asserted Rick Savage, "we hate singing about unemployment and such, and we hate bands that do sing about it. Everybody knows it's tough. A band can't change anything. Who wants to go to one of our shows to hear how bad life is." "It's all wine, women and song," echoed Joe Elliott. "Nothing annoys me more than records about politics this, Greenpeace that. Someone has to be the opposite, and that's us. All we are is total escapism."

MTV promoted the photogenic, escapist pop metal of Def Leppard through performance videos. Offering heavy rotation to clips of such songs as "Photograph," the music channel broadcast the band to the mass of teens. Coupled with constant touring, it successfully marketed *Pyromania* (1983), which sold more than 9 million copies. "1983 was our year," enthused Cliff Burnstein, co-manager of the group.

The music channel also contributed to the success of other pop-metal bands, some of which favored the outlandish costumes and antics of 1970s glam rockers. In 1981, Motley Crue played a West Coast version of video-ready glam rock. Nikki Sixx (a.k.a. Frank Ferranno) on bass, vocalist Vince Neil, guitarist Mick Mars (a.k.a. Bob Deal), and drummer Tommy Lee began performing together around Los Angeles. Setting fire to their extravagant clothing and chain sawing mannequins on stage, the band gained a loyal following for their theatrical heavy metal.

The band identified Kiss as its major influence. "When I first saw Kiss I stood in line for six hours at the Paramount Theater in Seattle, Washington," recalled Nikki Sixx. "I was sitting in the front row, and when they took the stage I knew then that I wanted to have a band that was nothing less than what I saw. The theatre bug bit me. Rock 'n' roll from then on had to have an element of theatre to excite me."

In May 1983, after an unsuccessful debut, Motley Crue signed to Elektra Records. Four months later they released *Shout at the Devil*, which through heavy rotation on MTV entered the Top 20. By the end of 1984, the readers of *Hit Parader* and *Circus* magazines voted the band Rock Act of the Year. The glam rockers followed with the Top 10 *Theater of Pain* (1985).

Ratt came from the same Los Angeles heavy-metal scene. Put together in 1981 by guitarist Robbin Crosby and singer Stephen Pearcy, the band played an escapist pop metal. "We have more melody in our music," noted Crosby as he compared the group to such heavy-metal pioneers as Led Zeppelin. "We talk about love and sex and reality and fantasy—just down-to-earth, fun stuff."

The band members affected a glam image to increase their popularity. "When we first got together, we were a real heavy-metal band—black leather, studs, the whole thing," admitted Robbin Crosby. "We showed up at our first gig—and everybody else had the same stuff. Me and Steve were going, 'This is not cool. We've got to do something to get away from this.' . . . We started wearing more fashionable clothes," Crosby continued. "Started dressing real sharp. A lot of the metalers said, 'Whoa! These guys are faggots!' But it's more of a mass appeal kind of thing."

The band proved its popular appeal with the help of MTV. In 1984, they released *Out of the Cellar* and filmed corresponding videos. By

Motley Crue, ca. 1983
Frank Driggs Collection

293

the next year the group had cracked the Top 10 and had sold more than 2 million copies of the debut. The next year Ratt repeated its success with *Invasion of Your Privacy*.

MTV also began to show clips of such pop-metal bands as Bon Jovi. Formed in 1983 by singer Jon Bon Jovi (a.k.a. John Bongiovi) and quickly signed to Mercury Records, the band toured extensively to promote its first, self-named LP. Three years later, the group released *Slippery When Wet* and filmed matching videos, which MTV aired ceaselessly. By late 1987, Bon Jovi had sold more than 12 million copies of its chart-topping second album. They followed with the number-one *New Jersey* (1988). "The success of such current hot groups as Bon Jovi," observed *Time*, "is largely traceable to the saturation airplay given their videos on MTV."

The MTV-based success of Bon Jovi opened the doors for a pop-metal explosion during the late eighties. "The majors are now going nuts. Everyone's out there trying to sign up a metal band," reported Bob Chiappardi, co-owner of the metal-oriented Concrete Marketing retail firm. The major labels signed such acts as Poison, Winger, White Lion, Tora Tora, Kix, Kingdom Come, and countless others. In 1986, Van Halen topped the charts with *5150* and followed with the number-one *OU812* (1988), both of which benefited from videos that received continual play on MTV. After a four-year hiatus, Def Leppard topped the charts with *Hysteria*, which sold more than 5 million copies. In 1987, Motley Crue neared the top with *Girls, Girls, Girls* and topped the chart with *Dr. Feelgood* (1989). Bon Jovi, observed *Billboard* columnist Paul Grein, "opened the floodgates the same way Michael Jackson did in 1983 for Prince, Lionel Richie and others."

The success of pop-metal and electro-pop bands and the unparalleled achievements of Michael Jackson indicated the importance of MTV. "At any one time, 130,000 homes are watching MTV, according to Nielsen," observed Len Epand of Polygram Records. "If the video is in power rotation—15 or 16 plays a week—and that audience tunes in 10 times, that's 1.3 million people hearing the record and deciding whether they like it or not. If they like it, they'll buy it." "There isn't a national radio station. That's where MTV comes in," added Laura Foti, director of marketing for RCA video productions. "That's where they have their power: immediately showing everyone in the country this new band." Joe Jackson, the singer who hit the chart in 1979 with *Look Sharp*, complained about the dominance of MTV: "Things which used to count, such as being a good composer, player or singer, are getting lost in the desperate rush to visualize everything. It is now possible to be all of the above and still get nowhere simply by not looking good in a video, or worse still, not making one."

The marketing clout of MTV translated into profits. In the first half of 1984, after the *Thriller* hysteria had abated, MTV registered $8.1 million in profits from sales of $30.3 million. In 1986, after Viacom International purchased the network from Warner Amex, it grossed $111 million and turned a profit of $47 million. Though its ratings began to decline in 1986, MTV tied USA Network and Cable News Network for first place among the cable channels.

MTV, broadcast on more than 5000 cable outlets to more than 46 million viewers in 1989, had helped define eighties rock-and-roll. It had fostered and successfully promoted electro-pop and pop metal and had created a frenzy over Michael Jackson's *Thriller*. To a large extent the music network had replaced radio as the preeminent trendsetter in rock. As *Billboard* noted in its wrap-up of the decade, "MTV is singularly responsible for one of the most basic changes in the current music fan's vocabulary: Where somebody might have said ten years ago, 'Yeah, I've heard that song,' that same person now might likely say, 'Yeah, I saw that video,' or, even more revealing, 'Yeah, I saw that song.' " During the 1980s, MTV had packaged and delivered rock-and-roll to the TV generation.

15

The Promise of Rock-and-Roll

"In the '80s, which is a barren era, we look back at the '60s as a great reservoir of talent, of high ideals, and of the will and desire to change things."

Bono

"I'm a romantic," Bruce Springsteen confessed to a reporter in 1980. "To me the idea of a romantic is someone who sees the reality, lives the reality every day but knows about the possibilities, too. You can't lose sight of the dreams. That's what great rock is about to me, it makes the dream seem possible." Rock, added Springsteen, is "a promise, an oath."

The romanticism of Bruce Springsteen, rooted in a sixties idealism, became prevalent from the mid-eighties into the nineties. It appealed to baby boomers who during the sixties had protested for a better world and against the war in Vietnam. The return to a sixties sensibility led to numerous benefit concerts, which revived the careers of some sixties rockers and revitalized the rock industry. It also influenced a nineties country-rock boom, which captured the attention of the baby-boom generation. From the mid-eighties to the mid-nineties, baby boomers embraced a sixties-inspired, cause-oriented rock that provided a stark contrast to the entertaining, glossy, sexy images on MTV.

The return to sixties ideals occurred around mid-decade, when the economy started to decline and the social order became increasingly stratified. In 1981 and 1982, after nearly three decades of prosperity in the United States, economic conditions began to worsen as unemployment increased to almost 10 percent. Though expanding at an encouraging 8 percent annual growth rate in the first half of 1984, the U.S. economy again began to falter later in the year. Wage gains slowed, unemployment stood at nearly 8 percent, and personal consumption declined. "The economy," noted one analyst in early 1985, "appeared to be teetering on the brink of a recession, having swung from boom to bust conditions in one quarter."

Economic stratification added to concerns. While indicating an increase in the number of families that earned more than $50,000 a year, a Census Bureau study in 1984 reported that nearly 66 million Americans in 36 million households received government benefits in the third quarter of 1983. Of the total, which represented nearly 30 percent of the U.S. population, about 42 million Americans received food stamps, welfare, subsidized housing, or Medicaid. From 1980 to 1986, as the number of families that earned more than $50,000 a year increased by nearly 323 percent, the number of families living on less than $2500 remained constant.

Many baby boomers who expected the prosperity of their youth especially felt the effects of the recession. "When we grew up in the '50s and '60s, we were told the world would be our oyster," explained Richard Hokenson, a 46-year-old demographer in New York City. "Now life's turned out to be more of a struggle than we were told it would be." In 1984, *U.S. News and World Report* referred to the baby boomers as "the disillusioned generation, people in their 20s and early 30s who wonder whatever happened to the American dream."

The Boss

Bruce Springsteen, nicknamed the Boss, sang about Americans who felt the hard times. The son of a bus driver, Springsteen grew up in Freehold, New Jersey. At the age of 13 he learned guitar, which, as with many other rockers, provided Springsteen with solace. "Music saved me," he told an interviewer. "From the beginning, my guitar was something I could go to. If I hadn't found music, I don't know what I would have done."

Springsteen, armed with a guitar, joined a series of bands. In 1966, he passed an audition to become a member of the Castiles, which performed at local clubs, parties, and school dances, recorded two unreleased demos, and within a year played at the Café Wha? in New York City. Upon graduation from high school the New Jersey guitarist worked with the power trio Earth, and in 1969 started Child, later renamed Steel Mill, which traveled to California to play on New Year's Eve at the Esalen Institute. "I've never been out of New Jersey in my life and suddenly I get to Esalen and see all these people in sheets," remembered Springsteen. Disbanding Steel Mill in 1971, he formed the short-lived Dr.

Zoom and the Sonic Boom and then the ten-piece Bruce Springsteen Band, which included David Sancious on keyboards, bassist Gary Tallent, Steve Van Zandt on guitar, drummer Vini Lopez, keyboardist Danny Frederici, and Clarence Clemons on saxophone. "I've gone through a million crazy bands with crazy people who did crazy things," the New Jersey rocker told *Time* in 1975.

Working as a solo act by early 1972, the Boss signed a contract with manager Mike Appel, who arranged an audition with Columbia Records talent head, John Hammond. "The kid absolutely knocked me out," recalled Hammond, who had discovered Bob Dylan, Aretha Franklin, and Billie Holiday. "I only hear somebody really good once every ten years, and not only was Bruce the best, he was a lot better than Dylan when I first heard him." Within a week Hammond had signed Springsteen to his label.

The newly signed Springsteen initially failed to fulfill the expectations of John Hammond. In January 1973, he and a re-formed version of the Bruce Springsteen Band released his folk-tinged debut, *Greetings from Asbury Park*, which, though touted by Columbia as a masterpiece by the "new Dylan," in the first year sold only 12,000 copies, mostly to fans on the Jersey shore. They toured to promote the album, mismatched as an opening act for the band Chicago. In May 1973, Springsteen made a disastrous appearance at the CBS Records Annual Convention in San Francisco. "It was during a period when he physically looked like Dylan," Hammond told *Time*. "He came on with a chip on his shoulder and played too long. People came to me and said, 'He really can't be that bad, can he, John?' " At the end of the year Springsteen and his group, renamed the E Street Band after a road in Belmar, New Jersey, released *The Wild, the Innocent and the E Street Shuffle*, which sold only 80,000 copies in nearly a year.

Bruce Springsteen and the E Street Band
Courtesy of Columbia Records

The next year Springsteen received some encouragement. In April 1974, at Charlie's, a small bar in Harvard Square, Cambridge, Massachusetts, the guitarist was spotted by *Rolling Stone* journalist Jon Landau, who wrote: "I saw the rock and roll future and its name is Bruce Springsteen." "At the time," Springsteen told *Newsweek*, "Landau's quote helped reaffirm a belief in myself. The band and I were making $50 a week. It helped me go on. I realized I was getting through to somebody." Within a year, he hired Landau to co-produce his third album, *Born to Run*.

Springsteen displayed his many influences in *Born to Run*. Besides the obvious Dylan elements that surfaced in his rapid-fire lyrics and harmonica playing, he borrowed the dramatic stylings of Roy Orbison, the wails of Little Richard, and the operatic sweep of Phil Spector, which he labeled "the sound of universes colliding." The Boss also adopted the pounding piano of Jerry Lee Lewis, the intensity of R & B exemplified by the honking sax of Clarence Clemons, and Chuck Berry's chugging guitar sound and his preoccupation with girls and cars. "I was about 24 and I said, 'I don't want to write about girls and cars anymore,'" recalled Springsteen, who cherished his own 1957 yellow Chevy convertible customized with orange flames. "Then I realized, 'Hey! That's what Chuck Berry wrote about!' So it wasn't my idea. It was a genre thing." In one record Springsteen had incorporated several aspects of the history of rock-and-roll to produce a signature sound.

Executives at Columbia Records decided to launch an unprecedented promotional campaign to market *Born to Run*. They spent $40,000 on radio spots in 12 major geographic regions to promote Springsteen's first two albums, which entered the chart in mid-1975. In mid-August, Columbia Records and Appel organized an exclusive performance by Springsteen at The Bottom Line in New York City, reserving almost 1000 of the 4000 tickets for the press and radio disc jockeys. "It was a very intelligent use of an event," remarked Stan Snadowsky, co-owner of the club. "Columbia got all the right people down there." After releasing *Born to Run* in September 1975, they spent an additional $200,000 to advertise the record in the press and on radio and $50,000 for television spots. "These are very large expenditures for a record company," admitted Bruce Lundvall, then vice-president of Columbia. Columbia brass engineered cover stories in the October 27 issues of both *Time* and *Newsweek*.

The promotional blitz had mixed results. *Born to Run*, though hailed by the critics and reaching the number-three slot, sold less than a million copies in the first year after its release. The title cut from the album peaked at number 23 on the singles chart. *Darkness on the Edge of Town*, Springsteen's next album, released in 1978 after a lengthy legal dispute with manager Mike Appel, stalled at number five on the charts. A single from the album, "Prove It All Night," failed to crack the Top 30.

After his thirtieth birthday in 1979, Springsteen began to change along with other baby boomers. "I'm a different person now," he told a rock critic in late 1980. "When you're in your 30s or late 30s, the world is different. At least, it looks different."

Springsteen's music reflected his changed attitude. Rather than dealing exclusively with cars, girls, and images of street toughs, his music began to deal with the plight of average Americans trapped by circumstances. The transition started with *Darkness on the Edge of Town*; in addition to such Beach Boy-type paeans as "Racing in the Street," the album included such songs as "Factory" which, in the words of the Boss, described "people who are going from nowhere to nowhere." The double album *The River* (1980) continued to combine such car-and-girl-oriented songs as "Cadillac Ranch," "Crush on You," and "You Can Look (But You Better Not Touch)" with the title song, which told of a factory worker who lost both love and his job because of a collapsing economy.

The 1982 stark, acoustic album *Nebraska* completed the transition. It chronicled the alienation of aging baby-boom Americans who had abandoned their sixties idealism. "I think what happened during the seventies was that, first of all, the hustle became legitimized. First through Watergate," Springsteen told *Musician* magazine. "In a funny kind of way, *Born to Run* was a spiritual record in dealing with values. *Nebraska* was about a breakdown of all those values and all those things. It was kind of about a spiritual crisis, in which man is left lost. It's like he has nothing left to tie him to society anymore. He's isolated from the government. Isolated from his job. Isolated from his family."

In 1984, Springsteen fused his vision with the infectious rock-and-roll of the E Street Band to create his masterpiece, *Born in the U.S.A.* He sang in "Downbound Train" about a lumber worker who had lost his job and his wife when hard times hit. In the brooding "My Hometown," the Boss detailed the bleak changes affecting a town located in the depressed heartland of industrial Middle America: "Now main street's whitewashed windows and vacant stores/Seems like there ain't nobody wants to come down there no more/They're closing down the textile mill across the railroad tracks/Foreman says these jobs are going boys and they ain't coming back/to your hometown." Springsteen gave a powerful statement in the title song, wailing about the dead-end fate of a working-class Vietnam veteran ten years after the war. In "Glory Days," he sang about the aimlessness of an ex-high school baseball star and a divorced ex-prom queen.

The album dealt with the loss of innocence experienced by an aging baby-boom generation. "I think *Born in the U.S.A.* kind of casts a suspicious eye on a lot of things. That's the idea. These are not the same people anymore and it's not the same situation," he remarked. "It certainly is not as innocent anymore. But, like I said, it's ten years down the line. . . . I wanted to make the characters grow up," he continued. "You got to. Everybody has to. It was something I wanted to do right after *Born to Run*. I was thinking about it then. I said, 'Well, how old am I?' I'm this old, so I wanna address that in some fashion. Address it as it is, and I didn't see that was done a whole lot [in rock lyrics]."

Despite an unadorned realism, Springsteen sought a renewed commitment to a sixties social consciousness. "We've abandoned a gigantic part of the population—we've just left them for dead. But we're gonna have to pay the piper some day," he insisted. "I mean, I live great, and plenty of people do, but it affects you internally in some fashion, and it just eats away at whatever sort of spirituality you pursue." In an interview with *Rolling Stone*, Springsteen pledged a return "to the social consciousness that was part of the sixties," which during the seventies seemed to become "old fashioned."

The Boss backed his words with action. As early as September 23, 1979, his thirtieth birthday, he performed at Madison Square Garden in New York City at a concert organized by Musicians United for Safe Energy (MUSE), who protested against the proliferation of hazardous nuclear power plants. A year later he played six benefit concerts for Vietnam veterans.

Springsteen intensified his benefit appearances on the *Born in the U.S.A.* tour. He plugged and donated $5000 to Washington Fair Share, which forced the cleanup of an illegal landfill in Washington State. "This is 1984 and people seem to be searching for something," he told the sellout crowd at the Tacoma Dome. In Oakland, California, he urged listeners to donate to the Berkeley Emergency Food Project; in New Jersey he donated $10,000 to a soup kitchen. He sent money to unemployed steelworkers, striking copper miners, and food banks across the country. In January 1985, he contributed lead vocals to a USA for Africa benefit disc, "We Are the World," to help starving, famine-plagued Africans. "One of the things I can do is play benefits and help people out that need help, people that are struggling, you know, trying to get something goin' on their own," he told *Rolling Stone* in December 1984.

Born in the U.S.A., reflecting Springsteen's social awareness, appealed to many baby boomers who had protested the war in Vietnam and during the 1960s had hoped for a better world. Snapped up by Springsteen fanatics, who on the average were 31 years old, the album reached the top of the U.S. and British charts and remained there for two years. The LP yielded five Top 10 singles and by the end of the decade had sold 11 million copies.

The Benefits

Benefit concerts such as Band Aid and Live Aid further demonstrated a reawakened interest to better the world. Started after singer Bob Geldof of the Boomtown Rats saw a report on the Ethiopian famine, Band Aid united a number of English musicians who recorded the song "Do They Know It's Christmas," which was featured at an Ethiopian Benefit Concert at Royal Albert Hall in December 1984 and sold 3 million copies. Live Aid, also conceived by Geldof to aid the starving masses in Africa, involved a simultaneous, televised 16-hour concert on July 13, 1985 at Wembley Stadium in London and at JFK Stadium in Philadelphia. It boasted such sixties rockers as Eric Clapton, Mick Jagger, Neil Young, Pete Townshend, and Paul McCartney. "This concert is the ultimate expression the pop industry can make," stated Bob Geldof. It was watched by more than 1.5 million people and raised over $120 million in cash and goods, most of which helped alleviate the situation of famine victims. "I think Live Aid and Band Aid were the beginning of an awareness," observed Jackson Browne, the seventies singer/songwriter who helped organize the MUSE benefit.

Other rock-and-rollers, most from the sixties, organized benefits. The Grateful Dead, having played countless free concerts during their heyday, organized a benefit to protect the world's rain forests. "It's a problem we must address if we wish to have a planet that's capable of supporting life," said the Dead's Bob Weir. Pete Townshend of The Who donated $10,000 to San Francisco's Hearing Education and Awareness for Rockers (HEAR) Foundation, which championed a cause important to rock stars such as Townshend, who had become partially deaf after years of loud rock-and-roll. Peter Gabriel, formerly of Genesis, which had fashioned a theatrical folk-based English rock, united with Bruce Springsteen to tour in support of Amnesty International, which sought to free political prisoners around the world. "The great challenge of adulthood is holding on to your idealism after you lose your innocence," Springsteen, who donated more than $200,000 to the charity, told one sellout crowd on the tour.

Steve Van Zandt, nicknamed Little Steven, organized rock-and-rollers against racism in South Africa. In late 1985, after leaving the E Street Band for a solo career, he established Artists United Against Apartheid, a cause that lashed out against the brutal discrimination toward blacks in South Africa, particularly the $90 million, white-only Bophuthatswana resort, Sun City, which had hosted Rod Stewart, Linda Ronstadt, and Queen. Little Steven planned an album, book, and video to combat apartheid, enlisting the support of such rock stars as Springsteen, Pete Townshend, Ringo Starr, Bob Dylan, Keith Richards, and Lou Reed. Taking the civil rights movement into the international arena, Little Steven donated nearly a half-million dollars to causes supporting the anti-apartheid struggle.

The Artists United Against Apartheid reinforced the growing interest in African music among rock musicians. Though an essential element of rock since its inception, during the eighties African music became a dominant aspect in the work of some rock musicians. At the turn of the decade David Byrne of the Talking Heads and Brian Eno produced *My Life in the Bush of Ghosts*, an album based upon African rhythms and voodoo tales. The same year the Talking Heads relied upon African elements in the Eno-produced *Remain in Light*. "We were really intrigued and excited by the formal aspects of African music," recalled Byrne. "I saw how African and Afro-American songs were put together in similar ways. I saw there were social parallels to the music and a kind of sensibility and philosophy and even metaphysics that's inherent in the way the music's constructed." Two years later Peter Gabriel established the World of Music Arts and Dance (WOMAD) festival, which brought together artists from around the world.

The interest in African pop and world music peaked when Paul Simon released *Graceland*. Half of the successful folk-rock duo Simon and Garfunkel, and a respected songwriter who had participated in USA for Africa, in late 1984 Simon traveled to South Africa to record with South African musicians. "To go over and play Sun City, it would be exactly like going over to do a concert in Nazi Germany at the height of the holocaust," Simon reasoned. "But what I did was go over and essentially play to the Jews." He hoped the record, featuring the South African choir Ladysmith Black Mambazo, would serve as a "powerful form of politics" that would attract people "to the music, and once they hear what's going on within it, they'd say, 'What? They're doing that to these people.' " The record met Simon's expectations. In 1985, *Graceland* topped the British chart and climbed to the number-three slot in the United States.

The sensitivity to international racism, embodied in the anti-Sun City project and an interest in South African music, helped rejuvenate the careers of some sixties rock stars. After a string of disappointing albums, Bob Dylan performed at the anti-Sun City benefit, Live Aid, the USA for Africa recording session, and a concert celebrating the first Martin Luther King Jr., Day in the United States. In 1986, he released a five-record boxed set of retrospective material, *Biograph*, which reached number 33 on the charts. Two years later Dylan joined with Tom Petty; Jeff Lynne, formerly of the Electric Light Orchestra; Roy Orbison; and George Harrison, who in 1971 had organized the Concert for Bangladesh, one of the first large-scale benefits that aided famine victims. They released the *The Traveling Wilburys*, which hit the top of the charts. By the early nineties Dylan had returned to his acoustic folk roots with *Good As I Been to You* (1992) and *World Gone Wrong* (1993).

Other baby-boom rockers benefited from a return to the idealism of the 1960s. Lou Reed, the former glam rocker and songwriter/guitarist for the Velvet Underground, turned to serious political issues after his participation in Artists United Against Apartheid. "We're in this terrible morass of people absolutely not giving a shit about anybody but themselves," he told *Rolling Stone*. "And a mean-spirited government that is essentially attacking people that can't defend themselves. That's the weakest people—the kids, the sick, the elderly. And I think we should fight back. . . . The days of me being aloof about certain things are over," Reed added. In 1989, he released *New York*, which detailed American racism, poverty, and hopelessness; it outsold all his previous efforts.

Many psychedelic bands received renewed attention. The Grateful Dead, continuing to attract die-hard Deadheads during the seventies, continued to tour during the eighties. In 1987, the band released their first Top 10 album, *In the Dark*, which included their first hit single, "Touch of Grey." At the end of the decade the Jefferson Airplane re-formed and released an album. Even Blue Cheer, the loud, psyche-

Paul Simon, Graceland tour, 1987
Photo © Jack Vartoogian

delic blues outfit, regrouped. "Speaking of '60s artists," *Billboard* informed its readers in a wrap-up of the decade, "one of the more notable trends of the late '80s was the commercial success of many bands that made their commercial debut more than 20 years ago." "And, as the fairy tales say, it seemed that it might be time again for legends," added *Time* in late 1989. "Twenty years later there was suddenly on every side the familiar sound of the '60s."

Radio helped promote the sixties rockers. Largely ignoring the TV generation, which preferred images on MTV, it programmed oldies for the baby boomers, who still purchased the greatest number of records and served as the prime target of most advertisers. In 1988, of the roughly 10,000 stations in the country, more than 500 radio stations broadcast oldies exclusively. The next year, contended Ken Barnes, editor of the trade magazine *Radio and Records*, at least 40 percent of all radio programming fell into the "classic rock" or "oldies" categories.

In early 1990, oldies station WCBS-FM grabbed the number-one spot in the New York market. Radio, observed CBS Records president Al Teller, seemed to be "chasing the yuppie generation to its grave."

The Compact Disc

The compact disc helped revive an interest in classic rock and rescued a troubled music industry. Introduced to the mass market in late 1982, it provided record buyers with a high-quality, digital, durable, long-lasting format. The compact disc, commonly called the CD, contained millions of digitally encoded pits, which held musical information that could be converted into almost noise-free sound through a low-powered laser beam. Less than five inches in diameter, the polycarbonate plastic disc warped only at temperatures over 220 degrees Fahrenheit, could not be scratched like a vinyl record, and produced up to 75 minutes of music with a dynamic range of 90 decibels.

The silver platter quickly became more popular than its vinyl counterpart. During its first two years on the market, the CD appealed primarily to jazz and classical music fans, who appreciated the expanded dynamic range. As the price of compact disc players plummeted from about $900 in 1983 to less than $150 in 1987, and as the cost of a compact disc declined from $18 to $14 during the same period, the convenient CD began to sell to the rock record buyer. In 1985, 16.4 million CDs were purchased worldwide. Three years later more than 390 million compact discs were sold internationally, to account for sales of more than $6 billion, compared to 295 million vinyl LPs sold for $2.8 billion. Cassette tapes, becoming the most popular format for music during the late 1970s and registering even greater sales after the introduction of the portable Walkman cassette player in 1981, outperformed both with sales of more than $6.7 billion for 787 million units sold. In late 1990, the CD even began to outsell the cassette in such retail outlets as Tower Records.

At the end of the decade, many industry executives predicted the demise of the vinyl LP. "I assume the death knell has been sounded, and there's not much we can do about it," mused Joe Smith, president of Capitol Music-EMI. "It's gasping for breath," agreed Russ Solomon, founder and president of the Tower Records chain. "We'd like to hold on, but unfortunately the world is not going that way." "Our little flat friend the record is what drove the business for a long time, but we're going to be out of the business," mentioned Bob Sherwood, senior vice-president of Columbia Records.

Industry predictions began to become reality. In 1989, the Camelot Music chain of 229 stores dropped vinyl albums from its inventory; other retailers such as the 85-store Disc Jockey chain, the 119-store Hastings Books and Records, and the 60-store Music Plus severely limited vinyl selections. The Hauppauge Record Manufacturing plant, pressing more than 100,000 vinyl records a day during the early eighties, discontinued operations. By 1992, vinyl records, which only ten years earlier had accounted for more than 42 percent of music sales, had shrunk to 1.4 percent of the market. "They're just not a factor anymore," explained Stan Goman, senior vice-president of retail operations for Tower Records. "You just don't think about LPs. They're just not there."

The predominance of compact discs over vinyl encouraged many baby boomers to replace their old, scratched LPs with CDs. "Talk about trends," observed *Billboard* in early 1990, "If the CD did anything in the '80s, it convinced consumers that they needed to buy their favorite albums all over again. Little wonder, therefore, that artists such as the Beatles were charting all over again in the '80s with records they'd recorded 25 years earlier." *Time* magazine called the compact disc the technology "most likely to bring Elvis back to life. With revolutionary speed, music lovers are replacing their favorite old scratched-up 45s and 33s with shiny compact discs." By 1992, purchases of previously released rock-and-roll accounted for more than 40 percent of record sales.

A slumping U.S. recording industry was revitalized by the geometric growth in sales of compact discs, created in part by baby boomers who rebought the music of their youth. After hitting a high point with sales of $4.13 billion in 1978, the U.S. record industry experienced a sharp decline. In 1979, it sold only $3.67 billion in records and tapes despite a high rate of inflation, a downturn that resulted in the loss of 2500 music industry jobs. Over the next four years the industry stabilized and by 1983 reported only $3.81 billion in total sales despite price hikes, MTV, and the phenomenal success of Michael Jackson.

The U.S. record industry experienced a boom after the introduction of the CD, which cost about 90 cents to manufacture, excluding packaging. In 1986, it exceeded its previous record, shipping $4.65 billion of CDs, records, and tapes. "The rise in profitability," wrote one reporter at the time, "is attributed primarily to the soaring sales of compact discs which carry a retail price of $12 to $20 as opposed to the $8.98 or $9.98 for records and cassettes." A year later the industry sold $5.57 billion and in 1988 $6.25 billion in records, tapes, and discs. In 1989, the industry registered $6.46 billion, with sales of more than 800 million units, bolstered by a 38 percent increase in CD sales compared to the previous year. The next year sales peaked at $7.5 billion. According to one report, the recording industry registered the highest rate of pretax operating income growth in the communications industry, expanding 26 percent from 1983 to 1987.

The record industry grew at the same pace internationally, dominated by six corporations—Time-Warner (WEA), Sony/CBS, Bertelsmann Music Group (BMG), MCA-Matsushita, N.V. Philips of Holland, and Thorn-EMI(CEMA)—which by 1990 sold more than 93 percent of the records in the United States. After a drastic downturn from 1979 to 1987, by 1988 the industry sold more than $14 billion and a year later nearly $17 billion in records, tapes, and CDs. Japan, dominated by the CBS/Sony giant, increased sales to $2.4 billion in 1987, a 10 percent gain from the previous year. In West Germany—dominated by BMG, which had purchased RCA during the decade—sales skyrocketed to $1.56 billion in 1987 and exceeded $1.82 billion by 1989. "The German music market is in a healthy state of growth and with East Germany opening up, it will develop even more," predicted Manfred Zumkeller, president of the Federation of German Phonographic Industry in early 1990. In 1989, the United Kingdom, the fourth-largest market in the world, had sales of $1.5 billion.

The increased sales translated into profits. In 1988, Warner Communications, the largest company in the field, posted sales of $2.04 billion and profits of nearly $319 million. The next year, after merging with Time Inc., Warner generated music revenues of $2.54 billion and profits of nearly $500 million. In 1987, CBS earned $202 million in profits on $1.75 billion in total sales. The next year EMI, the British conglomerate, sold $1.2 billion in products for a profit of $70.3 million. BMG showed remarkable growth, building sales from $663 million in 1986–87 to $1.1 billion in 1989–90 and increasing profits from $56 million in 1987–88 to $85.4 million in 1989–90. "The ultimate shot in the arm the record industry was craving, the CD allowed companies to rake in the bucks on a product that, in some cases, was one step away from actually being deleted," observed *Billboard* in late 1989.

Children of the Sixties

A renewed interest in the sixties spirit, fostered by the CD, shaped a number of new bands, notably U2. Formed in Dublin by schoolmates Bono (Paul Hewson), The Edge (David Evans), Adam Clayton, and Larry Mullen, Jr., the band won a talent contest sponsored by Guinness beer in March 1978. After two years of local gigs, it released a debut single, "11 O'Clock Tick Tock," which failed to chart. The group recorded two albums, *Boy* (1980) and *October* (1981), which attracted critical attention but sold few copies.

U2 began to infuse its music with a political message. In October 1982, during a concert in Belfast, Northern Ireland, Bono introduced the song "Sunday Bloody Sunday," which detailed the historic political troubles in Ireland. A few months later the band released *War*, combining rock with the various strands of punk. "Punk had died," recalled The Edge. "We couldn't believe it had happened, and *War* was designed as a knuckle buster in the face of the new pop. . . . We loved the Clash's attitude early on and Richard Hell and the Voidoids, the Pistols," continued the guitarist. "We wanted love and anger. We wanted a protest record, but a positive protest record." "It was an unsettled time, a year of conflict," added bassist Adam Clayton. "We focused on that." As a show of support for a sixties-type protest, in July 1984 Bono sang a duet with Bob Dylan on "Blowing in the Wind" at a Dylan concert in Ireland.

The band continued to demonstrate its commitment to the sixties

U2
Photo by David McIntyre, courtesy of D.M.B.B. Entertainment

spirit. Though beginning to replace hard-driving guitars with more ethe-real, echo-laden sounds engineered by producer Brian Eno, U2 dedi-cated its 1984 hit "Pride (In the Name of Love)," to Martin Luther King, Jr. It contributed to Band Aid, played in the Live Aid spectacular in Wembley Stadium, appeared on the anti-Sun City project, and per-formed on Amnesty International's twenty-fifth anniversary tour. In 1986, the band raised funds for the unemployed, performed with Lou Reed in San Francisco for another Amnesty International benefit, and symbolically was joined onstage in Philadelphia by Bruce Springsteen. By 1987, when it hit the top of the charts with *Joshua Tree*, U2 had be-come a prime example of the renewed interest in a sixties-style protest. As Bono remarked in 1987, "in the '80s, which is a barren era, we look back at the '60s as a great reservoir of talent, of high ideals, and of the will and desire to change things." Like his counterparts in the sixties, the singer was interested in "a revolution of love. I believe that if you want to start a revolution you better start a revolution in your own home and your own way of relating to the men and women around you."

Midnight Oil, an Australian band formed in 1976 when Jim Moginie, Rob Hirst, and Martin Rotsey of the hippie band Farm teamed with law student and singer Peter Garrett, applied sixties ideals to its own country. "I grew up loving people like John Fogerty," remembered drummer Hirst, "people who commented on what America was going through during the Vietnam War. It was rather natural that this band would choose to comment on the country that it knows better than anywhere else." In their first two LPs, the band decried the nuclear arms race and the dominant presence of U.S. military forces in Australia. In *Diesel and Dust* (1986), which sold 3 million copies, they protested white Australian oppression of the indigenous aborigines, touring the back country to demonstrate their support of aboriginal attempts to regain traditional lands. With *Blue Sky Mining* (1990), Midnight Oil told the tale of Wittenoon miners who contracted asbestos-induced cancer on the job during the 1950s and 1960s and who first secured redress from mine operators in 1988. "What Midnight Oil does have is an underlying belief in the human spirit," remarked Peter Garrett, who in 1984 ran for the upper house of the Australian Parliament on the Nuclear Disarmament Party ticket and served as the president of the Australian Conservation Foundation.

The sixties spirit also inspired a late-eighties folk boom led by Tracy Chapman. Born to a poor family in Cleveland, Chapman had always been interested in social issues. "As a child," she told *Rolling Stone*, "I always had a sense of social conditions and political situations. I think it had to do with the fact that my mother was always discussing things with my sister and me—also because I read a lot." While at Tufts University in Medford, Massachusetts, she began performing on the Boston folk club circuit.

One day in 1986, while playing at a Boston coffeehouse called the Cappuccino, Chapman met fellow Tufts student Brian Koppelman, who introduced the protest singer to his father Charles, the head of the largest independent music publishing firm in the world. Within a few months, with the help of the elder Koppelman, she landed a contract at Elektra Records and secured as manager Elliot Roberts, the manager of Bob Dylan. "You don't have to be a genius to see that words are coming back in a large way, that there's more social consciousness in people, and the apathy that there was for years seems to be slowly declining," observed Roberts in late 1988. "These are going to be exciting times, and I see Tracy as someone who will be at the forefront of these times." In 1988, Chapman released her first, self-named album, which hit the top of the chart; the next year she followed with the Top 10 *Crossroads*.

Other female folk singers began to achieve popularity. Discovered in 1986 at the Kerrville Folk Festival in Texas, Michelle Shocked hit the charts in 1988 with *Short Sharp Shocked*. A veteran of the Greenwich Village folk scene, in 1987 Suzanne Vega combined the New York influences of Bob Dylan and Lou Reed to produce the hit "Luka," a song decrying child abuse. By the end of the decade, other folksters such as the Indigo Girls, who lobbied for Amnesty International and the Coalition for the Homeless, began to attract attention.

R.E.M. delivered a socially conscious message through folk-rock. Formed in 1980 by vocalist Michael Stipe, guitarist Peter Buck, Mike Mills on bass, and drummer Bill Berry, the group perfected a Byrdsian guitar-driven sound. After four albums which garnered a cult following, in 1987 the band hit the Top 10 with *R.E.M. No. 5: Document* and followed with *Green* (1988), which urged listeners to protect the environment. R.E.M. lobbied for Greenpeace, voter registration, liberal political candidates, and the protection of the environment. "Well, just because these things [social ills] don't touch us personally doesn't mean we aren't affected by them," Peter Buck contended. "You've got to believe that what's happening to the lower man is an indignity to all men."

Country Boomers

As the nineties approached, baby boomers flocked to a country rock that squarely confronted social issues. During the first four years of the decade, more than 21 million Americans, mostly baby boomers, became country music fans. By 1994, many of the nearly half of all Americans who listened to country fit the baby-boom profile: 42 percent owned a house, 40 percent had a college education, and 36 percent lived in households with incomes of more than $60,000 a year. "By their sheer demographic weight, the nation's 76 million baby boomers continue to determine America's musical preferences," observed *Time* in 1992. "And what America currently prefers is country."

These country boomers caused an upsurge in all formats of country music. In 1984, only 19 country releases sold more than 500,000 copies. Eight years later, 53 country discs went gold, and more than 30 sold more than 1 million copies. In 1992, sales of country discs and tapes reached $660 million, a more than 50 percent increase from the previous year. In 1980, about 1500 radio stations played country music. Twelve years later more than 2500 stations catered to country listeners. On television, The Nashville Network (TNN) grew from 7 million viewers at its inception in 1983 to 54.5 million subscribers in 1992. From 1990 to 1992, *Country America* doubled its subscriptions to almost 1 million.

The nineties country boom centered around Garth Brooks, who owed a musical debt to rock and reflected the social concerns of the baby boomers. Unlike most country performers of previous decades, Brooks started his career after graduating from college in 1984. Although he was the son of a former country singer—Colleen Carroll Brooks, who had performed with Red Foley on "Ozark Jubilee"—and was attracted to the music of George Jones and George Strait, Garth drew his inspiration from rock. After attending a Queen concert, Brooks became convinced that he wanted to perform. "My ears are still ringin' from that concert," he enthused. "I was thinking, one day I'm going to feel this feeling— only it's gonna be me up there on that stage." He hoped to duplicate "the seventies-arena-rock thing."

Folk-rock also shaped Brooks. He listened to "a sixties wave of singers: Peter, Paul and Mary, Tom Rush, Townes Van Zandt, Arlo Guthrie, Janis Joplin, Janis Ian, Rita Coolidge, that kind of music. It was very warm, but you had to step inside it to see what was going on. From

312

Garth Brooks at Farm Aid, 1990
Photo © Ebet Roberts

that moment on, that's the kind of music I was attracted to. Off that, I went to James Taylor, Dan Fogelberg, the more writer-type artists."

Brooks combined folk-rock and seventies theatrics for superstardom. In 1989, he released a self-titled debut, which sold well. In 1990, Brooks topped the chart with *No Fences*, which sold more than 10 million copies in three years. He followed with the blockbuster *Ropin' the Wind*, which outdid his previous effort. During the summer of 1992, he hit the Top 5 with a Christmas album and topped the chart with *The Chase* (1992) and *In Pieces* (1993). By early 1993, Brooks had sold more than 30 million discs and tapes to create a country craze.

In his music, Garth Brooks addressed current social concerns. He supported gay rights and chose such antiwar songs as "Last Night I Had the Strangest Dream" for his concerts. In "Thunder Rolls" he sang about the effects of domestic violence. His "Face to Face" dealt with date rape. Garth Brooks, fashioning a rock-based country that explored socially relevant issues, had created music for nineties baby boomers.

Brooks led the way for other country rockers. Clint Black, who used James Taylor's "Steamroller Blues" in concert, climbed the chart. Also citing James Taylor as a major influence, Mary Chapin-Carpenter hit with *Shooting Straight in the Dark* (1990). Travis Tritt, who called his songs "country music with a rock 'n' roll attitude," blended the Eagles and the Allman Brothers into nineties success. Naming Linda Ronstadt as a role model, Trisha Yearwood and Patty Loveless scaled the nineties charts. "A lot of people turned to country because it's more like seventies rock and roll," observed Neil Young, who had played folk-rock with Buffalo Springfield and Crosby, Stills and Nash. "Pop and rock have just changed their name to country." From the mid-eighties to the mid-nineties, the baby-boom generation listened to socially responsible music that resembled the sounds of their youth. As they attended benefit concerts and bought country rock, the baby boomers confronted the harsh, rebellious, desperate music of a new generation.

16

The Generation X Blues

We had to grow up with this idealization that was never going to fucking come true.

Courtney Love of Hole

In the nineties, a post-baby-boom generation set the direction of rock-and-roll. They defined nineties rock with an angry metal/punk and rap, which reflected their fears, frustration, desperation, and hopes.

The post-baby-boom generation in the United States faced a grim economic situation. In 1992, the average American worker earned $391 a week; after adjustment for inflation, this was $18 less than the average worker brought home every week in 1979. As wages declined, unemployment rose. Official unemployment rates increased from between 4 and 5 percent during the baby-boom era to 7 percent during the eighties. In 1992, the official unemployment rate stood at 7.4 percent, a number that skyrocketed to nearly 13 percent after adding underemployed and discouraged workers to the equation. The remaining jobs shifted from manufacturing to the less-well-paying service sector. During the eighties, the retail and service industries created more than three quarters of all new jobs, many of which paid minimum wage. "The economy is failing nearly every American," contended Lawrence Mishel, chief economist at the Economic Policy Institute, in late 1992.

Post-baby boomers, nearly 50 percent of the population by the early nineties, especially felt the economic troubles. In 1992, 20 percent of teens not in school could not find jobs. More than 11 percent of young men and women between the ages of 20 and 24 were officially unemployed, compared to a 6.7 percent unemployment rate among the baby-boom generation.

The new generation, called Generation X by the press, found little stability in their families. Although fewer people divorced by the mid-eighties, the baby boomers had separated from their partners in record numbers during the seventies, leaving many post-baby boomers in single-family households. In 1970, single-parent households accounted for only 11 percent of homes that housed children. By 1992, households headed by one parent comprised more than 26 percent of homes with children under 18.

The turbulent American family caused frustration, pain, and fear among Generation X. "I know my parents don't mix, like water and oil," confided one nineties teenager. "I used to dream about them getting together, but as I get older I knew it really wouldn't work out. I wonder if I'll end up like my parents did." "I spent my life believing that I had this perfect family and making my friends believe we had this perfect family," confessed Nina Gordon of the band Veruca Salt. "A huge and miserable divorce . . . rewrote my entire life." "The bottom line is that most of us come from broken homes," explained Jesse Malin of the group, D Generation. "We have this self-destructive thing. We'd get a kick out of breaking up the band. And we do it with a lot of relationships with girlfriends and everybody, because that was our first impression from when we were 7 years old: seeing people split."

Aside from confronting the divorce of their parents, many youths also suffered abuse, often within the family. In 1991, reported the National Committee for the Prevention of Child Abuse, 2.7 million children, or 4 percent of all youths under 18 in America, were abused. The number represented a 40 percent increase in only six years.

"I do think that having no family structure, having no sense that there's shelter from the storm, drives people insane," commented Elizabeth Wurtzel, the young author of *Prozac Nation: Young and Depressed in America*, in 1995. "The level of uncertainty we function under in a personal realm is daunting. And obviously, economically, things are very uncertain. So altogether, this is not a pretty way to live."

Confronted with few economic prospects and a painful, sometimes brutal home life, many youths became violent. Most post-baby boomers had witnessed violent actions daily on television. According to the American Psychological Association, in the eighties the average child had watched 8000 murders and 100,000 other acts of violence by the sixth grade. In the eighties and nineties, many youths followed the celluloid images by carrying guns. "For youth today, I don't care where you live, what class you are, or whether you're white, black or Hispanic, it's cool to carry a gun," complained Colonel Leonard Supenski of the Baltimore County police department. "Owing to a lot of things, primarily the entertainment industry, it's a macho thing to do." In 1990, more than 4 percent of all high school students surveyed by the Centers for Disease Control had carried a gun, especially the semiautomatic 9-millimeter pistol, at least once in the previous month.

Many of the youths used the guns they carried. In the Seattle city school system, 6 percent of high school juniors confessed to carrying a gun into school, and one third of the gun-toting students fired the weapons at another person. Many of the youths evidently hit their human targets. In the United States during 1987, almost 1500 youths aged ten to 19 died from gunshot wounds, usually inflicted by another youth. Two years later, nearly 2200 youths died as a result of gun violence.

Many gun-carrying youths banded together in urban gangs across the country. By 1985, nearly 45,000 Los Angeles youths had formed together in more than 450 gangs, an increase of 25 percent in gangland activity in just five years. By 1992 in Los Angeles, 150,000 disgruntled youths joined more than 1000 gangs. Though highly visible due to press coverage, the Los Angeles gangs reflected a national trend. Seeking security in an insecure world, eighties youths started gangs in such diverse locales as Davenport, Iowa; Chicago; New Haven; Jackson, Mississippi; and Portsmouth, Vermont. By 1994, gangs existed in 187 U.S. cities. "The kids are all on the edge," warned Chicago social worker Sharon Brown. "Brush against them, and they're ready to fight."

The desperate generation, which followed the baby boomers, was drawn to a loud, aggressive, angry music. "A lot of people our age and younger have been brought up with these notions of Reagan-era fueled affluence," noticed Jonathan Poneman, co-owner of Sub Pop Records, in 1992. "Then when you suddenly see a lot of those dreams subside because of this particularly brutal recession, and class warfare, race warfare, it makes you very angry, very fearful, very alienated. And those are qualities that lead to an unusually rebellious, passionate rock."

The Hardcore Generation

Rock-and-roll music, especially hardcore, thrash, grunge, and rap, reflected the frustration and fear of the post-baby-boom generation. The desperate, angry version of punk known as hardcore began during the late 1970s in Los Angeles, the smog-filled fairyland gone sour. Bands such as X fused the hyperactive roar of punk with lyrics describing a society that had degenerated beyond repair. In late 1977, X began performing a punk characterized by the thunderous drumming of Don Bonebrake, the rockabilly-tinged guitar of Billy Zoom (a.k.a. Tyson Kindale), and the lyrics of John Doe (a.k.a. John Nommensen) and poet Exene Cervenka. "I saw the Ramones. That made me decide to play the kind of music we play now in X," Billy Zoom explained at the time.

On their 1979 debut, *Los Angeles*, released by Slash Records, which had evolved from the punk-rock fanzine of the same name, X applied the energy of the Ramones to such tales of despondency as

"Nausea" and "Sex and Dying in High Society." "In 1979 or '80, people realized everything was fucked up, and they couldn't do anything about it, and they didn't want to," recalled John Doe.

X set the desperate tone for other punk bands from the suburbs of Los Angeles. The Germs, first performing at The Whisky in Los Angeles in 1977, featured the staccato fuzz guitar of Pat Smear and the barking vocals of Darby Crash (a.k.a. Paul Beahm). In concert and on their first LP, *(GI)*, they sang such dark songs as "Suicide Madness." In December 1980, Darby Crash symbolically committed suicide as a tribute to his hero, Sid Vicious.

Black Flag, the prototypical hardcore group, emphasized the same themes of hopelessness. Unlike the lower-class British punks, the band consisted of suburbanites from middle-class, sometimes dysfunctional, families. Henry Rollins, who joined Black Flag in 1981 and wrote many of the group's songs, contended that "I've always been privileged, I've got it all going for me." But as with many of the band's fans, Rollins confessed he was "a classic product of a typical dysfunctional family. I don't know jack shit about love, or about feeling a relationship with a blood relative. That shit means nothing to me."

Vocalist Henry Rollins shouted songs about personal dysfunction over a thrashing, fuzzy, chaotic, guitar-based sound. In 1978, Black Flag recorded *Nervous Breakdown*; three years later they released the album *Damaged*, which included the hardcore anthems "Rise Above" and "Revenge." It followed with a flurry of albums that contained such despair-ridden songs as "Depression," "Dead Inside," and "Life of Pain." "Pain is my girlfriend; that's how I see it," explained Rollins. "I feel pain every day of my life. When you see me perform, it's that pain you're seeing coming out. I put all my emotions, all my feelings, and my body on the line. People hurt me, I hurt myself—mentally, physically." In contrast to the politicized British punk, explained Rollins in 1983, "there are no songs telling you to do anything. There are no political songs, there are no songs that speak out on some topic."

The Los Angeles media began to promote such pain-filled music. Rodney Bingenheimer, calling himself Rodney on the ROQ, played hardcore on his regular show on radio station KROQ. In 1981, filmmaker Penelope Spheeris released *The Decline of Western Civilization*, which documented the lifestyle and live performances of Los Angeles punk. Punk fanzines such as *Slash* and *Flipside* also promoted the new scene.

Local independent record companies were established to record and distribute hardcore. Lisa Fancher, a former employee at the Los Angeles-based Bomp Records, started Frontier Records in 1981. She initially recorded the Circle Jerks, a group of young, middle-class teens from the suburbs. "As it happened," Fancher recalled, "no one wanted to put out the Circle Jerks' LP *Group Sex*. It was total providence. I said, 'I'll do it.' . . . It's a classic, classic punk record, and it's what made everything else fall into place for me," she continued. "After them I did the Adolescents' [first album] and TSOL [True Sounds of Liberty]. I was on a roll." In 1983, Fancher recorded the Suicidal Tendencies single

"Institutionalized!," and their first album which, according to the label owner, sold "absolute shitloads: five hundred thousand copies to date [1993]."

Other labels specialized in hardcore. Posh Boy recorded Red Cross, the initial TSOL release, and punk compilations selected by Rodney Bingenheimer. Brett Gurewitz, bassist for the California hardcore outfit, Bad Religion, started Epitaph to record his own band and, within a decade, hit the Top Ten with the Offspring which sold 3 million copies of *Smash* that became the best-selling record released by an independent company. Two members of Black Flag, guitarist Gregg Ginn and drummer Chuck Dukowski, started their own label, SST, to record themselves. Almost immediately they began to press the music of other local hardcore punk bands such as San Pedro's Minutemen, who debuted with *Paranoid Time* (1980).

Ginn and Dukowski also documented the burgeoning national hardcore scene, which spread from Los Angeles to other urban areas across the nation. They recorded Husker Dü from Minneapolis. When guitarist Bob Mould heard the first Ramones' record, he said, "I gotta get back into music. This is something." In 1981, he joined with drummer Grant Hart and bassist Greg Norton in Husker Dü, which played loud, fast songs of alienation, reflected in the title of their 1982 studio debut, *Everything Falls Apart*. Like Black Flag, Husker Dü delivered songs of personal angst. "I don't write about politics because I'm not an expert," commented Bob Mould in 1985. "We're sort of like reporters in a way. Reporters of our own mental state."

In Minneapolis, Husker Dü shared the hardcore spotlight with the Replacements. This band was inspired by the punk that blasted forth from Southern California. "We were spawned by power-pop and hardcore, which were both offshoots of punk, so we were a product of that environment," pointed out singer Paul Westerberg. In May 1980, Westerberg dropped off a demo tape at Oar Folkjukeopus Record Store for manager Peter Jesperson, who since 1978 also had co-owned Twin/Tone Records. "I know it sounds like a fairy tale," remembered Jesperson, "but I knew how special it was the minute I heard it." The band signed to the label, which late the next year released *Sorry Ma, I Forgot to Take Out the Trash*, which included the hyperactive "Shut Up," "Kick Your Door Down," and "I Hate Music." Though most of the band members such as bassist Tommy Stinson later decried their early days as a "suck-ass hardcore band" after turning to a more mainstream rock, the early Replacements delivered a memorable, frantic version of eighties hardcore.

Other cities experienced the growth of a hardcore contingent. In Washington, D.C., Minor Threat carried the hardcore banner. In 1978, recalled singer Ian MacKaye, "I heard the Clash and the Sex Pistols." Hooked on punk, he formed the Teen Idles and, with friend Henry Rollins, later of Black Flag, "thought California was were it was at. We had heard Black Flag's single, it was our favorite, and *Slash* and *Flipside* were like our Bible." In fall 1980, MacKaye and Teen Idles drummer Jeff

Black Flag
Courtesy of Cam Garrett/S.C.V.D. Studio

Nelson started their own label, Dischord, to release their first single. They also decided to record the expanding Washington, D.C., hardcore community, first recording Rollins's band, SOA [State of Alert], and following with the first single of their renamed band, Minor Threat. Dischord continued to record local hardcore outfits such as Youth Brigade and Government Issue. "We thought, 'This is so cool, we'll do a little label, and everyone will get their own seven-inch.' "

The premier hardcore band in San Francisco, the Dead Kennedys, ensured artistic control with a label of their own, Alternative Tentacles. The band distinguished itself from other hardcore bands by its leftist politics. Leader Jello Biafra (a.k.a. Eric Boucher), who had attended the University of California at Santa Cruz and by 1980 was in his twenties, had become enamored with a politicized British punk. As he told it, "punk was an outbreak of new talent that happened all over the world and opened the door to a whole new generation of people who had ideas to replace the bankrupt swill that was being regurgitated [by people] who blew a lot of their talent and shot their wads in the sixties, but who maintained a strangehold on the airwaves in the seventies."

The Dead Kennedys, formed in 1978, embraced the message of British punk, merging a buzz-saw guitar sound with lyrics that lambasted U.S. imperialism, the moral majority, and the creeping fascism among hardcore youths who began to wear Nazi armbands. In 1979, on their own Alterative Tentacles label, they released their first single, "California Uber Alles," which criticized California Governor Jerry Brown and "zen fascists." On their first LP, *Fresh Fruit for Rotting Vegetables* (1980), the Dead Kennedys blasted U.S. involvement in Southeast Asia in "Holiday in Cambodia" and tackled the issue of poverty in "Let's Lynch the Landlord" and "Kill the Poor." The band continued to deliver such social commentaries as "Terminal Preppie," "Trust Your Mechanic," "Winnebago Warrior," and "Nazi Punks Fuck Off" until they disbanded in 1986 amid a controversy over censorship of the album cover to the LP *Frankenchrist*. "I think what we are witnessing in this country is the slow but inevitable fall of an empire that got too comfortable," asserted Biafra.

Jello Biafra became disillusioned with the embittered generation of hardcore fans who exhibited a violent aggression. "Some of us had talked for years about how great it would be for us to get our music to younger kids and how once they saw the energy they'd automatically like it," he explained. "But what we didn't realize is that they might not like it on our terms. So when younger people did start coming to shows in droves, they brought the arena rock mentality with them, including fights, jumping off the stage just to see if you could hit people." At hardcore concerts, members of the audience slammed into each other and at times leapt from the stage onto the mass of slam dancers. They called the ritual *moshing* and referred to the dance floor in front of the stage as the *mosh pit*. "It's a good outlet for aggression," reasoned one Seattle slam dancer. "I save it all week long, come in here and bang people up. It feels good." Sometimes shaving their heads in military style, the desperate middle-class fans of hardcore who cared little for left-wing rhetoric acted out the pain in their lives on the dance floor.

Thrash Metal

The aggressive, dissatisfied youth of the eighties also began to listen to thrash metal, which originated with the New Wave of British Heavy Metal. The New Wave of British Heavy Metal (NWBHM) stemmed from the conditions that helped foster English punk. Poor British youths with no apparent future formed bands to express their frustration by means of a violent, explosive sound. In 1976, four working-class youths from Stourbridge in the West Midlands near Birmingham, an area that had produced original heavy metal bands such as Black Sabbath and Led Zeppelin's Robert Plant and John Bonham, banded together as Diamond Head. "We started on June 26th, 1976. It was the last year of our school, about to leave to get jobs or go on the dole, whatever," recalled lead guitarist Brian Tatler. Around the same time, when British punk began to take shape, many British youths in similar circumstances formed other heavy metal bands with names that indicated a dark militancy: Saxon, Venom, the Tygers of Pan Tang, Angelwitch, and Iron Maiden.

These bands owed a musical debt to the heavy metal of the early seventies. Iron Maiden favored the Led Zeppelin sound. Venom and Angelwitch leaned more toward Black Sabbath. Diamond Head, remembered Tatler, first learned Black Sabbath's "*Paranoid* 'cause we thought it'd go down well."

Though modeling themselves on a blues-based style, the new wave of heavy metal delivered a harsh-sounding, fist-pumping music that shared the spirit of their British punk counterparts. "What people were looking for in punk is what they are looking for in heavy rock," observed Saxon vocalist Biff Byford. "We were the ones breaking down the barriers between band and audience, and we were doing it with complete honesty and no b.s."

The new wave of metal coalesced with the help of disc jockey Neil Kay and the media. Kay constantly promoted the albums of such struggling bands as Iron Maiden at his heavy metal club, London's Soundhouse. In May 1979, he helped stage a concert that featured many of the new metal acts and prompted Alan Lewis and Geoff Barton, editors of the British music magazine *Sounds*, to coin the phrase New Wave of British Heavy Metal. In August 1980, the British television show "20th Century Box" aired a special on the new music.

Heavy metal magazines such as *Kerrang* also helped to create an underground of metal fans who spread the word to one another. "The number one source [of support] is fanzines," contended Bret Hartman, the manager of A & R at MCA. "Getting demos with good songs is the bottom line, but the sources to expose the band are word of mouth, fanzines, and magazines, especially for metal." Metal fans, remarked Roadrunner Records executive Michael Schnapp about the grassroots spread of metal, "print fanzines, they talk to each other all the time on the phone, they are pen pals; you have that family type of atmosphere."

By the turn of the decade, the new metal bands began to offer records to the swelling ranks of the metal underground. In 1980, Diamond Head, mirroring the do-it-yourself punk attitude, released their first album on their own Happy Face label. The same year, the Tygers of Pan Tang cut *Wildcat* for MCA Records. Saxon debuted in 1979 and during the next three years provided fans with four more albums. In 1981, Angelwitch cut its debut, and Venom released *Welcome to Hell*.

AC/DC, the blues-powered Australian band that formed in 1974 and struggled for acceptance during most of the seventies, benefited from the exposure given to the New Wave of British Heavy Metal. In 1977, they first charted in Britain with *Let There Be Rock*. Two years later, amid the furor over the NWBHM, the band hit the British Top 10 with *Highway to Hell*; the next year they topped the British charts and reached the Top 5 in the United States with *Back in Black*. In 1981, they topped the U.S. chart with *For Those About to Rock (We Salute You)*.

During the early eighties, Iron Maiden, another commercially successful NWBHM band, gained a following. In November 1979, the band distributed by mail order their first effort, *The Soundhouse Tapes*. Early the next year they unveiled their self-named, major-label debut, which hit the Top 4 on the British chart. During the early eighties, Iron Maiden continued to chart with *Killers* (1981); *The Number of the Beast* (1982), which topped the British album chart; and the million-selling *Piece of Mind* (1983). By the end of 1983, readers of the new British heavy metal magazine *Kerrang* voted *Piece of Mind* and *The Number of the Beast* as the best two heavy-metal albums of all time.

Motorhead stood at the vanguard of the new metal explosion.

Banding together in 1975, Motorhead consisted of guitarist "Fast" Eddie Clarke, drummer Philthy Animal (a.k.a. Phil Taylor), and bassist and vocalist Lemmy Kilmister, a former member of Hawkwind and an ex-roadie for Jimi Hendrix. The trio, boasting that "we're the kind of band that if we moved next to you, your lawn would die," played a fast, aggressive, loud brand of metal. In 1979, they launched their vinyl career with *Overkill* and *Bomber*, the titles of which suggested the destructive intent of the music. The next year the band hit the British Top 5 with *Ace of Spades*. In 1981, as the NWBHM swept across the United Kingdom, Motorhead reached the top of the chart with the live album *No Sleep Till Hammersmith*.

Metallica combined the various elements of the New Wave of Heavy Metal to create a new genre called *thrash* or *speed metal*, which swept across the United States during the mid-eighties. The band initially grew from a passion for metal, which drove Danish-born Lars Ulrich. In 1980, Ulrich, the son of a professional tennis player, moved to Los Angeles with his parents. "I got very pissed off being in L.A.," related Ulrich, "so the summer of '81 I just upped and went back to Europe, kind of a hang-out trip. So I'd go hang out with Diamond Head for a while, and then try and find Iron Maiden, or try and find Motorhead, and sit outside of Motorhead's rehearsal room and wait." After returning to the United States, continued the drummer, "I wanted to get a band together in America that had some of those qualities I [had witnessed in Europe]." Ulrich placed an ad in a Los Angeles newspaper and found guitarist and vocalist James Hetfield, who "listened to a lot of Black Sabbath in the early days." The duo added lead guitarist Dave Mustaine and bassist Ron McGovney, Hetfield's roommate, to form Metallica.

The band first mimicked the New Wave of British Heavy Metal. "When we started doing clubs," recalled Hetfield, "we were doing mostly covers of the new wave of British metal bands, and because nobody had heard these records [in the United States], all the bangers thought we were doing our own songs."

Metallica, prodded by the California crowds that were embracing a moshing West Coast punk, began to speed up the already fast, loud, propulsive metal music. "That whole fast-tempo thing started with a lot of the songs we had for the first album," explained James Hetfield. "When we started writing our own songs, they weren't fast at all. Then we got a few more gigs, and we got a little more pissed off at the crowd and how people weren't appreciating our stuff. So they gradually got faster and faster as we got more aggressive. Instead of going, 'Please like us,' we were like. . . . 'AAAHH! Fuck you!'"

The speeded-up sound of Metallica became known as *thrash* or *speed metal*. "Metallica really created a form of music," contended Brian Slagel, the metal enthusiast who started Metal Blade Records. "When they came out, there was no speed metal or thrash metal. They were doing something new." *Rolling Stone* called the new sound "a marvel of precisely channeled aggression."

Metallica, which now included bassist Cliff Burton, who had replaced McGovney, and guitarist Kirk Hammett, who took the place of Mustaine, snagged a record contract through the metal underground. The band recorded a demo tape of its songs, which Ulrich, an avid metal tape swapper, sent along the metal underground. "All we wanted to do was to send it out to the traders, get mentioned in some fan magazines," mentioned Ulrich. "The cool thing about the metal scene is that you could pass out ten copies of your tape to people who were really into it and within a week know that 100 people would have it, and another 100 a week later." In 1982, the tape landed in the hands of Jon Zazula and his wife Marsha, New Jersey record store owners who recently had started the label Megaforce. The next March, Metallica signed with Megaforce and traveled to New York to record *Kill 'Em All*, originally titled *Metal Up Your Ass*. The next year they cut *Ride the Lightning* for Megaforce.

The band began to attract a national following at mid-decade, at a time when seminal California punk bands such as Black Flag and the Dead Kennedys disbanded. In early 1986, they released *Master of Puppets* and embarked on a six-month tour behind metal legend Ozzy Osbourne. Osbourne "told us, 'Man, you guys remind me of Sabbath in their early days—hungry, all the energy," enthused James Hetfield. With little radio play and virtually no support from MTV, which characterized metal as "very polarizing music," Metallica slowly climbed to the U.S. Top 30. As the metal army grew, the band hit the Top 10 with . . . *And Justice for All* (1988) and *Metallica* (1991). "It's a cultlike audience," claimed Geoff Mayfield, director of retail research for *Billboard*. "A record like *Metallica* can sell without airplay and without MTV."

Slam Dancer
Courtesy of Cam Garrett/S.C.V.D. Studio

James Hetfield
of Metallica, at
Woodstock, 1994
Photo © Ebet Roberts

Metallica delivered a somber, angry message similar to the desperate ranting of Southern California punk. "*Puppets* was about manipulation, *Ride the Lightning* was about death and dying, and *Justice* talked about the American dream and how that doesn't always work out anymore," explained James Hetfield.

Capturing the alienation and frustration of youth, Metallica paved the way for a legion of thrashers. In 1988, Megadeth, fronted by ex-Metallica guitarist Dave Mustaine, who listed Motorhead as a major influence, hit the charts with *so far, so good . . . so what!* The same year Anthrax, the New York thrash band influenced heavily by Iron Maiden, AC/DC, and the Ramones, hit the Top 30 with *State of Euphoria*. By the beginning of the nineties, asserted *Time*, "heavy metal is white-hot."

Grunge

Grunge, growing in the Seattle offices of the independent Sub Pop Records, combined hardcore and metal to top the charts and help define a generation. In 1979, Bruce Pavitt moved to Olympia, Washington, to attend the experimental Evergreen State College, where he worked at the alternative radio station KAOS and started the fanzine *Subterranean Pop*. After graduating in 1983, he relocated to nearby

Seattle, where he wrote a column in the local music paper, *The Rocket*, and landed a job as a disc jockey on the University of Washington radio station, KCMU, hosting a show called "Sub Pop U.S.A." In 1986, after opening an unsuccessful record store, Pavitt expanded his concept of regional-band cassette compilations, which had accompanied his *Subterranean Pop* fanzine, into a record label. "I could always see that the real essence of the punk work was the Dead Kennedys putting stuff out themselves," reasoned Pavitt, "and people taking control of their own culture." To inaugurate the label he released a collection of local Northwest bands, *Sub Pop 100*, and followed with an extended play by the local punk band, Green River. After the initial releases, Pavitt joined with fellow KCMU jockey Jonathan Poneman to launch Sub Pop Records as a joint venture.

Sub Pop scored its first success with Soundgarden. In 1987, Pavitt and Poneman borrowed money to record *Screaming Life* by the band, which included vocalist Chris Cornell and guitarist Kim Thayil, who had attended Evergreen State College and had been a disc jockey at KCMU with Pavitt. The band fastened upon a new sound, which Ponemen characterized as "a bastardization of the '70s revisionist guitar thing, with a healthy dose of punk-rock aesthetic. It wasn't orthodox metal, and it wasn't a bunch of people moshing in the pit either. . . . Basically," summarized the label co-owner, "it was hardcore and post-hardcore stuff." Attracting fans with their musical hybrid, Soundgarden began to gain the attention of other record labels. In 1988, they recorded *Ultramega OK* with SST, the company owned by Black Flag members Greg Ginn and Chuck Dukowski, and the next year released *Louder Than Love* on A & M Records.

Encouraged by their success with Soundgarden, Sub Pop signed other grunge bands, including Nirvana, which would become the pacesetter of new music. Nirvana vocalist and guitarist Kurt Cobain had grown up in Aberdeen, Washington. The musical impetus behind the band, Cobain, first became enraptured with the Beatles and then such seventies metal bands as Led Zeppelin and Black Sabbath. By his teens, remembered the singer, "I was looking for something a lot heavier, yet melodic at the same time, something different from heavy metal, a different attitude."

Cobain found his niche with punk rock. He became friends with Buzz Osborne, leader of the Aberdeen punk band the Melvins. When he heard the Melvins for the first time, recalled Cobain, "it just blew me away, I was instantly a punk rocker. I abandoned all my friends, 'cause they didn't like any of the music. And then I asked Buzz to make me a compilation tape of punk rock songs and I got a spiky haircut." Osborne also took Cobain to his first rock concert, a show by Black Flag.

By the mid-eighties, Cobain had decided to start a band that would showcase his musical influences. He joined with fellow Aberdeen resident and bassist Chris Novoselic to form a band. Cobain observed that the band "sounded exactly like Black Flag, totally abrasive, fast, punk music. There were some Nirvana elements, some slower songs, even then. And some heavy, Black Sabbath-influenced stuff, I can't deny Black Sabbath or Black Flag."

In 1987, Cobain, Novoselic, and drummer Chad Channing, together now named Nirvana, signed a record contract with Sub Pop. In late 1988, the trio released the seven-inch Nirvana single "Love Buzz/Big Cheese." The next year they released the band's first album, *Bleach*, recorded for $606.17, which showed hardcore and metal influences.

The band added a new musical dimension as they entered the studio to record their second Sub Pop album. Recording the songs that would become *Nevermind*, Nirvana added a melodic, Beatlesque element, which had shaped Cobain, Novoselic, and new drummer Dave Grohl. "We might as well just play Beatles covers for the rest of our careers," joked Novoselic. "They started it, they did it best, they ended it." "When it comes down to pop, there's only one word—the B word, Beatles," agreed Grohl.

By 1990, the band realized that Sub Pop had fallen into financial difficulties and used their demo tape to search for a new label. In January 1990, they signed to David Geffen's DGC label, which paid Sub Pop $75,000 for the Nirvana contract.

As Nirvana moved toward a pop/metal/punk hybrid, the Seattle scene began to garner media attention through the efforts of Sub Pop. From its inception, Sub Pop had tried to market the Northwest scene. "The thing that we've done here is we've taken a number of bands that sound similar," remarked Poneman in 1989. "We've given them a similar marketing look in terms of dynamic, live, portrait-oriented covers. We're using a precedent set by Tamla/Motown and Stax, where you have the scene that is being born in a particular region and then you just have a machine that you use to refine and perfect your product. You create a sensation, like Great Britain in 1962 through 1965. All of a sudden there are all these bands coming out of this part of the world, there's good press, it's romantic."

Rather than the slick Motown image of suits and dinner gowns, Sub Pop helped to create a downtrodden punk/metal fashion unique to the Northwest. They signed bands who dressed in faded flannel shirts or T-shirts, ripped jeans or baggy shorts, and worn boots or tennis shoes. The mostly male band members favored long hair, which had become a trademark among heavy metal fanatics. In 1992, Poneman wrote the copy for a *Vogue* article on grunge fashion that featured the Northwest look.

Sub Pop marketed their acts through a singles-of-the-month club. They introduced their bands to the metal/punk underground by starting a subscription service, modeled after the cassette compilations Poneman had included in his *Subterranean Pop* fanzine, to interest diehard fans and collectors. For $20, the label sent to subscribers six limited-edition singles such as "Room 1,000 Years Wide" by Soundgarden.

To promote their bands, the label also courted the press. In 1989, they paid for a visit from a journalist who wrote for the British music magazine *Melody Maker*, which subsequently called Sub Pop the "life force to the most vibrant, kicking music scene encompassed in one city for at least ten years." Within a year the label attracted the attention of the national press. *The New York Times* referred to the Northwest as "America's latest music mecca," and articles about Sub Pop appeared in the *Los Angeles Times*, the *Wall Street Journal*, Tower Records' *Pulse*, and other newspapers and magazines across the country. "At long last, Seattle is suddenly hot," observed *Billboard* in November 1990.

By the end of 1990, Sub Pop had help to create the image of Seattle as the site of an exciting, emerging music scene. "Bruce and I like to compare what's going on here in Seattle with what happened in San Francisco in 1967," Poneman told the *Seattle Times*. "People are moving out here to become part of a scene," added Pavitt. "No matter how silly it sounds, Seattle has become a mecca."

Television and film helped to solidify the image of Seattle as the new mecca. In spring 1990, David Lynch premiered the ABC television show *Twin Peaks*, generating further interest in the Northwest lifestyle. *Northern Exposure*, which became the most popular show on television at the time, extolled the virtues of the Northwest and was filmed a few miles from Seattle. In early 1991, director Cameron Crowe started to film the movie *Singles*, about the punk/metal Seattle scene, which included music of Northwest bands and band members in cameo roles. By early 1992, when *Singles* aired in theaters across the country, the national media had embraced Seattle as the newest sensation. "I really wanted the movie to have a real private kind of feel to it," remarked Crowe about *Singles*. "Now you get people going, 'Oh, it's about Seattle? How trendy.' "

Benefitting from media which had begun to lionize the Northwest, Nirvana became a national phenomenon. The band released their major label debut, *Nevermind*, on September 24, 1991. After MTV placed their video of "Smells Like Teen Spirit" in heavy rotation, in early 1992 Nirvana hit the top of the chart. The band appeared on *Saturday Night Live* and was featured in *Rolling Stone*, *Spin*, and most other music publications. Within a year the band had sold 10 million copies of their debut and entered the chart at the number-one position with their follow-up, *In Utero*.

Pearl Jam followed Nirvana to the top of the chart. The band had been established in Seattle by hardcore/British heavy-metal fans Jeff Ament and Stone Gossard, who had been members of Green River, the first band to record for Sub Pop, and had played together in Mother Love Bone. They added Black Sabbath-influenced guitarist Mike McCready, vocalist Eddie Vedder, and eventually drummer Dave Abbruzzese to complete the lineup. In September 1991, Pearl Jam released their first album, *Ten*. After waiting 20 weeks to crack the Top 200, the band topped the chart in the wake of Nirvana's success. The next year, matching Nirvana's track record, the band entered the chart at number one with *Vs.*

Other Northwest metal/punk bands found similar success. In 1992,

Kurt Cobain of Nirvana, 1993
Photo © Ebet Roberts

Alice in Chains, described by the band's guitarist, Jerry Cantrell, as "not entirely metal, not entirely grunge, but all of the above," released the million-selling *Dirt*. The next year they topped the chart with the more pop-sounding *Jar of Flies*. In 1993, Soundgarden, the first Seattle band to land a major label deal, topped the chart with *Superunknown*. Mudhoney, formed by Mark Arm and Steve Turner, who had played in the influential Green River, charted as well. By 1993, Seattle bands dominated the national album chart.

These bands played music for a post-baby-boom generation. "There's millions and millions of people in their 40s who think they're so fucking special," railed Kim Thayil of Soundgarden. "They're this ultimate white-bread, suburban, upper-middle-class group that were spoiled little fuckers as kids 'cause they were all children of Dr. Spock, and then they were stupid, stinky hippies, and then they were spoiled little yuppie materialists. . . . They thought they had a monopoly on rock 'n' roll," Thayil sneered, "and all of a sudden they realize they don't. It belongs to someone else now."

Seattle bands articulated the fears and frustrations of their many post-baby-boom fans. Kurt Cobain, who suffered through the divorce of his parents at the age of eight and drifted in and out of his mother's home as a teenager, sang about abandonment in *In Utero*. Eddie Vedder, who grew up believing his biological father was his uncle, wrote about the lethal effects of parental neglect in "Jeremy." Chris Cornell's lyrics "deal with inner struggles he's gone through, but a lot of people can relate to them," remarked Soundgarden drummer, Matt Cameron, about the band's songs. "I think the angst this generation is experiencing is very valid, and I think it's a pretty important change that this generation of bands is actually dealing with those issues." "I guess the music industry didn't predict that this generation of songwriters was going to plug in so accurately and so unanimously to the group of people who were buying records," mentioned Cornell himself. "It's a representation of the generation that wasn't being accurately represented."

Even the marketing of Sub Pop reflected the mood of a new generation. In 1989, the label dubbed a showcase of Sub Pop bands as a "Lamefest" and billed the event as "Seattle's lamest bands in a one-night orgy of sweat and insanity." They sold Sub Pop T-shirts emblazoned with the word *loser*. "That shirt really hit home," explained Poneman. "There were an incredible number of young people out there who weren't making it. It was a real anti-yuppie statement."

Many Northwest bands expressed the disillusionment which enveloped many post-baby boomers. "We had to grow up with this idealization that was never going to fucking come true, and it turned us into a bunch of cynics— or a bunch of drug addicts," explained Courtney Love, who fronted the grunge band, Hole. The overdose deaths of Mother Love Bone singer Andrew Wood and Hole bassist Kristen Pfaff emphasized the desperate mood of a generation which turned to such drugs as heroin. The shotgun suicide of Kurt Cobain, probably the most important figure in Northwest grunge and the husband of Courtney Love, highlighted the desperation of a generation. "I think there's gonna be more and more people who just give up hope," predicted Chris Cornell. "I mean, that's the way *I* feel. I'm successful in what I do, but I don't really have a clue where I'm going or how I fit into the rest of society." As it had done during the late sixties, rock-and-roll once again provided a new generation with the soundtrack of their anger, frustration, and disillusionment.

The Rap Attack

African-American youths, facing greater hardships than their white counterparts, used rap music to chronicle their plight and create a community of support. Though the African-American middle class increased in numbers as a result of the civil rights movement, during the eighties

331

Afrika Bambaataa
Photo by Al Pereira

African-Americans generally experienced hard times. By 1980, more than 31 percent of African-Americans lived in poverty, nearly three times the percentage of impoverished whites. Six years later, 14 percent of African-American families earned less than $5000 a year, compared with 9.6 percent in 1970, and more than 30 percent had a yearly income of less than $10,000.

African-American youths especially confronted forbidding economic prospects. The percentage of African-American males under 24 who never held a job increased from 9.9 percent in 1966 to 23.3 percent in 1977. By 1987, more than 34 percent of African-American teens were unemployed, compared to 17 percent of white teens, and more than 21 percent of African-Americans between the ages of 20 and 24 could not find jobs, compared to less than 10 percent of their white counterparts. Five years later, nearly 40 percent of African-American teens and 24 percent of African-Americans in their early 20s found themselves on the unemployment rolls.

Many of these poor unemployed youths lived in single-parent, single-income households usually headed by a mother. In 1964, roughly 25 percent of African-American children lived in female-headed households. Abetted by a welfare system that rewarded fatherless families, in 1980 the figure increased to 40 percent. In 1984, the number of female-headed, single-parent African-American families skyrocketed to more than 50 percent, compared to 14 percent among white families. By 1992, the figure had increased to 59 percent among African-Americans.

Having free time, little money, and less parental care than children in two-parent families, many inner-city African-American youths became involved with drugs, especially an inexpensive type of cocaine called crack, sometimes dealing the drug for profit. "When a nigga sells drugs around here," explained rapper OMB of the rap group OFTB [Operation from the Bottom], "he ain't selling for no big thing, 'cause his family is starving, he's starving, so he's gotta make some kind of move to get what he gotta get, and I mean dope is the most popular and quickest way he can get money. If you don't have no way out, you would do the same muthafuckin' thing."

To gain an identity and support in an unstable environment, others joined gangs such as the notorious, warring Crips and Bloods in Los Angeles. "There's a lot of admirable qualities in gang membership," suggested rapper Ice-T. "A guy will look at you and say, 'If something happens to you I'll be the first one to die.' There's a lot of love." "The gang was like your family," added rap pioneer Afrika Bambaataa, who had been a member of the Black Spades in New York City. "Sometimes a gang is more your family than a real family is, and that's what a lot of people don't understand," added B-Real (a.k.a. Louis Freeze) of Cypress Hill. "Why do you want to be in a gang? Well because my homeboy loves me more than my fuckin' mother or father does."

Many times, the gang-dominated street life led to violence. From 1986 to 1989, the number of African-American teen homicide victims increased from under 1000 to more than 1600. By 1992, homicide had become the leading cause of death among African-American teenagers. "The other day I was looking at an old picture from back when I used to play Pop Warner football," reported rapper Snoop Doggy Dog, who would later be charged with murder, "and like of 28 homies on the team, 12 are dead, seven are in the penitentiary, and three of them are smoked out."

The violent, economically bleak conditions that faced inner city African-American youths created a sense of despair. "We not living no American Dream," remarked rapper Kam. "We in a nightmare. Like I said, this is hell for us. Anything else would be an improvement, you know what I'm saying, we can't get no lower, we can't get no farther back."

Rap music arose from and helped shape the African-American desperation in the inner cities, many times decrying poverty, drugs, and gang-inspired violence. The music originated in the ghettos of New York City. As disco started to become popular in New York during the early seventies, some disc jockeys in the Bronx and Harlem began to play for parties. Rather than play an entire song, some record spinners such as Kool DJ Herc (a.k.a. Clive Campbell) began to play, or sample, short fragments, usually the percussion breaks, which the dancers requested. Starting in 1973, he "took the music of Mandrill, like 'Fencewalk,' certain disco records that had funky percussion breaks and he just kept that beat *going*," recalled Afrika Bambaataa, who began spinning records three years after Herc. "It might be that certain part of the record that everyone waits for."

The rap pioneers sampled all types of music. As Afrika Bambaataa explained, "The music itself is colorless 'cause you can't say, I don't like R & B, I don't like heavy metal, when half the shit that's out comes from all the different styles of records that's out there."

Though having eclectic tastes, rappers favored polyrhythmic funk over the more simplistic disco. "We was against the disco that was happenin', we had the funk back 'cause they wasn't playing James, Sly or Parliament no more," remarked Bambaataa. "How the funk came back on the scene was through hip-hop, through the street," agreed Jazzy Jay, a member of one of Bambaataa's groups. "All of them—James Brown, George Clinton, Parliament, all that—that was almost dead. Disco was in, everybody was hustling, and the disco deejays were talking over. Well, what happened, the kids just rebelled. They wanted something that they couldn't hear on the radio and everything. They wanted something else."

Kool DJ Herc started to add special effects to the samples of the funky music. Following the lead of his fellow Jamaican, reggae musician King Tubby (a.k.a. Osbourne Lawrence), he altered the rhythm track by using echo and reverb to create a dub version of the song. Using a special stylus, Herc and other spinners such as Theodore Livingston rotated, or scratched, the records back and forth to produce a unique rhythmic pattern. Kool DJ Herc sometimes mixed the beat with two turntables, quickly fading one song into another. Through these methods he wove together intricate polyrhythms into a staccato sound that mimicked the short, abrupt changes of commercial television.

Building upon the African oral history tradition and copying Jamaican U Roy, who had spoken, or toasted, to the dubs of King Tubby, Kool DJ Herc began to talk along with the halting, polyrhythmic sounds. Afrika Bambaataa remembered, "Herc took phrases, like what was happening in the streets, what was the new saying going round the high school like 'rock on my mellow,' 'to the beat y'all,' 'you don't stop,' and just elaborated on that."

Soon other disc jockeys such as rap pioneer Bambaataa and DJ Hollywood, who played disco records at the Apollo Theater during breaks, started to rap to their sampled music. "To attract their own followings, some of these DJs would give little raps to let the crowd know who was spinning the records," explained rapper Kurtis Blow. "As time went by, these raps became more elaborate, with the DJ sometimes including a call-and-response 'conversation' with the regulars in the house." "We just took the Jamaican style and put it to American records," summarized Bambaataa.

To allow greater dexterity and creativity with the funk-based music, some disc jockeys asked friends to rap, or emcee, for them. "The first MC that I know of is Cowboy [Keith Wiggins], from Grandmaster Flash and the Furious Five," related Lil Rodney Cee of the rap duo Double Trouble. "He was the first MC to talk for Grandmaster Flash [Joseph Saddler] and say how great Flash was—you know, 'the pulsating, inflating disco shaking, heartbreaking, the man on the turntable.' "

During the seventies, the number of disc jockeys who rapped to the funky samples of effect-laden music began to multiply. "After myself, Herc and Flash, crazy amounts of DJs started springing up everywhere," mentioned Bambaataa. "They always wanted to challenge or battle somebody. It was no joke. . . . If you lost you could kiss your career goodbye."

Many of these disc jockeys, ready for sonic battle, began to perform at prominent disco clubs. By September 2, 1976, Grandmaster Flash, nicknamed for his speed on the turntable, had progressed from parties on Fox Street and small clubs such as the Back Door to the Audubon Club, which held a maximum of 3000 patrons. "The pinnacle of a DJ group's career, before it was recording, was who can make it to the Audubon," indicated the Grandmaster. "Once you played there you were famous throughout the five boroughs" of New York City. By the late seventies, popular jockeys such as Afrika Bambaataa had found jobs at well-known downtown discos. After playing the Mudd Club, Bambaataa performed in Negril. "Then it got too big for Negril. One time the fire marshals closed the whole place down so we moved to the Danceteria," he related. "Then it got too big for Danceteria. Finally, we made home at the Roxy. It started slow building at the Roxy, and now Friday nights is always 3000, 4000."

A youth culture partly based upon disco began to develop around rappers such as Grandmaster Flash and Afrika Bambaataa. "Not only did our fans want to talk like we did," remembered Kurtis Blow, a member of Grandmaster Flash and the Furious Five, "but they dressed like we did, and seemed to be trying to live out the fantasies we were kicking in our raps." Calling themselves b-boys and fly girls, the rap fanatics in the inner cities of New York, Philadelphia, and Baltimore wore disco-like heavy gold chains and oversized gold rings. They extended disco by perfecting break dancing, a complex form of dance that hit the public with the films *Flashdance* (1983) and *Breakin'* (1984), and was perfected by such dancers as Crazy Legs and the Rock Steady crew.

As a reaction to the extravagance of disco, the poor, urban rappers grafted a street element to their counterculture, which they called hip-hop. They adopted a fashion style that included baseball caps with upturned bills, Adidas or 69er Pro Keds tennis shoes, and T-shirts. Learning from the rappers, the b-boys and fly girls used a street language that reflected their everyday concerns and included such words and phrases as "chill out" (calm down), "sweat" (hassle), "dope" (great), "posse" (gang), "def" (good), and "wack" (bad). Using subway trains and buildings as their canvases, individual artists and gangs such as the Vanguards, Magic, Inc., the Nod Squad, and the A Last Survivors refined the low-budget art of graffiti.

Like the eighties heavy-metal underground, the growing number of rap fans bought and traded tapes of their favorite performers. "Cassette tapes used to be our albums before anybody recorded what they called rap records," Bambaataa pointed out. "People started hearing all this rapping coming out of boxes. When they heard the tapes down in the Village they wanted to know, 'Who's this black DJ who's playing all this rock and new wave up in the Bronx?' " "I mean, we had tapes that went platinum before we were even involved with the music industry," added Jazzy Jay.

Independent companies eventually heard the tapes and recorded the new music. In 1979, Sylvia Robinson, a former vocalist with Savoy Records, heard several rap tapes that her children played at home. "Hey, if my kids like this, all the kids around the world will like this!," she reasoned. With her husband, Joe, she started Sugarhill Records and recorded the Sugarhill Gang's "Rapper's Delight," which reached the Top 5 on the R & B chart and cracked the national Top 40.

Grandmaster Flash and the Furious Five, the next Sugarhill signing, infused rap with a social awareness. The group was comprised of disc jockey Flash, Cowboy, Melle Mel (Melvin Glover) and his brother Nathaniel (Kid Creole), Duke Bootee (Ed Fletcher), and Kurtis Blow. In 1979, following in the path of such African-American musicians such as the Last Poets ("Niggers Are Scared of Revolution" and "White Man's Got a God Complex") and Gil Scott-Heron ("The Revolution Will Not Be Televised"), they released the socially charged "Freedom." In 1982, the group recorded "The Message," a bleak tale of life on the streets, which hit the charts in Britain and the United States. In November 1983, before fracturing into different bands, they produced the anti-cocaine

Run-D.M.C.
Courtesy of Rush Artist Management

"White Lines (Don't Do It)." Rap, asserted Kurtis Blow at the time, provides "a way for the people of the ghetto to make themselves heard."

Run-D.M.C. brought inner-city rap to the masses of American teens by combining it with heavy metal. The group banded together in 1982 after graduating from St. Pascal's Catholic School in New York. The next year, disc jockey Jason Mizel and rappers Darryl McDaniels and Joseph "Run" Simmons, the last of whom had worked as a disc jockey behind Kurtis Blow, released their first LP, which after a year on the chart became the first gold rap album.

The group followed its initial success with *King of Rock*, which reached number 52 on the charts through the use of the heavy-metal-like guitar of Eddie Martinez. "Run-D.M.C. used to rap over rock records a lot," mentioned Jam Master Jay Mizel. "I used to mix rock tunes, and have the guitar come in a little bit, and then play the drum over and over again. *Toys in the Attic*, Aerosmith, that was the best." The band secured airplay on MTV for its videos of "King of Rock" and "You Talk Too Much," two of the first rap videos aired on the network. Through its heavy-metal rap, Run-D.M.C. began to appeal to white teens. "Does the band have white crossover fans?" rhetorically asked Bill Adler, who helped manage the group. "I'll tell you, a typical letter we get is from someplace like North Dakota. They say, 'I'll bet I'm the only white person ever to write you, but I love Run-D.M.C.' All the white people think they're alone, but they're not."

Run-D.M.C. increased its white audience by collaborating with Aerosmith, a mid-seventies, Rolling Stones-influenced hard-rock outfit that neared the top of the chart with *Rocks* (1976). In 1986, they combined the polyrhythms of rap with heavy metal to hit the top of the singles chart with a remake of Aerosmith's "Walk This Way," which featured Aerosmith's Joe Perry on guitar and Steven Tyler helping with vocals. The band sold more than 3 million copies of the Top 5 *Raising Hell*, the album that contained the hit single and, according to Darryl "D.M.C." McDaniel, "put rap into a lot of people's living rooms."

The popular Run-D.M.C., like Grandmaster Flash, used rap to highlight the sobering conditions that confronted young urban African-Americans. They delivered such social commentaries as "It's Like That" and "Hard Times." To demonstrate their interest in social justice, they joined with the rock elite and such rap pioneers as Afrika Bambaataa, Kurtis Blow, Duke Bootee, and Mel Melle to form Artists Against Apartheid.

As the economic and social condition of young urban African-Americans continued to deteriorate during the eighties, many rappers graphically described the violent life in the inner cities to create "gangsta rap." Schooly-D, a former member of the Parkside Killers in North Philadelphia, started the trend with the shocking description of gang warfare in "PSK—What Does It Mean" (1986). Formed in 1987 by Eric "Eazy-E" Wright, N.W.A. [Niggaz With Attitude] perfected gangsta rap. They sold a million copies of their second album, *Straight Outta Compton* (1988), which included "Fuck the Police," a song that chronicled police violence against young African-Americans. They followed with "Sa Prize (Part 2)," which continued their "Fuck the Police" message. Ice Cube (a.k.a. Oshea Jackson), the rhymer who split from N.W.A. in 1989, rapped about the consequences of police and gang violence in his debut, *AmeriKKKa's Most Wanted* (1990) and "Dead Homiez" and "The Product" on *Kill at Will* (1990). The Geto Boys penned "City Under Siege" about police harassment and Cypress Hill wrote "Pigs." Ice-T (a.k.a. Tracy Marrow) dwelt on the same theme with *O.G. Original Gangster*, *Body Count*, and the controversial "Cop Killer" which Warner Brothers deleted after the first issue of the CD.

The angry gangsta rappers, though sometimes glorifying the street-wise gun culture, considered themselves reporters on the urban African-American beat. "I show white America about the black community, and I hold a mirror up to the black community to show them about themselves," contended Ice Cube. "I just look at it as, if there wasn't rap, where would the voice of the eighteen-year-old black male be?," asked Ice-T. "He would never be on TV, he ain't writin' no book. He is not in the movies."

During late April 1992, the observations of the rappers became evident when rioting erupted in Los Angeles after the acquittal of police officers who had brutally beaten African-American Rodney King. Angry African-Americans took to the streets in response to the actions of a jury that had seemingly disregarded videotaped evidence of police brutality. They burned and looted buildings until dispersed by 2000 National Guardsmen and 4500 federal troops dispatched by President George Bush. "When rap came out of L.A., what you heard initially was my voice yelling about South Central," remarked Ice-T. "People thought, 'That shit's crazy,' and ignored it. Then N.W.A. came out and yelled, Ice Cube yelled about it. People said, 'Oh, that's just kids making a buck.' They didn't realize how many niggas with attitude are out there on the street. Now you see them."

Besides reporting the stark realities of the African-American community, rappers such as the militant Public Enemy delivered an updated late-sixties soul message of African-American pride. "Black men and women are treated like bullshit," declared Chuck D (a.k.a. Carlton Ridenhour) of the group during a concert at Riker's Island prison. "You've got to know the rules of the game so we won't be falling into traps and keep coming back to places like these! . . . Our goal in life," continued the rapper, who started Public Enemy while a student at Adelphi University in Long Island, "is to get ourselves out of this mess and be responsible to our sons and daughters so they can lead a better life. . . . My job is to build 5000 potential black leaders through my means of communication in America. A black leader is just someone who takes responsibility." By the end of the decade Public Enemy had sold more than 1 million copies of *It Takes a Nation of Millions to Hold Us Back*, a pointed discourse on drugs, inner-city poverty, and African-American self-determination. They also contributed the song "Fight the Power" to director Spike Lee's controversial popular film *Do the Right Thing*, which pictured life in the inner city. In 1990, the group hit the Top 10 with *Fear of a Black Planet*, released by Def Jam Records, which was the largest African-American-owned label since Motown and which was co-owned by Russell Simmons, brother of Run-D.M.C.'s Joseph Simmons.

Arrested Development scaled the chart with its call for African-American self-respect. "We wanted to recognize all the bad things going on—the killings, the shootings, AIDS and everything that's crushing the communities," insisted Speech (a.k.a. Todd Thomas), who had been a gangsta rapper before forming the group. "But we wanted to make people understand that you've got to still be alive in order to change it." In 1992, they released their debut, *3 Years, 5 Months and 2 Days in the Life of . . .*, which included such hopeful songs as "Raining Revolution," hit the Top 10 and sold 2 million copies. Based upon their initial effort, the group snagged Artist of the Year honors from *Rolling Stone* and *Musician*.

During the late eighties and early nineties, others used rap to convey a sense of African-American self-worth. The Jungle Brothers fused rap and R & B "to bring about peace and unity. . . . We always felt that spreading a message was the way to go," indicated the group's Mike G. (a.k.a. Michael Small), a nephew of the legendary New York rapper Red Alert. In 1990, the group embarked on the "Politics of Nature" tour, which included speaking engagements about African-American consciousness. Big Daddy Kane rapped about African-American pride in "Young, Gifted and Black" and "Ain't No Stoppin' Us Now." As African pendants replaced gold chains, female rapper Queen Latifah emphasized an Afrocentric "show of pride for ancestors from whom we

Chuck D of Public Enemy
Photo by Al Pereira

descended" to create a sense of unity among African-Americans. In 1991, L.L. Cool J. (a.k.a. James Todd Smith) released *Mama Said Knock You Out*. "It's about truancy, drug abuse, teen-age pregnancy," he explained. "It's about knocking out all the ills of society." Eric B and Rakim rapped about African-American pride in "In the Ghetto" (1990), and the rap duo of Eric "E" Sermon and Parrish "P" Smith, known as EPMD, addressed the same topic in "Sayin'." Even rap pioneer Kool Moe Dee, who had been a member of the Treacherous Three, which in the early eighties recorded for Sugarhill, switched from boasting to rap about African-American unity in *Knowledge Is King* (1989).

Some rappers, having pride in their race, warned against the damaging effects of drugs on the African-American community. De La Soul delivered the sobering "My Brother Is a Basehead" and Kool Moe Dee offered the same message in "Monster Crack." "We guide a lot of kids," mentioned Queen Latifah. "When kids constantly hear rappers saying, 'don't do drugs, don't do drugs,' there's a chance it will sink in."

KRS-One, an acronym for Knowledge Reigns Supreme Over Nearly Everyone, organized rappers into action. After abandoning gangsta rap, in 1988 KRS (a.k.a. Kris Parker) helped organize Stop the Violence. By the next year he had convinced a number of leading rappers such as Chuck D. and Flavor Flav of Public Enemy, Just-Ice, Heavy D, Kool Moe Dee, and MC Lyte to denounce gang warfare on the inner-city streets in the single "Self-Destruction," which sold a half-million copies. He donated the $500,000 in royalties to the National Urban League, which promised to use the money to combat illiteracy. "We wanted to reach the kids most affected by black-on-black crime" that many times resulted from "unemployment which can be the result of illiteracy," noted Ann Carli, Jive Records vice-president of artist development who helped KRS-One organize Stop the Violence. "Rap records," added Carli, "can be a tool that can be used in education today; young adults will listen to rap and what rap artists have to say."

KRS-One continued his educational efforts. In 1991, with the help of Queen Latifah and Run-D.M.C., he started H.E.A.L. Yourself and released a video. The rapper gave profits from the video to Human Education Against Lies, which printed and distributed books to high schools. The next year he joined with Rutgers-educated rapper and activist Sister Souljah (a.k.a. Lisa Williamson) to advocate a ten-point program to empower African-Americans. The program "addresses all areas of African-American life, economics, education, culture, spirituality, defense and everything," explained Sister Souljah. "It's not a militant message but one of truth and common sense. We have to be educated on our own ethnicity."

By the mid-nineties, many rappers followed the socially active path of KRS-One and Sister Souljah. In 1990, Michael Conception, a former gang member and Grand Jury Records president, organized such rap performers as Tone Loc, Eazy-E., M. C. Hammer, Ice-T, and N. W. A. for the anti-violence rap single and video project "We're All in the Same Gang." "I hope it generates a lot of money and we can get it to the people who really need it," Conception told *Billboard*. "If anyone can convince the black gangs, it's somebody who was in one." Female rapper Yo-Yo started the Intelligent Black Woman's Coalition. L.L. Cool J visited schools to advise students about drug abuse, and X-Clan organized voter registration drives and anti-crack seminars. Even M. C. Hammer (a.k.a. Stanley Burrell), who sold 6 million copies of the chart-topping *Please Hammer Don't Hurt 'Em*, which blended rap with melodic hooks, worked with inner-city schoolchildren in his hometown of Oakland. "I make an active role model to kids," he explained. "They need people to show them there's another way." By the nineties, the rappers had directly faced the problems that confronted African-American youths.

The militant message of rap, though sometimes including a Black Muslim-inspired separatism, also reached discontented white teens. "Rap music in the '90s is developing a more socially aware conscience. For example: Public Enemy, [the KRS-One-led] Boogie Down Productions, X-Clan and Harmony," observed Troi Torain, R & B alternative promotion director for Virgin Records in late 1990. "These artists are committed to broadening the state of awareness, which is being acknowledged by more and more young people." "Now more than ever the rap market had reached a level of acceptance," agreed Ernie Singleton, the president of black music at MCA.

The white teens became aware of rap through television, the medium that helped expose a previous generation to rock-and-roll. In 1987, MTV began to air more rap videos and a special feature on rap, "Yo! MTV Raps," hosted by Fab 5 Freddy. "That wall between rock and hip-hop is falling down, especially with our younger audience," explained Andy Schuon, senior vice president of MTV. "We've created an environment where Aerosmith can be programmed right next to Snoop [Doggy Dog], and people will accept that." Filling a void created by radio, which seldom played rap, other networks programmed rap shows such as Fox's "Pump It Up" and BET's "Rap City" and began to use rap rhythms and rhymes in commercials. By 1991, noticed Rick Rubin, cofounder of Def Jam Records, "rap has moved into the suburbs. Ice Cube, N.W.A., Public Enemy—I'd say 90 percent of their audience is white."

As the nineties unfolded, many disgruntled thrash metal groups and grunge bands who initially had dismissed rap joined with angry rappers to create a united front of a desperate generation. Building upon the eighties rock-rap collaboration of Aerosmith and Run-D.M.C. and ex-Sex Pistol John Lydon and Afrika Bambaatta, the thrash metal band Anthrax combined with Chuck D. to record a thrash/rap version of Public Enemy's "Bring On the Noise" (1991), and subsequently toured with the rappers. "These two kinds of music have always been similar in attitude, I never understood why there wasn't more of a crossover," wondered Anthrax guitarist Scott Ian. In 1993, the grunge band Pearl Jam recorded with rappers Cypress Hill. "We listen to that kind of music anyway," insisted B-Real of the rap group, "so it wasn't hard to click with them." "The Pearl Jam shit is dope because we put hard B-boy rhymes on top of some heavy-metal-sounding shit," added Sen Dog of Cypress Hill. Sir Mix-a-Lot, the Seattle rapper who released an African-American version of the national anthem, rapped over the grunge band Mudhoney. "I was wondering when we'd bring rap and rock together in a big way," remarked Mix-a-Lot, "because the fans are a lot alike."

Ice-T exemplified the marriage between rap and punk/thrash/ grunge. On his 1992 album *Body Count*, he used a heavy-metal band as a background for his angry rhymes about prison, drug addiction, and police abuse. Ice-T admired the "more evil sounds" of such metal bands as Black Sabbath and the "punk energy" of Black Flag and the Dead Kennedys. For *Body Count*, he "wanted a group that has the attack of [thrash metal band] Slayer, the impending doom of Sabbath, the drive of Motorhead and groove-oriented . . . like what Anthrax does." As the rapper observed, "Rock-and-roll's not dead—it's just gotta open its doors and realize where it came from. I'm trying to get rap kids to realize that it's all rock-and-roll. When rock-and-roll first started, it was black and white kids together—I'm trying to get it back together." During the nineties, disaffected young whites and African-Americans joined together to claim rock-and-roll for a new generation.

Bibliography

This bibliography consists of the material I found most useful in the preparation of this book. It does not pretend to be a comprehensive survey of the thousands of books and articles on rock-and-roll, but rather offers the reader a concise guide to rock as social history. The many quotes and statistics used in this book have been gleaned from these materials.

General

CHAPPLE, STEVE, AND REEBEE GAROFALO. Rock 'n' Roll Is Here to Pay: The History and Politics of the Music Industry. Chicago: Nelson-Hall, 1977.

CURTIS, JIM. Rock Eras: Interpretations of Music and Society. Bowling Green: Bowling Green State Press, 1987.

FONG-TORRES, BEN, ed. The Rolling Stone Rock and Roll Reader. New York: Bantam, 1974.

———, ed. What's That Sound? New York: Anchor, 1976.

FRITH, SIMON. Sound Effects—Youth, Leisure and the Politics of Rock. New York: Pantheon, 1982.

HENDLER, HERB. Year by Year in the Rock Era. Westport: Greenwood, 1983.

HOLT, SID. The Rolling Stone Interviews: The 1980s. New York: St. Martin's, 1989.

JONES, LANDON. Great Expectations: America and the Baby Boom Generation. New York: Coward, McCann & Geohegan, 1980.

KIEFER, KIT, ed. They Called It Rock: The Goldmine Oral History of Rock 'N Roll, 1950–1970. Iola: Krause, 1991.

LAZELL, BARRY, ed. Rock Movers and Shakers. New York: Billboard, 1989.

LOGAN, NICK, and BOB WOFFINDEN. The Illustrated Encyclopedia of Rock. New York: Harmony, 1977.

MARSH, DAVE, and JOHN SWENSON, eds. The Rolling Stone Record Guide. New York: Random House, 1979.

MILLER, JIM, ed. The Rolling Stone Illustrated History of Rock and Roll. New York: Random House, 1976.

NITE, NORM. Rock On. New York: Popular, 1974.

PARELES, JON, and PATRICIA ROMANOWSKI, eds. The Rolling Stone Encyclopedia of Rock and Roll. New York: Summit, 1983.

POLLACK, BRUCE. When the Music Mattered: Rock in the 1960s. New York: Holt, 1983.

Rolling Stone, editors of. The Age of Paranoia: How the Sixties Ended. New York: Pocket, 1972.

———. The Rolling Stone Interviews. New York: Paperback, 1971.

———. The Rolling Stone Interviews. Vol. 2. New York: Warner, 1973.

Roxon, Lillian. *Rock Encyclopedia*. New York: Grosset & Dunlap, 1969.

Shaw, Arnold. *The Rock Revolution*. London: Collier, 1969.

Smith, Joe. *Off the Record: An Oral History of Popular Music*. New York: Warner, 1988.

Stambler, Irwin. *Encyclopedia of Pop, Rock and Soul*. New York: St. Martin's, 1977.

Ward, Ed, Geoffrey Stokes, and Ken Tucker. *Rock of Ages*. Englewood Cliffs: Prentice Hall, 1986.

Wienberg, Max. *The Big Beat*. Chicago: Contemporary, 1984.

Chapter 1
The Blues, Rock-and-Roll, and Racism

"B.B. King." *Living Blues* (May/June 1988), pp. 10–22.

Cohan, Lou. "Bo Diddley: The Man with the Beat." *Thunder Road* (June 1980), pp. 26–29.

Corritore, Bob, Bill Ferris, and Jim O'Neal. "Willie Dixon." *Living Blues* (July/August 1988), pp. 16–25 and (September/October 1988) pp. 20–31.

DeCurtis, Anthony. "Living Legends." *Rolling Stone*, September 21, 1989, pp. 89–100.

———. "Willie Dixon and the Wisdom of the Blues." *Rolling Stone*, March 23, 1989, pp. 109–114.

Dezutter, Hank. "Willie Dixon." *TWA Ambassador* (July 1980), pp. 39–41.

Escott, Colin. "The Everly Brothers: Brothers in Arms." *Goldmine*, June 25, 1993, pp. 14–42.

———. "John Lee Hooker: King of the One-Chord Boogie." *Goldmine*, March 20, 1992, pp. 10–12.

Gillett, Charlie. *Making Tracks*. London: Sunrise/Dutton, 1974.

Golkin, Pete. "Blacks, Whites, and the Blues: The Story of Chess." *Living Blues* (September/October 1989), pp. 22–30.

Guralnick, Peter. *Feel Like Going Home*. London: Dutton, 1971.

———. *Lost Highways*. New York: Vintage, 1982.

"Howlin' Wolf Interview." *Living Blues* (Spring 1970), pp. 13–17.

"Intermission with Fats." *Living Blues* (November/December 1977), pp. 16–19.

Jackson, John. *Big Beat Heat! Alan Freed and the Early Years of Rock 'n' Roll*, New York: Schirmer, 1991.

Larner, Jeremy. "What Do They Get from Rock and Roll?" *Atlantic Monthly* (August 1964), pp. 44–49.

O'Neal, James, and Amy O'Neal. "Eddie Boyd Interview." *Living Blues* (November/December 1977), pp. 11–15.

———. "Jimmie Rogers Interview." *Living Blues* (Autumn 1973), pp. 11–20.

———. "Jimmy Reed Interview." *Living Blues* (May/June 1975), pp. 16–37.

———. "John Lee Hooker Interview." *Living Blues* (Autumn 1979), pp. 14–22.

PALMER, ROBERT. *Deep Blues.* New York: Penguin, 1982.

———. "Muddy Waters: The Delta Son Never Sets." *Rolling Stone,* October 5, 1968, pp. 15–17.

PENN, ROBERTA. "Bo Diddley." *The Rocket* (September 1983), p. 19.

RESSNER, JEFFREY. "Pat Boone." *Rolling Stone,* April 19, 1990, pp. 89–91.

ROESER, STEVE. "An Interview with Steve Allen." *Goldmine* (December 11, 1992), pp. 24–32.

ROONEY, JAMES. *Bossmen: Bill Monroe and Muddy Waters.* New York: Dial, 1971.

ROWE, MIKE. *Chicago Blues: The City and the Music.* New York: Da Capo, 1981.

SIDERS, HARVEY. "Talking with a King: B.B. King." *Downbeat,* March 30, 1972, pp. 14–15.

STEARNS, MARSHALL. *The Story of Jazz.* New York: Mentor, 1958.

STUCKEY, FRED. "Chuck Berry: Exclusive." *Guitar Player* (February 1971), pp. 20–23.

SUMLIN, HUBERT. "My Years With Wolf." *Living Blues* (September/October 1989), pp. 10–18.

"Top Ten." *Rolling Stone,* February 13, 1986, p. 37.

"Turkish Tycoons: The Erteguns." *Time,* July 28, 1967, p. 43.

WELDING, PETE. "John Lee Hooker: Me and the Blues." *Downbeat,* October 3, 1968, pp. 15–17.

———. "Muddy Waters—Last King of the South Side?" *Downbeat,* October 8, 1964, pp. 18–19.

WHITE, CHARLES. *The Life and Times of Little Richard.* New York: Harmony, 1984.

Chapter 2
Elvis and Rockabilly

"Beware Elvis Presley." *America,* June 23, 1956, p. 295.

CONDON, E. "What Is an Elvis Presley?" *Cosmopolitan* (December 1956), pp. 54–61.

Congressional Record, 86th Congress, 1st session, 1959. Vol. 105, pt. 3, p. 3203.

"A Craze Called Elvis." *Coronet* (September 1956), pp. 153–57.

"Elvis: A Different Kind of Idol." *Life,* August 27, 1956, pp. 101–109.

"Elvis Presley: He Can't Be But He Is." *Look,* August 7, 1956, pp. 82–85.

ESCOTT, COLIN, and MARTIN HAWKINS. *Sun Records.* New York: Quick Fox, 1975.

FLANAGAN, BILL. "Johnny Cash, American." *Musician* (May 1988), pp. 97–111.

FRICKE, DAVID. "Ricky Nelson, 1940–85." *Rolling Stone*, February 13, 1986, pp. 16–20.

GOLDBERG, MICHAEL. "The Wisdom of Solomon." *Rolling Stone*, November 22, 1984, pp. 39–40.

GOLDROSEN, JOHN. *Buddy Holly.* New York: Putnam, 1979.

"Great Elvis Presley Industry." *Look*, November 13, 1956, pp. 98–100.

HILBURN, ROBERT. "Invincible Jerry Lee Lewis." Reprinted in the *Seattle Times*, November 29, 1981, p. E14.

HOPKINS, JERRY. *Elvis: A Biography.* New York: Warner, 1971.

"Howling Hillbilly Success." *Life*, April 30, 1956, p. 64.

ISLER, SCOTT. "The Everly Brothers in Arms." *Musician* (July 1986), pp. 38–48.

KAYE, ELIZABETH. "Sam Phillips Interview." *Rolling Stone*, February 13, 1986, pp. 53–88.

"Lonely and All Shook Up." *Time*, May 27, 1957, p. 101.

MABLEY, JACK. "Radio and Video." *Downbeat*, August 8, 1956.

MCGEE, DAVE. "Carl Perkins." *Rolling Stone*, April 19, 1990, pp. 73–77.

PALMER, ROBERT. "Billy Burnette Rekindles the Family Magic." *Rolling Stone*, November 27, 1980, pp. 16–17.

———. *Jerry Lee Lewis Rocks.* New York: Delilah, 1981.

PATOSKI, JOE. "Rock 'n' Roll's Wizard of Oz." *Texas Monthly* (February 1980), pp. 101–104.

POND, STEVE. "Roy Orbison, 1936–1988." *Rolling Stone*, January 26, 1989, pp. 22–33.

"Presley Spells Profit." *Newsweek*, February 18, 1957, p. 84.

"Rock 'n' Roll Battle." *Collier's*, October 26, 1957, p. 101.

"Rock 'n' Roll Riot." *Time*, May 19, 1958, p. 50.

"Roll Britannia." *Time*, February 25, 1957, p. 60.

SWENSON, JOHN. *Bill Haley: The Daddy of Rock and Roll.* New York: Stein and Day, 1984.

Chapter 3
Dick Clark, Don Kirshner, and the Teen Market

ARONOWITZ, ALFRED. "The Dumb Sound." *Saturday Evening Post*, October 5, 1963, pp. 91–95.

BUNZEL, PETER. "Music Biz Goes Round and Round." *Life*, May 16, 1960, pp. 118–20.

"Challenging the Giants." *Newsweek*, December 23, 1957, p. 70.

CLARK, DICK. *Rock, Rolls, and Remembers.* New York: Popular, 1978.

COX, HERB. "The Heart and Soul of the Cleftones." *Goldmine*, February 21, 1992, pp. 16–18.

Girl Groups. (Film.) Steven Alpert, director, MGM, 1983.

"Jockeys on a Rough Ride." *Newsweek*, December 7, 1959, p. 98.

"Jukebox" *Time*, July 27, 1959, p. 33.

"Payola Blues." *Newsweek*, November 30, 1959, p. 94.

"Rock 'n' Roll Rolls On 'n' On." *Life*, December 22, 1958, pp. 37–43.

"St. Joan of the Jukebox." *Time*, March 15, 1963, p. 50.

SCHIPPER, HENRY. "Dick Clark." *Rolling Stone*, April 19, 1990, pp. 67–70.

SPITZ, ROBERT. *The Making of Superstars*. New York: Doubleday, 1978.

"Tall, That's All." *Time*, April 14, 1958, p. 64.

U.S. Senate, 85th Congress, 2nd Session. *Hearings Before the Sub-committee on Communications of the Committee on Interstate and Foreign Commerce: Amendment to the Communications Act of 1934.*

Chapter 4
Surfboards and Hot Rods: California, Here We Come

ALEXANDER, SHANA. "Love Songs to the Carburetor." *Life*, November 6, 1964, p. 33.

BURT, ROB. *Surf City, Drag City*. New York: Blandford, 1986.

LEONARD, GEORGE. "California." *Look*, September 25, 1962, pp. 27–31.

NICOLOSI, VINCE. "Jan and Dean Interview." *Trouser Press Collector's Magazine* (March/April 1980).

"The No. 1 State: Booming, Beautiful California." *Newsweek*, September 10, 1962, pp. 28–38.

"Surf's Up." *Time*, August 9, 1963, p. 49.

"Two 'Empire States'—How They Compare." *U.S. News and World Report*, December 24, 1962, pp. 44–49.

WALTON, SAMUEL. "The Endless Summer of the Beach Boys." *Saturday Evening Post* (October 1976), pp. 52–53.

"A Way of Life." *Life*, September 1, 1961, pp. 47–53.

"What To Know and What To Look For." *Life*, October 19, 1962, pp. 69–70.

WOLFE, TOM. *The Kandy-Colored Tangerine Flake Streamline Baby*. New York: Farrar, Straus & Giroux, 1966.

Chapter 5
Bob Dylan and the New Frontier

"Angry Young Folk Singer." *Life*, April 10, 1964, pp. 109–16.

BLUESTEIN, GENE. "Songs of the Silent Generation." *New Republic*, March 13, 1961, pp. 21–22.

CARMEN, WALT. "The Children of Bobby Dylan." *Life*, November 5, 1965, pp. 43–50.

CHAPLIN, RALPH. *I. W. W. Songs*. (32nd ed.). Chicago: Chaplin, 1968.

"The Faculty." *Time*, June 16, 1961, p. 56.

"The Folk and the Rock." *Newsweek*, September 20, 1965,
    pp. 88–90.
"Folk Girls." *Time*, June 1, 1962, pp. 39–40.
"Folk Singers and Their Fans." *Look*, August 27, 1963, pp. 49–59.
"Fourth Man Makes the Trio Tick." *Business Week*, February 23,
    1963, pp. 56–58.
FRICKE, DAVID. "Roger McGuinn." *Rolling Stone*, August 23, 1990,
    pp. 107–10.
GLEASON, RALPH. "The Times They Are A-Changin." *Ramparts* (April
    1965), pp. 36–48.
HENTOFF, NAT. "Profiles." *New Yorker*, October 24, 1964, pp. 64–90.
"Hoots and Hollers on the Campus." *Newsweek*, November 27, 1961,
    pp. 84–85.
"It's Folksy, It's Delightful, It's a Craze." *Newsweek*, June 6, 1960,
    pp. 112–13.
"Just Playin' Folks." *Saturday Evening Post*, May 30, 1964, pp. 24–29.
LEONARD, GEORGE. "The Big Change in Teen Listening Habits." *Look*,
    January 3, 1961, p. 60.
"Let Us Now Praise Little Men." *Time*, May 31, 1964, p. 40.
"Like From Halls of Ivy." *Time*, July 11, 1960, pp. 56–57.
LODER, KURT. "Bob Dylan Interview." *Rolling Stone*, June 21, 1984,
    pp. 14–24.
O'CONNOR, RORY. "Albert Grossman's Ghost." *Musician* (June 1987),
    pp. 25–32.
"Real Long Hair." *Newsweek*, July 9, 1962, p. 53.
RODINTZKY, JEROME. *Minstrels of the Dawn*. Chicago: Nelson-Hall,
    1976.
SCADUTO, ANTHONY. *Bob Dylan*. New York: New American Library,
    1979.
SHELTON, ROBERT. *No Direction Home: The Life and Music of Bob
    Dylan*. New York: Ballantine, 1986.
"Sybil With a Guitar." *Time*, November 23, 1962, pp. 54–60.
"Take a Boy Like Me." *Time*, March 29, 1963, p. 40.

Chapter 6
The British Invasion of America

"Air Pollution." *Newsweek*, August 16, 1965, p. 76.
BARNES, RICHARD. *The Who: Maximum R & B*. New York: St. Martin's,
    1982.
"Beatlemania." *Newsweek*, November 18, 1963, p. 104.
Billboard, January 25, 1964.
———, February 15, 1964.
BOOTH, DAVE. "Chris Barber: The Original Sultan of Swing." *Gold-
    mine*, July 10, 1992, pp. 36–45.
BROWN, MICK. "A Conversation with George Harrison." *Rolling Stone*,
    April 19, 1979, pp. 71–75.

"Building the Beatle Image." *Saturday Evening Post*, March 21, 1964, p. 36.

BURDON, ERIC. "An Animal Views America." *Ebony* (December 1966), pp. 160–70.

COTT, JONATHAN. "Mick Jagger: The King Bee Talks." *Rolling Stone*, June 29, 1978, p. 45.

Daily Express, May 19, 1964, p. 1.

Daily Mirror, May 18, 1964.

DALTON, DAVID. *The Rolling Stones: The First Twenty Years*. New York: Knopf, 1981.

DAVIES, HUNTER. *The Beatles*. New York: McGraw-Hill, 1968.

"Evolution." *Time*, February 17, 1967, p. 76.

GAMBACCINI, PAUL. "A Conversation with Paul McCartney." *Rolling Stone*, July 12, 1979, pp. 39–46.

GARBARINI, VINCE, and JOCK BAIRD. "Has Success Spoiled Paul McCartney?" *Musician* (February 1985), pp. 58–64.

"George, Paul, Ringo and John: The Beatles in the U.S." *Newsweek*, February 24, 1964, pp. 54–57.

HEATLEY, MICHAEL. "The Yardbirds." *Goldmine*, June 12, 1992, pp. 15–30.

HENKE, JAMES. "Eric Clapton." *Rolling Stone*, October 17, 1991, pp. 42–49.

HOTCHNER, A.E. *Blown Away: The Rolling Stones and the Death of the Sixties*. New York: Simon & Schuster, 1990.

"Interview with John Lennon and Yoko Ono." *Playboy* (January 1981), pp. 75–106.

"Keith Richards Interview." *Playboy* (October 1989), pp. 59–65.

"Letters to the Editor." *Newsweek*, September 13, 1965.

LEWIS, RICHARD WARREN. "When Four Nice Guys Go Ape." *Saturday Evening Post*, January 28, 1967, pp. 24–27.

"Mick Jagger and the Future of Rock." *Newsweek*, January 4, 1971, pp. 44–48.

"Monkee Do." *Time*, November 11, 1966, p. 84.

MURPHY, MARTY. "I Took Paul and Ringo to the Space Needle." *Seattle Times*, February 12, 1984, pp. F1–4.

"New Madness: R & B Quartet Called the Beatles." *Time*, November 13, 1963, p. 64.

New York Times, February 17, 1964, p. 20.

"Pop's Bad Boys." *Newsweek*, November 29, 1965, p. 94.

"The Real John Lennon." *Newsweek*, September 29, 1980, pp. 76–77.

"Rolling Again." *Newsweek*, November 17, 1969, p. 137.

"Romp! Romp!" *Newsweek*, October 24, 1966, p. 102.

SANCHEZ, TONY. *Up and Down with the Rolling Stones*. New York: Morrow, 1979.

SCADUTO, TONY. *Mick Jagger: Everybody's Lucifer*. New York: Berkeley, 1974.

SCHAFFNER, NICHOLAS. *The British Invasion*. New York: McGraw-Hill, 1983.

Washington Post. February 12, 1964.

WENNER, JANN. *Lennon Remembers: The Rolling Stone Interviews.* San Francisco: Rolling Stone, 1971.

ZIMMER, DAVE. *Crosby, Stills and Nash: The Authorized Biography.* New York: St. Martin's, 1984.

Chapter 7
Motown: The Sound of Integration

GEORGE, NELSON. *Where Did Our Love Go? The Rise and Fall of the Motown Sound.* New York: St. Martin's, 1985.

GOLDBERG, MICHAEL. "Berry Gordy." *Rolling Stone,* August 23, 1990, pp. 67–77.

"No Town Like Motown." *Newsweek,* March 27, 1965, p. 92.

"Recorddom's Berry Gordy." *Ebony* (February 1966), pp. 33–39.

"The Supremes Make It Big." *Ebony* (June 1965), pp. 80–84.

GORDY, BERRY. *To Be Loved: The Music, the Magic, the Memories of Motown.* New York: Warner, 1994.

TARABORRELLI, RANDY. *Motown.* New York: Doubleday, 1986.

WILSON, MARY. *Dreamgirl: My Life as a Supreme.* New York: St. Martin's, 1986.

Chapter 8
Acid Rock

BROWN, JOE, ed. *The Hippies.* New York: Time, 1967.

FONG-TORRES, BEN. "Love Is Just a Song We Sing." *Rolling Stone,* February 26, 1976, pp. 58–87.

FRICKE, DAVID. "Lou Reed Interview." *Rolling Stone,* May 4, 1989, pp. 37–42.

GINSBERG, ALLEN. *Howl and Other Poems.* San Francisco: City Lights, 1959.

GLEASON, RALPH. "The Flower Children." *Encyclopedia Britannica Book of the Year 1968.* Chicago: Britannica, 1969, pp. 790–91.

—— *The Jefferson Airplane and the San Francisco Sound.* New York: Ballantine, 1969.

GOLDBERG, MICHAEL. "The San Francisco Sound." *Rolling Stone,* August 23, 1990, pp. 91–96.

GOODMAN, FRED. "Jerry Garcia Interview." *Rolling Stone,* November 30, 1989, pp. 66–74.

GRAHAM, BILL. *Bill Graham Presents: My Life Inside Rock and Out.* New York: Doubleday, 1992.

GUSTAITIS, RASA. *Turning On.* New York: New American Library, 1969.

HANSEN, JAY. *The Other Guide to San Francisco.* San Francisco: Chronicle, 1980.

"The Hippies." *Time*, July 7, 1967, pp. 18–22.

"Jerry Garcia: In Search of the X Factor." *Musician* (October 1981), pp. 64–73.

JOHNSON, JON. "Janis." *Pulse* (April 1985), p. 23.

JOPLIN, LAURA. "Love, Janis." *Rolling Stone*, September 3, 1992, p. 59.

KUNEN, JAMES SIMON. *The Strawberry Statement*. New York: Avon, 1970.

"Marty Balin." *Spin* (August 1990), p. 68.

"Open Up, Tune In, Turn On: The Airplane." *Time*, June 23, 1967, p. 53.

PECK, ABE. *Uncovering the Sixties: The Life and Times of the Underground Press*. New York: Pantheon, 1985.

PERRY, CHARLES. "From Eternity to Hell." *Rolling Stone*, February 26, 1976, pp. 38–55.

———. *The Haight-Ashbury*. New York: Vintage, 1984.

"The Rock Family." *Life*, September 24, 1971, pp. 46–53.

"Star Plunged from Heights to Depths: Skip Spence." *Seattle Times*, November 1, 1981, p. F12.

SWARTLEY, ARIEL. "Lou Reed Reconsidered." *Mother Jones* (June 1985), pp. 16–19.

"Swimming to the Moon: Jim Morrison." *Time*, November 24, 1967, p. 106.

"This Way to the Egress: The Doors." *Newsweek*, November 6, 1967, p. 101.

"Timothy Leary Interview." *Playboy* (September 1966), pp. 93–112.

WATROUS, PETER. "Touch of Gray Matter." *Musician* (December 1989), pp. 35–45.

WOLFE, BURTON. *The Hippies*. New York: New American Library, 1968.

Chapter 9
Fire from the Streets

"After the Riots." Newsweek, August 21, 1967, pp. 18–19.

"An American Tragedy: 1967." *Newsweek*, August 7, 1967, pp. 18–34.

Berkeley in the Sixties, transcript of film.

BROWN, JAMES. *James Brown: The Godfather of Soul*. New York: Macmillan, 1986.

"Cities." *Time*, August 4, 1967, pp. 13–18.

CLEAVER, ELDRIDGE. *Soul on Ice*. New York: Delta, 1968.

ELLISON, MARY. *The Black Experience*. New York: Harper, 1974.

FLEXNER, STUART BERG. *I Hear America Talking*. New York: Van Nostrand, 1976.

GARLAND, PHYL. "Eclipsed Singer Gains New Heights." *Ebony* (October 1967), pp. 47–52.

GURALNICK, PETER. *Sweet Soul Music.* New York, Harper & Row, 1986.

HIRSHEY, GERRI. *Nowhere to Run: The Story of Soul Music.* New York: Times Books, 1984.

JONES, LEROI. *Blues People.* New York: Morrow, 1963.

"Lady Soul: Singing Like It Is." *Time,* June 28, 1968, pp. 62–66.

LLORENS, DAVID. "Wilson Pickett." *Ebony* (October 1968), pp. 130–35.

"Pop Singers: James Brown." *Time,* April 1, 1966, p. 75.

"The Races: Hot and Cool." *Newsweek,* April 22, 1968, pp. 24–66.

"Rampage and Restraint." *Time,* April 19, 1968, pp. 15–17.

SANDMEL, BEN. "Katie Webster." *Musician* (April 1990), p. 16.

SANTORO, GENE. "James Brown." *Pulse* (October 1986), pp. 27–31.

SHAW, ARNOLD. *The World of Soul.* New York: Coronet, 1971.

"Singers: Aretha Franklin." *Time,* January 5, 1968, p. 48.

"Take Everything You Need Baby." *Newsweek,* April 15, 1968, pp. 31–34.

Chapter 10
Militant Blues on Campus

"At War With War." *Time,* May 18, 1970, pp. 6–14.

BOOTH, STANLEY. "Bring Billy Gibbons His Burden." *Musician* (September 1988), pp. 70–79.

CLARK, RICK. "Wayne's World: Wayne Kramer Talks About the MC5." *Goldmine,* April 17, 1992, pp. 16–22.

"Class of '69." *Newsweek,* June 23, 1969, p. 63.

COX, BILLY. "Jimi Hendrix." *Guitar Player* (May 1989), p. 47.

CROWE, CAMERON. "Jimmy Page and Robert Plant Talk." *Rolling Stone,* March 13, 1975, pp. 33–37.

"A Dignified Protest." *Time,* March 29, 1968, p. 56.

FELDER, ROB. "Black Sabbath." *Rolling Stone,* October 19, 1978, p. 28.

GILMORE, MIKAL. "The Allman Brothers." *Rolling Stone,* October 18, 1990, pp. 77–85.

HENDERSON, DAVID. *Jimi Hendrix: Voodoo Child of the Aquarian Age.* New York: Doubleday, 1978.

"Lean, Clean and Bluesy. John Fogerty." *Time,* June 27, 1969, p. 58.

"Lifting a Siege." *Time,* May 10, 1968, pp. 77–79.

"The Rebellion of the Campus." *Newsweek,* May 18, 1970, pp. 28–33.

"Rebirth of the Blues." *Newsweek,* May 26, 1969, pp. 82–85.

REDDING, NOEL. "Inside the Jimi Hendrix Experience." *Musician* (August 1986), pp. 64–78.

ROSENMAN, JOEL, JOHN ROBERTS, and ROBERT PILPEL. *Young Men with Unlimited Capital.* New York: Harcourt Brace Jovanovich, 1974.

"Rose Petals and Revolution." *Time,* November 28, 1969, p. 90.

SHERIDAN, KEVIN, and PETER SHERIDAN. "T-Bone Walker: Father of the Blues." *Guitar Player* (March 1977), pp. 22–56.

"Singing Is Better Than Any Dope." *Newsweek*, October 19, 1970, p. 125.

"Voice of Experience: Jimi Hendrix." *Newsweek*, October 9, 1967, pp. 90–92.

WELCH, CHRIS. *Hendrix*. New York: Flash, 1973.

"Woodstock Remembered." *Rolling Stone*, August 24, 1989, pp. 61–92.

Chapter 11
Soft Sounds of the Seventies

"Down to Old Dixie and Back." *Time*, January 12, 1970, pp. 42–46.

EDER, BRUCE. "The Moody Blues: Veteran Cosmic Rockers." *Goldmine*, October 28, 1994, pp. 14–40.

"ELO: America Sees the Light." *Rolling Stone*, August 24, 1978, p. 12.

"Elton John Interview." *Playboy* (January 1976), pp. 57–70.

FLANAGAN, BILL. "Songwriter Heaven." *Musician* (November 1992), pp. 79–83.

"The Girls Letting Go." *Newsweek*, July 14, 1969, pp. 68–71.

HERBST, PETER. "Linda Ronstadt Interview." *Rolling Stone*, October 19, 1978, pp. 57–59.

———. "James Taylor Interview." *Rolling Stone*, September 6, 1979, pp. 38–43.

"James Taylor: One Man's Family of Rock." *Time*, March 1, 1971, p. 45.

"Return to Good-Times Rock." *Time*, June 2, 1975, pp. 59–60.

"Rock and Roll's Leading Lady: Joni Mitchell." *Time*, December 16, 1974, pp. 63–66.

"Rock Goes to College." *Time*, September 23, 1974, pp. 90–91.

ROWLAND, MARK. "Life's Lessons: Jackson Browne and Bonnie Raitt." *Musician* (August 1989), pp. 57–90.

RUHLMANN, WILLIAM. "Poco." *Goldmine*, August 20, 1993, pp. 48–67.

———. "Steely Dan." *Goldmine*, January 22, 1993, pp. 10–20.

SHARP, KEN. "Roy Wood." *Goldmine*, Sseptember 30, 1994, pp. 57–70.

SOOCHER, STAN. "The Poco Reunion." *Musician* (February 1990), pp. 94–98.

"Timothy Leary." *MacLean's*, November 15, 1976, p. 4.

VALLELY, JEAN. "Linda Ronstadt Interview." *Playboy* (April 1980), pp. 85–116.

WHITE, TIMOTHY. "Old Wounds, New Bandages: James Taylor on the Mend." *Musician* (April 1988), pp. 70–80.

Chapter 12
The Era of Excess

BERNSTEIN, PETER. "Growth Rocks the Record Industry." *Fortune*, April 23, 1979, pp. 59–68.

CHRISTOPHER, RITA. "Every Night Fever." *MacLean's*, May 15, 1977, pp. 55–59.

CROWE, CAMERON. "David Bowie Interview." *Playboy* (September 1976), pp. 57–72.

DI PERNA, ALAN. "Back from the Dawn of Funk: Billy Bass." *Musician* (December 1993), pp. 69–73.

"Disco Takes Over." *Newsweek*, April 2, 1979, pp. 56–64.

FRICKE, DAVID. "George Clinton." *Rolling Stone*, September 20, 1990, pp. 75–77.

GILMORE, MIKAL. "Stan Cornyn." *Rolling Stone*, November 30, 1978, p. 40.

GOLDMAN, ALBERT. "The Disco Style: Love Thyself." *Esquire*, June 20, 1978, pp. 76–78.

"The Gorillas Are Coming." *Forbes*, July 10, 1978, pp. 41–46.

GREENBERG, PETER S. "Rock and Big Bucks." *Playboy* (January 1981), pp. 201–70.

GREENE, BOB. *Billion Dollar Baby*. New York: New American Library, 1974.

HARRIS, CARTER. "George Clinton." *Pulse* (December 1993), pp. 57–66.

HEIBUTZKI, RALPH. "Sly and the Family Stone." *Goldmine*, February 18, 1994, pp. 14–33.

"Hotspots of the Urban Night." *Time*, June 27, 1977, pp. 56–57.

ISLER, SCOTT. "Gregg Geller." *Rolling Stone*, February 22, 1979, pp. 28–29.

"The Man Who Sells the Sizzle: Al Coury." *Time*, December 25, 1978, pp. 48–49.

MCCARDELL, CHARLES. "Kraftwerk." *Trouser Press* (November 1981), p. 14.

"Now, the Self-Centered Generation." *Time*, September 23, 1974, pp. 84–85.

"Pop Records: Moguls, Money and Monsters." *Time*, February 12, 1973, pp. 61–63.

POST, HENRY. "Sour Notes on the Hottest Disco." *Esquire*, June 20, 1978, pp. 79–86.

RESSNER, JEFFREY. "Freddie Mercury: 1946–1991." *Rolling Stone*, January 9, 1992, pp. 13–17.

"The Rockets Are Rolling in It." *Forbes*, April 15, 1973, pp. 28–39.

ROSENBLUM, CONSTANCE. "Discomania." *Human Behavior* (November 1978), p. 27.

SWENSON, JOHN. "15 Years of Making Kisstory." *Billboard*, January 21, 1989, p. K5–25.

"Tyrannical King Coke." *Time*, April 16, 1973, pp. 69–70.

"Vaudeville Rock." *Time*, October 30, 1972, p. 81.

"Where Have the Flowers Gone?" *Newsweek*, September 5, 1977, pp. 24–30.

WOLFE, TOM. *Mauve Gloves and Madmen, Clutter and Vine*. New York: McGraw-Hill, 1976.

Chapter 13
Punk Rock and the New Generation

"Anthems of the Blank Generation." *Time*, July 11, 1977, pp. 46–47.

AZERRAD, MICHAEL. "Searching for the Cure." *Rolling Stone*, September 7, 1989, pp. 47–50.

BURGESS, ANTHONY, and JOHN LOMBARDI. "Plastic Punks." *Psychology Today* (November 1977), pp. 120–26.

CIOE, CRISPIN, and RAFI ZABOR. "The New Reggae." *Musician* (November 1981), pp. 48–50.

"The Clash." *Musician* (May 1981), pp. 45–72.

"Commando Squad Attacks Musicians' Coop." *In These Times*, June 13–19, 1979, p. 20.

CONSIDINE, J. D. "The Police." *Musician* (December 1981), pp. 59–65.

DANCIS, BRUCE. "Artistic Control and Records Too." *In These Times*, June 4–17, 1980, pp. 20–21.

———. "Reggae Today." *In These Times*, October 25–31, 1978, p. 23.

———. "Tom Robinson Talks to ITT." *In These Times*, May 16–22, 1979, p. 24.

DAVIS, JEROME. *Talking Heads*. New York: Vintage, 1986.

DROZDOWSKI, TED. "Full Metal Justice." *Musician* (January 1989), pp. 44–52.

FLANAGAN, BILL. "Frontman: John Lydon." *Musician* (July 1994), p. 7.

GILMORE, MIKAL. "The Clash: Anger on the Left." *Rolling Stone*, March 8, 1979, p. 22.

———. "The Talking Heads." *Rolling Stone*, November 29, 1979, pp. 23–24.

HALASA, MALU. "The English Beat Can't Stop Dancing." *Rolling Stone*, November 13, 1980, pp. 24–25.

HAMSHER, JANE. "Stiv Bator and the Dead Boys." *Damage* (July 1980), p. 12.

HEY, JOHN D. *Britain in Context*. Blackwell: Oxford, 1979.

HEYLIN, CLINTON. *From the Velvets to the Voidoids: A Pre-Punk History for a Post-Punk World*. New York: Penguin, 1993.

HOCHSWENDER, WOODY. "Slam Dancing." *Rolling Stone*, May 14, 1981, pp. 29–32.

HOPKINS, TOM. "Dada's Boys." *MacLean's*, June 13, 1977, p. 42.

ISLER, SCOTT. "Blondie." *Trouser Press* (June 1981), pp. 19–23.

———. "Fear and Loathing on the West Coast." *Trouser Press* (June

1980), pp. 20–23.

Kozak, Roman. *This Ain't No Disco: The Story of CBGB*. Boston: Faber & Faber, 1988.

Lydon, John. *Rotten: No Irish—No Blacks—No Dogs*. New York: St. Martin's, 1994.

McCormick, Moira. "Richard Hell." *Trouser Press* (November 1982), p. 14.

McNeil, Legs. "The Devil Finds Work for Idol Hands to Do." *Spin* (September 1990), pp. 29–32.

———. "We're a Happy Family." *Spin* (August 1986), pp. 66–71.

Marcus, Greil. "Pete Townshend Interview." *Rolling Stone*, June 26, 1980, pp. 34–39.

———. "Wake Up!" *Rolling Stone*, July 24, 1980, pp. 38–43.

Marsh, Dave. "It Takes a Lot to Laugh: The Punks." *Rolling Stone*, September 21, 1978, p. 21.

"Mick Jones." *Musician* (June 1995), pp. 46–48.

Palmer, Robert. "Joy Division." *Musician* (August 1988), pp. 85–88.

"Prep or Punk." *Mademoiselle* (June 1980), pp. 182–84.

"Rock Bottom: Punk Fashions." *Newsweek*, June 20, 1977, pp. 80–81.

"Rock on Right." *Billboard*, August 22, 1981, p. 53.

"The Sky Above, the Beat Below." *Time*, April 7, 1980, p. 75.

Sommer, Tom. "Adam Ant." *Trouser Press* (July 1981), p. 13.

Stevenson, Ray. *Sex Pistols File*. London: Omnibus, 1980.

Watrous, Peter. "Sting." *Musician* (December 1987), pp. 60–74.

Wild, David. "Elvis Costello Interview." *Rolling Stone*, June 1, 1989, pp. 59–68.

Young, Charles M. "Visions of Patti." *Rolling Stone*, July 27, 1978, pp. 51–54.

Zabor, Rafi. "John Lydon's PiL." *Musician* (November 1984), pp. 42–48.

Zuckerman, Ed. "The Rise of Rock Against Racism." *Rolling Stone*, December 14, 1978, pp. 40–41.

Chapter 14
I Want My MTV

Barol, Bill. "1989: MTV." *Newsweek*, July 3, 1989, pp. 50–51.

Connelly, Christopher. "Ratt: Lap Dogs of the Devil?" *Rolling Stone*, December 6, 1984, p. 50.

"The Copycats That Are Chasing Music Television." *Business Week*, September 3, 1984, pp. 57–58.

DeMartino, Dave. "Decalog." *Billboard*, December 23, 1989, pp. D8–12.

Dutka, Elaine, and William Tyson. "MTV Faces a Mid Life Crisis."

Time, June 29, 1987, p. 67.

"The Eurythmics." *Trouser Press* (October 1983), p. 13.

FARREN, MICK. "Surface Noise." *Trouser Press* (August 1982) p. 46.

FLANAGAN, BILL. "We Three Kings: The Top Managers." *Musician* (April 1991), pp. 52–68.

FOLTZ, KIM. "Michael Jackson Inc." *Newsweek*, February 27, 1984, pp. 66–67.

GREEN, JIM. "Culture Club Comes Clean." *Trouser Press* (June 1983), pp. 16–18.

"His Highness of Haze: Prince." *Time*, August 6, 1984, p. 62.

"Human League." *Trouser Press* (August 1982), p. 35.

JAFFE, LARRY. "What Hath Video Wrought, Parts I & II." *Pulse* (September 1986), pp. 32–35; (October 1986), pp. 57–59.

JEFFREY, DON. "Growth Levels Projected in Music Video." *Billboard*, June 17, 1989, p. 4.

"JVC Celebrates Shipping 200 Million Units." *Billboard*, January 14, 1989, p. 58.

KAPLAN, PETER. "MTV: 21st Century Box." *Esquire* (March 1983), p. 222.

LEARNER, MICHAEL. "The Heavy Metal Frenzy." *Newsweek*, August 10, 1987, p. 59.

LODER, KURT. "Dress Right." *Rolling Stone*, June 23, 1981, pp. 14–19.

LUPO, JANE. "Spandau Ballet." *Trouser Press* (September 1981), pp. 16–17.

McDONALD, PATRICK. "Whitney Houston Rocks to the Top." *Seattle Times*, October 4, 1987, p. L1.

MacKAY, GILLIAN. "The New Wizard of Pop." *MacLean's*, July 23, 1984, pp. 38–43.

MILANO, BRETT. "Def Leppard Roars Back." *Pulse* (September 1987), pp. 46–51.

MILLER, JIM. "Britain Rocks America—Again." *Newsweek*, January 23, 1984, pp. 50–57.

PERRY, STEVE. "Prince in the Purple Decade." *Musician* (November 1988), pp. 83–99.

"The Peter Pan of Pop: Michael Jackson." *Newsweek*, January 10, 1983, pp. 52–54.

PORTER, MARTIN, and STEVEN SCHWARTZ. "Madonna." *Seattle Times*, April 7, 1985, p. L1.

ROCKMAKER, DEIRDRE. "Def Leppard: The Heavy Metal Band You Can Bring Home to Your Mother." *Goldmine*, June 11, 1993, pp. 14–40.

ROWLAND, MARK. "Dreaming: Def Leppard." *Musician* (April 1992), pp. 52–61.

SALEWICZ, CHRIS. "Kemp: A Revolt into Style." *The Face* (October 1982), pp. 25–26.

"Sing a Song of Seeing." *Time*, December 26, 1983, pp. 54–64.

SWAN, CHRISTOPHER. "Rock Video Quakes." Reprinted in *Seattle Times*, June 2, 1985, p. E1.

TANNENBAUM, ROB. "George Michael: Artist or Airhead?" *Musician* (January 1988), pp. 27–36.

"Top 100." *Rolling Stone*, November 16, 1989, pp. 55–121.

"The Tour, the Money and the Magic." *Newsweek*, July 16, 1984, pp. 64–70.

"Why He's a Thriller." *Time*, March 19, 1984, pp. 54–63.

YOUNG, CHARLES. "Def Leppard Pulls Out of the Fast Lane." *Musician* (December 1987), pp. 76–82.

Chapter 15
The Promise of Rock-and-Roll

COCKS, JAY. "Roll Them Bones." *Time*, September 4, 1989, pp. 58–62.

COLEMAN, MARK. "The Revival of Conscience." *Rolling Stone*, November 15, 1990, pp. 69–80.

"Compact Disc Players." *Consumer Reports* (May 1987), pp. 283–84.

DECURTIS, ANTHONY. "Ropin' The Wind." *Rolling Stone*, April 1, 1993, pp. 31–35.

DIMARTINO, DAVE, and ED CHRISTMAN. "CD Edges Up on Cassette as Top Format." *Billboard*, June 23, 1990, p. 1.

FLIPPO, CHET. "Bruce Springsteen." *Musician* (November 1984), pp. 53–58.

FRICKE, DAVID. "All Star Line-Up for Band-Aid Shows." *Rolling Stone*, July 18/August 1, 1985, p. 17.

———. "Lou Reed: Back on the Streets." *Rolling Stone*, March 9, 1989, p. 26.

———. "Rage and Roll." *Rolling Stone*, June 28, 1990, pp. 49–57.

GRAHAM, BILL. "U2 Give Themselves Away." *Musician* (May 1987), pp. 79–90.

"Grateful Dead Aid Rain Forests." *Rolling Stone*, November 3, 1988, p. 17.

GRIEST, STEPHANIE. "Kickin' Up a Storm." *Seattle Post-Intelligencer*, August 2, 1994, p. C1–3.

HENKE, JAMES. "Springsteen." *Rolling Stone*, August 6, 1992, pp. 38–44.

HILBURN, ROBERT. "Bruce Springsteen." *Oregonian*, October 24, 1980, p. G1.

HIRSHBERG, CHARLES. "He's Garth Brooks." *Life* (July 1992), pp. 55–63.

HUNTER, NIGEL. "Key Global Markets Love That CD," *Billboard*, March 11, 1989, p. 1.

HUTCHINSON, JOHN. "Luminous Times: U2." *Musician* (October 1987), pp. 68–78.

LICHTMAN, IRV. "Music Shipments Hit New Mark." *Billboard*, March 18, 1989, p. 1.

LIGHT, ALAN. "Forever Young." *Rolling Stone*, January 21, 1993, pp. 36–37.

LODER, KURT. "Bruce Springsteen Interview." *Rolling Stone*, December 6, 1984, pp. 19–22.

McBEE, SUSANNA. "Are Today's Young a Disillusioned Generation?" *U.S. News and World Report*, January 23, 1984, pp. 40–42.

MacDONALD, PATRICK. "Vinyl's Final Days." *Seattle Times*, January 21, 1990, p. L1.

"Making of a Rock Star." *Newsweek*, October 27, 1975, pp. 57–63.

MARSH, DAVE. *Born to Run.* New York: Dell, 1981.

MEHLER, MARK. "Recorded Music Ranks Highest in Growth." *Billboard*, December 10, 1988, p. 75.

NELSON, PAUL. "Springsteen Fever." *Rolling Stone*, July 13, 1978, p. 13.

PAINTON, PRISCILLA. "Country Rocks the Boomers." *Time*, March 30, 1992, pp. 62–68.

POND, STEVE. "On Her Own Terms: Tracy Chapman." *Rolling Stone*, September 22, 1988, pp. 55–63.

PUTERBAUGH, PARKE. "Gone But Not Forgotten." *Rolling Stone*, October 29, 1992, p. 28.

RESSNER, JEFFREY. "Going, Going, Gone?" *Rolling Stone*, April 20, 1989, p. 15.

"Rock's New Sensation." *Time*, October 27, 1975, pp. 48–58.

SPAHR, WOLFGANG. "West German Record Industry." *Billboard*, February 17, 1990, p. 3.

STOUT, GENE. "Rock Radio Drags On." *Seattle Post-Intelligencer*, July 17, 1988, p. F1.

TANNENBAUM, ROB. "Country's New Gold Rush." *Rolling Stone*, April 16, 1992.

"Technology." *Time*, January 1, 1990, p. 104.

THOMPSON, DAVID. "David Byrne." *Rolling Stone*, April 21, 1988, pp. 42–52.

Chapter 16
The Generation X Blues

ARNOLD, GINA. *Route 666: On the Road to Nirvana.* New York: St. Martin's, 1993.

AZERRAD, MICHAEL. "Inside the Heart and Mind of Kurt Cobain." *Rolling Stone*, April 16, 1992, pp. 37–41.

———. "Public Enemy." *Rolling Stone*, September 22, 1988, p. 32.

———. "When Things Get Heavy." *Rolling Stone*, November 3, 1988, p. 112.

"Bad Rap." *Time*, September 1, 1986, p. 20.

BERMAN, ERIC. "The Godfathers of Rap." *Rolling Stone*, December 23, 1993/January 6, 1994, pp. 137–142.

BOOK, JOHN. "Seattle Heavy." *Goldmine*, April 17, 1992, pp. 46–54.

BOSC, MICHAEL. "Street Gangs No Longer Just a Big City Problem."

U.S. News and World Report, July 16, 1984, pp. 108–109.

Conally, Michael. "Hip-Hopping to the Beat: The Reggae Rap Connection." *Billboard*, June 9, 1990, pp. R3–4.

Demott, John. "Have Gang Will Travel." *Time*, December 9, 1985, p. 34.

DiMartino, Dave. "A Seattle Slew." *Rolling Stone*, September 20, 1990, pp. 23–24.

Drozdowski, Ted. "Full Metal Justice." *Musician* (January 1989), pp. 42–52.

Ehrlich, Dimitri. "Phat Cats and Punks." *Rolling Stone*, August 19, 1993, p. 18.

Fernando, S.H. *The New Beats: Exploring the Music, Culture and Attitudes of Hip-Hop*. New York: Anchor, 1994.

Flanagan, Bill. "Black History: Speech Meets Curtis Mayfield." *Musician* (June 1993), pp. 58–67.

Flipside, Al. "Core." *Trouser Press* (August 1982), pp. 23–26.

Fricke, David. "Heavy Metal Justice." *Rolling Stone*, January 12, 1989, pp. 42–49.

———. "Life After Death—Courtney Love." *Rolling Stone*, December 15, 1994, pp. 59–67.

Fuchs, Lawrence. *The American Kaleidoscope*. Hanover: University Press of New England, 1991.

Gaar, Gillian. "A Band Called Alice." *Goldmine*, August 5, 1994, p. 54–58.

———. "The Dark Side of Innocence: Nirvana and the Rise of the Seattle Sound." *Goldmine*, December 10, 1993, pp. 38–58.

Garcia, Guy. "Heavy Metal Goes Platinum." *Time*, October 14, 1991, p. 85.

Gardner, Elysa. "Watching the Detectives." *Musician* (October 1994), pp. 28–33.

George, Nelson, Sally Barnes, Susan Flinker, and Patty Romanowski. *Fresh: Hip Hop Don't Stop*. New York: Random, 1985.

Gitter, Mike. "Somber No More?" *Pulse* (September 1991), pp. 82–85.

Gold, Jonathan. "The Day of the Dre." *Rolling Stone*, September 30, 1993, pp. 39–43.

Goldberg, Michael. "Punk Lives." *Rolling Stone*, July 18/August 1, 1985, pp. 28–32.

Greene, Jo-Ann. "Pearl Jam: Intrigue and Incest and the Secret History of Seattle." *Goldmine*, August 20, 1993, pp. 14–43.

Griffin, Brian. "AC/DC Classic Big Rock." *Pulse* (August 1985), p. 34.

Halbersberg, Elianne. "The Majors." *Billboard*, May 6, 1989, pp. H3–25.

Hamilton, Tish. "Rap It Up." *Rolling Stone*, July 12–26, 1990, p. 109.

Henk, Ronald. "Kids Are Killing, Dying, Bleeding." *Fortune*, August 10, 1992, pp. 62–69.

359

HOCHMAN, STEVE. "NWA: Keeping Attitude Alive." *Musician* (March 1991), pp. 59–61.

"Is Rock and Roll Dead?" *Rolling Stone*, December 13–27, 1990, p. 176.

KELLY, CHRISTINA. "D Generation." *Rolling Stone*, February 9, 1995, pp. 19–20.

KOEPP, STEPHEN. "Teenage Orphans of the Job Boom." *Time*, May 13, 1985, pp. 46–47.

LELAND, JOHN. "Rap and Race." *Newsweek*, June 29, 1992, pp. 47–52.

LIGHT, ALAN. "Ice." *Rolling Stone*, August 20, 1992, pp. 29–31.

———. "L.A. Rappers Speak Out." *Rolling Stone*, June 25, 1992, pp. 15–21.

———. "Rappers Sounded Warning." *Rolling Stone*, July 9/23, 1992, pp. 15–17.

McADAMS, JANINE. "A Message of Peace Outta Compton." *Billboard*, May 5, 1990, p. 26.

MacNIE, JIM. "Soundgarden's Full Punk Power Slide." *Musician* (February 1990), pp. 30–38.

MOORE, JOHN. "Diamond Head: Living on Borrowed Time." *Goldmine*, June 11, 1993, pp. 52–58.

MORRIS, CHRIS. "Bob Mould: Shaken, Stirred and Fueled." *Musician* (October 1994), pp. 19–26.

———. "Nirvana." *Musician* (January 1992), pp. 28–35.

MUNDY, CHRIS. "Nirvana." *Rolling Stone*, January 23, 1992, pp. 39–41.

NATHAN, DAVID. "Jungle Brothers Bear Civilized Message." *Billboard*, March 3, 1990, p. 30.

———. "Rap." *Billboard*, December 24, 1988, pp. R1–80.

NEELY, KIM. "Into the Unknown." *Rolling Stone*, June 16, 1994, pp. 46–52.

PARELES, JON. "Henry Rollins: The Loner." *Musician* (April 1993), pp. 35–41.

———. "How Rap Moves to Television's Beat." *New York Times*, January 14, 1990, Section 2, pp. 1–2.

———. "Run-D.M.C." *Rolling Stone*, July 18/August 1, 1985, p. 24.

PERRY, STEVE. "Achin' to Be Understood." *Musician* (February 1989), pp. 63–70.

PODHORETZ, JOHN. "Metallic Rock That's Designed to Shock." *U.S. News and World Report*, September 7, 1987, pp. 50–51.

POSTEL, ERIC. "Heavy Metal Thunder!" *Pulse* (September 1983), pp. 1–12.

PUNK, DONNY. "The Dead Kennedy's State of Confusion." *Spin* (February 1986), pp. 47–48.

RAMIREZ, MARC. "Bliss Out." *Pacific Magazine, Seattle Times/Seattle Post-Intelligencer*, April 26, 1992, pp. 7–29.

REID, LARRY. "Smells Like Prozac." *Rocket*, September 28 – October 12, 1994, p. 29.

RESSNER, JEFFREY. "Thrashers Pay Tribute to Rap." *Rolling Stone*, August 8, 1991, p. 21.

ROESNER, STEVE. "Anthrax: Spreading the Metal." *Goldmine*, April 17, 1992, pp. 26–29.

ROWLAND, MARK. "Crap Killer." *Musician* (January 1993), pp. 37–40.

RUHLMANN, WILLIAM. "X: They're Still Desperate, But They're Used to It." *Goldmine*, February 4, 1994, pp. 52–99.

RULE, SHEILA. "Rappers Words Foretold Depth of Blacks' Anger." *New York Times*, May 26, 1992, p. B1–2.

RUSSELL, LISA. "M. C. Hammer." *People*, June 24, 1990, pp. 59–60.

SAMUELS, DAVID. "Yo! MTV Unwrapped." *Spin* (September 1991), pp. 44–45.

SOMMER, TOM. "Black Flag." *Trouser Press* (June 1983), pp. 23–24.

STOUT, GENE. "L.L. Proves Cool." *Seattle Post-Intelligencer*, May 17, 1991, What's Happening, p. 5.

———. "Rockin' and Rollin' the Boat." *Seattle Post-Intelligencer*, March 24, 1990, p. C1–2.

TOOP, DAVID. *Rap Attack 2: African Rap to Global Hip Hop*. New York: Serpent's Tail, 1991.

UCHITELLE, LOUIS. "America Isn't Creating Enough Jobs, and No One Seems to Know Why." *New York Times*, September 6, 1992, section 4, pp. 2–3.

WEIDENBAUM, MARC. "Flipside." *Pulse* (September 1990), p. 132.

WHITE, RICHARD. "Sub Pop." *Pulse* (Independent Special 1989), pp. 27–29.

WYMAN, BILL. "Who Is Veruca Salt?" *Musician* (March 1995), pp. 22–28.

361

Index